Northern Ireland
The Politics of War and Peace

Second Edition

Paul Dixon

First edition 2001
Second edition 2008

Published by
PALGRAVE MACMILLAN

Palgrave Macmillan in the UK is an imprint of Macmillan Publishers Limited, registered in England, company number 785998, of Houndmills, Basingstoke, Hampshire RG21 6XS.

Palgrave Macmillan in the US is a division of St Martin's Press LLC, 175 Fifth Avenue, New York, NY 10010.

Palgrave Macmillan is the global academic imprint of the above companies and has companies and representatives throughout the world.

Palgrave® and Macmillan® are registered trademarks in the United States, the United Kingdom, Europe and other countries.

ISBN-13: 978–0–230–50778–4   hardback
ISBN-10: 0–230–50778–6   hardback
ISBN-13: 978–0–230–50779–1   paperback
ISBN-10: 0–230–50779–4   paperback

This book is printed on paper suitable for recycling and made from fully managed and sustained forest sources. Logging, pulping and manufacturing processes are expected to conform to the environmental regulations of the country of origin.

A catalogue record for this book is available from the British Library.

Library of Congress Cataloging-in-Publication Data

Dixon, Paul, 1964-
   Northern Ireland : the politics of war and peace / Paul Dixon.– 2nd ed.
      p. cm.
   Includes bibliographical references and index.
      ISBN-13: 978–0–230–50778–4 (alk. paper)   1. Northern
Ireland—Politics and government.   2. Political
      violence—Northern Ireland.   3. Peace movements—Northern Ireland.
   I. Title.
   DA990.U46D598 2008
   941.6—dc22   2008020978

10   9   8   7   6   5   4   3   2   1
17   16   15   14   13   12   11   10   09   08

Printed and bound in China

For mum and dad

Contents

List of Maps, Figures and Tables

Acknowledgements

Since the first edition of this book was published I have moved from the University of Ulster (UU) (1997–2005) to become a Senior Lecturer at Kingston University in south-west London. I am grateful to Kingston University for facilitating this unexpectedly rapid move in such an understanding way. The staff in the UU library and the superb Linen Hall Library in Belfast were excellent in tracking down sources and making helpful suggestions for my research.

The Dixon family have been solid in their continuing support, and Jack and Tom an absolute pleasure to be around. Thanks to Nick Garland, who has provided a dog of tea, computer hardware and internet access. Carrie is a dote, as they say in Tyrone. I would like to thank again those friends in Northern Ireland for their support during my time there, particularly the 'Sisters of Tyrone' and long-time housemate Cait. I have had a long and fruitful relationship with Methody College Hockey Club, aka Belfast Harlequins, stretching back as far as 1992. Injury, and a rapid departure from my job at Ulster, meant that I did not get the chance to say goodbye and wish them all the best. Lunchtime soccer at UU was immense fun, sometimes reflecting communal tensions; but at other times the virtues of common interests in transcending communal divisions! Most of the time the possession of a white shirt and a positive attitude to passing the ball was the most important aspect of identity. . .. Best wishes to the regulars, including Mervyn, Steven, Richard, Brendy, Paul, Kevin, Kenny . . . even Pat.

Teaching students at the University of Ulster was very enjoyable and stimulating. They tolerated with great humour and (perhaps undue) respect, an Englishman teaching them about Northern Irish and Irish politics. It has been wonderful to see these students doing so well, particularly in the fields of politics and journalism. Thanks to Gordon Anderson for his work on my website, and Aeneas Bonner for being such a good guy! During my time in Belfast I benefited from the friendship of Cathal, Anne and Marie McCall. I enjoyed frank and free exchanges with Dr McCall under 'Vicos House Rules' as much as I enjoyed the pizza afterwards (no greater compliment. . .). Belfast just isn't the same without Ski Bunnies.

In recent years I have also had the benefit of the wisdom of the 'Usual Suspects' of the Irish politics group of the Political Studies Association. In particular, I would like to thank Professor Jon Tonge, whose generosity towards me has been magnified by his very different perspective on the North of Ireland. Professor Mick Cox has shown similar integrity by promoting the work of a critic. Dr Eric Kaufmann, co-President of Southfields Irish Society, has been a very welcome discussant of the twists and turns of Northern Irish politics, even if he does play the wrong kind of hockey. At Palgrave, Steven Kennedy has proved, again, to be an excellent publisher. I am grateful for the diligent work of my editor Keith Povey. I was very grateful to the Weatherhead Center for International Affairs at Harvard University for hosting me for a few months in 2004, during which the Boston Red Sox ended the curse. In particular, thanks go to Jim Cooney, Michelle Eureka, Tom Murphy and Thomas Oatley for making me so welcome.

I have revised the first edition of this book. In particular I have edited down and combined Chapters 3 and 4 into one chapter in this new edition to make way for a major chapter on the period 1998–2007. I have also attempted to edit down elsewhere and improve the way I have expressed my arguments. This new edition also indicates that my thinking on the conflict is developing (particularly in terms of understanding the complexity of the politics of conflict) and this will also be expressed in my book on *The Northern Ireland Peace Process: Choreography and Theatrical Politics* (Routledge, 2009).

PAUL DIXON

List of Abbreviations

AIA	Anglo-Irish Agreement
ANC	African National Congress
APL	Anti-Partition League
APNI	Alliance Party of Northern Ireland
CAJ	Committee on the Administration of Justice
CC	Cabinet Conclusions
CDU	Campaign for Democracy in Ulster
CIRA	Continuity Irish Republican Army
CLMC	Combined Loyalist Military Command
CP	Cabinet Papers
CSJ	Campaign for Social Justice
DCAC	Derry Citizens Action Committee
DHAC	Derry Housing Action Committee
DSD	Downing Street Declaration
DUP	Democratic Unionist Party
EEC	European Economic Community
EU	European Union
FARC	Revolutionary Armed Forces of Colombia
FEA	Fair Employment Agency
GAA	Gaelic Athletic Association
GFA	Good Friday Agreement
GOC	General Officer Commanding
HCL	Homeless Citizens League
IGC	Intergovernmental Conference of the AIA
IMC	Independent Monitoring Commission
INLA	Irish National Liberation Army
IRA	Irish Republican Army (the Provisional IRA)
LVF	Loyalist Volunteer Force
MP	Member of Parliament (UK)
MLA	Member of the Legislative Assembly (NI)
NATO	North Atlantic Treaty Organisation
NIC	Northern Ireland Committee of the Parliamentary Conservative Party
NICRA	Northern Ireland Civil Rights Association
NILP	Northern Ireland Labour Party

NILT	Northern Ireland Life and Times
NIO	Northern Ireland Office
NIWC	Northern Ireland Women's Coalition
OIRA	Official IRA
PIRA	Provisional IRA
PREM	Prime Minister's Office
PRO	Public Record Office
PSNI	Police Service of Northern Ireland
PTA	Prevention of Terrorism Act
PUP	Progressive Unionist Party
RIR	Royal Irish Regiment (a regiment of the British Army comprising the UDR and Royal Irish Rangers)
RIRA	Real IRA
RUC	Royal Ulster Constabulary
SAS	Special Air Service
SDLP	Social Democratic and Labour Party
SF	Sinn Féin
TUAS	Tactical Use of the Armed Struggle
UDA	Ulster Defence Association
UDP	Ulster Democratic Party
UDR	Ulster Defence Regiment
UFF	Ulster Freedom Fighters
UK	United Kingdom
UKUP	United Kingdom Unionist Party
USC	Ulster Special Constabulary
UUC	Ulster Unionist Council
UUP	Ulster Unionist Party
UUUC	United Ulster Unionist Council
UVF	Ulster Volunteer Force
UWC	Ulster Workers' Council
VUP	Vanguard Unionist Party
VUPP	Vanguard Unionist Progressive Party

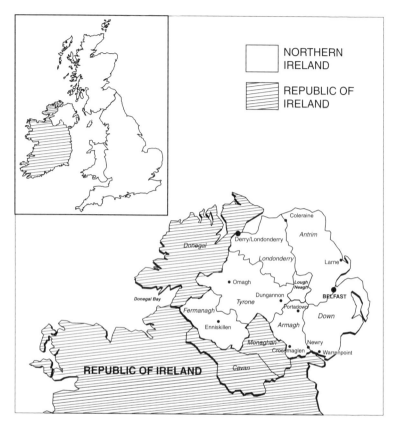

Map 1.1 Northern Ireland

1
Introduction

This chapter aims to give a short background and introduction to the conflict in Northern Ireland, by presenting a brief history, introducing nationalist and unionist perspectives on the conflict, and considering also the extent of violence and segregation. The popular historical accounts given by nationalists and unionists of the history of the conflict in Northern Ireland are very different. These accounts are not merely of historical interest but are deployed by politicians to win advantage in the propaganda war over the future of Northern Ireland. Past grievances are used to justify current claims to justice. Although these highly 'propagandistic' accounts of history are often undermined by historical research, these 'myths' continue to persist. Do these very different accounts of the history Northern Ireland, including the recent period of conflict covered by this book, contribute to the continuation of the conflict?

The following chapter presents 'The Approach and Argument' of the book and will pick up on the concepts of 'power', 'ideology' (and the propaganda war) and 'reality' which are the key, interrelated, themes. Power, it is argued, is deployed in the two interconnected wars being fought over Northern Ireland: the 'real war' and the propaganda war. The 'real war' is aimed at winning advantage through physical means, violence, demonstrations and repression. But these are also deployed in the propaganda war to shift the political agenda. The ideological, public rhetoric of the propaganda war by the various parties to the conflict can be contrasted with the 'realities' of the conflict, which are sometimes only privately acknowledged.

A Few Generalizations

A few generalizations can be useful to get an initial grasp on the Northern Ireland conflict. These generalizations, however, are distortions and cannot do justice to the nuances and complexities of the situation. The conflict in Northern Ireland can be most easily and quickly understood as being between two main groups. First, there are unionists, who comprise about 60 per cent of the population of Northern Ireland, who tend to see themselves as British and want Northern Ireland to continue to remain part of the UK. In this book I use the term 'British' as a simple way to refer to the population living in England, Wales and Scotland. This should not be taken to imply that there are no British people living in Northern Ireland. These unionists are mainly Protestant, but there are some Catholic unionists. Second, there are nationalists, who make up an increasing proportion of the Northern Ireland population, about 40 per cent at the time of writing, who tend to see themselves as Irish and aspire to be part of a united Ireland. These nationalists are overwhelmingly Catholic. There is a much smaller third group, perhaps a few per cent of people in Northern Ireland, who reject the domination of nationalism and unionism and see themselves as occupying the 'moderate' centre ground between the two dominant unionist and nationalist communities. While the labels 'Catholic' and 'Protestant' are used to describe the principal contending communities, the conflict is not to any great extent about religion or religious dogma. The terms 'Protestant' and 'Catholic' are usually used to indicate someone who is either unionist or nationalist. Northern Ireland can be seen as a place where the British and Irish nations overlap and their co-nationals, British unionists and Irish nationalists, aspire to be part of two different states. This is not such an unusual state of affairs – in Eastern Europe, for example, where borders have shifted back and forth down the centuries, minorities have frequently been caught on the 'wrong side' of a border, under the sovereignty of a state that is not run by their co-nationals.

A Brief History of the Conflict

In the historical debate between nationalists and unionists there is some dispute over which group has first claim to Northern Ireland. Nationalists can point to their Celtic 'forefathers', while some unionists have claimed that their ancestors, the Cruthin, were in the territory now called Northern Ireland even before the Celts. This is not a unique debate: where there is conflict over territory there is often historical debate over 'who was here first' since this can be used in political argument to justify one or other group's legitimate claim to a territory.

Nationalists usually date Ireland's woes to the Anglo-Norman invasion of 1169 and England's domination of Ireland ever since. When Henry VIII broke with Rome in the sixteenth century, England became Protestant while Ireland remained Catholic and rebellious. In 1603, the conquest of Ireland was complete. In 1609, the plantation of Ulster began, the Catholic Irish were dispossessed and (mainly Scottish) Protestant settlers were established in present-day Northern Ireland. Some Catholics can still point out the lands that were taken over by the settlers. During the seventeenth century, Protestant landownership in Ireland rose from 5 per cent to over 80 per cent at the expense of the Catholics. In 1641, the Irish rose up against the Protestants and massacred some of them, but Cromwell triumphed bloodily over the Irish in 1649–52. In 1690, King William of Orange defeated James II, the Catholic King of England and Scotland, at the Battle of the Boyne, ensuring Protestant dominance. At the end of the seventeenth century and the beginning of the eighteenth, 'penal laws' were passed which further established Protestant domination in Ireland. Anglican Protestants enjoyed privileges over both Catholics and Nonconformist Protestants. In 1798, the Protestant Wolfe Tone led the United Irishmen, combining Catholics and Presbyterians, in a republican uprising, to establish Ireland's independence from England. Again, this was defeated, and in 1801 the Act of Union was passed integrating the Irish Parliament into the Parliament of Great Britain and Ireland.

During the 1820s and 1830s, Daniel O'Connell led a successful movement for Catholic representation in Parliament and an unsuccessful one for the 'Repeal of the Union'. The Irish famine (1845–51) resulted in the deaths of over a million Irish, and the emigration of another million within a decade. This diaspora has continued to play a role in Irish politics ever since, particularly in the United States. Nationalists continued to agitate against English domination. The Fenians turned to violence and bombings to oust the English. A constitutional movement for Irish Home Rule developed at the end of the nineteenth century and succeeded in winning considerable land reforms for the Irish, but by the outbreak of the First World War it had failed to achieve the implementation of Home Rule for Ireland. Throughout Ireland, the unionists, mainly the Protestant descendants of the plantation, led resistance to Home Rule, fearing Catholic domination in an all-Ireland assembly. Unionists were particularly concentrated in Ulster, and between 1912 and 1914 they mobilized, declaring their willingness to fight against Home Rule. In this they were supported by the Conservative Party and had the sympathy of important sections of the British Army. By 1914, England faced civil war over the 'Irish Question' between the Conservatives and their unionist allies in Ireland, and the Liberals (and Labour) who were sympathetic to the Home Rule demand of nationalists.

The First World War changed the political landscape drastically. Both Irish nationalists and unionists fought for Britain in the war, with the Ulster Division taking heavy casualties on the Somme. At Easter 1916 a small group of republicans entered the General Post Office in Dublin and declared an Irish republic. The 'Easter Rising' was initially unpopular and defeated by the British, but when its leaders were executed there followed a wave of public sympathy for the republicans. Public opinion shifted away from the Irish Parliamentary Party and Home Rule and towards the republicans and their demand for independence. In 1918, the republican party, Sinn Féin, decisively won the last all-Ireland election. The 'War of Independence' of 1919–21 was fought by the Irish Republican Army (IRA) to drive the British state out of Ireland. On the other hand, the unionists continued to resist incorporation into a united independent Ireland. In 1920 the British government partitioned Ireland. Northern Ireland, which had its Parliament at Stormont in Belfast, consisted of six of the nine counties of Ulster. Unionists comprised a majority in just four of the six counties, but held a clear majority in Northern Ireland. The Irish Free State (as the South of Ireland was known after partition until the declaration of the republic in 1948), with a Parliament in Dublin, was to rule the other twenty-six counties of Ireland. The treaty signed between the British government and Sinn Féin in December 1921 gave the Irish Free State dominion status within the British Empire and set up a boundary commission to consider redrawing the border with Northern Ireland.

The partition of Ireland was widely seen as a temporary measure, and provision was made for its voluntary reunification. The British hoped that Irish unity would be achieved within the Empire/ Commonwealth, while republicans favoured an independent, united Ireland outside the Empire/Commonwealth (see Chapter 3). However, the division between the majority Protestant Northern Ireland state and the overwhelmingly Catholic state in the South grew after partition. In 1937, the new Constitution of the Irish Free state recognized the special position of the Catholic Church, and in Articles 2 and 3 claimed as the national territory the whole island of Ireland. The Catholic minority within Northern Ireland was discriminated against by a unionist regime concerned to establish its control in the face of an IRA threat from the South. British politics had been dominated by the 'Irish Question' for much of the late nineteenth and early twentieth centuries. British politicians now handed over responsibility for the North to the subordinate Stormont Parliament, ignored abuses of Catholics' civil rights and minimized its involvement in Irish politics (see Chapter 3). By the 1960s, unionists were concerned that their position within the Union was becoming undermined. In 1964 there was rioting during the Westminster General Election campaign and in 1966 the newly-formed, loyalist paramilitary Ulster Volunteer Force (UVF) murdered two Catholics. The civil rights movement drew attention to abuses occurring under the Stormont government but, when that failed to bring about change, it took politics into the streets. The result was escalating conflict and violence, which finally forced the British government to intervene more directly. First the British put pressure on the Stormont government to reform, and then troops were deployed on the streets as communal rioting spiralled beyond the control of the local police – the Royal Ulster Constabulary (RUC): see Chapter 4. Republicans took to the streets to defend Catholic areas from attack by unionists, but also went on the offensive, seizing their opportunity to drive the British out of Ireland. Unionist paramilitaries mobilized to strike back against the IRA by killing Catholics. In 1972, after a further escalation in violence, the British government suspended the Northern Ireland Parliament and introduced direct rule (see Chapter 4). Between 1972 and 1974 a serious attempt was made by the British government to introduce power-sharing between unionists and nationalists alongside an all-Ireland body. Unionist opinion turned against this first 'peace process' and it ended in failure (see Chapter 5). Opinion in Northern Ireland was polarized, and the prospects for resuscitating an accommodation between unionists and nationalists receded.

The British government and the IRA settled down for a 'Long War'. The British attempted to criminalize republican prisoners who resisted, resulting in the deaths of ten republicans during the Hunger Strikes of 1980–1. The IRA's political wing, Sinn Féin, contested elections after the Hunger Strikes and performed well (see Chapter 6). The British and Irish governments embarked on an initiative which Margaret Thatcher intended would reap security benefits for Britain in the battle against the IRA (see Chapter 7). In 1985, the Anglo-Irish Agreement was signed by the two governments, giving the Irish an input into the governance of Northern Ireland. Unionists were alienated by this development, and a polarization of public and political opinion followed the Agreement. However, this Agreement may have accelerated a rethink within the republican movement which, while the IRA continued its 'armed struggle', adjusted its ideological stance and entered into secret contacts with the British government between 1990 and 1993 (see Chapter 8). In 1994, the IRA announced a ceasefire and negotiations began around the conditions upon which Sinn Féin would be admitted into all-party negotiations with unionists. Unionists and the British government insisted that some decommissioning of IRA weapons must take place before Sinn Féin could be allowed to sit at the negotiating table. A proposal was put forward to abandon the demand for decommissioning in return for elections to a Northern Ireland Forum, a unionist demand. Republicans rejected this, and the IRA ended its ceasefire in February 1996. Following the election of a Labour government in 1997, the IRA renewed its ceasefire and entered negotiations with unionists in September 1997. On 10 April 1998 the 'Good Friday Agreement' was reached between unionists and nationalists on new power-sharing institutions for Northern Ireland and a programme of reform (Chapter 9). The Agreement continues to be dogged by controversy, particularly over the issue of decommissioning IRA weapons. There were several periods of devolution; in the first two periods, Sinn Féin/IRA did get into government twice without giving up any guns (December 1999–February 2000 and May 2000–October 2001), and a third time after an unspecified amount of IRA arms had been put beyond use (November 2001–October 2002). In May 2007, a fourth period of devolution was initiated when the now dominant hard-line parties, Sinn Féin and the DUP, agreed to share power (see Chapter 10).

Nationalist Views of the Conflict

In Northern Ireland, Irish nationalists and British unionists have very different perspectives on the conflict and its history. History and contemporary events are used to apportion blame and justify contrasting analyses and 'solutions' to the conflict. Yet, while unionists and nationalists are divided, there are also divisions within both unionism and nationalism in their analysis of the conflict and prescriptions for settling it. Nationalist and unionist ideologies are not static but dynamic, shifting over time in response to changing circumstances. The term 'nationalist' is often used to describe someone who aspires to a united Ireland but is opposed to the use of violence to achieve it, while a 'republican' often shares much of the analysis of the 'nationalist' but is prepared to use violence; so all republicans are nationalists, but not all nationalists are republicans. But these terms are contested, and some nationalists resent the way that the term republican has been appropriated by the IRA and other violent organizations. Republicans tend to come disproportionately from the working classes.

Nationalist and Republican Views

Nationalists argue that 800 years of English oppression have followed the Anglo-Norman invasion of 1169, during which a succession of nationalist heroes have striven to drive out the English invader who has brought nothing but trouble to Ireland. However, some nationalists go even further back and draw inspiration from an idyllic Celtic past.

A consistent theme of nationalist/republican history is the brutality of the invading English/British. The propensity of the English to oppress the Irish brutally is established, from Cromwell's massacres of the Irish during the 1640s, through the execution of the Easter Rising martyrs in 1916 and the atrocities perpetrated by the British 'Black and Tans' during the War of Independence, to the Bloody Sunday 'massacre' in 1972. The responsibility of the English for the Irish famine, or genocide as some call it, is used to establish the guilt of the English then and, by implication and analogy, now, both for the events of the 1840s and Ireland's stunted development ever since (Ireland's population was 25 per cent of that of the UK in 1845 but just 10 per cent by 1914). A story is told that emphasizes the continuity of English/British oppression in Ireland and therefore its inevitability: 'Nothing but the same old story', according to the title of one book.

Irish history becomes a morality tale in which the brave, principally male, heroes of nationalist history take up the struggle of centuries against the English/British oppressor (the O'Neills of Tyrone, Wolfe Tone, the Fenians, Daniel O'Connell, Michael Davitt, Charles Stewart Parnell, James Connolly, Patrick Pearse, Michael Collins, Bobby Sands). As the struggle against the English continues, new events and heroes are added to the pantheon. During 'the Troubles' republicans and nationalists have commemorated Bloody Sunday and the introduction of internment. Bobby Sands and the 1981 hunger strikers are placed in the tradition of the men of 1916.

The role of Irish Protestants in the nationalist tradition is often highlighted, from Tone to Parnell, to show the way for contemporary unionists. From this perspective, unionists are seen as Irish people who have been duped by the English/British into believing they are

British. Once the British leave Ireland the unionists will reassess their position and realize that they are Irish after all. Alternatively, unionists are seen as illegitimate settlers with no right to remain in Ireland. They should be encouraged to leave when the British colonial power withdraws.

For both nationalists and republicans, the partition of Ireland was seen as an undemocratic imposition by the British to maintain their domination, rather than a compromise between the competing forces of nationalism and unionism. The 1918 all-Ireland election demonstrated the desire of the Irish people for unity and independence. Partition is undemocratic and artificial, since the border was not drawn with respect to the will of the people but as a result of power and the threat of force. The British could have imposed a united Ireland and the unionists would not have resisted, because they had no particular place to go. It is the British prop that has sustained unionist resistance.

Republicans view developments during 'the Troubles' in a different way from nationalists. The IRA justifies its lack of popular support for its 'armed struggle' among nationalists by reference to the Easter Rising of 1916. The Rising did not have popular support at the time (many nationalists had relatives serving in the British Army in France) but subsequently won widespread sympathy. Republicans emphasize loyalist or unionist responsibility for the recent outbreak of the conflict, pointing to the emergence of the loyalist UVF in 1966, or the brutality of the Stormont regime against the civil rights protesters. The British rather than the unionists then become the primary focus of the enmity of republican ideology. The British are held to be responsible for the establishment of an oppressive security regime, including abuses of human rights, torture, Bloody Sunday, internment without trial, 'shoot to kill', the suspension of civil liberties, and collusion between the British state and loyalist paramilitaries. Republicans, on the other hand, were forced to respond to British oppression and defend the Catholic community. Republicans reject the nationalist view that the British are 'neutral', and have argued that the British have economic, strategic and political reasons for retaining Northern Ireland within the Union.

Both republicans and nationalists argue that Irish unity is inevitable (see Chapter 2). Since partition, British neglect of Northern Ireland has allowed the perpetuation of civil rights abuses by the Unionist government at Stormont. During the 1960s there was a shift towards participation in the Northern Ireland state, with Catholics emphasizing 'British rights for British citizens' rather than an end to the border. When this conciliatory stance was rebuffed by the unionists, Catholics took to the streets to secure their civil rights and were met with unionist brutality (see Chapter 3). The violence of the British Army polarized the situation in Northern Ireland. Republicans stress the repressive nature of the Stormont era and subsequent British policy in order to justify the IRA's 'armed struggle' after 1969.

Republicans deemed nationalists to be collaborators for supporting power-sharing in 1974, and tried to undermine it. Nationalists argued that the British Labour government betrayed the power-sharing executive by not taking stronger action to defend it against unionist opposition or subsequently push the unionists hard enough towards reviving power-sharing. Unlike republicans, however, nationalists have tended to accept that Britain is 'neutral' in its attitude towards Northern Ireland, meaning that it has no overriding interest in retaining the Union. Nationalists argue that the Anglo-Irish Agreement of 1985, which gave the Republic a say in the affairs of Northern Ireland, was further evidence of British neutrality and argued that the IRA's violence was counterproductive to achieving Irish unity. The key problem in Northern Ireland for nationalists is not so much the British government as a division among the people of Northern Ireland themselves, between unionists and nationalists. Unionists are not simply, as republicans claim, the puppets of the British; they have a considerable degree of independence or autonomy. The republican leadership presents the peace process and the Good Friday Agreement as further steps towards the inevitable unity of Ireland.

The Social Democratic and Labour Party (SDLP, www.sdlp.ie*)* The SDLP was founded in 1970 and has been the main exponent of the nationalist view of the conflict. It is overwhelmingly Catholic in membership and support. A centre-left party with working-class support, it none the less tends to do better among middle-class Catholics. In its founding constitution the SDLP supported the proposition that the unity of Ireland could only come about with the consent of the majority within Northern Ireland. The SDLP has long supported joint authority of the British and Irish governments over Northern Ireland; but it has also supported power-sharing between nationalists and unionists, along with an 'Irish dimension' to express the Irishness and national aspiration of the minority community. In the mid-1970s factions within the SDLP supported a declaration of British intent to withdraw and independence for Northern Ireland – some as a transition stage before Irish unity; and others in order to reach accommodation with unionists. The principal divide within the SDLP has been between those around John Hume, who have emphasized the importance of the Irish dimension (North/South bodies and an increased role for the Republic of Ireland in the North), and others who have prioritized power-sharing and accommodation with unionists within Northern Ireland. On security, the SDLP has been critical of the security forces, the police and the army, and refuses to 'support' the police or encourage Catholics to join the RUC. However, the SDLP has also been very strong in its condemnations of all republican and loyalist violence. The SDLP's principal electoral rivals have been, first, the moderate Alliance Party, second, in the late 1970s and early 1980s, the small, 'more nationalist' Irish Independence Party; and third, throughout the 1980s and 1990s, Sinn Féin, the political wing of the IRA. Although the republicans did not contest elections in the 1970s, they nevertheless represented a challenge to the SDLP for the support of the nationalist community. The SDLP championed the Northern Ireland peace process and the Good Friday Agreement 1998, but by May 2001 had been overtaken as the largest nationalist party by Sinn Féin. The SDLP has been led by Gerry Fitt (1970–9), John Hume (1979–2001) and Mark Durkan (2001–).

Sinn Féin/Irish Republican Army (SF/IRA, www.sinnfein.ie)   Since 1969, the republican movement has split into various factions. In 1969, the IRA split into the Official IRA and the Provisional IRA (which is the full name of the IRA at the time of writing). The Official IRA (OIRA) was more left-wing than the Provisionals, emphasized the unity of the Protestant and Catholic working class, and took a more defensive military stance. It declared a ceasefire in 1972. In 1975, the Irish National Liberation Army (INLA) split away from the OIRA and mounted a terrorist campaign against the security forces. The Provisional IRA (PIRA) was more Catholic, right-wing and militaristic in its outlook. It took the offensive against the British Army in 1969–70 and emerged as the dominant group within the republican movement. In 1986, Sinn Féin voted to end their traditional boycott and take their seats in the Irish Dáil (assembly). Republican Sinn Féin (www.rsf.ie) broke away from the Provisionals in 1986 over this decision and formed a military wing called the Continuity IRA. The 'Real IRA' (RIRA) split from the Provisionals in the autumn of 1997 over growing dissatisfaction with Sinn Féin's involvement in the 'peace process'. The political wing of the RIRA is

Table 1.1   Election results, 1973–2007 principal parties, percentage shares

Election			Political parties					
			Democratic Unionist	Vanguard Unionist	Ulster Unionist	Alliance	Social Democratic & Labour Party	Sinn Féin
May	1973	L	4.3	2.1	41.4	13.7	13.4	–
Jun	1973	A	10.8	10.5	29.3	9.2	22.1	–
Feb	1974	W	8.2	10.6	32.3	3.2	22.4	–
Oct	1974	W	8.5	13.1	36.5	6.4	22.0	–
May	1975	C	14.7	12.7	25.8	9.8	23.7	–
May	1977	L	12.7	1.5	29.6	14.4	20.6	–
May	1979	W	10.2	–	36.6	11.9	18.2	–
Jun	1979	E	29.8	–	21.9	6.8	24.6	–
May	1981	L	26.6	–	26.5	8.9	17.5	–
Oct	1982	A	23.0	–	29.7	9.3	18.8	10.1
Jun	1983	W	20.0	–	34.0	8.0	17.9	13.4
Jun	1984	E	33.6	–	21.5	5.0	22.1	13.3
May	1985	L	24.3	–	29.5	7.1	17.8	11.8
Jun	1987	W	11.7	–	37.8	10.0	21.1	11.4
May	1989	L	17.7	–	31.3	6.9	21.0	11.2
Jun	1989	E	29.9	–	22.2	5.2	25.5	9.1
Apr	1992	W	13.1	–	34.5	8.7	23.5	10.0
Jun	1993	L	17.3	–	29.3	7.6	22.0	12.4
Jun	1994	E	29.2	–	23.8	4.1	28.9	9.9
May	1996	F	18.8	–	24.2	6.5	21.4	15.5
May	1997	W	13.6	–	32.7	8.0	24.1	16.1
May	1997	L	15.9	–	27.8	6.6	20.7	16.9
Jun	1998	A	18.1	–	21.3	6.5	22.0	17.6
Jun	1999	E	28.4	–	17.6	2.1	28.1	17.3
May	2001	W	22.5	–	26.8	4.8	21	21.7
May	2001	L	21.4	–	22.9	5.2	19.4	20.7
Nov	2003	A	25.7	–	22.7	3.7	17	23.5
Jun	2004	E	31.9	–	16.5	–	15.9	26.3
May	2005	W	33.7	–	17.7	3.9	17.5	24.3
May	2005	L	29.6	–	18	5	17.4	23.2
Mar	2007	A	30.1	–	14.9	5.2	15.2	26.2

Notes:
(i) Type of election is indicated by letter:
 A = Assembly, W = Westminster Parliament, C = Convention, E = European Parliament, F = Forum, L = Local Council Elections.
(ii) The symbol (–) indicates the party did not exist or did not contest the election.
(iii) Figures do not add up to 100 per cent, as assorted minor parties and independents also contested elections.
Source: www.ark.ac.uk/elections

the 32 County Sovereignty Committee (www.32csm.org). The CIRA and RIRA continue their 'armed struggle', the latter being responsible for the Omagh bombing in the summer of 1998, which killed 29 and injured 310.

The evidence points overwhelmingly towards an inextricable link between the IRA and Sinn Féin, in spite of the attempts in recent years, for propaganda reasons, for Sinn Féin to claim a distance between itself and the IRA. Sinn Féin had long been subordinate to the military wing, but during the 1980s began to play a more prominent role in the partnership, contesting elections and taking its seats on local councils. The republican movement did not accept partition and argued for British withdrawal and a democratic socialist Irish republic. The IRA opposed power-sharing during 1972–4 and escalated its campaign to topple that experiment. In 1975–6 it announced a ceasefire in the expectation that the British were about to withdraw. 'Hardline' elements within the republican movement opposed this development and, when the British did not withdraw, the IRA leadership were discredited. The new northern leadership of Gerry Adams and Martin McGuinness became dominant within the IRA and settled down for the 'Long War' by attempting to mobilize a political campaign alongside the military struggle. Following the Hunger Strikes in 1981, this emerged as the 'Armalite and ballot box' strategy: the PIRA continued its military campaign while the political wing, Sinn Féin, fought elections. The Provisionals continued to oppose any partitionist, power-sharing settlement in Northern Ireland on the grounds that it represented a return to the bad old days of the 'Stormont regime'. Nevertheless, the Sinn Féin leadership supported the Good Friday Agreement, which accepted the principle that the constitutional position of Northern Ireland should not change without the consent of the people. Sinn Féin emerged by May 2001 as the largest nationalist party and consolidated this position in subsequent elections. In July 2005, the IRA declared the 'armed campaign' was over and ordered IRA units to dump arms and in May 2007 entered a power-sharing Executive with the DUP.

Republican paramilitaries have been responsible for approximately 2,139 (58.8 per cent) (PIRA 1,771) out of the 3,636 'Troubles'-related deaths in Northern Ireland (McKittrick *et al.* 2004). Sinn Féin/IRA alone were responsible for over 50 per cent of all deaths (Fay *et al.* 1999, p. 178). They have killed police officers, prison staff, those working for the security forces, soldiers, and both Protestant and Catholic civilians (see Figure 1.2 on page 29). Responsibility for these deaths is complicated by the role of the security forces in running and protecting their agents within republican paramilitary organizations. Reviewing the statistics of violence, Fay *et al.* argue that the IRA has 'Essentially . . . been an offensive rather than defensive organization, with little evidence that it was able to protect the Nationalist population from either the security forces or sectarian attack' (Fay *et al.* 1999, p. 178). Ruairí Ó Brádaigh was President of Sinn Féin (1970–83), while Gerry Adams was Vice-President of Sinn Féin (1978–83) and has been President since 1983.

Unionist Views of the Conflict

The term 'unionist' describes a supporter of the Union who tends to be opposed to the use of violence and uses more constitutional means to defend the Union, while a 'loyalist' is used to describe a unionist who tends to employ or advocate more militant methods to defend the Union, sometimes including violence. Loyalists tend to be drawn disproportionately from the working class.

Unionist and Loyalist Views

In recent years, loyalist historians have argued that the Cruthin were the original inhabitants of Northern Ireland, and when the Scottish settlers settled in Ulster during the seventeenth century this was simply a return of the Cruthin to their original homeland. Unionist history highlights the plantation of the seventeenth century and suggests that the Protestant settlers brought with them 'progressive' ways to a backward land. The Irish rebellion of 1641 against the settlers is remembered as a warning to Protestants of the hostility of Catholics, and the consequences of not being vigilant. At the Siege of Derry in 1689 the Protestant Apprentice Boys slammed the gates of Derry shut when the Protestant leader, Governor Lundy, proposed to surrender to the forces of the Catholic King James II. The siege was subsequently lifted, and in 1690 the Protestant King William of Orange defeated James at the Battle of the Boyne. These events are highlights of the unionist marching season, commemorated annually on 14 August and 12 July, respectively. The Siege of Derry is used to remind unionists that a defiant 'no surrender' posture can bring victory. Those who are perceived to be selling out the unionist cause are called 'Lundies'. Another key date in unionist history is the mobilization of unionism, under the leadership of Sir Edward Carson, during the Ulster Crisis of 1912–14, when unionists rallied to demonstrate their opposition to Home Rule for Ireland and their willingness to resort to arms to avoid it. During the Battle of the Somme in 1916, the Ulster Division suffered heavy casualties, demonstrating 'Ulster's' commitment to the Union in blood, and consequently Britain's debt to Northern Ireland. The loyalty of Northern Ireland was again demonstrated during the Second World War, when Britain 'stood alone' against the Nazis – in contrast to the neutrality of Southern Ireland. During 'the Troubles' unionists have also moved to preserve its heritage, celebrate new heroes and commemorate new events. For example, following the Drumcree stand-off in 1995, a commemorative medal was struck.

Unionists see the partition of Ireland as being democratic and resulting from the South's decision to secede from the Union. The border of Northern Ireland is formed in a similar way to most others, being the result of conflicts of power rather than just following natural geographical features. The threat to the new Northern Ireland state from the IRA is emphasized to justify discrimination against Catholics, or else that discrimination is denied or its impact minimized (see Chapter 3). The emergence of the civil rights movement in the 1960s is seen as a Communist/republican-inspired campaign to re-open the border question, rather than a movement genuinely seeking reform. The growing involvement of 'untrustworthy' British governments prevented unionists from taking the necessary repressive measures to deal with the terrorist threat. The British government's weakness was manifested in its negotiations with the IRA, suspension of Stormont and ambiguity on Northern Ireland's constitutional position. This encouraged IRA violence and resulted in a mobilization of unionists to defend the Union (see Chapter 4). The Republic of Ireland, with a territorial claim on the North in its Constitution and its failure to suppress the IRA, encourages and legitimizes the IRA campaign against Northern Ireland. The British-inspired power-sharing experiment of 1972–4, particularly its hated Irish dimension, was designed to manipulate Northern Ireland out of the Union, and only a popular revolt by unionists prevented this. The Labour government of 1974–9 cracked down on terrorism and began to rule Northern Ireland like any other part of the UK. This resulted in a decrease in violence. The Conservative governments during 1979–97 turned their backs on unionists, beginning an Anglo-Irish process in 1980 that culminated in the great 'sell-out' of 1985, when the Anglo-Irish Agreement was signed, giving the Republic a role in the running of Northern Ireland. For some loyalists this represented yet another turn of the ratchet in the expulsion of Northern Ireland from the Union. From this perspective, the 'peace process' represents a 'surrender process', with Northern Ireland pushed further and further to the edge of the Union. Unionists are more likely to see the agreement as a historic accommodation from which the Union benefits and emerges stronger, ending Northern Ireland's slide from the Union.

The Ulster Unionist Party (UUP, www.uup.org)   This was the dominant party during the Stormont era: 1921–72. It is a centre-right party that draws support from all classes but disproportionately from the middle class. After partition, the Ulster Unionist Party (UUP) lacked a serious rival until it was challenged by the Northern Ireland Labour Party in the late 1950s and early 1960s. In the 1960s, it was riven by conflict over reform and how to deal with the British government's interventionism. During the 1970s the UUP began to fragment. The most serious division within its ranks was over the power-sharing experiment of 1974. The leader of the UUP, Brian Faulkner, signed up for power-sharing and an Irish dimension, but this split his party and Faulkner resigned. Following the collapse of power-sharing, unionism shifted away from any further power-sharing settlements. Subsequently, the principal division has been between the 'devolutionists', who favour a strong devolved assembly in Northern Ireland, and the 'integrationists', who (before the devolution of power to Scotland and Wales in 1999) preferred the region to be ruled, like any other part of the UK, directly from Westminster. The UUP favoured the restoration of the powers of local government and an improvement in the way Northern Ireland's affairs were dealt with under direct rule as a step towards integration. The party has been united against any Irish dimension beyond 'normal' North–South co-operation. The Good Friday Agreement split the UUP into those supporting the Agreement and those who felt, among other things, that the Agreement did not make explicit enough the link between IRA decommissioning and participation in government. During the recent conflict, the party's principal rival has been the hardline Democratic Unionist Party (DUP) which has succeeded in making inroads into its support, most notably in the early 1980s when it almost became the leading unionist party. At the Assembly Elections in November 2003 the DUP beat the UUP and became the dominant unionist party, and this position was strengthened in subsequent elections. The UUP has been more conciliatory, more middle-class and slightly less hardline on security than its DUP rival. The UUP's most recent leaders have been Terence

O'Neill (1963–9), James Chichester-Clark (1969–71), Brian Faulkner (1971–4), Harry West (1974–9), James Molyneaux (1979–95) David Trimble (1995–2005) and Sir Reg Empey (2005–).

*The Democratic Unionist Party (*DUP, www.dup.org.uk*)*   This loyalist party was founded by the Reverend Ian Paisley and some members of his Free Presbyterian church in September 1971. During the 1960s, Paisley had warned against the apparent softening in the UUP's attitude towards Catholics and the Republic of Ireland, and these warnings appeared to be vindicated by the turn of events (see Chapter 3). The DUP, after initially supporting the integration of Northern Ireland into the UK, favoured the return of a majority-rule Northern Ireland Assembly, albeit with some safeguards for the nationalist minority. The DUP is more opposed to power-sharing and an Irish dimension than the UUP, and there has been some sympathy for Ulster independence. In the late 1970s it demolished its rival, the Vanguard Unionist Party (VUP), which had a more open relationship with the loyalist paramilitaries, and in the early 1980s its hardline stance threatened to make it the biggest unionist party. Ian Paisley regularly tops the poll for the Northern-Ireland-wide European elections, illustrating that his popularity extends beyond his party. The party opposed the Good Friday Agreement but did take up its ministerial positions in the executive. At the November 2003 Assembly Elections the DUP emerged as the largest party in Northern Ireland. In May 2007, the DUP agreed to share power with Sinn Féin and devolution was restored.

The DUP tends to take a more 'repressive stance' on security issues than does the UUP, leaning towards conservatism on social issues (contraception, and gay and women's rights), but it is less conservative on economic issues, perhaps reflecting its more working-class support. There are two DUP voting constituencies – rural evangelicals and urban, working-class loyalists. The DUP was led by Dr Ian Paisley from 1971 to 2007.

The Loyalist Paramilitaries   The Ulster Defence Association (UDA) was formed in 1971 to co-ordinate working-class, loyalist vigilante groups that had grown up to 'defend' loyalist areas. The peak of UDA membership was probably in 1972 when it had about 40,000 members. It has been involved in violence against Catholics, and its political wing has tended towards support for an independent Ulster. The UDA was banned in August 1992 and carries out paramilitary activities under the name the Ulster Freedom Fighters (UFF). The political wing of the UDA was the Ulster Democratic Party (UDP), which participated in the all-party talks that led to the Good Friday Agreement but, with only 1.1 per cent of the vote, it failed to win any Assembly seats in 1998 and was dissolved in 2001. The UDA became increasingly disillusioned with the Agreement and eventually came out in opposition to it, although it did support power-sharing between the DUP and Sinn Féin in May 2007.

The modern UVF was established in 1966, but after the organization murdered two Catholics it was proscribed by the Northern Ireland prime minister shortly after. It is a smaller, more elite grouping than the mass membership UDA but has been responsible for more deaths during the recent conflict. The political wing of the UVF is the Progressive Unionist Party (PUP, www.pup-ni.org.uk) which is a left-of-centre party, while the UDA tends to be more right-wing. The PUP won 2.6 per cent of the vote in the 1998 Assembly Elections, securing two seats, but by March 2007 this had declined to 0.6 per cent of the vote and one seat, held by Dawn Purvis. The initial support of the UVF and UDA for the 'peace process' resulted in a split in the UVF, with Billy Wright breaking away to form the Loyalist Volunteer Force (LVF) in 1995. Wright was murdered in prison in December 1997. In 1998, the LVF declared a ceasefire and in December of that year was the first paramilitary organization to decommission any weapons.

Loyalist paramilitaries have been responsible for approximately 983 deaths during the recent conflict, 27.4% of the total. Of these deaths, 858 out of the 983 victims were 'civilians', 65 were other loyalist paramilitaries (in feuds), and just 26 were republican paramilitary deaths. Of those deaths for which an organization could be identified as responsible, 254 were attributed to the UVF and 177 to the UDA/UFF (Fay *et al.* 1999, p. 169; and Hayes and McAllister 2001, p. 904, give figures of 439 and 254, respectively). Responsibility for the deaths is complicated by some degree of collusion between the security forces and loyalist paramilitaries. There has been some recent discussion about the winding up of both the UVF and UDA in response to the 'standing down' of the IRA.

A Centrist View of the Conflict

*The Alliance Party (*APNI, www.allianceparty.org*)*   This is the only party in Northern Ireland that attracts significant cross-community support. The party opposes and wants to overcome 'tribal politics', and its members refuse to designate themselves as either nationalist or unionist in the Assembly (although in November 2001 they redesignated to ensure that devolution was achieved). The party argues that there can be no constitutional change without the consent of the people of Northern Ireland. It was founded in April 1970 among people with little previous political background, and drew support from liberals in the UUP and the Northern Ireland Labour Party. The party supported the 1974 power-sharing experiment and after its collapse argued that there was no need for a Council of Ireland to achieve co-operation with the Republic. The Alliance Party draws its support principally from the Greater Belfast area, but when it gave conditional support to the Anglo-Irish Agreement in 1985 it lost some Protestant support. The party has favoured power-sharing and been more supportive than the UUP of the Irish dimension. The party endorsed the Good Friday Agreement but has been critical of aspects of the accommodation that reinforces communal identities. It has more middle-class support and its principal electoral rivals have been the nationalist SDLP and the unionist UUP. The most recent leaders of the Alliance Party have been Oliver Napier (1972–84), John Cushnahan (1984–7), Lord John Alderdice (1987–98), Sean Neeson (1998–2001) and David Ford (2001–).

History and the Current Conflict

Politicians are not necessarily interested in the 'truth' of what actually happened in history, but rather in telling a story about history that is useful in the propaganda war for political advantage now. Their stories imply guilt and blame for the conflict that has occurred, and who should be entitled to what in current negotiations. Both nationalists and unionists have very different views of history, which justify their political positions. History has been used to emphasize past injustices and patterns of oppression, and these are used to legitimize violence to redress these grievances. As the historian, Paul Bew, has commented, 'The difficulty is that many people on "both sides" as a result of the "troubles" have an investment in a highly partisan reading of that history that validates their suffering or indeed suffering they have inflicted on others.'

Historians are conscious of the way that history has been used to justify violence. A so-called 'Revisionist' movement of professional historians has developed to undermine the 'myths' of popular unionist and nationalist history. In the 1930s and 1940s, a school of professional Irish historians believed that their 'value-free' approach to history could demythologize the dominant official and popular histories. This was seen as even more necessary after the 'Troubles' exploded in the late 1960s, and history was used by the protagonists on all sides to justify their violence. The revisionists criticized history as a morality tale and emphasized the discontinuities and complexity of history; they rejected and sought to explode the 'simplistic hero cults' of nationalism and unionism. Inevitably, these 'revisionists' revised the demonic, propagandistic portrayal of Britain in nationalist history and portrayed it in a more sympathetic light. Revisionists also took on unionist history and showed the support of the Pope for William of Orange in 1690, and the conciliatory character of Sir Edward Carson in the early twentieth century, in contrast to his 'no surrender' unionist stereotype. A more accurate (and empathetic) understanding of history and contemporary history, it could be argued, promotes the kind of understanding that can undermine the crude 'propagandistic', ideological history which (some argue) sustains the conflict.

A traditionalist or nationalist school of history has criticized revisionists for using history to justify the partition of Ireland by emphasizing historical divisions and sectarianism of unionists and nationalists. They were also accused of playing down famine and massacres in history in order to portray the British more favourably. 'Revisionists' have been accused of 'neo-colonialism' or 'anti-nationalism', and one historian has claimed they are part of British counter-insurgency strategy. Traditionalists argued that nationalism and its 'myths' could be a positive force in uniting and fortifying a community in its struggle against the British imperialistic enemy (Boyce 1995).

'Myths' are used by the various parties to the conflict in Northern Ireland in the propaganda war to mobilize support and shift the political agenda in their direction (for more on the propaganda war, see Chapter 2). In attempting to communicate with and mobilize a mass audience, politicians use versions of history that resonate with popular ideologies rather than necessarily what is more 'historically accurate' (which, of course, is debatable). These myths may not reflect the latest historical findings, but they may reflect certain 'truths' experienced by the people, which the politician seeks to put across to an audience using historical 'stories'. The imperatives of the propaganda war also override the need for historical accuracy, since 'distortion' can be more useful politically than 'truth'. The historical account is not necessarily about, for example, the history of past English atrocities, but about English oppression now. Michael Ignatieff argues that the 'atrocity myth' does not deny that atrocities happen:

> What is mythic is that the atrocities are held to reveal the essential identity of the peoples in whose name they were committed. The atrocity myth implies an idea of a people having some essential genocidal propensity toward the other side. All the members of the group are held to have such a propensity even though atrocity can only be committed by specific individuals. The idea of collective guilt depends on the idea of a national psyche or racial identity. The fiction at work here is akin to the nationalist delusion that the identities of individuals are or should be subsumed into their national identities. (Ignatieff 1996, p. 116)

Generally, 'myths' have to contain some portion of 'truth' in order to be accepted and, depending on their intent, we may be sympathetic to the sentiment and ignore the historical inaccuracy. These, often competing, 'myths' about Ireland were created by the protagonists during 'the Troubles' to reinforce their ideological positions and mobilize supporters in the propaganda war (O'Doherty 1998, chs 3 and 4). This means that, as this book makes clear, there is considerable conflict over the interpretation of Northern Ireland's recent history (Boyce and O'Day 1996). In the run-up to and during the peace process, the British government has attempted to address historical grievances in the hope that this will aid the process of reconciliation. The British prime minister has apologized for Britain's role in the famine of the 1840s, ministers have regretted England's role in Irish history, an inquiry has been set up into the events of 'Bloody Sunday' 1972, and a commission has been established to examine the victims of the conflict. There has been some debate about whether a 'Truth Commission' should be set up to investigate the recent conflict.

There are contrasting views on the impact of history and myth. To what extent does a 'distorted' view of Irish history motivate and exacerbate the conflict? Or is the debate over history more a symptom than a cause of 'the Troubles'? If nationalist and unionist ideologies have deeper, even primordial, cultural or ethnic roots, then revisionist history is less likely to be effective, since it will not 'resonate' with the ideologies of the national communities. On the other hand, if nationalism and unionism are modern and malleable ideologies, then we can be optimistic that 'revisionism' may be able to dent nationalist and unionist histories by promoting empathy and a less simplistic view of the conflict. There is also the issue of how history has impacted on Northern Ireland and its people, constraining the extent to which political actors can change and shape the future.

Segregation and Sharing

There are contrasting views about the impact of segregation and integration on the Northern Ireland conflict. Those who are segregation-orientated, such as consociationalists (see Chapters 10 and 11), argue that antagonistic unionist and nationalist identities are either impossible or very difficult to change. The priority for those who manage conflict should, therefore, be to manage and work around these identities, and prevent or limit contact between the two groups. This will pacify the people and allow the political elites to reach agreement over the heads of the antagonistic population. Consociationalists argue that, while people may claim to be integrationist their behaviour is segregationist, which is a more telling indicator of what people really think.

By contrast, integrationists, such as those who support the Civil Society approach (see Chapters 10 and 11) favour mixing and contact between members of different groups in order to breakdown prejudices and hostile ideological views about 'the other' group. They argue that segregation creates very different socialization experiences for nationalists and unionists, who often attend different schools, and socialize and work separately. This, they argue, creates an environment in which prejudice and violence against the 'other side' is tolerated and encouraged instead of being challenged. To promote the management of conflict, it is argued, cross-community contact, among other things, should be promoted (see Dixon 1997a, 1997c, 1997d, 2005 for a detailed review of these approaches). Opinion polls tend to suggest that there is considerable popular support for integration; people prefer to work in mixed-religion workplaces; live in mixed-religion areas; marry people of the 'other' religion; and send their children to mixed-religion schools (see Table 1.2, and other survey data at www.ark.ac.uk). There is a large body of research suggesting that contact can be effective in reducing inter-group conflict.

While there is evidence of segregation, and some see a 'growing apartheid' in Northern Ireland, others argue that this research is flawed and exaggerated. Residential segregation does not necessarily mean social segregation, and more fluid behaviour patterns and significant social mixing have been perceived, particularly in the workplace (Anderson 2004).

Education

Research suggests that even pre-school children develop sectarian attitudes. The overwhelming majority of both Catholics and Protestants are educated in single-denomination Catholic or state (that is, Protestant) schools. This limits opportunities for cross-community contact. Some attempt has been made during the conflict to establish integrated schools, but these have been met with opposition from both the Protestant and Catholic churches. Just 6 per cent of students attend integrated schools, but Catholics can be found in largely Protestant grammar schools and in non-Catholic nursery schools. The school curriculum has come under scrutiny for its role in contributing to a less antagonistic society.

Residence

There has always been some degree of residential segregation in Northern Ireland, particularly in working-class areas. The rioting of the late 1960s and early 1970s precipitated what was until then the largest movement of population in Western Europe after the Second World War. Catholics fled from Protestant areas to find safety with their co-religionists and, to a lesser extent, Protestants fled Catholic areas. Since the early 1970s there has been a gradual trend towards further residential segregation as a result of force (intimidation and fear of attack) and voluntary movement. Boyle and Hadden conclude, 'in urban areas the two communities are moving into what they regard as safe areas, while in rural areas they are staying put on their land' (Boyle and Hadden 1994, p. 7). By 1991, 'About half of the province's 1.5 million population live in areas more than 90 per cent Protestant or more than 90 per cent Catholic', and 'In the past two decades, the number of predominantly Catholic wards increased from 43 to 120. Areas almost exclusively Protestant rose from 56 to 115' (*Independent on Sunday*, 21 March 1993). In 2007 there were 46 'peace walls' and

Table 1.2 Northern Irish public opinion over time for selected questions

	1989	1990	1991	1993	1994	1995	1996	1998	1998a	1999	2000	2001	2002	2003	2003a	2004	2005	2006
Percentage saying that the long-term policy for Northern Ireland should be for it to remain part of the United Kingdom (rather than a united Ireland)																		
Protestants	93	93	92	89	89	86	85	84	87	87	83	79	83	82	84	85	84	85
Catholics	32	33	35	36	24	34	35	19	22	16	20	15	22	21	27	24	25	22
NR	83	68	78	71	67	68	54	58	67	65	53	46	53	45	53	51	46	46
Percentage saying that a united Ireland in the next 20 years is 'very' or 'fairly' unlikely																		
Protestants	64	–	70	68	58	48	62	44	46	49	49	39	49	56	54	–	–	–
Catholics	65	–	66	71	67	59	70	39	48	40	47	38	55	49	56	–	–	–
NR	77	–	77	76	55	54	65	46	47	45	47	33	50	57	64	–	–	–
Percentage describing themselves as British																		
Protestants	66	–	64	69	70	64	59	67	76	72	72	70	75	66	71	73	63	63
Catholics	10	–	10	12	9	11	10	8	10	9	9	8	10	8	10	12	8	11
NR	55	–	40	41	56	46	47	34	60	51	45	40	46	36	43	43	30	35
Percentage saying they would prefer to live in a mixed-religion neighbourhood																		
Protestants	67	–	64	67	–	73	81	66	62	68	67	59	67	68	–	80	76	75
Catholics	75	–	76	82	–	83	85	74	67	79	73	72	82	76	–	83	81	80
NR	78	–	80	89	–	87	87	85	77	77	81	79	81	82	–	84	88	87
Percentage saying relations between Protestants and Catholics are better than they were 5 years ago																		
Protestants	20	–	29	25	26	51	43	44	29	42	37	25	26	42	46	53	51	54
Catholics	23	–	31	27	26	62	47	60	42	60	52	33	37	49	61	59	54	60
NR	28	–	19	23	28	61	47	48	41	47	40	30	28	41	43	58	44	54

Notes: NR – No religion; 1998a – Northern Ireland Election and Referendum Study; 2003a – Northern Ireland Assembly Election.
Source: www.ark.ac.uk/sol, Northern Ireland Life and Times.

11 'gates' constructed to prevent conflict between Protestants and Catholics at sectarian interfaces. Map 1.2 illustrates, albeit very crudely, residential segregation in Derry/Londonderry and Belfast. Although 94 per cent of social housing is segregated the British government has encouraged the development of new, cross-community housing estates (*Guardian*, 13 November 2006). The picture of integration/segregation is more complex and less clear cut than these statistics suggest, however; for example, people can mix socially while being segregated geographically.

Employment

Following discrimination during the Stormont period (see Chapter 3) there have been attempts to correct the religious imbalance in the workforce. Residential segregation has compounded the problems of achieving this balance, and Protestants and Catholics are deterred from taking jobs in areas dominated by members of the opposite religion, for safety reasons. Catholics make up just 5 per cent of the workforce in companies in Protestant-dominated areas, while 8 per cent of the workforce in Catholic-dominated areas are Protestants (*Belfast Telegraph,* 12 January 2002). Also, particularly in smaller firms, employment by social network, word of mouth or overt discrimination has resulted in a high degree of segregation in employment (Boyle and Hadden 1994, p. 46). This led to a situation in which Catholics were far more likely to be unemployed than Protestants. In 1971, Catholic *male* unemployment was estimated at 17.7 per cent, nearly three times the Protestant male rate. The ratio of Catholic to Protestant unemployment approached 2.5 during much of the recent conflict. In 1999 this dropped below 2, and by 2001 approached 1.6. The unemployment rate dropped from about 17 per cent in 1984 to under 4 per cent by 2005. In spite of this, Northern Ireland is one of the most deprived regions of the UK, and there has been increasing inequality (Coulter 1999, ch. 2). Reform of the police has increased the percentage of Catholics from 8 per cent to 21 per cent in the Police Service of Northern Ireland. There have been government initiatives to deal with religious discrimination and inequality in the workplace. Anderson argues that the number of highly polarized workplaces fell during the 1990s and the proportion of employees in mixed workplaces increased substantially (Anderson 2004, p. 6).

BELFAST

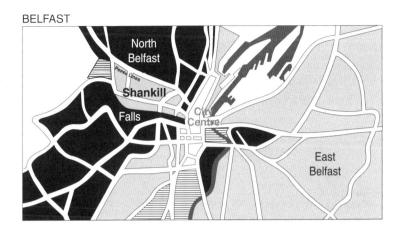

DERRY/LONDONDERRY

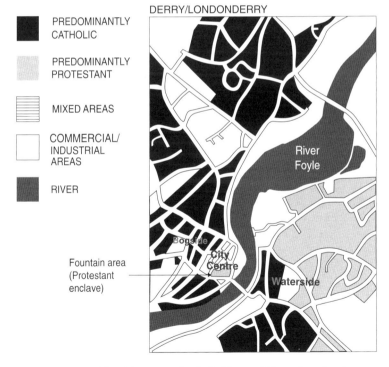

PREDOMINANTLY
CATHOLIC

PREDOMINANTLY
PROTESTANT

MIXED AREAS

COMMERCIAL/
INDUSTRIAL
AREAS

RIVER

Map 1.2   Residential segregation in Belfast and Derry/Londonderry
(a very rough guide)

Northern Ireland's economy has been highly dependent on public expenditure and public-sector employment during the conflict. By 2006, Great Britain's subsidy to Northern Ireland stood at £5–6 billion per year, about 20–25 per cent of Northern Ireland's gross domestic product (GDP). Northern Ireland's GDP is approximately £25 billion, and per capita is estimated at £14,600 (Portland Trust 2007).

Social

The levels of church attendance in Northern Ireland are disproportionately high for the UK. Social activities associated with the church tend therefore to reproduce segregation. In addition, sports are often segregated, with Catholics playing the 'Gaelic sports' (such as hurling, camogie, Gaelic football) while Protestants play the more 'British sports' (such as hockey, rugby, cricket). Even sports that are 'shared', such as soccer, are not necessarily played in a cross-community context. The Orange Order was founded in 1795 and now has approximately 100,000 members. One of its objectives was to defend the Protestant succession to the British throne, and it commemorates Protestant victories in Irish history by parading every year. Catholics are excluded from membership. Catholic organizations include the Ancient Order of Hibernians and the Gaelic Athletic Association. These organizations are often associated with social or community activities: 'It is highly unlikely that anyone who frequents any of these clubs or premises will ever meet anyone from the other community there' (Boyle and Hadden 1994, p. 39). There are data which suggest that 8.3–10.6 per cent of marriages are 'mixed-marriages', up from 6 per cent in 1969 (Niens *et al.* 2003, pp. 129–30).

Population

The population of Northern Ireland is 1,685,261, according to the 2001 census, with about 500,000 living in the urban area around Belfast (the population of the Republic is approximately 3.9 million). The higher Catholic birthrate in Northern Ireland did not lead to an increasing Catholic proportion of the population between 1926 and 1961 because of its higher emigration rate. But since 1971 the Catholic proportion of the population has increased – from about 33 per cent to 40 per cent in 1991, and to 44 per cent in the 2001 census, with Protestants making up 53 per cent of the population. This has raised nationalist expectations that there will be a Catholic, and therefore a nationalist, majority by about 2020, which could vote itself into a united Ireland. In the 2001 census, however, 13.9 per cent did not see themselves as affiliated with any religion and the growth in the size of the secular group has come mainly from former Protestants, who are more likely to be pro-Union (though this no-religion group is also more likely to reject a unionist or a nationalist identity). Since some Catholics are also unionists, then even a Catholic majority might not vote for a united Ireland.

Violence and the Conflict: Who Did What to Whom

Between 1966 and 2006 approximately 3,720 people were killed as a result of the conflict. Violence between 1966 and 2006 was not constant, but varied with time and place. In 1966, there were 3 killed as a result of the conflict, and then none for 1967 and 1968. The biggest death toll was in 1972, when 497 people were killed, and the worst period was 1972–6, when 1,638 people were killed (328 on average per year), representing 44 per cent of all those who died in the conflict. Between 1977 and 1994, the year of the IRA's first ceasefire, 1,656 people were killed (92 on average per year). Since the IRA's first ceasefire on 31 August 1994 and 2006 192 people were killed (on average 16 per year). Three areas saw most of the violent incidents: Derry, Mid-Ulster and Belfast. North and West Belfast have seen approximately 40 per cent of all deaths, and there were 600 deaths in North Belfast alone in 1969–93 (*Irish News*, 25 January 1993). Fay *et al.* argue that there is not one conflict in Northern Ireland but 'a mosaic of different types of conflict. Accordingly, the "reality" of the Troubles is different for people in different locations and in different occupations' (Fay *et al.* 1999, p. 136).

The interpretation of the statistics of violence during the recent conflict is highly contentious, because they can be used to establish victimhood and legitimize political violence. It can be difficult to establish responsibility for deaths, particularly in the light of increasing knowledge about the 'dirty war' fought between the security forces and the paramilitaries. Unionists and nationalists have strongly contrasting views as to who is responsible for the violence, and what is a legitimate response to it (Fay *et al.* 1999, pp. 156–7).

There are two contrasting academic perspectives on the impact of violence. The first emphasizes the extent of the violence in Northern Ireland and sees this as an incentive for people and policymakers to turn away from the abyss of all-out civil war and towards

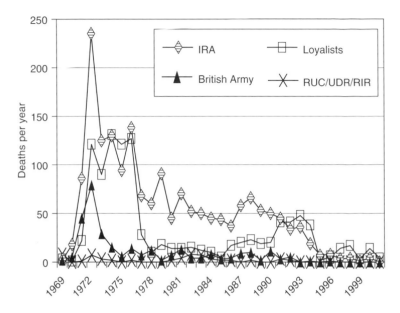

Figure 1.1   Responsibility for deaths, 1969–2001
Source: http://www.incore.au.uk

accommodation. Nearly 2 per cent of the population of Northern Ireland has been killed (0.22 per cent) or injured (1.78 per cent) during the recent conflict (see Figure 1.2) and comparative evidence is produced to argue that the Northern Ireland conflict is 'very intense' (O'Leary and McGarry 1996, pp. 13, 20). While more than 3,600 people have been killed, 'around 100,000 people in Northern Ireland live in households where someone has been injured in a Troubles-related incident' (Fay *et al.* 1999, p. 204). It has been estimated that, by 1998, one in seven of the adult population reported direct experience of violence, one in five had a family member or close relative injured or killed, and more than half personally knew someone who had been injured or killed (Hayes and McAllister 2001, p. 910). Padraig O'Malley argues against this use of comparative data:

> Scale alters the perception of the breadth of conflict: we do not think in terms of proportionality but in terms of absolutes. A bomb that kills one person in a population of 1.5 million is not the same thing, nor is it perceived as such, as a bomb that kills one hundred people in a country with a population of one hundred-fifty million people. (O'Malley 1994, p. 16)

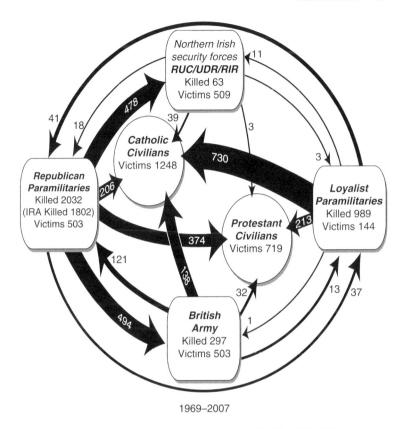

1969–2007

Figure 1.2   'Who killed whom during "the Troubles"', 1969–2007

Note: The primary source for this diagram is McKittrick *et al.* (2004) but where necessary this has been supplemented by figures from Sutton (1994, 1999), Fay *et al.* (1999), O'Leary and McGarry (1996) and www.cain.ulst.ac.uk. These figures are from varying sources with different methods of classification, therefore the figures are approximate and do not add up. Nevertheless they give an idea of the perpetrators and victims of the violence. The concept of using this type of diagram to map the perpetrators and victims of violence in Northern Ireland was originated by O'Leary and McGarry (1996).

He draws attention to the extent of the killing in Sri Lanka (50,000 killed out of 17 million population in ten years) and Angola (100,000 killed during its civil war).

A second interpretation of the violence suggests that it is because the violence in Northern Ireland has been localized and contained that many have been unaffected by the conflict and are therefore reluctant to become involved in resolving it (Boyle and Hadden 1994,

p. 107; O'Malley 1994). There is less risk of sudden death (as a result of terrorism/murder or road deaths) in Northern Ireland than in the USA: 'most people in Northern Ireland have less direct contact with death or injury from the conflict than from ordinary accidents'. They conclude, 'The vast majority of people in Northern Ireland live perfectly normal lives in the midst of the conflict' (Boyle and Hadden 1994, pp. 105–6). However, deaths caused by violence are often intentional and create terror among the civilian population in a way that road deaths do not.

Lost Lives: The Stories of the Men, Women and Children Who Died as a Result of the Northern Ireland Troubles documents the circumstances of every life lost during the recent conflict. It is a valuable contribution to our understanding of the situation, because it brings home the immense human tragedy of the conflict which risks being lost in the discussion of statistics and in the broad sweep of general analyses (McKittrick *et al.* 2004).

Generalization, Complexity and Integration

The generalizations presented in this opening chapter (and in the rest of this book) can be useful in giving an initial grasp of the conflict, but they are at the same time distortions that cannot do justice to the nuances and intricacies of the situation. Simplification and categorization are used to make sense of a conflict, but this simplification necessarily distorts the complex reality. This is why there has been so much scepticism over much of the comparative literature on Northern Ireland (Whyte 1990, pp. 254, 252). There is a further problem that simplification of a complex reality – by dividing the social world into in-groups and out-groups, and attributing stereotypes to them – can create conditions for conflict (Kremer and Schermbrucker 2006, p. 160). Generalizations and simplifications, if they are not acknowledged, can prevent a closer understanding of the conflict and, at worst, reproduce some of the communal stereotypes that, arguably, contribute to the persistence of antagonism.

Generalizations about the conflict can blind the observer to a more complex reality when it is observed more closely. Willie Frazer, a prominent, hard-line unionist and campaigner for 'Families Acting for Innocent Relatives', was brought up in a predominantly nationalist area and, while a Protestant, played Gaelic football for Whitecross GAA Club. Danny Morrison was a prominent member of Sinn Féin and from a republican family. His sister met a British soldier in 1969 and married him. Ronnie Bunting was the son of Major Ronald Bunting, a leading loyalist activist and supporter of Ian Paisley. He was 'associated' with the Irish National Liberation Army, a very violent, republican Marxist organization, and was murdered in 1979. The first policeman to be shot in the recent conflict was killed by the loyalist UVF. One source claims that the first six British soldiers to die in Northern Ireland were all Catholic. Seán MacStiofáin, the Chief of Staff of the IRA between 1970 and 1972, was born John Stephenson in London and spoke with an English accent.

The definition of the terms discussed in this chapter are *highly contested* (see Chapter 2, 'The War of Words' pp. 45–47). For example, I have defined 'republicans' here as people who have nationalist views but are prepared to use violence to achieve their goals. This definition is one that has been popularly used in Great Britain and Northern Ireland to refer to the IRA. But there are others in the island of Ireland who contest the IRA's appropriation of this label and try to claim the term back from violent republicanism. Furthermore, the IRA's definitions of republicanism are not static but have changed over time. Among unionists, there is also not quite the sharp divide between violent loyalists and non-violent unionists described here, but rather a spectrum along which unionists move between violence and non-violence. Loyalists have often been more accommodating than people described as 'unionists', such as Robert McCartney (Dixon 2004b). There has been a significant percentage of 'Catholics' who favour Northern Ireland remaining in the Union; between 1989 and 2006 this fluctuated between a high of 36 per cent in 1993 to a low of just 15 per cent in 2001. An average of about 10 per cent of 'Catholics' described themselves as 'British' between 1989 and 2006 although, significantly, only 1 per cent identified themselves as unionists (see Table 1.2 on page 23 and data at www.ark.ac.uk).

The degree of segregation has been exaggerated, and this can lead to a distorted understanding of the conflict. For example, US President Clinton believed that it was only because of his visit to Belfast and under the cover of darkness that unionists and nationalists came out on to the streets together to hear his speech. This perception is mistaken; nationalists and unionists do shop alongside each other in daylight hours in Belfast, and there is a degree of mixing at work, in education and socially.

2

The Approach and Argument: Power, Ideology and 'Reality'

Introduction

This chapter explains the approach and argument of the book to analysing the conflict in Northern Ireland. It stresses the dynamic nature of the conflict and the inter-relationship between power, ideology and 'reality', which reveal the constraints and opportunities affecting the various parties (individuals, groups and governments) to the conflict. The argument of this chapter will be enlarged upon as the book progresses.

The power of the various parties to pursue their interests is distributed unevenly, with considerable constraints operating on the British government's ability to control the conflict (see the Conclusion to this book).

- *Power* is used to fight both a 'real war' and an ideological or propaganda war over Northern Ireland. The 'real war' involves the use of physical force in an attempt to destroy an opponent's armed forces.
- *Ideology* is deployed in the propaganda war in which rhetoric and propaganda are used to realize the party or government's interests. In the propaganda war, participants attempt to sustain the determination and morale of the domestic audience, win external support and shift the political agenda in their favour, while at the same time attempting to break their opponent's will to resist. The 'real war' and the propaganda war are inextricably interrelated.
- *'Reality'* – an attempt is made to distinguish between the ideological propaganda and rhetoric deployed in the 'propaganda

war' and shape perceptions, and the underlying 'realities' of the conflict. However, attention is drawn to the difficulties of this exercise, in particular the problems of objectivity and the problem of distinguishing between false 'propaganda' and 'reality'.

Defining Power: Structure and Agency

The problems of one-dimensional and static explanations of the Northern Ireland conflict – based solely or largely on materialism, religion, social-psychology, ethnicity or culture – have been exposed elsewhere (Whyte 1990). However, while one factor may not explain everything, it could explain something. For example, the unemployment rate may not be related directly to the statistics of violence (McGarry and O'Leary 1995, p. 289), but this does not mean that unemployment has no indirect impact on violence and the conflict. Areas of high deprivation have been associated with high levels of violence and support for paramilitary activity. Static and one-dimensional explanations tend not to consider the dynamics of the conflict, its peaks and troughs, and how the impact of its prime factor varies over time and by context (Dixon 1996b). The great difficulty is attempting to weigh the importance of various factors (structural, rational and cultural) that affect the conflict, and how they interrelate (Lichbach and Zuckerman 1997, p. 273).

This book seeks a more dynamic explanation of the conflict in Northern Ireland. It focuses on the inter-relationship of power, ideology and reality. Power is an elusive but useful concept which can be defined as the ability to shape perception and, therefore, action (and here the power of ideologies to shape perception action is emphasized). By considering the *structures* (political, economic, ideological, cultural) that empower or constrain the various *agents* (individuals, parties, organizations and governments) that seek to exert influence on the conflict we can make an assessment of the power these agents have to pursue their interests, and how this power varies over time. There is an attempt to combine the political scientist's eye for the general, structure-orientated explanation and the journalist's or contemporary historian's more agency-orientated approach, with an eye for chronology, detail and nuance (Hay 1995; Marsh *et al.* 1999; Marsh and Stoker 2002).

Agency-orientated Explanations

There is a tendency among some historians and journalists to become caught up in the minutiae of the conflict and not to see the wood for the trees, or the trees for the leaves. There is an overemphasis placed on the individual's capacity for agency (an agent's capacity to take decisions and act upon a situation), where the agents are conceived of as being 'knowledgeable and intentional subjects with complete control over the settings which frame their actions' (Hay 1995, p. 189). Agents or individuals are constrained by the realities of their world, but do have the choice to decide on different courses of action.

Some proposals for conflict management, for example, seem to suggest that initiatives designed to build good personal relations between the political leaders of different groups, perhaps in a place away from the conflict, is sufficient to resolve a conflict. This agency-orientated explanation is limited, for three reasons. First, good personal relations among political elites are compatible with the persistence of strong political disagreements. Second, the Sinn Féin-DUP power-sharing deal of 2007 suggests that bad and hostile personal relations between political elites are perfectly compatible with the achievement of political agreement. Third, in a 'back-stage' area, away from the media and the gaze of the audience, political actors may be able to enjoy good personal relations and find a degree of agreement, but when they return to the stage there are often a variety of structural reasons – such as audience expectations, or the hostility of other actors – that prevent them from playing a more accommodating role. For example, on a personal level, Ian Paisley and John Hume appear to have enjoyed a good relationship, but this did not prevent the two from being strong political adversaries. The public hostility of the loyalist PUP and Sinn Féin did not prevent the development of good personal relations between some members of those parties, partly based on shared socialist and working-class identities. Agency-orientated accounts play down the structural constraints, influences and long-term processes that shape the individual's, government's or group's (agent's) identity, experience and strategic orientation (Marsh *et al*. 1999, p. 217).

An agency-orientated account of the Northern Ireland peace process by historians and journalists, for example, might be drawn towards the historical minutiae of who said what to whom, the recollection of politicians, and the nature of the personalities in explaining the outcome of the process. In *The Fight for Peace*, the peace process is explained as the result of 'great men' and forceful personalities such as John Hume, Gerry Adams, Albert Reynolds and Father Alec Reid who, largely through their determination and political skill, produce an IRA ceasefire (Mallie and McKittrick 1997). The politicians (agents) are seen as exerting a powerful influence, and so there is a focus on their intentions, strategies and perceptions. In these agency-orientated accounts, politicians have complete responsibility for what they do because they are free to have done otherwise. The British government attracts particular criticism for failing to win an IRA ceasefire. Little attention is paid to the structural constraints that operate on British policy, in particular the need to bring republicans *and unionists* simultaneously into any all-party talks process (see Chapters 9 and 10, and the Conclusion to this book). Even if the British prime minister had included republicans in an all-party talks process, there was little likelihood that he could have forced unionists to attend. An agency-orientated account therefore attaches less weight to the context and constraints that operate on the politicians, such as the political, ideological, social and economic context (the 'structure') in which the politicians make their decisions, and the constraints these impose upon politicians (Hay 1995, p. 195).

Structural Explanations

The tendency of some political scientists, particularly comparativists, is to stand so far back that they can only see the wood and not the trees, branches or leaves. They emphasize the objective structures that constrain or are held to determine the behaviour of agents (individuals, groups, governments) and which may even lie outside the understanding of those individuals. A structuralist argument attributes little importance to the autonomy and influence of agents, it is not interested in the ways in which people perceive change or contribute to it. Actors are like robots, programmed or determined by the environment or structure in which they find themselves. Agents have the illusion that they have free will but in fact they are determined by ideological, social and economic structures. The actors appear as 'the unwitting products of their context, helpless individuals with minimal control over their destiny, floundering around in a maelstrom of turbulent currents' (Hay 1995, p. 189). If actors are like robots, we cannot hold them responsible for their actions because those actions are programmed into them and therefore beyond their control.

A strong structuralist account of the peace process would play down the role of politicians who are seen simply as the product of a situation largely determined by social, political, historical, ideological and economic forces which it is beyond their ability to control or manipulate. There is little focus on the role of agents and their ability to impact on the conflict (see Ruane and Todd 1996, 1999 for structure-orientated accounts). A 'structuralist account' might, for example, emphasize the history of antagonism and 'ancient hatreds' which makes conflict 'inevitable'. The socioeconomic disparity between Catholics and Protestants combines with social segregation to nurture widely contrasting ideologies which perpetuate division and conflict. Reflecting this polarization, the structural constraints operating on the agents are such that the ability of political leaders to move towards the centre ground of politics, or even to effect change in Northern Ireland, is highly constrained. Public opinion may demand a non-compromising approach from the politicians and make it very difficult to move away from an 'intransigent' stance. The activities of politicians, parties and governments do not and cannot make a difference to a conflict that is beyond their ability to influence, let alone control. Agency-orientated accounts attribute great power to agents (individuals, groups, governments) whereas structuralist accounts emphasize the limits on their power. Strong, structuralist accounts of the Northern Ireland conflict find it difficult to explain the remarkable changes, such as the Good Friday Agreement 1998 and the Sinn Féin–DUP deal 2007, that have occurred since the first IRA ceasefire in 1994. They tend to fall back on problematic explanations that stress the end of the Cold War, European integration and changes in British policy (Dixon 2006a) rather than exploring the structure/agency relationship.

The Strategic-Relational Approach

Structure and agency can be separated for the purposes of explanation but they are better thought of as an alloy of two metals. The strategic-relational approach is structure-orientated but leaves scope for agency (Hay 1995; Marsh *et al.* 1999). Structure conditions agency and the potential strategies that agents may use to realize their intentions. These structures tend to favour some strategies over others, and the more powerful actors. All agents are not equally powerful and strategic opportunities are unevenly distributed; this reflects structures of power and social inequality, which are constantly evolving and transforming (Marsh *et al.* 1999, pp. 39–41). Structures constrain agents, but agents also have the potential to impact on the structures in which they operate and thereby attempt to improve their scope for taking action and wielding power. The structural constraints operating on an agent will vary depending on the context in which the agent wishes to wield power. Agents' strategies are dependent on their perceptions or misperceptions of the world around them and they take decisions based on the information available to them. Ideology and culture are therefore relevant in explaining the perceptions and behaviour of agents. Agents can be unpredictable and make 'mistakes'; and outcomes may be intended or unintended. These agents have to respond to contingencies, events that occur by chance or have unforeseen causes. But these agents can also 'learn' about the structures operating on them and thereby improve their ability to maximize their opportunities to exert power. As Karl Marx put it:

 Men make their own history but they do not do so just as they please; they do not make it under circumstances chosen by themselves, but under circumstances directly encountered, given, and transmitted from the past.

The strategic-relational account of the peace process given later (see Chapters 9–10 and the Conclusion) is structure-orientated and emphasizes and assesses the limits of the power of the various agents to the conflict (politicians, groups, governments) to impact on the structures by which they find themselves constrained. Particular attention is paid to the perceived interests of the various agents and their attempts to realize these interests, and the structural constraints they face in trying to do this. This highlights the distribution of, and limits to, the power of the various parties to the conflict. Although this strategic-relational account is 'structure-orientated', the focus of the study is on the structural limitations facing the power of agents rather than on the structures themselves (which is well done by Ruane and Todd 1996).

The relevance of the strategic-relational approach can be seen when we consider the attempts of some politicians to lead their political activists and supporters to the 'centre' ground of Northern Irish politics (see, in particular, Chapters 3, 4, 6, 9 and 10). In order to understand the power of political elites to effect change in Northern Ireland we have to understand and interpret the structural constraints operating on those politicians. Gerry Adams (Sinn Féin) and David Trimble (Ulster Unionist Party) have attempted to move the Good Friday Agreement forward, but both have been constrained by what their activists and voters will accept. If either moves 'too far', they stand to lose support to their political rivals. Indeed, David Trimble and the UUP were eclipsed by the anti-Agreement DUP in the 2003 Assembly Elections. Gerry Adams was probably less concerned by the nationalist electorate, Sinn Féin having gained electoral support, than by the threat of a significant minority of republican activists splitting away and restarting the 'armed struggle'. In 1997, a split in the IRA led to the formation of the 'Real' IRA, which was opposed to the peace process. During and after the negotiations of the Good Friday Agreement the tactical issue was who should be expected to move first in negotiations, and how far – Adams or Trimble? By considering the structural constraints on each agent (Adams and Trimble), we attempt to understand what room for manoeuvre they have. Who has the power to move, and by how much? This is a highly political and sensitive process as we are attempting to distinguish between:

(a) the moral question of who *should* move; and
(b) the pragmatic or tactical question of who *can* move.

These moral and pragmatic issues are difficult to disentangle, and there is a tendency to argue that those who should move can move. Those sympathetic to republicanism are likely to emphasize the constraints operating on Adams in order to put pressure on unionists to move, whereas unionist sympathizers are likely to do the opposite. Mo Mowlam argued that 'we always had to judge how serious the threat of a split was and how much it was a ploy to maximize their negotiating position' (Mowlam 2002, p. 173). The more immediate constraints are probably related to a host of other, more long-term, structural influences (economic, political, social, historical, ideological and so on) which have constructed and reproduced a population as divided and suspicious as that in Northern Ireland, and which form the wider context in which Adams and Trimble have to operate.

Power is more obviously manifested in a 'top-down' fashion by political and other elites. For example, the power of the British state is seen clearly in the strength of its army and the resources it has at its disposal in the propaganda war. In this view, all aspects of popular daily life are formed by the dominant economic and political forces. The subordinate social groups are reduced to the status of passivity with little or no scope for independent action. But power can also manifest itself from the 'bottom-up', in the culture of daily life and lived experience. National identity, for example, 'is produced, reproduced and contested in the taken-for-granted details of social interaction, the habits and routines of everyday life' (Ozkirimli 2005, p. 191; Billig 1995). The Civil Society approach to the Northern Ireland conflict has been highly critical of the political elites for their communalism, incompetence and maliciousness in failing to reach a settlement to the conflict. This instrumentalist understanding of political elites has problems in explaining why the people have been so responsive to these communal appeals and voted increasingly for the most communal parties. Political elites, to be successful in a democracy, require popular prejudices to which they can appeal. The interrelationship between elite, top-down, and mass, bottom-up, practices should be considered in order to assess opportunities for agency and change. But even this is also too crude a model to understand the politics of managing conflict and the complex interactions between political elites, other elites, internal actors, external actors and the various audiences to the conflict (Dixon 2009).

The strategic-relational approach raises important questions about the scope and limits of the power of politicians and other agents to effect change and pursue their interests. Some agents have more power in certain contexts than others, but who has that power and how do we determine this? What resources do actors have, or can they mobilize, in order to alter the structural pattern of constraint and opportunity in which they find themselves? What is the role of agents such as the British government, Irish government, US government and civil society in Northern Ireland to bring about change? How can the structures that constrain agents be altered to maximize the power of politicians to sustain a centrist accommodation? Or are these constraints too strong to be manipulated, and the gap between politicians too wide to bridge? A focus on the relationship between structure and agency allows us to understand the strategic problems facing the political elites, as well as the extent and limits of their power. It should be remembered that a politically possible accommodation or settlement (such as the Good Friday Agreement) may not be a 'just' one.

The Ideological or Propaganda War

Ideology is a highly controversial concept, but arguably a useful one for analysing the conflict in Northern Ireland. Ideology is used here to describe a set of related ideas shared by a significant number of people, which is connected to the nature of power within a society. Ideologies (nationalism, republicanism, unionism, loyalism, socialism, conservatism):

- first, claim to describe the world as it is;
- second, prescribe a vision of the ideal society of the future that can be used to inspire and mobilize support; and
- third, provide a strategy for achieving the ideal society.

Ideologies serve either to sustain or to undermine the legitimacy, or rightfulness, of a socio-political order. Importantly, ideologies are not just the preserve of political and intellectual elites but shape the common-sense, conscious and unconscious, assumptions of the people too. Ideologies are apparent in the rhetoric of politicians and political publications – which seek to persuade the electorate – but extend also into the politics and culture of everyday life, such as everyday conversation, marching and demonstrations, the arts and sport. These ideologies shape people's perceptions and motivate behaviour (they can have an emotional as well as a rational appeal), and can be considered part of the structure within which politicians and other agents operate, but which agents also attempt to change (Cash 1996).

Ideology is deployed to win support and pressurize opponents in the propaganda war that has been fought over Northern Ireland. The propaganda war has been fought alongside and is inextricably bound up with the 'real war'; that is, the physical, military and material power struggle. Leading figures in the republican movement accepted that they could not physically kill all the soldiers in the British Army, but they felt they could, through a combination of their military and propaganda activities, attempt to undermine the British will to remain in Northern Ireland, as anti-imperialist movements had done to the British in the days of Empire. According to the IRA's 'Green Book', the organization was waging a 'politico-military' struggle, 'Military action is an extension of political action therefore the military campaign being waged by the Irish Republican Army is in effect a political campaign' (O'Brien 1993, p. 291). Leading British soldiers have argued from the beginning of 'the Troubles' that there was no purely military solution to the conflict, and that the army could only 'hold the ring' or promote a climate in which a political settlement could be found, perhaps by sapping the will of the enemy to resist. In the propaganda war, the British government could not declare publicly that the conflict in Northern Ireland was a 'war', since that ran the risk of conceding legitimacy to the IRA's violence and the political nature of its struggle. This, in turn, would increase support for the IRA within Northern Ireland and internationally and take its struggle forward. However, the British behaved as though the conflict was a 'war' because of the threat it posed to the state. This was reflected in the government's attempts to extend its influence over the media, since the belief was that impartiality has no place in war. As the British prime minister, Ted Heath, privately commented in 1972, referring to 'Bloody Sunday', 'we were in Northern Ireland fighting not only a military war but a propaganda war' (*Guardian*, 10 November 1995).

The British have attempted to undermine support for the IRA's military campaign (and the loyalists) through its rhetoric in the propaganda war, attempting to criminalize the republican movement and reduce its base of support both inside and outside Northern Ireland. Yet privately the 'reality' is that, over the course of the conflict, the British have maintained contacts and even negotiated with the IRA, accepting implicitly the political nature of the republican movement. The IRA's Hunger Strike in 1981 represented in part an attempt to fight back against the British in the propaganda war, and to have the republican movement's political rather than criminal interpretation of their struggle recognized (see Chapter 7). The contrast between public rhetoric and private reality has been a particular feature of British politicians' attitudes towards Northern Ireland, and explains important apparent contradictions and inconsistencies in British policy (Dixon 1994b; 1995a, pp. 173–8; 2001b; 2009).

Modern political propaganda has been defined as 'the deliberate attempt to influence the opinions of an audience through the transmission of ideas and values for a specific persuasive purpose, consciously designed to serve the interest of the propagandists and their political masters, either directly or indirectly' (Welch 1999, p. 26). The participants in the conflict in Northern Ireland have conflicting ideologies and interpretations of history and political events, and these are used to fight a propaganda war for the 'hearts and minds' of Irish, British and international opinion. Propagandistic rhetoric, while it bears some relationship to 'truth', can be contrasted with the 'realities' (which may be privately acknowledged) that under-lie the conflict. Ideological positions may be adopted not because they are 'true' – the limitations of the different positions are often painfully apparent (O'Malley 1983; Whyte 1990) – but because they are effective in mobilizing public opinion.

Ideology is not necessarily 'false', rigid or dogmatic, but, when used to mobilize political support in the propaganda war, it can simplify in a way that distorts 'reality'. Contrary to popular perceptions, propa-ganda does not have to be untrue, and the purveyors of propaganda may or may not regard it as being true. As a result, propaganda that is based on 'truth' and reflects 'reality' is more likely to be effec-tive. It has been argued that the IRA soon realized that deceiving the media in an obvious way lost it credibility, and that being more 'truthful' could be more effective in the propaganda war (Curtis 1984, p. 268). The British Army used 'black propaganda' (the spreading of deliberate lies to undermine an opponent) against both loyalist and republican paramilitaries. When the extent of this became known, it undermined the effectiveness of the government's propaganda effort and the army's unit was wound up.

The propaganda war played to at least three different audiences:

- First, by waging a propaganda war directly *against the enemy gov-ernment/organization and population* to undermine its will to resist and win over the support of waverers. This can be promoted by 'white'/'true' propaganda or by 'black propaganda', which involves the planting of deliberate lies and false stories to mislead and undermine the enemy; or, in the case of a 'civil war', to win over the 'hearts and minds' of the people living in the affected territory.
- Second, the propaganda war is waged to win the *support and sym-pathy of international opinion*, which may support one side or the other materially, ideologically (through propaganda) or through diplomatic pressure.
- Third, the government attempts to break the opponent's will to resist in the propaganda war by showing *the determination of the domestic government, military and public opinion* to overcome the enemy. This might be achieved by demonizing the opponent by telling stories (sometimes false) of atrocities in order to whip up popular support for war. Morale may also be sustained by cen-soring reports of defeats or reversals, or exaggerating successes against the enemy. The British Army has been sensitive to the morale of public opinion and the perceived impact this can have

on soldiers. Creating the appearance (if not necessarily the reality) of the determination of public opinion strengthens the position of the government in negotiations with the enemy. It could result in victory with more 'limited' use of force, or even without any need to resort to force (for example, in Kosovo: see Dixon 2003). On the other hand, demonizing your opponent can make it more difficult to negotiate with them at a later stage, and whipping up popular opinion could result in an unstoppable momentum to war or even to withdrawal. Not enough domestic interest in a conflict fails to demonstrate determination to win, whereas too much could have an impact on elite control of policy.

British counter-insurgency strategy placed a great premium on winning the propaganda war against the IRA through political determination. If the British government showed complete determination to defeat the IRA this would sap the will of republicans and their supporters to resist. The government was concerned that the republicans would defeat the British, not so much by physical military means, but by sapping the will of the British public and political elite to resist the IRA. The bipartisan approach of the British political parties to the conflict was designed to maintain unity and stifle domestic dissent in order to demonstrate political determination against the IRA's challenge (see Chapter 4). In 'war', some argue that censorship is necessary to defeat the enemy; the importance of the propaganda war in maintaining morale and defeating the enemy explains British censorship during the Second World War, the Falklands/Malvinas conflict, and over Northern Ireland (Dixon 2000a).

The British government is not the only participant in the propaganda war. Since early on in 'the Troubles' the IRA leadership has demonstrated an appreciation of the importance of the propaganda war and of establishing its own legitimacy. The 'armed struggle' could be seen as a tool in the propaganda war – 'armed propaganda' according to Gerry Adams – to put pressure on the British to win a better settlement for republicans, if not outright withdrawal. Violence is a tool for increasing pressure, and the propaganda war is necessary to maintain and increase the pressure of republican and nationalist opinion against the British government. The IRA, like other parties to the conflict, was addressing and attempting to tailor its propaganda to different audiences. For example, in the USA, republicans tended to emphasize nationalism and Catholic Irish imagery, playing down their socialism. Socialism was played up when attempting to win sympathy among the British Left, particularly in the early 1980s. Republicans also understood the legitimacy that talks with the British government lent to the 'armed struggle' (Wright 1991, pp. 94–7). This helps to explain the reluctance of both the British and Irish governments to embark on making *public, official* contact with the republican movement.

Republicans have also demonstrated an awareness of the propaganda impact of army casualties on British public opinion. These have contributed to polls that suggest consistent majority support for a British withdrawal since the early 1970s (Dixon 2000a). Since the mid-1970s, leading figures in the republican movement may have realized that they could not win by forcing the British army to withdraw, but nevertheless continued to make intransigent demands and employed the rhetoric of ultimate victory to maintain republican morale and sustain their 'struggle'. The IRA's 'Green Book' points out, 'It is not an easy thing to take up a gun and go out and kill some person without strong convictions of justification' (O'Brien 1993, p. 290). Sustaining the propaganda war would maintain morale and maximize the IRA's negotiating position in any future peace process. Republicans, again like other parties to the conflict, demonize their opponents to legitimize their violence (see Cash 1996 on loyalist demonization). Joanne Wright describes the importance of 'supporting propaganda' for sustaining the IRA's violence:

[it] emphasizes the supreme importance of the cause and of the collective over the individual, thus helping to resolve any moral dilemma individuals may have about the acts they have committed or will commit. The theme of a 'war situation' is dominant, with constant references to a long war and the inevitability of victory. Also to maintain morale among active volunteers, the terrorist organization's treatment of its imprisoned members is vital. It is essential for volunteers to believe that even if captured they will retain a place in the overall struggle, and that attempts will be made to release them. For the volunteer killed in action there is the promise of martyrdom. (Wright 1991, p. 140; see also Chapter 7 in this book)

The Irish government has also participated in the propaganda war. It has kept up pressure on the British by advocating and demanding Irish unity and (until 1999) retaining Articles 2 and 3 of its Constitution, which laid claim to Northern Ireland. This power to influence the attitudes of Irish nationalism, both North and South, and to be more or less co-operative over security, can be used as a bargaining counter in negotiations with the British. Privately, however, Irish governments have often acted in a more accommo- dating way than their public nationalist posturing would suggest. In the mid-1970s, the Irish government privately opposed British withdrawal from Northern Ireland on the grounds that this would lead to civil war. Privately, the Irish government agreed to the British armed forces flying up to five miles inside the Republic, but publicly the Irish government denied this for fear that it would be politically damaging (Miller 1993). Whether the use of propa- ganda by the political elites is as consciously cynical as suggested here is debatable, as is the extent to which people believe their own propaganda.

The War of Words

The propaganda war is contested by political elites, pressure groups, journalists and academics, but also by the people in the politics of everyday life. The language used to describe the conflict can influence an observer's understanding of it. External opinion, perhaps with lit- tle time for the details of the conflict, can more readily grasp that a conflict fits into a pre-existing category such as 'colonial', 'ethnic', 'anti-terrorist' or 'criminal'. Some argue that the use of 'inappropri- ate' language and characterizations has contributed to the conflict by reproducing sectarian perspectives and stereotypes. Definitions of words are strongly contested, and the most obvious conflicts occur, for example, over whether 'paramilitaries' in Northern Ireland are 'terrorists', 'freedom fighters' or 'guerrillas'. (Inverted commas are used during the text to highlight the particularly contested nature of some of these terms.) In Northern Ireland, one of the ways of indi- cating whether someone is a nationalist or a unionist is their choice of language. Unionists who want to emphasize the separateness of Northern Ireland from the rest of the island tend to refer to Northern Ireland as 'Ulster', while nationalists who want to stress the illegiti- macy of Northern Ireland refer to it as the 'six counties' or the 'north of Ireland'. Since Sinn Féin has attempted to distance itself from the IRA, unionists more often refer to Sinn Féin as Sinn Féin/IRA to stress that the two are inextricably linked or IRA/Sinn Féin to suggest the priority of the military wing.

Conor Cruise O'Brien has gone so far as to argue that, in a political and ideological struggle, 'words are weapons' and the use or otherwise of the term 'terrorism' had 'a bearing on how long the political violence is likely to continue and how many lives it will cost'. He argues that by failing to describe the IRA as 'terrorists', people are intentionally or unintentionally giving them the legitimacy that sustains their violence. The grounds on which this propaganda war is fought extends from party politics through to culture. There were calls in Britain for the banning of the film *Michael Collins* for fear that its romanticized portrayal of the IRA lent legitimacy to the contemporary IRA's 'armed struggle'.

Politicians have expressed a consciousness of the impact their pronouncements can have on the conflict. A clear connection is often perceived between aggressive political rhetoric, party ideology and political violence. Ideology and political rhetoric are seen to have 'real' effects, directly inciting violence or creating a permissive culture in which political violence is more likely. Nationalists, particularly in the case of Ian Paisley, tend to draw the link between the rhetoric and actions of unionist politicians and political violence. Since the 1960s, some loyalists have claimed they were incited to violence by Paisley's rhetoric and actions. The IRA justified the murder of Unionist MP Robert Bradford on the grounds that he was 'responsible to a considerable degree for motivating the series of purely sectarian attacks on ordinary nationalists, and while they do not pull the trigger they provide the ideological framework for the UDA and UVF gunmen who do the murdering' (*An Phoblacht*, a republican newspaper quoted in Wright 1991, p. 157).

Unionists have complained that Sinn Féin has not been banned, despite the fact that the political wing of the IRA has publicly advocated violence against the mainly Protestant RUC. It is argued that the common goals of nationalists and republicans lend legitimacy to the IRA's violence. The failure of nationalists to support the police, their support for the Hunger Strikers in 1981, for Irish unity and Articles 2 and 3 of the Irish Constitution have all been cited by some unionists as legitimizing the IRA's campaign of murder against them. In 1991, Joanne Wright argued that the eradication of the IRA would only be achieved by de-legitimizing or redefining the common ideological ends that nationalists (particularly in the Republic) and republicans seek. The British, by avoiding 'security force blunders', could contribute to choking off the propaganda on which the IRA thrives (Wright 1991, p. 219).

There does appear to be evidence to support some relationship between the ideologies of public opinion and violence (Burton 1978; Sluka 1989). To some extent, the paramilitary 'fish' require a 'sea' of at least some public support or acquiescence in which to swim. When the IRA's political wing, Sinn Féin, launched itself into electoral politics in the 1980s and 1990s there developed a tension between the violent activities of the IRA which, if they went 'too far', could alienate nationalists, and the electoral struggle of Sinn Féin to win votes (see Chapter 8 below; Wright 1991, pp. 117–21; Darby 1994, pp. 62–3). Nationalists have expressed concern from time to time that the IRA was provoking loyalist retaliation (Wright 1991, p. 215). On the loyalist side, there also seems to be a relationship between the violence of loyalist paramilitaries and the perceptions of the wider unionist community. During times of extreme stress, when Northern Ireland's constitutional position appears to be under threat, unionists are more tolerant of (and likely to engage in) paramilitary activity (Bruce 1999, pp. 202-3).

The problem arises in attempting *to interpret the rhetoric and intentions* of politicians. Many politicians would deny the interpretation that their words are intended to incite violence. Ian Paisley could defend his 'anti-Catholic' rhetoric on at least two grounds: first, that the rhetoric was directed at the Catholic Church and not at Catholic people, and second, that the rhetoric is directed to win and consolidate the support of unionists in competition with other unionist parties, rather than inspire violence against Catholics. Paisley's rhetoric could represent a means by which his supporters 'let off steam' and vent their frustrations, as an alternative to violence. Gerry Adams' rhetoric could be interpreted along similar lines: that the IRA's violence is directed at the forces of the British state whose representatives often just happen to be unionists; that the rhetoric is necessary to represent republicans, express their discontents and fend off challenges to his leadership rather than to incite more violence.

Ideology: Power Creates 'Reality'?

Some argue that the ideological contest over the 'truth' of any situation is not based on 'facts about reality' but on power. Ideology becomes 'true' because those with the power and authority to produce knowledge impose their definition of the 'truth' of the situation.

For example, during the propaganda war, the British state tried to criminalize the republican movement. Whether or not the IRA is 'really' a 'criminal' organization is beside the point if some body has the power to convince people that it *is* a criminal organization. However, this power to convince people is likely to be related not just to 'political spin' but also to people's direct experience of 'reality' and what they *perceive* that 'reality' to be. Those with a republican ideology, who may know republican activists or have personal experience of the conditions that have sustained the IRA, are less likely to be susceptible to British propaganda than the British public, who are probably already disposed to accept a hostile interpretation of the IRA as criminals.

Ideology may influence action but, to be effective, it has to bear some relation to material realities. The impact of class on the conflict can be seen in the concentration of violence in working-class areas and the disproportionate support of the working class for the more 'extreme' political parties. Archbishop Eames, the head of the Church of Ireland, expressed the significance of class: 'I've heard it said they're not fighting each other on the Malone Road [a middle-class suburban area of South Belfast]. It took me years to understand the implications of that remark. There are two communities here, and one is involved in violence, suffering, unemployment, and injustice. The demarcation is class.' (This is backed up by Fay *et al.* 1999. On class, see O Connor 1993; Bew *et al.* 1995; Ruane and Todd 1996, pp. 61–3, 73–5; Coulter 1999, ch. 2.)

The resources available to those who want to conduct a propaganda war vary. While the British government has enormous material resources this has not ensured domination. Other agents also have resources and a varying ability to put their message across (see the Conclusion). Nationalist or republican targets of British propaganda have alternative sources of information to draw upon, including their own ideological predispositions and experiences. Equipped with such ideologies, their receptivity to British propaganda is not likely to be passive but will be conducive to alternative explanations of events. Summarizing research on propaganda, David Welch argues that it 'is most effective when it reinforces already held ideas and beliefs'. Propaganda is not simply injected into a passive people through the mass media:

> individuals seek out opinion formers from within their own class or sex for confirmation of their own ideas and attitudes. Most writers

today argue that propaganda confirms rather than converts, and is most effective when its message is in line with existing opinions and beliefs of those it is aimed at. (Welch 1999, p. 26)

Ideologies tend to reflect and perpetuate contrasting socialization experiences and the structures that sustain them. These ideologies, although changing and adapting, also reproduce the contrasting assumptions and attitudes of the communities from which they spring, often with overtones of superiority and a lack of empathy for others. The attitude of external opinion, the British, Irish, Europeans and Americans, also reflects to some extent the cultural and ideological environment in these countries. British attitudes towards the conflict in Northern Ireland, particularly at its start, were permeated with assumptions, prejudices and a superiority that derive from a very different cultural environment (see Chapter 4). Their receptivity to republican propaganda – when it does get through – is likely to be hostile, given the cultural context and predisposition of the audience.

Ideologies are not closed; they undergo constant change and remaking. The potential exists for these ideologies to be transformed in a way that reduces the demonization of opponents, is more reflective of political 'realities' and promotes accommodation and understanding. This raises questions about the extent to which these ideologies can be transformed, and is this in turn dependent on structural change? How far can political actors remake an ideology without losing popular or party support?

Winding Down the Propaganda War

The propaganda war sees participants demonizing the enemy in order to mobilize support for the 'war effort', gain external support and exhibit determination to win. The triumph of propaganda over reality – it is argued – has succeeded in polarizing opinion, particularly within Northern Ireland. Expectations have been raised, while the gap between political rhetoric and political reality has widened and become entrenched. This has left would-be peacemakers with the difficult task of winding down the propaganda war, in order to create an ideological environment more conducive to accommodation, and at the same time sustaining the propaganda war to maximize leverage in negotiations.

In times of 'war' it is often argued that dissent and the 'truth' are luxuries that cannot be afforded. First, dissent and the 'truth' could undermine domestic morale and the group's determination to defeat the enemy. Second, this lack of will encourages the enemy to scent victory and to continue its own physical and propaganda campaign. Adherents of an ideology may or may not believe in the 'truth' of that ideology. Indeed, an ideology that is 'untrue' may prove to be a more effective tool in fighting the propaganda war, because of its ability to mobilize popular prejudices. The ends justify the means: censorship and distortion are justified by the political elite in order to fight the propaganda war and sustain the struggle of the group. The 'truth' could undermine 'the struggle' and is a luxury permitted, if at all, in peacetime. In 1981, the former British prime minister, Jim Callaghan, argued that it was now time for a full, frank and open debate on Northern Ireland:

> At the time of writing, every fresh discussion is constrained by self-imposed limitations – justifiable limitations, I admit. There is the fear that anything we may do will lead to the IRA being encouraged to renewed its efforts; the feeling that, of course, we must give no encouragement to it or to any terrorist organization. There is no doubt that this has inhibited discussion in the House. In my view, the time is ripe for a fundamental, free and open discussion at Westminster. That is the first step (Hansard, vol. 7, col. 1050, 2 July 1981).

Unionists and nationalists, at elite and popular levels, show sensitivity to how 'the truth' could aid the enemy in the propaganda war. This might apply, for example, to charges of discrimination; unionists may privately be aware that it occurred, but publicly would not confirm this because they felt it would help the IRA in its propaganda war, feed its armed struggle and strengthen its hand in negotiations. For nationalists to acknowledge that some Protestants may have been discriminated against or else to draw attention to IRA atrocities might weaken their side of the propaganda war against unionists and the British (O Connor 1993, pp. 332–3). The winding-down of the propaganda war and the re-evaluation of ideologies could take place when the climate is more peaceful and the 'real war' has de-escalated, but it could also be a precondition for that de-escalation.

The peace process has largely been pursued by elites who, while they have attempted to bring their supporters to accommodation,

have a highly limited ability to do so, given the accretion and polarization of propaganda (ideology) and violence in the 'real war' built
up over the years. This propaganda has had an adverse effect on the
ideological structures that constrain the politicians (and other agents)
who seek an accommodation between unionism and nationalism. The
difficulty comes for the political elites in attempting to bridge that ideological gap, wind down the propaganda war and 're-educate' their
communities for the 'new realities' of the post-conflict era (Dixon
2002a). The IRA's ceasefires may have opened up the space where
a more 'objective' investigation of 'the Troubles' and the abuses of
all sides can be investigated without giving rise to charges that this
is sustaining the violence of one side or the other in the propaganda
war. Investigations into 'Bloody Sunday', allegations of security
force collusion and the IRA's 'disappeared' could all be seen in this
context.

'Reality': The Hall of Mirrors

In this propaganda war it is difficult to tell the difference between
the political spin necessary to keep up the political pressure on opponents and sustain domestic support, and what is argued here as the
underlying political 'realities' of the conflict. Politicians may privately
acknowledge 'realities' which they cannot express publicly for fear of
jeopardizing public or party support. John Taylor, a leading member
of the UUP, has commented on the limits of leadership, 'in politics sometimes the logical thing is not necessarily what the people
will allow you to do. And in Northern Ireland such are the intense
feelings and deep seated fears that what an outside observer might
consider logical is not the kind of thing you can deliver politically'
(*Irish Times*, 27 September 1989). Public admissions of private 'realities' might provoke an adverse reaction, including violence. As Garret
Fitzgerald, Irish Taoiseach (prime minister) in the 1980s, put it:

> In any situation which is ultimately a negotiating situation, none of
> the parties are likely to disclose the whole of their minds in public.
> And that means there can be significant disparities between pub-
> licly stated attitudes and privately stated positions, you have the
> fact that the issues we are dealing with are ones which involve
> strong emotions in each of the areas – both within Northern
> Ireland on the Unionist and nationalist sides, in the Republic to a

degree also, and in Britain perhaps sometimes to a degree greater than appreciated. And that all operates as a constraint on people stating the whole of their thought in a public forum. (Quoted in O'Malley 1983, p. 253)

The difficulty lies in trying to distinguish between public attitudes and private positions. The observer is in a 'hall of mirrors' trying to go beyond the propaganda war to distinguish between the public rhetoric of propaganda and private 'reality'. How do we know what the underlying 'realities' of the conflict are? Or are these just the author's realities or ideology? Political elites tend to have a vested interest in producing propagandized accounts of events and may be embarrassed to admit publicly a gap between rhetoric and realities, while for some this gap may not exist.

The approach taken here represents an attempt to analyse these often private 'realities' through a careful interpretation of the recent history of the conflict, and by an assessment of the interests of the various parties to the conflict and how they sought to achieve them (see the Conclusion). Particular attention is paid to sources that indicate the attitudes of politicians when they are not in the public eye – for example, to newspaper off-the-record briefings, leaks of information to the press, politicians' gaffes, private papers, committee minutes and private communications between elites. One journalist wrote of interviewing politicians in Northern Ireland: 'On the record, one gets platitudes and clichés. Off the record, one can either hear unprintable sectarian bile, or well-thought-out ideas on the future' (O'Farrell 1998, pp. 102–3). The lack of available government documents is a disadvantage, though they do not provide direct access to the 'truth', but it seems likely that, if past experience is any indicator, some of these will be unavailable for a hundred years or so on the grounds of 'national security'. Nevertheless, even without government papers, it is possible for contemporary historians to construct an account of an event that proves reasonably accurate once papers are released.

Objectivity and Argument

There is an attempt in this book to present a 'balanced' account of the Northern Ireland conflict. However, this inevitably reflects the intellectual interests, preoccupations, conscious and unconscious assumptions and perspectives of the author (who is also 'structured') and so should be read – as all books should be – with a critical eye and a healthy dose of scepticism. Academics, as with journalists and politicians (whether wittingly or not), inevitably become caught up in the conflict they are trying to analyse and should not be blind to the political implications of their arguments. It has been argued that 'the conclusions of much of the scholarship on Northern Ireland are closely correlated with the background of those who reach the conclusions' (Fay *et al.* 1999, p. 3). While this is not necessarily so, it is a useful corrective to those who claim to be neutral or impartial. An awareness of the way the observer is structured can be used to counter any tendency towards communal bias. For this reason, in this book, where possible and with the limits of space, contesting perspectives and explanations are presented, analysed and evaluated, along with the author's conclusion. The attempt is to empathize (the ability to identify with and understand others), rather than sympathize, in order to understand how people interpret the world, but also to explain how that world operates. Not all explanations are equally convincing; it is argued that some, based on the evidence available, are more convincing than others. There is no claim here to offering 'absolute truth', but it is hoped that this exercise will encourage more critical thinking about the nature of what we know and how we know it, and that this will have an emancipatory effect. A consciousness of how we are socially constructed facilitates critical reflection on our ideological assumptions and actions (Ozkirimli 2005, ch. 7).

This book contributes to ongoing debates about the Northern Ireland conflict in several ways (the arguments of the book are brought together in its Conclusion):

1. There is a focus in this book on the role of politics in winding up the conflict in Northern Ireland, through violence and the propaganda war, and then the winding down of the conflict into a peace process and accommodation. It analyses the considerable difficulties in 'bridging the gap' between unionist and nationalist politicians and achieving an accommodation on the 'centre ground' of politics, such as the Good Friday Agreement 1998 and the Sinn Féin-DUP deal of 2007. Implicit is the assumption that such an accommodation is 'a good thing'. Civil Society and consociational approaches to managing the conflict are found to provide inadequate descriptions of the conflict and unrealistic prescriptions for managing it (see Chapter 10 in this book; Dixon 1997a; 1997b; 2005; 2009).

2. This book argues against nationalist and republican accounts of the peace process that are echoed in much of the literature. This literature claims the end of the Cold War in 1989 and closer European integration caused a shift in British policy, first, by declaring that it had no selfish or strategic interest in Northern Ireland, and second, by shifting from a political process that excluded paramilitaries to one that included them. By contrast, it is argued here that British policy towards Northern Ireland after 1972 was characterized by *continuity and tactical adjustments* in pursuit of a compromise settlement of power-sharing with some kind of Irish dimension. This settlement was pursued – and the options of Irish unity or integration into the UK rejected (see Chapter 6) – because it was thought most likely to result in a stable Northern Ireland. This is why the first peace process (1972–4) and the second (1994–2007) are similar (see Chapters 5, and 8-11 in this book; Dixon 1997a; 1997b; 2001b; 2009). The Anglo-Irish Agreement 1985 was not a 'volte-face' in British policy, and Margaret Thatcher did not sign the deal to 'coerce consociationalism' (see Chapter 7). The British government had declared its neutrality in the early 1970s and attempted to create an inclusive peace process at that time, but were rebuffed by the paramilitaries. British governments had every interest in choreographing the entry of the republican movement into a peace process and took significant political risks to bring this about, rather than deliberately obstructing the peace process (see Chapters 8–11 of this book; Dixon 2002a; 2009). The role of the international has been exaggerated (Dixon 2006a) and the peace process is better understood as the product of moves within the republican leadership to end the conflict and the role of other actors in facilitating this (Dixon 2009). The account of British policy presented here counters some of the popular and propagandistic accounts and may run the risk of presenting an overly sympathetic view of British policy.
3. Unionist fears of betrayal by the British government had more substance than republican fears that the British government was unequivocally opposed to a united Ireland. The British government did not have overwhelming selfish, strategic, political or economic reasons for maintaining the Union with Northern Ireland, and might have taken the path of least resistance towards a united Ireland if unionists had not mobilized to demonstrate their opposition. British policy has been more about a stable settlement than about manipulating Northern Ireland out of the Union

(Dixon 2009). This understanding of British policy leads to a more empathetic understanding of the plight of unionism, suggesting that there is substance, as well as paranoia, to unionist fears of being manipulated out of the UK.

4. Violence and the threat of violence by loyalist and republican paramilitaries has proved to be an effective means of exerting influence on the political process. It has produced significant gains and losses for its advocates, which may be uncomfortable to acknowledge but churlish to ignore. There is a grey area between 'constitutional' and 'unconstitutional' political actors in Northern Ireland; and 'constitutional' politicians have threatened and incited the use of violence. The British and Irish governments have refused publicly to deal with the 'men of violence' or legitimize the use of violence through concessions, but have been forced to recognize the importance of engaging with paramilitaries to bring an end to violence. The extent to which the British state has deployed illegitimate and repressive violence has become increasingly clear as investigations during the peace process have revealed collusion between the state and loyalist paramilitaries.

5. A key contribution of this book to the literature is to try and draw attention to the relationship between the British government's political and security strategy. The efforts of the government to find a power-sharing accommodation between nationalists and unionists in Northern Ireland was perceived by the military to have an impact on the security situation. Security policy also affected the government's ability to find agreement. This was most starkly apparent in the 1969–74 period (see Chapter 4), when the perceived requirements of the military's counter-insurgency strategy were in tension with the British government's attempts to reach a political settlement. The British became increasingly reliant on 'Protestants' to join the security forces so that the army could be taken out of the front line and the conflict could be Ulsterized. This created a persistent and structural bias of the security forces against the nationalist community. This bias can be seen in, the reluctance of the army to take on the loyalist paramilitaries during the period of the loyalist backlash (1971–6), when unionists took to the streets after the Anglo-Irish Agreement 1985 (see pp. 205–08) and again during the peace process, particularly the Drumcree standoff in 1996 (see pp. 258–61).

3

Partition and Civil Rights

The partition of Ireland in 1920 was an unhappy compromise between contending interests, and widely seen as a temporary measure until Ireland could be reunited. Republicans and nationalists tended to believe that Ireland would be reunited as a state independent of the UK. The British and unionists, on the other hand, looked forward to a united Ireland more closely tied to Britain, either through a closer relationship within the Empire/Commonwealth or even the re-entry of Ireland into the UK. The forces of history, geography, religion, demography, anti-colonialism and economics have all been invoked to argue that the reunification of Ireland is inevitable. Belief in the inevitability of Irish unity persists among many British and Irish politicians, but now it is more often assumed that a united Ireland would be independent rather than achieved within the Union.

The imposition of the devolved Stormont parliament on Northern Ireland allowed British governments to distance themselves from the 'Irish Question' and ignore the discrimination perpetrated by the Unionist political elite against the 'Catholic' minority. The civil rights campaign originated in the early 1960s, in part to deal with anti-Catholic discrimination, and became a mass movement when the second civil rights march was attacked by the RUC on 5 October 1968. This dramatic event drew the attention of the rest of the world to the conflict in Northern Ireland and involved the British government, once again, more closely in the affairs of the region.

This chapter reviews the period since partition, considering the impact of beliefs about the inevitability of Irish unity and analyses the debate over the origins of the civil rights movement and its impact (for more detail on these arguments, see Dixon 2001a, chs 3 and 4).

Modernization and the Inevitability of Irish Unity

'Modernization theory' suggests that the spread of economic integration and interdependence between states creates common interests among different social groups. These common interests then transcend, erode and ultimately end national and communal identities. Nationalists have argued that 'modernization theory' makes a united Ireland inevitable, while unionists have argued that the implication of 'modernization theory' is that the Republic of Ireland will rejoin the United Kingdom. It is a structural theory (see Chapter 2) because it emphasizes the inevitability of these modernizing forces and the powerlessness of actors to influence or resist this process.

'Modernization theory' suggests that old identities and prejudices are eroded in three ways:

(i)   Increased contact between people breaks down stereotypes, reduces prejudice and promotes understanding and tolerance;

(ii) by creating common material interests between people these rational economic interests come to take precedence over outdated communal or religious ones; and

(iii) the prosperity that modernization brings with it allows individuals to detach themselves from backward or primordial identities, based on religion, nation or ethnicity. These old cleavages are left behind and a new, modern politics emerges around material or class interests.

Confusingly, modernization theory is related to the notion of modernization which was used in the 1960s to mean a rejection of traditional sectarian attitudes and a growing interest in economic growth and consumerism. Modernization theory fails to predict the turn of events in Northern Ireland, but the widespread *belief* in the assumptions underlying modernization theory continues to affect the attitudes and actions of important actors in Britain and Ireland.

The Government of Ireland Act 1920, which partitioned Ireland, created two equal Irish parliaments and a 'Council of Ireland' providing for eventual Irish unity (Dixon 2001a, pp. 48–9). Nationalists, unionists and the British did not want the partition of Ireland. The British tended to see it as a temporary expedient that went against modern trends (Canning 1985, p. 312). The assumption among some key British politicians that a united Ireland within the Union was inevitable could justify a policy of non-interference in 'Irish' affairs in case this provoked the re-emergence of the Irish Question in British politics. Indeed, the British Parliament insulated itself from Northern Irish affairs by refusing to rule the country directly and imposing the Stormont Parliament. In addition, a 'Speaker's Convention' emerged at Westminster, which forbade the discussion of affairs held to be the responsibility of the Northern Ireland government. The British withheld royal assent for a Northern Ireland Bill abolishing proportional representation in local elections, because it threatened to entrench the domination of the Ulster Unionist Party, but when the Unionist cabinet threatened to resign, the British backed down.

Nationalists tended to assume that modernization, and other 'historical forces', were inevitably going to bring about Irish unity (O'Halloran 1987). From this perspective, unionist opposition to unification was an anachronism that would be worn down by the forces of 'progress'. Each episode of unionist resistance was interpreted as the last stand before unionists realized they were really Irish and succumbed to the inevitable: if Irish unity is inevitable, this removes the need to persuade unionists of its advantages.

Ireland: Years of Polarization, 1921–58

In 1925, the British, Northern Irish and Irish governments agreed to amend the Irish Treaty and transfer the powers of the Council of Ireland to the Parliaments of the North and South. It provided for the two governments to 'meet together as and when necessary for the purpose of considering matters of common interest arising out of or connected with the exercise and administration of the said powers'. However, this regular contact did not take place, and the prime ministers of Northern Ireland and the South did not meet for forty years.

During the 1930s, relations between Northern Ireland and the Irish Free State became polarized. As Unionist leaders infamously declared Northern Ireland a Protestant state, Nationalists in the South underlined the Catholicism of the Irish Free State. James Craig, the prime minister of Northern Ireland (1921–40), declared: 'In the South they boasted of a Catholic State. They still boast of Southern Ireland being a Catholic State. All I boast of is that we are a Protestant Parliament and a Protestant State.' Northern Ireland had been set up during a period of crisis: there was IRA activity in the North and unionists feared an invasion from the South.

Discrimination was justified against the Catholic minority on the grounds that they were a disloyal 'enemy within' who could not be trusted in positions of power. In 1933, Sir Basil Brooke, future prime minister of Northern Ireland, bragged that he did not have

> a Roman Catholic about his own place ... He would point out that the Roman Catholics were endeavouring to get in everywhere and were out with all their force and might to destroy the power and constitution of Ulster. There was a definite plot to overpower the vote of unionists in the North. He would appeal to loyalists therefore, wherever possible, to employ good Protestant lads and lassies.

The victory of the anti-Treaty party, Fianna Fáil, in the 1932 Free State elections brought Eamonn de Valera, the leader of the anti-treaty forces, to power. De Valera's protectionism and the advent of a 'trade war' between Britain and the Free State resulted in a decline of cross-border trade. The Catholic priorities of the Free State were becoming more apparent in the 1930s. De Valera began 'openly to stress specifically Catholic priorities', British heritage was dismantled and Protestants in the South claimed persecution as their numbers dropped by 32 per cent between 1911 and 1926. This culminated in the 1937 Constitution, which enshrined the special position of the Catholic Church in the South. After 1956, de Valera argued that the choice for unionists was 'either assimilation or emigration with compensation' (Bowman 1982, pp. 318–19). De Valera's confrontational approach to Britain and the creation of a more Catholic Ireland probably served to shore up the unionists' position within the UK.

James Craig claimed that the coming to power of the gunman 'forever destroyed any hopes of a united Ireland'. Lord Londonderry pointed out the benefit to unionism of a hostile administration in the South. With the 'doubtful friendship' of the more moderate Cosgrave governments in the South (1922–32), the unionist government would be under 'continual pressure' to make concessions to keep him in power. The 'more or less open opposition of a de Valera government' removed this pressure (Harkness 1993, p. 33).

British politicians hoped that, as in the First World War, Ireland might be reunited through the struggle of North and South against a common enemy. In 1940, when Britain 'stood alone' against the Nazis, an offer of unity was made to the Irish government by Neville Chamberlain. De Valera rejected the scheme because Britain looked likely to lose the war, and there was no guarantee that a united Ireland would result from their proposals. Furthermore, he 'could not imagine how the British could ever obtain a firm grasp upon Craigavon [the Prime Minister of Northern Ireland], let alone thrust him toward Dublin' (Fisk 1983, p. 216). In the aftermath of Pearl Harbor, Winston Churchill telegraphed de Valera: 'Now is your chance. Now or never. "A nation once again." ' Again, this was to be achieved out of common struggle, rather than British coercion of the unionists (Fisk 1983, pp. 324–5). Northern Ireland's loyalty to the Allies during the Second World War won it international credit, particularly in the USA, which traditionally had been sympathetic to the claims of Irish nationalism. The Free State's wartime neutrality weakened its international standing. De Valera sent his condolences to the German embassy on the news of Hitler's death, an incident that obscured the generally sympathetic position taken by the Free State government towards the Allies.

In the immediate post-war period, the Irish Free State launched an anti-partition campaign, raised the question of discrimination in Northern Ireland and left the Commonwealth by declaring itself a Republic in 1948. There was plenty of sympathy in the newly-elected Labour government for Irish unity, to come over time and through co-operation, but not for coercing Northern Ireland out of the Union. The Labour government gave Northern Ireland a guarantee that it would remain within the UK as long as its Parliament consented.

Autonomy under Threat: Northern Ireland and the UK

In the post-war period, the autonomy of the Northern Ireland state was began to be undermined by four developments:

1. The growth of the Welfare State after 1945 made Northern Ireland more dependent economically on Britain. The decision of the Stormont government to implement, more or less, British welfare legislation meant that it was acting increasingly as an agent of the British state. Local government assumed a new importance as the distributor of state resources, and this brought them into more contact and conflict with the population. Unionist dominance of local government in Northern Ireland and its discriminatory practices exacerbated the disadvantages experienced by the Catholic minority.

2. Stormont could not cope with its unemployment problem without the co-operation of Westminster. In the years following the Second World War, Northern Ireland became the most depressed region of the UK. The Northern Irish government complained of its powerlessness to meet the challenge alone, as all the major tools of economic management were in the hands of the British government. Since partition, successive British governments had been extremely reluctant to risk re-opening the 'Irish Question' by interfering with Northern Ireland's affairs. So, in spite of Northern Ireland's financial dependence on Westminster, Stormont was relatively autonomous. However, unionists were fearful of the possibility that some future, probably Labour, government in London might use its financial leverage to undermine Northern Ireland's constitutional position. During the early 1960s, the impression was given that Britain would take a more active and interventionist role in Northern Irish affairs. Both Conservative and Labour parties adopted policies that appeared to involve British politicians in taking decisions on Northern Ireland's economy. The Ulster Unionists required an increased role for Westminster in the affairs of Northern Ireland and yet, at the same time, feared this would lead to opportunities for nationalists to raise questions of civil rights abuse and partition.

3. The region's dependence on Westminster was underlined by the Conservative government's application to join the European Economic Community (EEC) in 1961, and its need to attract foreign investment. The British Conservative government's application to the EEC in 1961 underlined Northern Ireland's growing subjection to UK and international influences that it was beyond the Stormont Parliament's ability to control. The decision to enter the EEC was taken by the British Parliament without need for the consent of the Northern Ireland Parliament. The Euro-enthusiasts' modernizing assumptions were largely accepted and echoed in Northern Ireland by politicians across the communal divide, regardless of whether the implications of those assumptions were welcome. Nationalists favoured European integration since, for them, the logical corollary of a united Europe seemed also to be a united Ireland, while unionists feared that if the Republic had direct representation in the EEC, Northern Ireland's position may be viewed in an unsympathetic light (Dixon 1994a). The European question heightened unionist constitutional uncertainties at a time when they feared that the processes of modernization were

shifting power away from Northern Ireland and undermining Stormont's ability to control the future of the region. Attempts to attract foreign, particularly US, investment may have been a further factor in raising unionist insecurities, by increasing their reliance on international actors, who tended to be hostile to unionism.

4. The prospect of a Labour government at Westminster alarmed unionists, who feared this would make interference more likely. The bipartisan accord that had kept Northern Ireland out of British politics for so long was showing signs of weakening under the impact of the need for 'national' economic planning and politicians pressing to raise civil rights issues at Westminster. In Opposition, the British Labour Party used the plight of Northern Ireland's economy as an example of the Conservative government's poor management of the economy, and drew up proposals for the introduction of a UK-wide economic plan. The 'Speaker's Convention', ruling discussion of Northern Ireland affairs at Westminster out of order, was relaxed in order to permit discussion of the UK economy as a whole. Stormont was potentially vulnerable to political manipulation by Westminster because of growing integration into Britain's economic policy-making and the region's financial dependence on Westminster. At the 1964 Westminster General Election there was considerable unionist disquiet at the prospect of a Labour government, its UK-wide economic plan and the comments of the Labour leader, Harold Wilson, on civil rights in Northern Ireland. Wilson promised the Campaign for Social Justice (CSJ) 'that a Labour Government would do everything in its power to see that the infringements of justice to which you are so rightly drawing attention are effectively dealt with'. The Labour leader had probably not intended to raise communal passions in Northern Ireland, but the unintentional effect of Wilson's intervention, coupled with his party's 'national' planning policy and traditional sympathy for Irish nationalism, was probably to exacerbate unionist insecurity and its sense of vulnerability to Labour's power. Labour's narrow majority at the 1964 Westminster General Election focused the party's resentment on the twelve Ulster Unionist MPs at Westminster who were voting with the Conservative Opposition. This resentment fuelled the interest of the Labour Party in civil rights in Northern Ireland, leading to the formation of the Campaign for Democracy in Ulster in 1965.

O'Neill, Modernization Theory and Modernization

The emergence of Terence O'Neill as Prime Minister of Northern Ireland in 1963 led to a modernization of at least the rhetoric of unionism if not the substance. O'Neill's speeches were permeated by the assumptions of modernization theory, reflecting an awareness of the 'new economic and political realities' facing Northern Ireland in what appeared to be an increasingly integrated and interdependent world.

The old antagonisms between unionists and nationalists had been worn away and appeared a 'ludicrous anachronism' which, O'Neill's supporters claimed, he was trying to replace with 'normal twentieth-century politics, based on a division between Right and Left' (O'Neill 1969, p. 11). O'Neill's modernizing rhetoric mirrored that of the British political elite and alleviated the pressure on them to intervene (Dixon 1993).

Four themes stand out in O'Neill's speeches (for details, see Dixon 2001a, pp. 58–60):

1. *The economic and political dependence of Northern Ireland on Britain*, and the consequent need to win the support of British public opinion. This highlighted the vulnerability of the region's place in the UK to the whims and prejudice of British political and public opinion, which appeared to know or care little about Northern Ireland (Loughlin 1995).
2. *Northern Ireland's need to maintain a good name in order to win external investment from the rest of the UK and further afield, particularly the USA.*
3. *The improvement of relations with the Republic of Ireland and Catholics in Northern Ireland could increase prosperity and develop an understanding of the unionist position as well as to appease British pressure.*
4. *Economic interests and increased contact would and should win out over communal allegiances, resulting in a strengthening of the Union rather than its weakening* (O'Neill 1969, pp. 47, 114). O'Neill's famous 'Crossroads' speech in December 1968 asked, 'Is a freedom to pursue the un-Christian path of communal strife and sectarian bitterness really more important to you than all the benefits of the British Welfare State?' He hoped to rally 'the moderates', in particular the churches, against 'the raucous sound of extremism [which] is often heard much more loudly than the steady

ground-swell of moderation' (O'Neill 1969, pp. 142, 115, 130–1; Faulkner 1978, p. 41).

During the 1960s, both 'moderate unionists' and nationalists took comfort from an apparent acceleration of the modernizing process, believing such structural developments heralded the triumph of their ideology over the other. O'Neill's modernizing regime was met with opposition from both inside and outside his party, as he attempted to reassure unionists that his more conciliatory approach towards Catholics did not mean that the Union was in danger (O'Neill 1969, p. 51). Paradoxically, O'Neill's reformist efforts may have undermined the Union, not because these reforms were intended to achieve this end, but because British politicians interpreted this reformism as unionist weakness on the border issue: reformism sent out the wrong message to the British political elite.

North–South Co-operation and Wilson's 'Surrogate Nationalism'

During the 1950s, Dublin–Belfast relations were at a low ebb. The replacement of de Valera by Sean Lemass in 1959 was welcomed by the British, since Lemass wanted closer co-operation with the UK, 'partly for its own sake and partly in the hope of creating a more friendly climate of opinion between Northern Ireland and the Republic' (Bew *et al.* 1997, p. 25). By the 1950s, North/South trade was very limited and economic integration was an unlikely motor for Irish unity. However, in 1958, the Republic emerged from its state of relative economic isolation and introduced its 'First Programme for Economic Expansion', which recommended the opening up of the country to foreign investment and an industrial export drive as a means for generating economic growth. The Republic of Ireland was also emerging from diplomatic isolation and using international platforms to raise the question of partition.

Lemass, the Irish Taoiseach, successfully justified this radically new direction in the Republic's economic policy by claiming that it would undermine partition. At the same time, he took a more conciliatory position, recognizing that it was the unionist majority in Northern Ireland, rather than the British state, that represented the principal barrier to ending partition. In April 1964, after a visit to London where he met Sir Alec Douglas-Home and Harold Wilson, Lemass declared:

> I do not believe that there now exists in Britain either amongst its political leaders or the mass of its people any desire to maintain partition or any belief that it serves British interests... I am sure there would be a general and sincere welcome for any move to bring it to an end by agreement amongst Irishmen. This sentiment has not yet found clear political expression from British leaders – as I have urged of them – but this I believe to be now only a matter of time. (*Newsletter*, 14 April 1964)

In response to Lemass's overtures, O'Neill demanded the full constitutional recognition of Northern Ireland by the South, and appealed for a concentration on more immediately relevant issues. The meeting between Lemass and O'Neill at Stormont in January 1965 was the first between the prime ministers of Northern Ireland and the South since 1925.

There is contemporary evidence that Harold Wilson favoured Irish unity, or at least did not oppose it, which suggests that the British prime minister could see no overriding British strategic interest in Northern Ireland. The *Daily Telegraph* reported Wilson as favouring Irish unity within the Commonwealth (six years later, in November 1971, Wilson publicly supported this position: see Bew *et al.* 1997, p. 37). One press report claimed that Wilson wanted to be the prime minister who solved the Irish Question, and that he believed that increased trade, by helping to reduce tension between North and South, would promote this (*The Sunday Times*, 12 December 1965; Dixon 2001a, pp. 62–3).

The impact of modernization theory and the 'surrogate nationalism' of Harold Wilson may help to explain the growing concerns among unionists that Northern Ireland's autonomy and its constitutional position was being eroded. The British political elite, above all, wanted to avoid re-opening the 'Irish Question' in British politics. The process of modernization appeared to be accelerating with the O'Neill–Lemass meeting, and this held out the prospect of resolving the border issue alongside a profitable improvement in Anglo–Irish relations. Unionists had substantial reasons for their perception that events were running against them, and it is against this background of heightened unionist insecurity that their response to the emerging civil rights movement should be considered.

How Much Discrimination Was There?

The question of discrimination is still highly politically charged, and deployed in the propaganda war between the competing parties. Unionist politicians seldom acknowledge that discrimination occurred during the Stormont period, perhaps fearing that to do so would concede legitimacy to the IRA's violence. Some unionists attempt to minimize the extent of discrimination in order to vindicate Stormont, reject nationalist grievances and strengthen their arguments for a return to majority rule in local and regional government. Ian Paisley's DUP have tended to deny that nationalists were discriminated against, while nationalists tend to exaggerate the extent of discrimination in order to claim the moral high ground and put pressure on unionists to shift their position. Some republicans have compared the Stormont regime to Nazi Germany and apartheid South Africa.

There is little doubt that there was discrimination against Catholics during the Stormont period; the academic debate revolves around the *extent* of discrimination against Catholics (Whyte 1990, p. 64). Crude statistics are often misleading and there is complex debate over how to measure discrimination. There have been reasons advanced for disparities between Catholics and Protestants, other than overt discrimination, and these include: lower Catholic educational standards; Catholics discouraging their co-religionists from serving the state (in the RUC or civil service); differences in attitudes to work; inadequate knowledge of job opportunities; concentration of Catholics in peripheral areas and the uneven development of capitalism; the larger size of Catholic families; and the legacy of past discrimination (Teague 1993). The most authoritative survey of discrimination during the Stormont period ordered the different fields of overt discrimination in order of demerit (Whyte 1983), as shown below:

1. *Electoral practices*: local government boundaries were in some cases 'gerrymandered' to produce unionist majorities in Catholic majority areas. The abolition of proportional representation for local government elections in 1922 shifted some authorities to unionist control and prevented Catholic majorities from gaining

power. In 1967, the UUP secured 60 per cent of the seats on Londonderry Corporation with just 32.1 per cent of the vote.

2. *Public employment*: there was discrimination against Catholics, who tended not to reach the upper levels in public employment.

3. *Policing*: the composition of the police force – the Royal Ulster Constabulary – was disproportionately Protestant and biased against Catholics. The part-time Ulster Special Constabulary was found to be a 'Protestant militia'. The Northern Ireland Special Powers Act (1922) gave the Minister of Home Affairs draconian powers to 'take all such steps and issue all such orders as may be necessary for preserving the peace and maintaining order'.

4. *Private employment*: discrimination against Catholics, particularly since a majority of employers were Protestant.

5. *Public housing*: allocation unfairly favoured Protestants.

6. *Regional policy*: evidence that development was concentrated in the more Protestant East of the province rather than the Catholic West.

Discrimination against Catholics was particularly severe at the local authority level and in the predominantly nationalist area west of the River Bann, where unionists used it to secure their dominance. The area 'had less than a quarter of the total population of Northern Ireland yet generated not far short of three-quarters of the complaints of discrimination' (Whyte 1983, pp. 30–1). Housing was a key issue in the emergence of the civil rights movement and it was in these gerrymandered councils in the West that conflict was 'particularly intense' (Purdie 1990, p. 86). While local government has a poor record, the Stormont government did 'put through the original gerrymander which underpinned so many of the subsequent malpractices, and then, despite repeated protests, did nothing to stop those malpractices continuing' (Whyte 1983, p. 31). The problem of unequal life chances for Catholics persists; the Good Friday Agreement 1998 has established an Equality Commission to develop further strategies to deal with this problem and other reasons for inequality.

There is some evidence that Catholics have also discriminated against Protestants. The unionist *Newsletter* newspaper, responding to a report on discrimination by Labour MPs, argued: 'Discrimination in employment has never been denied. That it is practised by both sides does not make it any less deplorable' (*Newsletter*, 25 April 1967). According to Barritt and Carter, 'Many local councillors take it for granted that they are dispensers of patronage to their own side; and the exercise of this patronage is made easier by the custom of expecting personal canvassing of the Council or of its committee before appointments are made' (Barritt and Carter 1962, p. 99). In nationalist Newry in 1962, only 22 out of 765 council houses were occupied by Protestants, and no Protestants at all were employed by the council (Barritt and Carter 1962, p. 67; Gudgin 1999). Since local government was dominated by unionists, anti-Protestant discrimination would not have had the same impact as Protestant discrimination against Catholics. The socialist and civil rights activist, Bernadette Devlin, argued that:

> Both the Protestant Unionists and the Catholic Nationalists deny they discriminate against each other, but both use religion to divide and rule the working class. It is only less serious on the Catholic side because there are fewer Catholic bosses and fewer Catholic local authorities in a position to practise discrimination. (Devlin 1969, p. 57; see also Smith and Chambers 1991, p. 369; Boyle and Hadden 1994, p. 46)

She condemned the hypocrisy of 'Catholic slum landlords marching virtuously beside the tenants they exploited, Catholic employers marching in protest against the Protestants they excluded from their factories' (Devlin 1969, p. 155).

Unionists have responded in three ways to charges of discrimination:

(i) by saying that there was no discrimination;
(ii) by saying that there was no discrimination but you could not expect the Northern Ireland state to give nationalists who questioned the very existence of the state positions of influence within it (however, for much of the Stormont period, Northern Ireland was not in a state of war or siege, yet Catholics continued to be excluded); and
(iii) by saying that there was some discrimination during the Stormont period but that it has been exaggerated. Few unionist politicians will admit privately, or indicate publicly, that discrimination occurred. This is the context in which the Ulster Unionist Party leader, David Trimble, admitted in December 1998 that Northern Ireland during the Stormont period 'was a cold house for Catholics'.'

The 1960s: Polarization or Reconciliation?

There is debate over the climate of opinion in Northern Ireland during the 1960s. There is simultaneously evidence both of a thawing
in community relations *and* polarization. Optimists contrast the dis-
mal 1950s with the modernizing 1960s, portraying it as a period in
which Catholics were shifting their allegiances away from a united
Ireland and towards the pursuit of full participation and equality
in the Northern Ireland state, while O'Neill was holding out the
prospect of reconciliation with the Catholic minority. Between 1955
and 1959 the vote for republican candidates slumped from 23.7 per
cent to 11 per cent. The IRA's Border Campaign of 1956–62 was
called off because of 'the attitude of the general public whose minds
have been deliberately distracted from the supreme issue facing the
Irish people – the unity and freedom of Ireland'. The IRA subsequently began to pursue a more political path. The emergence of a
new, moderate, nationalist opposition at Stormont also encouraged
hopes for reconciliation. Other signs of reconciliation included the
growth of ecumenism; the 'Orange–Green talks' between the Orange
Order and the Ancient Order of Hibernians; and the confidence
of Catholics resulting from the election of the first Irish-American
Catholic president of the United States, John F. Kennedy. O'Neill's
more conciliatory approach to community relations and his rhetoric
of modernization was also taken as evidence for optimism.

The pessimists about the 1960s emphasize growing conflict over
expanding state resources, the impoverishment of the Catholic
working class and evidence of continuing sectarianism and rising
nationalist sentiment. The deployment of British troops was threatened by tensions surrounding the Divis Street Riots of 1964 and
the commemorations of the Battle of the Somme and the Easter
Rising in 1966. Loyalists were being mobilized against O'Neill by
Ian Paisley's Ulster Protestant Volunteers and the Ulster Committee
for the Defence of the Constitution. In 1966, the Ulster Volunteer
Force was established, murdered two Catholics and was banned by
the Stormont government. Meanwhile, recruitment to the IRA was
growing, perhaps stimulated by conflict over the flying of nationalist
flags and commemoration of the Easter Rising. While the emphasis of the organization had shifted towards political struggle, it still
continued to organize and prepare for a military campaign. More-
over, there were still numerous incidents involving republicans, and
the IRA was having difficulty controlling its activists (Purdie 1990,

pp. 10, 31, 44–6). With the benefit of hindsight, the surge of antagonism and violence that followed the civil rights march of October 1968 might suggest that the optimistic view of community relations in the 1960s was rather superficial.

The Campaign for Civil Rights

The election in 1945 of a Labour government, a party traditionally sympathetic to Irish nationalism, aroused nationalist expectations. The Anti-Partition League (APL) was formed in 1945 to press nationalist demands, and in the Irish Free State the government also launched an anti-partition campaign (Purdie 1986, p. 67). The APL was rurally based, traditionally nationalist and deeply Catholic. The APL presented a moderate face emphasizing discrimination to the British audience in order to delegitimize partition, while speaking to nationalists in the language of Irish nationalism. There was some limited sympathy for the APL among the Friends of Ireland group at Westminster, largely composed of Labour MPs, but there was a reluctance to re-open the 'Irish Question' (Purdie 1983). The Connolly Association's (see below) campaign to release republican prisoners after the end of the IRA's border campaign of 1956–62 suggested that Labour MPs could be mobilized around issues of civil rights more easily than partition. After maximizing the APL's vote 'there was little to do beyond going through the motions again and again' and the campaign fizzled out (Purdie 1988, p. 75).

The civil rights campaign of the 1960s included groups and individuals with very different political agendas and class backgrounds.

The Northern Ireland Labour Party

In the early 1960s and up to 1965, the strong performance of the NILP at the polls raised the possibility that an anti-UUP grand coalition that included nationalists could defeat the Unionist government at Stormont (Purdie 1990, p. 64). The NILP attempted to build from its base among Protestants to attract more Catholics to the party. Between 1958 and 1962 the party doubled its total vote at Stormont elections. Charles Brett, the NILP chairman, told his party at its 1963 conference, 'I believe that the time has come when we must challenge the Catholic vested interests as well as the Protestant ones' (Brett 1978, p. 85). The NILP probably benefited electorally during this period, both from its new liberal appeal to Catholics and its continued perception in the unionist community as a Protestant Labour party (Dixon 1993, p. 78).

The contribution of the NILP to the civil rights movement has been airbrushed from history by some nationalist writers who were perhaps too keen to draw a simple 'black and white' story of the civil rights period (Dixon 1996c). However, 'Throughout the 1960s, while concentrating on economic matters, the NILP plugged away at many of the issues that were taken up by the civil rights movement' (Purdie 1990, p. 69). The NILP annual conference overwhelmingly approved of the cross-communal direction in which the party was moving. It endorsed, by 18,300 votes to 900, the chairman's three-point action plan to combat religious discrimination in the region: first, to set up a Joint Tribunal to examine allegations of religious discrimination; second, to establish a joint working party to develop a points system for the allocation of housing; and finally, to appeal to employers to allocate jobs to applicants on merit alone (Dixon 1993, pp. 79–80).

The NILP, with its Protestant base of support, was sensitive to the communal interpretations that could be placed on the demand for civil rights. The party couched its appeal for civil rights demands in unionist terms, suggesting, for example, that civil rights reforms would give Stormont a greater degree of legitimacy. Reforms that could be interpreted as nationalist-inspired were advocated, such as measures against discrimination and on electoral law, but so too was a 'unionist' proposal to increase Northern Ireland's representation at Westminster by three more seats, to bring it into line with the region's population (Dixon 1993, p. 79). Its 'Electoral Reform Now' document avoided the more sensitive issue of discrimination in employment and housing, and the repeal of the Special Powers Act. Brett opposed open interference by the British government in Northern Ireland because it would 'arouse deep resentment', and might force Stormont into a defensive position from which 'it could not with honour retreat'. A Royal Commission would only 'stir up old issues and hatreds'. Reform was more likely to be secured by 'private and discreet' pressure by the Labour government on the Unionist government, making the granting of financial or economic aid dependent on progress with reforms. However, while 'Private representations of the strongest possible nature' had been made to the Labour government to have religious discrimination included in anti-race discrimination legislation, the government 'did not find it possible to accede to this pressure' ('Notes on Resolutions for the British Labour Party Annual Conference 1965', 11 August 1965, LPA, quoted in Dixon 1993, p. 104). In spite of the NILP's proclaimed loyalty, at the 1965 Stormont elections O'Neill claimed that Harold Wilson controlled the NILP and attacked it as an antipartitionist party; pamphlets were circulated with the slogan, 'If you want a Catholic for your neighbour vote Labour' (Purdie 1990, p. 64).

The Nationalist Party

During the 1960s the Nationalist Party was coming under fire from nationalists, who criticized the party's failure to contest elections, its lack of a modern regional party organization, failure to unite nationalists and provide leadership, ineffectiveness in winning redress for Catholic grievances, and emphasis on partition to the exclusion of social and economic issues (Purdie 1990; Lynn 1997, pp. 232–3). A nationalist pressure group, dominated by teachers and intellectuals, called National Unity, which later transformed itself into the National Democratic Party, urged the Nationalist Party to unite the opposition and recognize that Irish unity could only come about by consent (Lynn 1997, p. 184). In response, the Nationalist Party did attempt to transform itself into an orthodox, modern, democratic political party with an individual membership and national conference. In January 1964 the party launched 'Operation Truth and Justice', to bring to the attention of the British political parties 'the disabilities operating against Catholics in the Six Counties' (Lynn 1997, p. 171). The party became the official opposition at Stormont in 1965, after encouragement from the Irish Taoiseach, and continued to use constitutional methods in an unsuccessful bid to convince O'Neill and the British government to introduce reform into Northern Ireland. Austin Currie, a radical member of the Nationalist Party, wanted the party to use extra-parliamentary methods to raise civil rights issues, but the party leadership feared that this would result in violence (Lynn 1997, p. 202). In November 1967, the Nationalist Party leader, Eddie McAteer, appealed to O'Neill 'to try to find some basis of progress without either of us playing to the gallery', but he was rebuffed (Lynn 1997, p. 203).

The Connolly Association and the Republican Movement

The role of the republican movement and the Connolly Association in the origins of the civil rights movement has been underestimated. The British-based Marxist Connolly Association campaigned for Irish unity among the Irish in Britain, and had strong links with the Communist Party of Great Britain. During the 1950s, the organization argued that 'the way to a peaceful solution of the Irish problem was to discredit Ulster Unionism in Britain through exposing the discriminatory practices which occurred under the Stormont regime, in the process winning sympathetic allies for the cause of Irish reunification' (Coughlan 1990). The Association had won the support of half the Parliamentary Labour Party for the release of republican internees during the Border Campaign and now hoped to perform a similar role with civil rights. In the early 1960s, the Association organized a series of civil rights marches across England and the campaign was taken up by the National Council for Civil Liberties, the Movement for Colonial Freedom and later by the Campaign for Democracy in Ulster.

During the 1960s, the Connolly Association's civil rights approach influenced the republican movement in a more political direction. However, IRA membership was also expanding, from 657 members in 1962 to 1,039 members in October 1966 (*Independent on Sunday*, 4 January 1998) with the hope of participating in a military campaign (Patterson 1997, pp. 107, 111). The leadership's approach appears to have been to pursue the politicization of the republican movement while containing the pressure for military action by engaging in limited military activities. The hope was that popular Catholic agitation for civil rights would squeeze the unionist regime. The republican movement would break through to Protestants, and a united movement of Catholics and Protestants would bring down the Northern Ireland state (Patterson 1997, pp. 107, 111–12). However, as events unfolded it became clear that the civil rights movement had unleashed communal violence which divided rather than united Protestants and Catholics. The republican movement played the driving role in the establishment of the Northern Ireland Civil Rights Association and was active in stewarding marches.

The Campaign for Social Justice

This was founded in Dungannon, Co. Tyrone, on 17 January 1964 by Mrs Patricia McCluskey and her husband, Dr Conn McCluskey.

The CSJ grew out of the Homeless Citizens League (HCL), which they had also founded. The HCL was established after forty young Catholic housewives petitioned and sixty-seven picketed Dungannon Urban District Council over poor housing conditions and discrimination in housing allocation (Purdie 1990, p. 83). Nevertheless, the HCL's activities forced the council to make concessions by making representations to Stormont. It also revealed a 'gentleman's agreement' between unionists and nationalists to allocate housing on a sectarian basis, so that Catholics would become the tenants of 'Catholic houses' and Protestants the tenants of 'Protestant houses' (Purdie 1990, pp. 90–1). The success of the HCL demonstrated the effectiveness of direct action and contrasted with the failure of the Nationalist Party's parliamentary approach.

The CSJ was formed to oppose the policies of 'apartheid and discrimination' implemented by the Stormont government, and its first objective was 'to collect comprehensive and accurate data on all injustices done . . . and to bring them to the attention of as many socially minded people as possible'. The CSJ was composed of 'educated people' drawn from the Catholic, professional, university-educated, middle classes. The 13-strong committee contained no Protestants but included two consultant surgeons, two GPs, an architect and a science professor. The objectives of the group were equal rights within the UK, though most in the CSJ aspired towards Irish unity. The CSJ hoped to go over the heads of the Stormont government and appeal to Westminster by breaking the 'Speaker's Convention', which prohibited discussion of Northern Ireland, so that the government could legislate to protect minority rights (Purdie 1990). The CSJ did succeed in drawing Harold Wilson into saying that a Labour government would intervene to deal with discrimination, which threw unionism into a panic.

The Labour Government, 1964–6, and the Campaign for Democracy in Ulster

The slender, four-seat, majority that Labour won at the 1964 General Election focused attention on the twelve Ulster Unionist MPs at Westminster who held the balance of power and voted with the Conservatives. Labour MPs, incensed at the sight of Ulster unionists loyally trooping into the Opposition lobby at Westminster to vote on issues that did not relate to Northern Ireland, began to take a new interest in the region. The Campaign for Democracy in Ulster (CDU) was founded as an all-party pressure group for the reform of Northern Ireland. The use of 'Ulster' in the name of the pressure group was deliberate; the border question was deemed to be irrelevant to the CDU and the objective was to obtain 'full British rights for the people of Northern Ireland, to which they are entitled as British subjects'. However, at least two of its founding members were members of the socialist republican Connolly Association. The CDU and Gerry Fitt sought an investigation into the workings of the Government of Ireland Act, something that could be seen by unionists to strike at the very heart of partition. By early 1966, approximately forty Labour MPs tabled a motion calling for the establishment of a Royal Commission to inquire into the working of the Government of Ireland Act 1920.

The CSJ and CDU were comprised predominantly of people who aspired towards Irish unity and were probably seen by many Protestants as being anti-unionist and interventionist. The CSJ was all-Catholic in composition and 'did not want to be "contaminated" by any Northern Ireland politicians, except Gerry Fitt' (Purdie 1990, pp. 93–5). The CDU also gravitated more towards anti-partitionist civil rights supporters such as Fitt, elected MP for West Belfast in 1966, than the unionist NILP. Gerry Fitt told a Connolly Association conference that he was asking for 'British standards as they apply in the island of Great Britain', but he coupled this with a claim that unionists were in Northern Ireland 'by no right'. 'He is not there by his right of being an Irishman, because he disclaims any Irish nationality . . . He is there because he wants to maintain this little oasis of fascism in Northern Ireland' ('The Irish Question – Challenge to Democratic Britain', Report of Conference, 25 February 1967).

The simultaneous advocacy of civil rights, 'British rights for British citizens', with anti-partitionism and the overwhelmingly Catholic/nationalist membership of the civil rights movement led unsurprisingly to a perception that the two demands were linked. It was not just unionists who interpreted the attempt to raise civil rights as an anti-partitionist tactic. An editorial in the nationalist *Irish News* claimed, 'A big campaign to focus public attention on the question of partition in Ireland is at the moment going on quietly but effectively in Britain. In recent months the CSJ in Northern Ireland has been active with meetings and the various injustices imposed on the minority in the six counties' (*Irish News*, 8 September 1965). The NILP maintained its support for civil rights but, after its poor performance at the 1967 corporation elections, the Party's Secretary reported that 'A platform of civil rights will not win us any more votes' (Secretary's report on corporation elections, May 1967, quoted in Graham 1982, p. 248). The Executive of the NILP was generally critical of the interfering and pro-nationalist stance of the CDU, and pulled back from the civil rights platform which appeared to be identified increasingly with nationalism (Dixon 1993, pp. 135–6). The 1966 Westminster General Election produced a Labour government with almost a 100-seat majority. It removed the irritant of the influence of Ulster unionist MPs and the salience of the civil rights issue at Westminster declined.

O'Neill: Bridging the Gap?

The Divis Street Riots of 1964 and the violence surrounding the 1966 commemorations of the Battle of the Somme and the Easter Rising were reminders that communal tensions in Northern Ireland could require the deployment of British troops on the streets and precipitate the re-opening of the 'Irish Question' (*The Sunday Times*, 1972, p. 82). In 1966, the British government feared a campaign of IRA violence to mark the Easter Rising and was anxious that if troops were deployed, then any clashes between soldiers and the IRA should not be publicized as 'a people's uprising against the excesses of the Crown forces' (*Irish Times*, 1–2 January 1997; Rose 1999, pp. 18–20). The loyalist paramilitary Ulster Volunteer Force was formed to defend and uphold the Protestant North against the IRA. The UVF carried out a number of petrol bomb attacks on Catholic shops, homes and schools in February–April 1966, and in June 1966 was responsible for the murder of two Catholics. Wilson denounced the ultra-unionists as 'quasi fascist', and O'Neill banned the UVF. Ian Paisley, a Protestant fundamentalist preacher, was exploiting fears that improved North/South relations were undermining Northern Ireland's position in the UK (Faulkner 1978, pp. 42–3).

The Labour government put some pressure on O'Neill to reform Northern Ireland, but did not want to push him 'too far' in case this undermined him and he was replaced by hardliners within his own party. O'Neill did introduce some reform of Northern Ireland's constitutional system, met the Irish Taoiseach for the first time since 1925, took steps to open up his party to Catholics, and visited a Catholic school. This symbolism is usually derided, but it may have paved the way towards a more substantive, material and political accommodation with nationalists (Loughlin 1995, p. 177; Cash 1996, p. 129). There was hardline pressure against O'Neill's gestures towards Catholics from within his cabinet, unionist backbenchers, the largely autonomous constituency parties, and outside his party from the maverick Protestant unionist, Ian Paisley. Public pressure by the Labour government could make it difficult for O'Neill to introduce reforms because they would be seen to be the result of pressure from Westminster and a sign of weakness. The question was not so much the issue of reform but rather the pace at which reform could take place without undermining the reformist prime minister (*Belfast Telegraph* editorial, 4 October 1967). In a meeting with the Irish government in December 1966, Harold Wilson cited O'Neill's 'difficulties with the Rev Ian Paisley' as a reason not to push him further to reform; he also argued that O'Neill's position 'within his own party and cabinet was none too secure' (*Irish Times*, 1–2 January 1997). That month, O'Neill announced a package of reforms: abolition of the university constituency and instead creating four additional territorial constituencies; abolishing the business vote for Stormont elections; and setting up a statutory boundary commission. Roy Jenkins, the British Home Secretary and historian, argued that history showed that the English did not have a talent for solving Irish problems, and: 'Few issues in the past have shown a greater capacity to divert and dissipate the reforming energy of left-wing British governments than deep embroilment in Irish affairs' (*Hansard*, vol. 751, col. 1687, 25 October 1967). In May 1968, shortly before the civil rights movement took to the streets, Wilson told the House of Commons, 'in the last two or three years considerable advances have been made under the present Premier of Northern Ireland. Not enough, I agree, but what has been achieved has been remarkable in view of the prejudice he has to meet in that particular area of the UK' (*Hansard*, vol. 768, col. 732, 21 May 1968).

O'Neill's leadership skills are certainly open to question. He had an autocratic style and failed to consult with his party, most famously over his ground-breaking meeting with the Irish Taoiseach in 1965. O'Neill placed considerable hope in the ordinary decency and common sense of the people of Ulster (and civil society) to see the sense of his 'moderate' and modernizing way forward. At times, O'Neill considered himself to be English and 'was sufficiently removed from traditional unionism to be quite happy to ignore its symbols and its sacred history in favour of elements of an instrumental and rational

view of politics' (Bruce 1989, p. 71) but this tended towards the abandonment of all that was distinctive about unionist politics. His more
middle-class, liberal unionist circle was insulated from the world of
the Protestant working class, who were concerned at the direction
of O'Neillism and receptive to Ian Paisley's 'traditionalist' message
(Bruce 1989, pp. 70–1; Gailey 1995).

Ian Paisley led the opposition to O'Neill outside the UUP. This
'prophet in the wilderness' appeared to be increasingly justified in his
criticism of O'Neill by the turn of events. Paisley's populist appeal
was effective: 'A traitor and a bridge are very much alike for they
both go over to the other side.' He helped to establish the Ulster
Constitutional Defence Committee in April 1966, and the Ulster
Protestant Volunteers to defend the Union. He opposed ecumenism
and a march of his through 'republican territory' to the Presbyterian
Assembly, in June 1966, resulted in a riot (Bruce 1989, p. 81).

Politicians operate under constraints and whether even a more
skilful unionist leader could have delivered sufficient support for civil
rights reforms to meet Catholic demands without undermining his or
her position is open to question (Bruce 1989, p. 70; *Irish Times*, 1–2
January 1999). During this period, O'Neill struggled to control his
party and, at one point, the NILP chairman told Roy Jenkins that the
government should support the 'extremist' Brian Faulkner against
O'Neill 'as a man capable of carrying his party with him' (Brett 1978,
p. 135).

During the period 1966–8, both the NILP and the CDU tried
and failed to persuade the Labour government and the wider labour
movement of the importance of swift civil rights reform in Northern
Ireland. Between August 1966, when the use of the army in Northern
Ireland was first mooted, and October 1968, the Labour government
had taken no steps to improve its supervision of the region, and there
was little information available when the conflict erupted.

Politics in the Streets

The formation of the Northern Ireland Civil Rights Association
(NICRA) on 29 January 1967 originated with a decision taken by the
republican Wolfe Tone Society in August 1966. A 13-person steering
committee was drawn from the Amalgamated Union of Engineering Workers, the CSJ, the Communist Party of Northern Ireland,
the Belfast Wolfe Tone Society, the Belfast Trades Council, the

Republican Clubs, the Ulster Liberal Party, the National Democratic Party, the Republican Labour Party, the Ardoyne Tenants Association and the NILP; later, a liberal Young Unionist was co-opted on to the committee. NICRA was based on the National Council for Civil Liberties and its constitution 'emphasised the association's character as a body which would make representations on the broad issues of civil liberties and would also take up individual cases of discrimination and ill-treatment' rather than reflecting a commitment to militant protest (Purdie 1990, p. 133). But it did little between its founding and the proposal for the first civil rights march, which was suggested in June 1968 by the nationalist MP, Austin Currie (Purdie 1990, pp. 134–5; Lynn 1997, p. 206).

During 1967, Currie had been campaigning on the failure of Catholics to be allocated council housing by unionist-controlled councils. In October 1967, Currie drew attention to squatting by homeless Catholic families as an example of 'growing desperation and frustration', and he predicted 'more squatting, more acts of civil disobedience, more emphasis on the "other means" and less on traditional parliamentary methods'. He advocated direct action as the only means by which the nationalist population could improve their conditions (quoted in Lynn 1997, pp. 205–6). Currie also shared nationalist modernizing assumptions that Irish unity was inevitable, and that the religious and economic barriers to it were crumbling (*Irish Independent*, 18 September 1964).

The Nationalist Party rejected Currie's direct action tactic, feeling this had not been 'properly thought through' and could lead to widespread violence. Some of Currie's Derry Nationalist Party colleagues had been involved in the street protests of 1951 and 1952 which had resulted in serious public disturbances. After these experiences they were reluctant to take politics into the streets. By rejecting direct action, the Nationalist Party failed to put itself at the head of the civil rights movement and was subsequently marginalized when that movement took to the streets. Direct action swiftly won a reform package 'which far exceeded anything that the Nationalist Party had been able to gain in over 40 years' (Lynn 1997). In June 1968, Currie joined a Catholic family which was squatting in a house in Caledon and about to be evicted. The new tenant was to be a 19-year-old unmarried Protestant woman who was the secretary to a solicitor and unionist parliamentary candidate. Currie then proposed, and NICRA agreed to, a protest march from Coalisland to Dungannon. The march, organized by republicans, took place on 24 August 1968 to the accompaniment of nationalist bands (Devlin 1969, p. 91). NICRA refused to accept the re-routing of the march to the Catholic area of the town, since it would have implied that it was a sectarian march. Paisley's Ulster Protestant Volunteers counter-demonstrated and the police kept the two marches apart. When some of the marchers tried to attack the counter-demonstrators they were beaten back by the RUC. While the platform reminded the crowd they were demonstrating for civil rights, Gerry Fitt called for both civil rights and a 32-county Republic. One participant thought it was 'hilarious' to see how out of touch organizers of the march were with their civil rights beliefs compared to the republicanism of the marchers (Devlin 1969, pp. 93–4).

The second civil rights march took place on 5 October 1968 and was again a response by NICRA to a local initiative, this time from the left-wing Derry Housing Action Committee (DHAC) which was composed of left-wingers in the NILP and the republican movement. In Derry/Londonderry there had been the most flagrant case of gerrymandering, and while deprivation was distributed among both Catholics and Protestants, Catholics bore the brunt disproportionately. By the summer of 1968, a leading member argued:

> [the DHAC's] conscious, if unspoken, strategy was to provoke the police into over-reaction and thus spark off a mass reaction against the authorities. We assumed that we would be in control of the reaction, that we were strong enough to channel it. The one certain way to ensure a head-on clash . . . was to organise a non-Unionist march through the city centre. (McCann in Purdie 1990, p. 184)

The march was banned but an estimated 400–600 marchers defied the ban and were brutally attacked by the police. The march then descended into a general violent confrontation between the RUC and young Catholics in the adjoining Bogside, who had not been involved in the march (Purdie 1990, pp. 143–6). According to Purdie, 'the whole affair was a series of blunders and the violence resulted from a breakdown of control by the leaders of the march and the controllers of the police, and not from any pre-existing plan' (Purdie 1990, p. 146). The violence that met the 5 October march was captured by the television cameras and evoked attacks by the US police on black people in the Deep South. The broadcasting of the march outraged British, Irish and world opinion, and finally forced Ireland back on to the British political agenda. O'Neill told his cabinet that they were under pressure from Wilson to 'justify some of our practices' and that 'we have now become the focus of world opinion' (*Irish Independent*, 7 January 2000).

The 5 October march transformed the civil rights campaign from a collection of groups and activists into a movement with branches all over Northern Ireland where 'there was a significant Catholic population' (Purdie 1990, p. 156). As Catholics clambered aboard the civil rights bandwagon, the radicals of the DHAC were marginalized. The more 'respectable' and 'moderate' members of the Catholic community – 'mainly business and professional people, clergy, trade unionists and political leaders' – established the Derry Citizens Action Committee (DCAC) 'to harness the energies and enthusiasm of the people in a disciplined manner' (Frank Curran, former editor of the *Derry Journal*, quoted in Purdie 1990, p. 189). Its demands were modest and confined to 'civil rights': a two-year crash house building programme in Derry; 'some form of legal control in the renting of furnished accommodation'; and a fair points system for the allocation of housing (Ó Dochartaigh 1997, p. 25). The DCAC organized and carefully stewarded demonstrations in order to avoid violence and this enabled them to keep control for a few months (Purdie 1990, p. 191).

The RUC did not have enough power to control the big marches (over 15,000 strong) now being organized without the co-operation of the DCAC, who were themselves having problems controlling their supporters wishing to respond to loyalist provocation (Ó Dochartaigh 1997, p. 29; Purdie 1990, pp. 193–4). On 22 November, O'Neill, under pressure from the publicity surrounding the October march, announced a reform programme that included proroguing the Londonderry Corporation; A Development Commission was appointed to run the city. In December, O'Neill appealed successfully for calm (see Chapter 4) and was supported by the Nationalist Party, the DCAC and other 'moderates' in the civil rights movement.

At the end of 1968 the DCAC had been largely successful in policing and organizing demonstrations, but in 1969 its grip weakened as the conflict took on a more sectarian tone. In January 1969 a small left-wing student group, the People's Democracy, defied a NICRA moratorium and organized a march from Belfast to Derry. The march was attacked repeatedly and at Burntollet was ambushed by loyalists with clubs; approximately half of these were off-duty members of the

B Specials (a part-time overwhelmingly Protestant police force with a reputation for sectarianism). This violence reinforced the shifting focus of debate in Northern Ireland from political and economic issues to the more sensitive issue of reform of the state's security apparatus (Bew and Patterson 1985, pp. 16–18). Following police violence, republicans established 'Free Derry' by organizing local vigilante committees and barricades to keep the RUC out of the Bogside area of Derry. The DCAC were appalled by this, 'But blood was up and there was nothing they could do about it' (McCann 1974, p. 53). By early 1969 republicans could see the advantage of Catholic mobilization for achieving Irish unity (Ó Dochartaigh 1997, pp. 46–7).

Marches were continuing but were provoking serious confrontations with the RUC and getting out of the control of the DCAC. In April 1969, Samuel Devenney was beaten by police and later died. After April it was difficult 'to organize a demonstration which did not end in riot', but 'by ending the demonstrations the moderates took away from the youth any channel for expression other than riot. The rage and frustration which lay just beneath the surface of life in the Bogside could no longer be contained within the thin shell of the [D]CAC's timid respectability' (McCann 1974, pp. 57–8). The political agenda was shifting away from civil rights towards RUC brutality and the need to defend nationalist areas. Young rioters now ignored the persuasion of moderates or republicans to desist from attacks on the RUC (McCann 1974, (Ó Dochartaigh 1997, pp. 40–1, 53, 115).

The hope of republicans and socialists that confrontation with the Stormont government would produce a united working-class movement of Protestants and Catholics quickly appeared to be misplaced. By Easter 1969 'There had been a distinct resurgence of basic nationalist feeling in Derry' (Ó Dochartaigh 1997, p. 45). The socialist activist Eamonn McCann commented in early 1969 on the sectarian tone of some of the civil rights initiatives:

> the cry 'get the Protestants' is still very much on the lips of the Catholic working-class. Everyone applauds loudly when one says in a speech that we are not sectarian, we are fighting for the rights of all Irish workers, but really that's because they see this as the new way of getting at the Protestants.

In August 1969. Orange Order parades in Derry were the occasion for fierce rioting which the RUC could no longer contain. NICRA organized demonstrations across Northern Ireland to increase pressure on the RUC and relieve pressure on the rioters in Derry. In Belfast, republicans laid siege to an RUC station and the ensuing rioting resulted in the deaths of five Catholics (four killed by RUC gunfire) and two Protestants. On 14 August the British Army was finally deployed on the streets. Republicans did not make strenuous efforts to avoid conflict between loyalists, the RUC and nationalist youths. Ó Dochartaigh argues, 'It does not seem unreasonable to suggest that they saw 12 August as an opportunity to bring the very existence of Northern Ireland into question' (Ó Dochartaigh 1997, p. 116). In this they were encouraged by Jack Lynch, the Irish prime minister, who made anti-partitionist remarks, further raising fears among unionists of a nationalist agenda behind the civil rights movement, and of an Irish invasion from the Republic. The day before British troops were deployed, Jack Lynch called for a UN peace-keeping force and said that 'the Irish government can no longer stand by and see innocent people injured and perhaps worse'. 'Recognising ... that the reunification of the national territory can provide the only permanent solution for the problem, it is our intention to request the British government to enter into early negotiations with the Irish government to review the present constitutional position of the six counties of Northern Ireland' (*Irish Times*, 14 August 1969). Irish troops were moved to the border to set up field hospitals for the injured. In the Republic, members of the Fianna Fáil government were attempting to influence the character of Catholic insurgency and were involved in supplying arms to the emerging Provisional IRA in the North (Patterson 1997, pp. 130–4). The Scarman Report later criticized Lynch's speech: 'There is no doubt that this broadcast strengthened the will of the Bogsiders to obstruct any attempt by the police to enter their area, and to harass them by missile and petrol bomb attacks, whenever they appeared on the perimeter' (Scarman 1972). There were real concerns among unionists, including senior unionist ministers, that the Irish Army might invade (*Irish Times*, 3 January 2000). For nationalists, 'This put new heart into the fight. News that "the Free State soldiers are coming" spread rapidly', and they 'believed themselves within a whisker of a united Ireland' (McCann 1974, p. 60; Ó Dochartaigh 1997).

Debating the Origins of the Civil Rights Movement

A Republican/Communist Conspiracy?

The main response of the Ulster Unionist Party to the civil rights movement was to brand it a republican/Communist conspiracy to overthrow the Northern Ireland state and bring about a united Ireland. Christopher Hewitt has argued that the emergence of the civil rights movement and the subsequent violence was a result of 'nationalist indoctrination and foreign involvement rather than socio-economic disadvantage', which he argues was exaggerated (Hewitt 1991, p. 17). During the 1960s, Catholic nationalism was as strong as ever, and civil rights demands were used as a tactic to raise the question of partition and overthrow the Northern Ireland state (Hewitt 1991, pp. 28–9, 37). The evidence for this anti-partitionism is the failure of civil rights leaders to endorse the constitutional position of Northern Ireland and to condemn Catholic discrimination against Protestants, and the fact that many civil rights leaders went on to found the nationalist SDLP.

Nationalists and republicans did play a prominent role in the civil rights campaign. The socialist republican Connolly Association was influential on the IRA, the Campaign for Democracy in Ulster and the Labour Party in raising civil rights issues. The IRA were active in establishing NICRA, active in the DHAC (which called the Derry march) and in organizing and stewarding marches. While the IRA leadership may not have predicted the immediate consequences of the political, civil rights strategy, most republicans would probably have shared the primary objective of raising partition. Given close republican involvement in the campaign and that of other prominent anti-partitionists, as well as the past record of nationalists in using allegations of discrimination to raise the issue of partition, it is not so surprising that some unionists perceived that the civil rights campaign's goal was anti-partitionist (a view shared by the nationalist *Irish News*) or even a republican front, particularly in the context of growing unionist insecurity. Some of the most moderate elements in the civil rights movement favoured Irish unity, and John Hume saw the reform of Northern Ireland 'as a necessary prerequisite to the eventual and inevitable marriage of the two parts of Ireland' (*Derry Journal*, 13 March 1969, quoted in Ó Dochartaigh 1997, p. 60). The campaign for civil rights could be used to delegitimize Stormont and question the existence of Northern Ireland. For some, the campaign for 'British rights for British citizens' was probably a tactical move to win support in Britain among politicians who were happier to consider civil rights issues rather than re-open the constitutional question. Appeals for an investigation into the workings of the 1920 Government of Ireland Act could easily be interpreted as raising the border question. It seems reasonable to conclude that *some* of those involved in the civil rights movement did see it as a tactic to undermine Stormont and bring about a united Ireland, while others saw it as a shift away from the traditional mix of civil rights and anti-partitionism towards a primary focus on civil rights (and working-class unity), with Ireland's unity further down the road. Of course, there were some liberal and socialist unionists who believed that civil rights reform would strengthen the union.

This unionist view of the civil rights movement can be questioned on several counts. First, *by underestimating discrimination and Catholic grievance it is unable to explain the kind of mass violence that was provoked by the civil rights campaign and does not explain why the civil rights movement emerged and achieved success in the 1960s.* The increase in votes for the Nationalist Party can be interpreted as a shift away from republicanism and towards participation in the Northern State rather than as evidence of increased national feeling. When violence erupted it correlated with the nationalist vote but also with deprivation.

Second, *it does not recognize that at least for some of those nationalists in the civil rights campaign there was a shift towards an emphasis on civil rights rather than the border question during the 1960s.* That many, but not all, of those involved in the civil rights campaign were Catholics and nationalists does not detract from the justice of their cause. Indeed, given the disproportionate impact of discrimination on the nationalist community it is not surprising that nationalists were more likely to be involved in the civil rights movement and affect its character.

Third, *while accepting the key role played by republicans in the civil rights campaign, the evidence suggests that republicans and communists were not in effective control of NICRA* (Purdie 1988, pp. 33, 39). The thinking behind the IRA's civil rights strategy did not anticipate the resurgence of communal conflict that followed, and the opportunities that might later flow from that. After 5 October the republicans in NICRA urged restraint and a moratorium on demonstrations and marches (Purdie 1988, p. 39; Purdie 1990, pp. 157–8).

The New Catholic Middle-Class Thesis (Top-Down)

The 'new Catholic middle-class' thesis has been the 'orthodox' explanation for the emergence of the civil rights movement. The Cameron Commission, which reported on the background to the October 1968 violence, echoing Modernizing assumptions, argues that the civil rights movement was led and founded by a new, expanded and assertive Catholic middle class that emerged in the 1960s (Cameron 1969). This new middle class was the product of two developments, first, it was a product of the expansion and extension of the British welfare state to Northern Ireland, which also benefited Catholics. The 1947 Education Act in particular is singled out for its role in facilitating the emergence of a new, educated Catholic middle class. Second, economic modernization and an influx of international capital opened up new opportunities to middle-class Catholics and raised their expectations because it recruited personnel on a non-discriminatory basis. The extension of the Welfare State to Northern Ireland demonstrated the material benefits of British citizenship to the 'new Catholic middle class', opening up a disparity in the standard of living between North and South. The benefits of British citizenship made Catholics more British and weakened their enthusiasm for Irish unity. They encouraged Catholics to participate in and seek a fairer deal from the expanding British state. 'The Catholic middle class, while not abandoning their nationalist sentiments, began to seek the reform of Northern Ireland as their first goal; and before long for many it became the overriding goal.' The motivation of most of those in the civil rights movement is not Irish unity but civil rights (O'Leary and McGarry 1996, pp. 158, 160, 168). The civil rights movement is seen as a highly organized, disciplined, mass protest movement, under the strong control and leadership of the 'new Catholic middle class' located in NICRA. The replacement of the old rural, anti-partitionist Nationalist Party by the SDLP is seen as symbolic of this newly emerging, less traditional, rural and *urban* elite 'wholly different and separate in outlook, purpose and social background' (Morgan 1987, p. 103).

The 'new Catholic middle class' thesis is favoured by nationalists and republicans, since it is useful in the propaganda war for emphasizing the failings of unionists and the British who rebuffed the increasingly British-orientated 'respectable Catholic middle classes' who led the civil rights movement. It underlines the sincerity of the civil rights movement in seeking redress and in not raising the

question of the border, contrasting with the unionist 'republican conspiracy' argument. The unionists and the British government appear
all the more reprehensible in their failure to meet reasonable civil
rights demands. The escalation of the conflict from demonstrations
to anti-partitionism and the 'armed struggle' appears all the more
understandable, if not excusable. Some republicans have gone so far
as to suggest that the IRA did not exist at that time and was only
brought into being as a response to state repression.

The 'new Catholic middle class' thesis has been subjected to with-
ering criticism, principally by those who advance a more 'bottom-up'
perspective on the civil rights movement. There are four main points
of criticism.

First, *while there was an expansion in the Catholic middle class, this
took place before 1961 and therefore before the establishment of the
CSJ or NICRA.* There was 'virtually no change in the social structure
of the male Catholic population' between 1961 and 1971 (Bew *et al.*
1995, p. 151).

Second, *there is little evidence to link the expansion in higher education to activism in the civil rights movement.* Morgan argues that it
was only in the mid-1960s, after the civil rights movement began
to emerge, that the student population in Northern Ireland as a
whole began to expand and many Catholic and working-class students started to go through university. From the available evidence,
there was a gradual increase in Catholic university education in the
1950s and 1960s but the most dramatic increases came in the 1970s
(Morgan 1987, p. 108; McKeown 1997). Against this it could be
argued that it is the absolute increase in the number of Catholics in
higher education that is relevant here, but it would have to be shown
how this affected the civil rights movement.

Third, *the impetus for the civil rights campaign and movement
was a result of pressure from below and the locality, rather than any
central organization (such as NICRA) or the Catholic middle class.*
This propelled the CSJ, NICRA and Catholic middle-class activists
into action. The HCL and CSJ were formed after direct action by
Dungannon housewives. Austin Currie's support for direct action
followed from squatting by Catholics in his area, and it was he who
proposed the first civil rights march from Coalisland to Dungannon.
While NICRA was divided on the issue, an important factor in
winning over NICRA was the support of the republican movement and the locally-based CSJ. The impetus for the 5 October
march in Derry came from the DHAC, composed of republicans and

left-wing members of the NILP, who had already launched a number of direct actions to draw attention to bad conditions and discrimination in housing. The moderate organizations of the civil rights campaign, including NICRA, the CSJ, the DCAC and others, attempted to manage and restrain rather than to lead developments in the civil rights movement, and their attempts to lead, steward and control marches appeared to have a diminishing effect. Even the republicans struggled to control nationalist youths from rioting. The 'new Catholic middle-class thesis' 'fails to show why such a narrow impulse should have generated such broad appeal and impact'; 'it hardly shows why the movement was to acquire an irreversible momentum among the Catholic population at large' (Bew *et al.* 1995, p. 149). As one activist put it, 'I am not sure how many of our speakers mesmerised the masses. Certainly the masses mesmerised the speakers' (Eamonn McCann quoted in O'Clery 1986, p. 140).

Fourth, *the role of the Catholic middle class in the civil rights campaign was limited; it is questionable as to whether NICRA could be described as a 'middle-class' organization and whether any other civil rights body apart from the CSJ could be considered 'middle-class'.* Multinational investment did not disrupt traditional employment patterns, and few Catholics were employed in the newer financial and managerial sectors of the economy. Those from the middle class involved in the civil rights movement were largely not members of a 'new' middle class but members of the old, traditional middle class which serviced its own community. Teachers continued to dominate the Catholic middle class and political activism (Morgan 1987, pp. 62, 109). The initiative for the founding of NICRA came from the republican movement and the 13-person steering committee was drawn mainly from traditional organizations which showed little evidence of the impact of a new Catholic middle class (Purdie 1990, p. 133).

Finally, *the 'new Catholic middle class' thesis ignores the communal context into which the civil rights campaign marched.* It loses sight of why unionists were so sceptical of its non-sectarianism and had real grounds for suspecting it of anti-partitionism.

Growth of State Explanation (Bottom-Up)

The 'growth of the state' approach sees the rise of 'ethnic' politics since the Second World War as being related to the expansion of the state, and political and economic competition for state resources.

The segregated, communal division of labour is broken down by competition for state resources – public housing, public employment, public investment – which brings the communal groups into contact, competition and therefore conflict (this contrasts with modernization theory).

Since partition, a Catholic 'quasi-state within a state' has existed which, together with its own social infrastructure (church, sporting activities, Ancient Order of Hibernians, newspapers, businesses), provided an extensive network of communally-based services (education, welfare, social and health services) to the Catholic community. The 'quasi-state', dominated by the Catholic Church and staffed by the Catholic middle class, was involved in extensive informal negotiation between the Church and the state (Morgan 1987). The welfare reforms of the Labour government, largely adopted by Stormont, dramatically increased the state resources available for distribution, and Catholics looked increasingly beyond the Catholic quasi-state to the Northern Ireland state, where much higher levels of welfare provision and opportunities for employment might be achieved. Morgan and Taylor point out that nearly all the civil rights issues concerned aspects of state expansion that were dispensed largely through local government, which became increasingly a site of conflict (Morgan and Taylor 1988). After 1945 there was a massive increase in the provision of public housing, which led to growing complaints about how that housing was allocated. Between 1961 and 1971, the proportion of public rented housing increased from 21 per cent to 35 per cent (Whyte 1983, p. 18).

The thrust of the civil rights campaign and movement was from below, drawing its strength from the growing conflict over discrimination, access to state resources and the impoverishment of the Catholic working class (Morgan 1987; Bew *et al*. 1995). Between 1911 and 1961 the position of the Catholic working class deteriorated, providing the conditions of alienation out of which the civil rights movement could quickly mobilize significant support. The civil rights movement was 'loosely organised, often spontaneous', 'an immense wave of anger' that was 'suddenly released', bypassing the middle class elite (Morgan and Taylor 1988). The civil rights movement, having exhausted constitutional methods for the redress of its grievances, finally took to the streets. This tactic 'utilised the tensions produced by the threat that violence might rise from their activities, either because they had lost control of some of their supporters or because they had provoked their opponents' (Purdie 1990, p. 3). Some leading members of the civil rights movement may have been sincere in their view of the civil rights march as 'non-sectarian' but this was a 'perception which was not widely shared' (Purdie 1990, pp. 244, 186). The march upset the 'tacit understanding between the two communities about territorial divisions' and provoked a disproportionate and brutal response from the police. The advocates of direct action had been warned of the danger that taking politics into the streets would provoke communal clashes, but they may have felt that this was the only way that civil rights demands would be met. This sparked off a sectarian response that spiralled beyond the control, or probably even the intentions, of the civil rights leaders (Purdie 1990, pp. 247–8). The spontaneous mobilization of large sections of the Catholic community after the 5 October 1968 march and the difficulty that the leaders of the civil rights movement had in controlling this explosion is indicative of the discontent of the Catholic community and the 'bottom-up' thrust of the movement. The reappearance after 1969 of the republican movement 'amplified the effect of Catholic political mobilisation while simultaneously reducing the ability of its formal leadership to "deliver" support for any particular political compromise it was offered' (Bew *et al.* 1995, p. 156).

Growing conflict over state resources and the impoverishment of the Catholic working class help to explain why the civil rights movement erupted in the 1960s, but there were possibly three further triggers. First, the Labour Party raised the spectre of intervention in Northern Ireland affairs without any real desire to become involved. Catholic expectations, and unionist fears, had been heightened by the election of a Labour government in 1964 and this was a strong incentive for civil rights mobilization (for example, the CSJ and the CDU). Second, Catholics were disgruntled with the ineptitude of the Nationalist Party and were finding that direct action was a more effective means of redressing grievances. Third, heightened unionist insecurity and division meant that O'Neill was neither able to persuade unionism of the necessity for reform nor to deliver sufficient concessions to the civil rights campaign. Given the involvement of both nationalists and republicans in the civil rights movement, it was not surprising that unionists saw (inaccurately) the civil rights movement *solely* as an attempt to force Northern Ireland out of the Union. As O'Neill told his cabinet in October 1968, 'Of course, there are anti-Partition agitators prominently at work but can any of us truthfully say in the confines of this room, that the minority has no grievance calling for remedy?' (*Irish Times*, 1–2 January 1999).

Conclusion

Different accounts of the civil rights movement are used to promote different political agendas in the propaganda war for British, Irish and international opinion. The Labour government tried to avoid blame by claiming that it had not been warned about civil rights and the impending crisis. Nationalists argued that the civil rights movement was inspired solely by civil rights in order to win external sympathy for intervention. Republicans claim that their political violence after 1969 was reactive, the result of the violence and repression that met the peaceful civil rights campaign. Unionists and loyalists claimed that the civil rights movement was a republican/communist conspiracy designed to bring about a united Ireland. There is a degree of 'truth' in all these explanations, which is what makes them such effective 'myths' in the propaganda war.

The great problem is trying to discern the intentions of the various parties and organizations in the conflict. Certainly, the civil rights movement's claims were largely just (if exaggerated for impact) and deserved to be met regardless of whether they were raised tactically or not. Undoubtedly, some nationalists, and probably more republicans, believed that the end of partition could be brought nearer by advancing civil rights demands that were more effective in winning external support and intervention than traditional anti-partitionist campaigns had been. But there is no evidence that the subsequent violence and 'armed struggle' by the IRA was planned in advance. After October 1968 the republican movement may have increasingly felt, encouraged by the actions of the Irish government and the mobilization of the Catholic masses, that its opportunity to end the partition of Ireland had finally arrived. It had every incentive to provoke further conflict with the state.

The Unionist government's refusal to meet peaceful demands for reform was both unjust and counter-productive, allowing the republicans to plant the question of partition firmly on the political agenda. O'Neill, in spite of his personal commitment to reform and the backing of the British government and important elements of the media (see the Conclusion to this book), faced considerable opposition within his cabinet, on the backbenches and in his wider party towards a modernizing reform programme. It has to be doubted whether even a more skilful leader or unionist government might have been able to deliver reform in the face of such structural constraints. Unionists were completely outmanoeuvred and unprepared for the civil rights explosion. They were beaten hands down in the subsequent propaganda war. By January 1969, O'Neill was telling his cabinet that 'As things stand it [is] all too widely accepted throughout the UK that a sectarian government, directing a partisan force, is confronting a movement of idealists' (*Irish Times*, 3 January 2000). In Britain, public and political (both Labour and Conservative) opinion was sympathetic to the civil rights movement and hostile to the 'un-British' sectarian practices of the 'backward' Stormont administration.

The history of Britain and Ireland since partition presented here casts doubt on the credibility of modernization theory. The principal patterns of trade have been much more East to West than they are North to South. The dependence of the Republic of Ireland on Britain was such that, in 1952, a firm of American economists concluded that this economic dependence was incompatible with the status of political sovereignty. The South's economic dependence on Britain did not prevent the country from asserting and extending its political independence from Britain through neutrality during the Second World War and the declaration of the Republic afterwards. Neither does there seem to be any strong evidence that the process of modernization has made unionists more sympathetic to a united Ireland or northern nationalists any more sympathetic to remaining in the Union. While the Republic has become less economically dependent on Britain, Northern Ireland's dependence on the British subvention has grown. The South continues to be more dependent economically on the UK than the North has ever been on the South. What emerges from this review of the post-partition period is the importance of politics over economics. The economic fortunes of Ireland, both North and South, have ebbed and flowed, but the strength of the adherence of Southern nationalists to their independence and Ulster unionists to the Union has been solid. Nevertheless, in recent years, modernization theory has been boosted by some interpretations of globalization which share similar assumptions and predict similar outcomes.

Modernization theory is 'structure'-orientated and leaves little scope for 'agency'. It is *objective* historical forces such as economic integration that make Irish (or British Isles) unity inevitable. Agents (for example, politicians, governments) can only delay the inevitable working out of these forces. This neglects the impact of modernization theory itself in shaping the perceptions and therefore actions of politicians, governments and people. Since the 1960s the assumptions of modernization theory, while highly questionable, have continued to pervade the thinking of politicians in both Britain and Ireland. Such assumptions can be perceived in the Sunningdale Agreement 1973, the Anglo-Irish Agreement 1985, the Downing Street Declaration 1993, the Joint Framework Documents 1995, the Good Friday Agreement 1998, and the St Andrews Agreement 2006. Modernization theory continues to inform the assumptions of important political actors. Irish nationalists continue to interpret modernization as leading to a united Ireland, and by some unionists as drawing the Republic closer to the Union (Delaney 2001, pp. 335–7; Millar 2004, pp. 84–5). It has been a powerful influence on the thinking of the British Labour Party towards Northern Ireland throughout the recent conflict and has had some impact on the Conservative Party too (Dixon 1993). Modernization theory was influential on the thinking of the British Labour prime minister, Tony Blair (1997–2007), who, on the devolution of power in May 2007, described the Northern Ireland conflict as an 'irrational' one in the 'modern world'.

Modernization theory is useful to political actors because it can be effective in the 'propaganda war'. While moderate unionists such as O'Neill attempted to turn it to his advantage by arguing that it would lead to the unity of the British Isles, nationalists had more success in persuading British politicians that the inevitable result of modernization was Irish unity, and that unionist resistance flew in the face of history. The danger is that policy-makers make poor decisions based on an unrealistic appraisal of the political situation because they are informed by 'modernizing' assumptions that have little basis in 'reality'. Arguably, this was the case when policy-makers failed to fully anticipate the adverse reaction of unionists to the Sunningdale Agreement 1973, the Anglo-Irish Agreement 1985, the Framework Documents 1995 and the Good Friday Agreement 1998. A realistic appraisal of the political environment is important if policy-makers are to develop policies that will maximize the chances of political accommodation.

4

The Crisis of British Policy over Northern Ireland, 1968–73

British governments had tried to minimize their involvement in the Northern Ireland conflict. As they were drawn into deeper involvement they drew on the assumptions shaped by the experience of British and colonial politics. At first the British attempted to resolve the conflict by reforming Northern Ireland and bringing it up to 'British standards' of democracy in an attempt to undermine the material basis for communal division and replace nationalist/unionist divisions with 'normal' left/right politics based on economic interests. When violence did not subside, the conflict came to be seen increasingly in 'colonial' terms, and the use of repression was justified to subdue 'sinister forces'. The increasingly repressive nature of the unionist government's security policy in Northern Ireland by alienating nationalists made the task of finding a political accommodation between nationalism and unionism more difficult. The key questions facing the British government were: how could it avoid direct rule without supporting a unionist government that was polarizing opinion in Northern Ireland? Could the tension between the army's counter-insurgency strategy, which demanded political determination to defeat the IRA, be reconciled with the government's political strategy, which involved negotiations with nationalists and republicans in order to draw them into a 'peace process'? Would the British be able to conciliate nationalists without provoking a backlash from loyalists fearing that the Union was being sold out? This period saw the height of 'the Troubles' and exposes the limits on the British government's power to impose its will on the conflict.

British Nationalism and Irish Unity

The violent events of 5 October 1968 were an affront to British national pride, and shocked public opinion, which had been led to believe that its political system was a model for the rest of the world. This judgement appeared to have been vindicated by the absence of aggressive confrontations between 'violent students' and 'sadistic police', which had shaken every other major Western country during 1968. The media had not prepared the British public for the sudden confrontation with the 'political slum' in its own backyard. Press reaction was 'virtually unanimous' in its support for the Catholics' demands for civil rights, since these 'were seen to accord with what were considered British standards' (Kirkaldy 1984, p. 175).

British nationalism became the hallmark of the response of the British political parties to the conflict. It underpinned the bipartisan (or two-party) approach of the parties to the crisis, and informed the nature of its attempts to resolve the conflict through reform of the British model. As Harold Wilson pointed out, this was not just 'on our doorstep ... it is in our house' (Wilson 1974, p. 871). British politicians tended to see the conflict in Northern Ireland as a 'backward', 'religious' 'throwback' to the seventeenth century. By contrast, the 'British model' of liberal democracy had international respect for producing consensus and stability. The civil rights movement's demand for 'British rights for British citizens' appealed to patriotic sentiment, and it was hoped that these civil rights demands could be satisfied while avoiding the re-opening of the 'Irish Question'. The key to resolving sectarian divisions was therefore modernization, bringing Northern Ireland up to date and into line with the British model, which was at the forefront of the 'modern' world. In short, Northern Ireland had to be made 'more British'; once Northern Ireland, its people and institutions, were 'more like us' their outdated conflict would be consigned to history. By undermining the economic basis of sectarianism, the anachronistic bonds of religion would be severed and the unity of Protestant and Catholic workers forged around 'real' modern economic and social issues. The 'British model' was the standard for most of the reforms introduced into Northern Ireland, including the creation of 'normal', two-party, 'class' politics; a British 'bobby on the beat' police force; an ombudsman; 'one man, one vote'; and a revision of the Special Powers Act of 1971.

Northern Ireland appeared to be increasingly 'un-British' as the reform strategy failed and violence and sectarianism persisted.

A British nationalism was emerging that regarded England, Wales and Scotland as the 'nation', excluding Northern Ireland. British Labour *and Conservative* politicians increasingly contemplated more radical action, including Irish unity. The Labour Party in particular combined support for reform with a traditional sympathy for Irish unity as a natural, inevitable and just outcome of modernizing forces. Some believed that reform would undermine the material basis of sectarianism and lead to Protestant support for Irish unity. The interests of British and Irish nationalism coincided, the 'British' arguing that Northern Ireland was certainly not part of the British nation, and the Irish claiming it as part of their own nation.

Bipartisanship

There were three principal reasons behind the rapid establishment of a bipartisan approach by the Conservative and Labour parties to Northern Ireland in 1968 (Dixon 1995a).

First, perhaps the fundamental reason for the operation of bipartisanship is that an accord between the British political parties can help to promote a consistent British policy towards Northern Ireland and facilitate a resolution to the conflict, or at least help to contain the situation and stop it 'infecting' British politics. In the context of Northern Ireland, bipartisanship works through the two principal British parties broadly agreeing on the constitutional principles of their approach to the issue. They can then present a united British front to the contending communal groups, thus preventing those groups from exploiting the political differences between the British parties, playing one off against the other and holding out on the agreement. For example, if the British political parties were divided in their approach and became aligned with different factions in Northern Ireland (the most obvious case would be an alignment of Labour with the nationalists and the Conservatives with the unionists), each change of government at Westminster could result in the reversal of the previous government's Irish policy and the imposition of one more favourable to their respective allies in Northern Ireland. If this were to occur, the chances of reaching a permanent and stable solution to the conflict would be diminished. If Westminster maintains a sufficiently broad agreement on its approach, it reduces the likelihood of the contending groups in Ireland refusing to reach a settlement in the hope of the return of a British government more sympathetic to its cause.

The opposition party, whether as part of a bipartisan approach or not, is potentially in a position to wield considerable influence on government policy towards Northern Ireland. Outside a bipartisan relationship, the posture of the opposition can disrupt the government's attempts at accommodation by offering a more favourable settlement to one of the parties. This induces that party to hold out on any settlement with the government of the day in the hope that the next election will return a government more favourably disposed to its demands. If the political parties operate a bipartisan approach, then the government's policy has to be framed broadly enough to take the opposition with it.

In 1968, bipartisanship was used to bolster Terence O'Neill against his 'hardline' rivals. Both the Conservative leader, Edward Heath, and the British prime minister, Harold Wilson, were agreed that, for progress to be made in Northern Ireland, support must be given to those who were pursuing a 'moderate policy' against the 'extremists'. Wilson noted the importance of bipartisanship in presenting a united front to dampen the expectations of 'bigots' or 'zealots' who might have led the fight against O'Neill (House of Commons Debates, vol. 775, col. 582, 12 December 1968). O'Neill sold a five-point reform plan to his own community by pointing to Conservative/Labour unity and arguing that there was no alternative but to accept it (*Newsletter*, 10 December 1968, quoted in Gordon 1989, p. 135). William Whitelaw, formerly Secretary of State for Northern Ireland, recognized the importance of bipartisanship in delivering a political settlement. He wrote: 'We need to know that the Opposition can be relied upon to support us. A bipartisan approach is vital since if any of the parties in Northern Ireland think that they can look to the Opposition to oppose what we are doing and promised different things if they were to come to power, there is little hope that a settlement will stick' (Cabinet Papers (73) 27, 26 February 1973).

A second reason for the establishment of bipartisanship is to insulate the issue from British domestic opinion. The deaths of British soldiers in Palestine sparked off a populist revolt among British public opinion in favour of withdrawal, and the threat of another public revolt hung over politicians as they contemplated subsequent decolonizations. By presenting a united front to the contending parties in Northern Ireland, the British bipartisan approach could minimize inter-party conflict which might stimulate the demand for withdrawal among domestic British public opinion (Dixon 1995a, 2000).

Third, the 'legacy of the Irish Question' had left a scar on the collective memory of British politicians and it was hoped that a cross-party approach would help to contain both the conflict in Northern Ireland and its impact on British politics. In 1914, Britain had faced civil war over the 'Irish Question'. The bipartisan approach was not necessarily to promote any particular constitutional outcome, but there was support for the principle that Northern Ireland could only leave the Union with the consent of the people.

British Influence, Unionist Disaffection

British politicians had avoided direct intervention by leaving reform to O'Neill, and the 'hardline' opposition to his premiership cautioned the Labour cabinet from pushing him 'too hard' to deliver substantive reform. In private meetings with O'Neill, representatives of the Labour government urged further reform in the local government franchise, housing allocations and in the appointment of a Parliamentary Commissioner. There was concern for Britain's international image, which had tarnished the Special Powers Act and 'some aspects of the Londonderry outbreak' (Wilson 1974, p. 845). The outcome of the O'Neill–Wilson meeting was a five-point plan, announced by O'Neill in November 1968. This plan consisted of a points system for public housing allocation; the creation of a Parliamentary Commissioner for Administration; reform of local government; revision of the Special Powers Act; and the abolition of Londonderry Borough Council and its replacement by a non-elected Development Commission (Cunningham 1991, p. 19). This package dealt with most of the demands of the civil rights movement, except 'one man, one vote' in local government elections. In December 1968, O'Neill declared 'Ulster [is] at the crossroads' in a speech that resulted in 150,000 letters or telegrams of support and the return of a further 120,000 newspaper coupons.

Unionist hardliners urged O'Neill to resist British pressure to reform. Wilson exacerbated O'Neill's problems by claiming credit for pressurizing the Northern Ireland government to reform (Callaghan 1973, p. 93). Those unionists who had long suspected British behind-the-scenes interference in Northern Ireland's affairs were now finding evidence to substantiate their concerns. The joint statement released at the end of the Wilson–O'Neill talks repeated the constitutional guarantee contained in the Ireland Act (1949). However, Wilson warned O'Neill's unionist opponents that if the Northern Ireland

prime minister was overthrown he would 'need to consider a fundamental appraisal of our relations with Northern Ireland' (House of
Commons Debates, vol. 772, col. 690, 5 November 1968). This was
a none-too-subtle threat to raise the question of Northern Ireland's
constitutional position within the UK, which contradicted Labour's
reassurances that the constitutional position of Northern Ireland was
secure and that the border was not an issue. Although the British
prepared for the introduction of direct rule, they probably wanted to
avoid this option at all costs (*Independent on Sunday*, 2 January 2000).

These threats of intervention were a bluff (Bloomfield 1994,
p. 108), designed to bolster O'Neill's arguments for reform against
hardliners. Perversely, these kinds of threats from British politicians
seemed to undermine rather than bolster O'Neill's position within
unionism. Instead of pulling the UUP behind O'Neill's 'trust the
British' position, the threats suggested that the British could not
be trusted with the security of the Union. The implications of this
for unionist strategy were that power should therefore be kept, as
far as possible, within Northern Ireland and the hands of unionists.
A tougher line should be taken in dealings with a British government which – against its reassurances – appeared prepared to sell the
Union out.

Indirect Rule

The Labour government attempted to be even-handed in dealing with
the claims of nationalists and unionists in order to avoid becoming
more deeply involved in Northern Ireland. According to Callaghan,
'my short-term aim was to try to restore a sense of self-confidence in
the Ulster Unionist Cabinet . . . and to calm the fears of the Catholic
community without awakening those of Protestants' (Callaghan 1973,
p. 70; Crossman 1977, p. 622). The Secretary to the Northern Ireland
cabinet warned the British against introducing direct rule, arguing
that it might lead to a Protestant backlash, sectarian civil war and
the establishment of a provisional government headed by extremists
(*Irish Times*, 3 January 1999). The Labour government had had its
fingers burnt over Rhodesia, and Northern Ireland threatened to
repeat that scenario.

By encouraging O'Neill to pursue a programme of reform, the
Labour government could use its influence to maintain 'indirect rule'
through Stormont and so avoid becoming involved too directly in
the conflict. However, the extension of civil and economic rights

for Catholics was not necessarily compatible with non-intervention if these reforms resulted in the defeat of O'Neill. If Wilson pushed O'Neill too hard, then 'hardline' unionists might gain the upper hand within the UUP and oust the Northern Ireland prime minister. Such a course of events could then force the Labour government to become more involved in Irish affairs to secure reforms, and perhaps ultimately lead to the suspension of Stormont and the introduction of direct rule from Westminster. There was concern that the introduction of direct rule would be met with considerable resistance from within Northern Ireland, not least from the unionist-dominated police and civil service, therefore resulting in British military rule (*Sunday Times* Insight Team 1972, pp. 103–4). The alienation of unionists as well as republicans might well result in the Army's 'nightmare scenario' of fighting an unsustainable 'war on two fronts'. So, while Wilson was talking about getting tough with Stormont, he did not take measures to follow through with his threats in the event of unionist defiance.

On 3 February 1969, twelve unionist backbenchers called for O'Neill's resignation and in retaliation he called the 'Crossroads' election. The 1969 election underlined the rifts within the unionist bloc: unofficial pro-O'Neill unionists stood against official anti-O'Neill unionists. O'Neill himself was returned with only a 1,414 majority over the Reverend Ian Paisley. The result was also a blow to the modernizing hopes of the British government that had been built up by the media. Following UVF bombing attacks on public buildings and utilities, which were wrongly blamed on the IRA, O'Neill resigned in April 1969, to be succeeded by his cousin, James Chichester-Clark. The Labour government had prepared for the collapse of the Northern Ireland government in the winter of 1968–9. Following serious rioting in Derry and several bombings, British troops were posted in April 1969 to guard electricity, water and other public service installations in remote areas. The cabinet agreed with the British Home Secretary, James Callaghan, that 'the Northern Ireland government was genuinely going ahead with reforms. Our aim must be to influence while getting embroiled as little as possible' (Castle 1984, p. 640; Crossman 1977, pp. 453, 458). By May 1969, he was able to tell the cabinet that four out of the five demands the government had put to O'Neill had been met, and the review of local government franchise had been accepted in principle.

The loyalist marching season during the summer of 1969 provided an opportunity for both Protestants and Catholics to vent their frustrations with political developments in Northern Ireland.

After violence following the marches on 12 July, Wilson and Healey favoured the banning of all further parades in Northern Ireland. Callaghan was advised by the Northern Ireland Home Affairs Minister that the RUC had neither the resources nor the resolution to impose a parade ban, while Chichester-Clark told him he would fall from power if the marches were banned (*Sunday Times* Insight Team 1972, p. 102). The marches went ahead and the subsequent rioting led to the deployment of the British Army on the streets of Northern Ireland.

The Army: In and Out?

The British Army was not deployed on the streets of Northern Ireland on 14 August 1969 to protect Catholics against the largely Protestant RUC and rampaging loyalist mobs. Callaghan had been advised 'from all sides . . . on no account to get sucked into the Irish bog'. Such was the government's desire not to become embroiled in the 'Irish Question' again that Callaghan suggested that giving Northern Ireland independence might be preferable to the introduction of direct rule, but this was dismissed on the grounds that it would lead to civil war (*Irish Times*, 3 January 2000). The Labour government warned the Stormont government that the deployment of troops might result in direct rule, and this was also leaked to the newspapers. This was probably a bluff designed to ensure that the unionist government did not call for the use of troops until all its resources had been exhausted (Callaghan 1973, pp. 15, 42–3). These resources included the deployment of the infamous B Specials and the use of CS gas, an indiscriminate weapon that affected innocent and guilty alike. This was used only days before troops were finally deployed and calmed the rioting. On 11 August, ministers agreed that, as the overriding consideration was to avoid the use of troops, top priority should be given to the strengthening of the RUC and the deployment of the Ulster Special Constabulary (*Irish Times*, 3 January 1999). The Scarman Report later 'concluded that if [J./A.] Peacocke [Inspector-General of the RUC] had correctly appreciated the hopelessness of the police position . . . and not been so sensitive to the political pressures against calling the army, then Londonderry and Belfast might have been spared much of the ensuing tragedy' (Ryder 1997, p. 116). In this way the British government was able to force Stormont to exhaust its resources, regardless of the consequences for inflaming communal tensions, and then avoid responsibility for the resulting deterioration.

Chichester-Clark argued that the Labour government's threat to suspend Stormont was an incentive to rioters to keep up the pressure (letter from Chichester-Clark to Callaghan, 6 August 1969, PREM 13/2843).

The army was to be 'borrowed' by Stormont for a short holding operation, to enable reforms to be introduced to bring Northern Ireland up to 'British standards' of democracy and modernity. There was a precedent for military intervention and swift withdrawal from Northern Ireland. In 1935, following rioting in Belfast, the army was called out for just eleven days in aid of the civil power and then withdrawn once order was restored. In August 1969, the army were welcomed by nationalists and operated in a non-confrontational way, facilitating a quick withdrawal. An indication of the government's desire to limit the involvement of the army was the reduction of troop numbers there in the first days of August 1969, at a time when General Freeland was pleading for reinforcements. The General Officer Commanding (GOC) suspected that the 'honeymoon period' would not last and had 'strong misgivings' about the consequences of becoming involved in an urban guerrilla war (*Irish Times*, 3 January 2000). If Protestants resisted and Stormont collapsed, the Ministry of Defence projected that direct rule would require the deployment of 20–30,000 troops. In practice, according to one minister, Labour's policy was 'to do anything which would avoid direct rule' (*Sunday Times* Insight Team 1972, p. 103). Meanwhile, Callaghan considered drafting in British police officers to relieve the army of the burden of police duties (Cabinet Conclusions (69) 43rd Conclusions, Minute 3 Thursday, 11 September 1969, CAB 128/46).

Reform: Modern British Standards

On 19 August 1969 Callaghan put five recommendations to the cabinet:

1. for the 12,000 B Specials to be disarmed;
2. the transfer of some authority to Westminster;
3. for advisers to be attached to the Northern Ireland government;
4. that a coalition of more elements should be brought into the Stormont government; and
5. for the establishment of a community relations organization and possibly a minister for Northern Ireland (Callaghan 1973, p. 66, *The Times*, 27 August 1969).

Callaghan also considered proportional representation as a means of building cross-sectarian consensus, boosting such moderate forces as the NILP. The cabinet agreed that their negotiators should bargain for as many of Callaghan's recommendations as possible. Barbara Castle underlined the government's dilemma: 'Nobody wants us to have to take over political control, with all the trouble that implies – indefinite embroilment in Northern Ireland. Equally we have minimum demands that must be met' (Castle 1984, p. 700). Denis Healey, the Minister of Defence, was sympathetic to the plight of the Catholics but wanted to avoid the army's nightmare scenario of a war on two fronts. He argued that 'we must keep the Protestants quiet' (Benn 1988, pp. 196, 198).

Following negotiations 'The Downing Street Communiqué' was published on 19 August 1969 setting out 'the principles which should govern their future actions'. The key points were that the 'border is not an issue' and Northern Ireland would remain part of the UK so long as that was the will of the people and the Northern Ireland government. Troops were provided on a temporary basis and the momentum of reform was to be maintained. The GOC Northern Ireland was to assume command of all security operations. After a triumphant trip to Northern Ireland, Callaghan established two inquiries, one under Lord Scarman into the disorders of August 1969 and another under Lord Hunt into the police. The Unionist government declared its intention to establish machinery for investigating citizens' grievances, a Community Relations Board and joint working parties of the officials of Westminster and Stormont, to ensure fair allocation of housing, avoidance of discrimination in public employment and promotion of good community relations. Callaghan was pleased with the result of his negotiations with Stormont: 'the principal achievement, without doubt, was to have secured by agreement a very great extension of Westminster influence without facing the crisis that would have arisen if the Ulster Unionist Government had resigned' (Callaghan 1973, p. 99).

The border, as the Downing Street Declaration made clear, was still officially 'not an issue' but there were signs that it was already creeping on to the political agenda. The causes of 'the Troubles' were widely seen as being principally economic. The Cameron Report on the disturbances between June 1968 and January 1969 concluded that the causes of the trouble were both material (including housing provision and allocation, discrimination in local government appointments) and security-related ('resentment' among Catholics against the B Specials and the Special Powers Act). The assumption was that once these grievances had been dealt with, peace would be established and 'normal British-style class politics' would develop.

James Callaghan, while subscribing to the materialist analysis of the Northern Ireland conflict and keen to bring Northern Ireland up to British standards of democracy, also appeared to hint at the possibility of Irish unity by talking of raising the problem to 'a new plane' (Labour Party 1969, p. 184, Callaghan 1973, p. 107). The Home Secretary complained to the cabinet of the 'world-wide propaganda campaign' directed by the Irish government against the UK and Northern Ireland governments. He argued that if the Irish prime minister

> really wanted a united Ireland, he must conciliate Protestant opinion: but so far his tactics had done nothing but alarm it. Nevertheless, if there were to be any prospect of a final solution, relations between the North and South of Ireland and between the South and the United Kingdom must be lifted to a different plane. As things stood at present this was likely to take a long time. (CC (69) 43rd Conclusions, Minute 3 Thursday, 11 September, 1969, CAB 128/46)

When Callaghan published his reflections on Northern Ireland, in *A House Divided* (1973), the former Home Secretary publicly came out in favour of eventual Irish unity. The Irish minister, Charles Haughey, met the UK ambassador to Dublin and offered him Irish entry into the Commonwealth, and British or NATO access to Irish bases in return for Irish unity. The ambassador told Haughey that there would be a Protestant backlash in the North caused by British 'open dickering with the South' over the border. Haughey more or less accepted this (*Irish Times*, 7 January 2000).

The logical extension of Labour's strategy to extend the 'British model of democracy to Northern Ireland was to introduce a British class-based, two-party system. While the Labour Party undertook to revitalize the NILP as a non-sectarian party of labour, the Conservatives attempted to transform the UUP into a non-sectarian, conservative party (Hogg 1975, p. 242; Dixon 1993). An alternative strategy was to unite the predominantly Catholic opposition forces with the NILP to at least offer Catholics some prospect of a share in governmental power. The success with which the NILP and the wider labour movement had managed to combine Catholics and Protestants within its organizations impressed both Conservative and

Labour observers. The Northern Irish labour movement appeared a familiar haven of 'British normality' in a communal political culture which British politicians found disorienting. A proposal to merge the NILP with the British Labour Party collapsed under pressure from a number of civil rights activists, who later formed the Social Democratic and Labour Party (SDLP). One report claimed that the government did not want to alienate the civil rights leaders, on whom they depended 'not to let the civil rights movement get out of hand' (*Private Eye*, 13 February 1970).

Ulsterization

The British Army had been introduced on to the streets of Northern Ireland because of the breakdown of the local police force. A priority for the British, therefore, was the restoration of order and the strengthening of the local security forces so that the troops could be withdrawn. This would lower the chances of a conflict between either the forces of 'British imperialism and Irish nationalism' or even disaffected loyalists who resented British intervention. The police had become discredited within the nationalist community so the British favoured steps to see that the RUC and B Specials were reformed in such a way as to make them acceptable to nationalists. Unionists, however, tended to see the police not only as a force for law and order but also as a powerful bulwark against untrustworthy British politicians who might manipulate unionists into a united Ireland.

The strategy of 'Ulsterization' – the replacement of British Army personnel by locally-recruited forces – is conventionally seen to have begun in the mid-1970s. Yet Ulsterization seems to have been the strategy of the British from the moment troops were deployed on the streets in August 1969. The failure of the army to implement this policy until the mid-1970s was caused by the weakness of the local security forces and the ferocity of the IRA campaign. The mid-1970s did not represent a strategic switch but rather the opportunity to realize the goal of police primacy that had been pursued since 1969 (Rees 1985, p. 51; Urban 1992, p. 15).

The Hunt Report, published on 10 October 1969 proposed an unarmed, civil police force 'which will be in principle and in normal practice an unarmed force'. The paramilitary B Specials were to be disbanded and replaced by an RUC reserve and a locally recruited part-time military force of 4,000 (this became the Ulster Defence

Regiment, or UDR, with a strength much less than the 8,481 of the Ulster Special Constabulary, USC) under the control of the British Army. There was also to be a large increase in recruitment to the RUC since, according to the Hunt Report, it was 'seriously below effective strength'. In particular, 'vigorous efforts' were to be made to recruit Catholics, who made up only 11 per cent of the RUC (Hunt Report 1969, pp. 29–30, 43). The RUC was to be brought nearer to the British model through closer links with British forces, and the adoption of the British rank and promotion structure. It was even proposed that the RUC's uniform be changed to blue. An English inspector-general, Arthur Young, who had much experience of colonial policing, was appointed head of the RUC. As Callaghan wrote: 'The underlying theme of the Report was that policing in Northern Ireland should become more akin to policing in the UK' (Callaghan 1973, p. 113).

On 10 October 1969, Callaghan endorsed the Hunt Report. There followed two nights of rioting by loyalists on the Shankill Road, during which Constable Victor Arbuckle became the first policeman to be killed during 'the Troubles'. Three people were killed during the rioting and sixty-six injured, including fourteen soldiers and three policemen with shotgun wounds. Even before the Hunt Report there had been considerable conflict between the army and loyalists, resentful at British interference in Northern Ireland. Craig criticized Chichester-Clark for allowing the army to take over control of security. Paisley threatened a general strike if Protestant demands were not met. He presented Chichester-Clark with a petition signed by nearly 100,000 expressing opposition to the disarmament of the B Specials. Shots were fired at the army on the Shankhill, and fifty-four RUC and forty-eight soldiers were hurt in the rioting. Callaghan reacted to the continuing rioting, warning that the attainment of civil rights coupled with the proper structure of the police force 'has got to put an end to this nonsense in the streets. It has got to end' (*The Times*, 10 October 1969). Callaghan told Parliament that Protestant violence was 'based on a false appreciation of the situation and on rumours which have no relevance at all and no truth'. He completely failed to appreciate the importance of the police force to the unionist community in Northern Ireland and was puzzled by the sensitivity of the unionist cabinet to the Hunt Report (House of Commons Debates, vol. 788, col. 56, 13 October 1969; Callaghan 1973, pp. 110–11).

There were some misgivings within the cabinet about establishing the UDR. By 1973, a British military intelligence report, 'Subversion in the UDR', suggested that 5–15 per cent of UDR soldiers were or had been involved with 'Protestant extremist organizations'. The UDR was the 'best single source of weapons' for these groups, and some of the weapons had been used in the murders of Catholics. The British army's judgement on the UDR was that the first loyalties of many of its members were to 'Ulster' rather than the British government, and that in a conflict of loyalties the government would come off second best ('Subversion in the UDR' http://cain. ulst.ac.uk/publicrecords/1973/subversion_in_the_udr.pdf). To some extent the British cabinet had anticipated this problem but, as Barbara Castle recalled on the establishment of the UDR, '[we] were persuaded by the argument that this was the only way to prevent the 'B' Specials from going underground' (Castle 1984, p. 716; Fitzgerald 1991, p. 279). This has been a perennial security argument in Northern Ireland. The theory is that it is better to channel the frustrations of militant Protestants and their desire to defend the Union by bringing them into the official state security organizations, where a degree of control and discipline can be exerted, than to allow these disaffected people to express their frustration through non-state, paramilitary organizations, where the state has less control. By replacing the B Specials with the UDR, the members of this notorious force might be watered down with new (particularly Catholic) blood, but also disciplined through the control of the British Army and its officers. The rapid establishment of the UDR, which became operational on 1 April 1970 (with 18 per cent Catholic membership), again reflected the urgency with which the Labour government wanted to withdraw British troops. By February 1970, three out of the eight additional army units deployed in Northern Ireland had returned to Britain (Cunningham 1991, p. 32). Allowing UDA members to join the UDR also helped the army with its policy of Ulsterization. There were suspicions in British political and military circles that the loyalties of the locally-recruited security forces were to Ulster unionism rather than the British state, and that there were limits to which they could be pushed in order to police their own community (Donoughue 1987, p. 129; Urban 1992, pp. 51–2).

The False Dawn and 'Sinister Forces'

Towards the end of 1969, Northern Ireland had quietened down and the Labour government dared to hope that the programme of reform was beginning to take effect and would be sufficient to pacify Catholic grievances (Dixon 1993, pp. 214–16). By October

1969, John Hume's Independent Organization was claiming that when the proposed reforms were fully implemented, 'the civil rights movement in this country can be considered to have drawn to a hitherto unbelievably successful conclusion' (quoted in Ó Dochartaigh 1997, p. 141). Prime Minister O'Neill recalled in his memoirs, 'Any liberal-minded person must admit that the Civil Rights movements brought about reforms which would otherwise have taken years to wring from a reluctant Government' (O'Neill 1972, p. 111). Significantly, Callaghan's meeting with Chichester-Clark in January 1970 was concerned mainly with economic matters. The result of Labour's concern to tackle the economic basis of the violence was the 'Northern Ireland Development Programme 1970–75', which 'drew a direct link between improving employment prospects and housing, and reducing violence' (Cunningham 1991, p. 32).

Violence in Northern Ireland persisted in spite of the implementation of the reform programme. British definitions of the conflict began to shift; less and less was the conflict seen in optimistic 'liberal' terms of rational social, economic and security problems that were amenable to British reform. A more 'conservative' approach became apparent, which increasingly identified 'sinister' and 'irrational forces' to explain the continuing conflict and justify a more hardline security stance. The 'conservative' explanation had the added benefit for British political and military elites of placing blame for the continuing violence on the Northern Irish rather than on any British failing.

From its initial non-confrontational stance, the army began to patrol nationalist areas to enforce law and order. In Derry, 'relations between the army and sections of the Catholic community began to break down within weeks of the army's arrival' (Ó Dochartaigh 1997, p. 154). The 'heavy-handedness' of the army's operation diminished nationalist toleration for their presence and by January 1970 there were already clashes with the British army 'which it appears some Republicans helped to provoke' (Ó Dochartaigh 1997, p. 167, ch. 4). It seems reasonable to suggest that repressive army tactics helped to alienate nationalists, but at the same time some republicans were attempting to provoke just such a reaction. At the beginning of 1970, republicans were already preparing for military action, some for defence but others for offensive action to bring about a united Ireland (Ó Dochartaigh 1997, p. 195). On 1 April 1970, the first conflict between British troops and Irish Catholic civilians for two generations broke out at the Ballymurphy housing estate on the western edge of Belfast. The troops were now being attacked by the people it was thought they were there to defend. The victory of Ian Paisley and a fellow Protestant unionist at two Stormont by-elections in April 1970 indicated the growing polarization of Northern Irish politics and the deepening of the crisis. General Officer Commanding Ian Freeland issued a warning that anyone carrying or throwing petrol bombs was liable to be shot dead after a warning. He also spoke of 'sinister people' who were behind the youth gangs attacking the troops (*The Times*, 4 April 1970). Roy Hattersley, Deputy Minister of Defence, also blamed the violence on 'sinister elements' stirring up the Catholic masses. Conservative politicians were also impatient with the failure of the reform programme to end the violence. A Conservative minister later wrote, 'Seldom can a protest movement anywhere have so rapidly achieved so many of its initial objectives' (Windlesham 1975, p. 92). Enoch Powell argued that grievances had been exaggerated out of all proportion to serve the purposes of anarchy and Irish unity. Quintin Hogg believed the riots reflected 'sinister influences', people 'who seem to hate humanity as such'. This was a rude awakening for the Labour government, particularly with a General Election approaching. The Ballymurphy Riots undermined the optimistic belief that the reform programme introduced by the Labour government had met Catholic grievances and set the region on the road to 'normality'. Callaghan's initial optimism turned towards despair; he was exasperated with Catholics 'stringing the British government along, making fresh demands as soon as old ones were met', and he felt that only the people of Northern Ireland, not Britain, could solve the problems of Northern Ireland (*Sunday Times* Insight Team 1972, p. 222).

Security Policy and British Counter-Insurgency Strategy

In dealing with the Northern Ireland conflict, the army was able to draw on its colonial experience of counter-insurgency (Dixon 1997b). There were four principal interrelated requirements of British counter-insurgency strategy during this period:

- *First, and most important, the primary factor for victory is the determination of the political elite to defeat the insurgents.* The military accepted that neither side could win militarily, and that the army could only 'hold the ring' until a political solution was found (Heath 1998, p. 423; see also Hamill 1985; Dixon 1997c). However, if the insurgents won the battle for the 'hearts and minds' of the local population, then all was lost. An unswerving determination by the government to defeat the insurgents would help to win over the 'neutral mass' of the population to the government's side. This would end the prospect of success on which the insurgents depended to mobilize popular support. Bipartisanship demonstrated the determination of the British political parties to defeat insurgents and, by limiting party conflict, reduced divisions among public opinion. The media would play a complementary role in this propaganda war by maintaining the support of domestic public opinion and demonstrating British determination to defeat the insurgents. This would counter republican expectations of the inevitability of their victory, captured in the slogan *Tiocfaidh ar la!* (Our day will come!).

- *The second requirement of British counter-insurgency strategy emphasized the importance of winning 'the battle for hearts and minds' of the affected population.* The government, by showing its political determination to win, is more likely to win the 'battle for hearts and minds' by discouraging the public from supporting the insurgents. If, on the other hand, the local population think the government will lose they may well throw in their lot with their future masters, the insurgents. Success for the government in the battle for 'hearts and minds' not only robs the insurgents of the popular support that sustains their campaign, but also means that intelligence – a vital component of counter-insurgency operations – is more likely to be passed on by the public. 'Hearts and minds' were to be won by good government and nation-building, 'psychological operations' to persuade the local population, and 'minimum force' to avoid alienating the local population.

- *The third requirement of British counter-insurgency theory stressed the importance of police primacy and civil–military co-operation for providing the intelligence to track down insurgents.* British counter-insurgency doctrine tended to favour the primacy of the police in fighting insurgents and a more restricted role for the army, for several reasons. The police were more effective intelligence gatherers; more likely to be sensitive to local opinion, and therefore more effective at winning 'hearts and minds'; they helped to create an image of normality; they could be cheaper than the army; and they were better-trained for a 'peacekeeping' role. Police primacy also reduced the chances of British soldiers being killed and lead to domestic pressure for the troops to be brought home (Dixon 2000).

- *Fourth, the centralized co-ordination of effort on all fronts – political, economic, military, psychological – was required to bring the full force of the state to bear against insurgents.*

What was remarkable about the British counter-insurgency strategy was its dependence on political rather than military action. This dependence and the need to co-operate so closely with the civil authority was not something that came naturally to the army. The stress on the role of politicians in British counter-insurgency doctrine also provided a convenient excuse for military failure. The army's failure to defeat insurgents could be blamed on the lack of resolve of the politicians or the 'restrictive' framework of law that prevented it from doing its job properly. The higher profile of 'the Troubles' in domestic British politics, compared with counter-insurgency campaigns in the far-flung Empire, resulted in greater political involvement in security operations. This exacerbated tensions in civil–military relations.

Northern Ireland: 'Minimum Force' and Escalation

The replacement of a Labour government by a Conservative one (seen as traditionally pro-unionist) in June 1970 prepared the way for a more repressive security policy in Northern Ireland. The Falls Road Curfew of 3–5 July 1970, following close to the Conservatives' June election victory, confirmed in the minds of some the new trajectory of British policy. The Curfew ranks alongside the introduction of internment as one of the most disastrous army operations. Significant supplies of arms were found, but five civilians were killed and sixty injured. Sixteen hundred canisters of CS gas were fired into the Lower Falls area. The army later admitted that fifty-eight allegations of looting and other misconduct 'were of such a nature as to suggest that an offence might have been committed, but there was no evidence on which action could be taken' (*The Times*, 18 September 1970). As a result of the Curfew, many Catholics became alienated from the army, and IRA recruitment accelerated. According to the IRA's 'Green Book', 'In September of 1969 the existing conditions dictated that Brits were not to be shot, but after the Falls curfew all Brits were to the people acceptable targets. The existing conditions had been changed' (quoted in O'Brien 1993, p. 292). By early 1971, both the Official and the Provisional IRA were involved in offensive operations against the British Army (Smith 1995, p. 95), and in February 1971 the first British soldier was killed. In May 1971, off-duty soldiers

could visit friends in nationalist parts of Derry, but after the introduction of internment in August 1971 this was no longer possible (Ó
Dochartaigh 1997, p. 16).

The Northern Ireland prime minister, Chichester-Clark, called on
British prime minister Heath to introduce more repressive security
measures to reassure unionists. When this was refused, he resigned in
March 1971 and was replaced by Brian Faulkner, who was perceived
to be more 'hardline' on security issues and favoured 'a strategic shift
to a short-run policy of aggression' (Bew *et al.* 1995, p. 167). The
British government was caught between its anxiety to avoid direct
rule, thereby increasing its entanglement in the conflict, and opposition to Stormont's requests for a harsher security policy, which might
escalate the conflict and precipitate direct rule in any case.

John Hume, member of the SDLP, announced that the army's
'impartial role has now clearly ended' after the British Army killed
two Catholics in Derry. The government's failure to hold an inquiry
into the deaths resulted in the SDLP's withdrawal from Stormont.
The introduction of internment in August 1971 ended what remaining hopes there were that the nationalists would co-operate with the
Stormont regime. The British were reluctant to reject Faulkner's
request for internment, fearing this would precipitate direct rule.
Internment was a response to the growing intensification of the IRA's
offensive and, while it was welcomed widely in Britain at the time,
it was a serious blunder. Internment was directed solely at the
nationalist community: to have picked up Protestants might have
compounded Faulkner's political problems. Not only did it prevent
any political accommodation with nationalists in Stormont but it also
resulted in a massive escalation of violence. In the two years prior to
internment, sixty-six people were killed, including eleven soldiers. In
the first seventeen months after internment, 610 were killed, including 146 soldiers. The use of 'interrogation in depth' techniques by the
army against some internees led to substantiated allegations of torture. The escalation of violence following internment led to increased
pressure on Faulkner from 'hardliners' to crack down even harder on
terrorism.

On 'Bloody Sunday', in January 1972, thirteen innocent Catholic
civilians were killed by the British Army, further escalating the
conflict. Lord Widgery led an inquiry into Bloody Sunday which
concluded that there would have no deaths if the illegal march had
not gone ahead, thus making a clash inevitable. Although in one
instance the paratroopers 'firing bordered on the reckless', there was

found to be 'no general breakdown in discipline'. The details of the Widgery Report are more damning than the conclusions that largely exonerated the army. Subsequently, it has been found that none of the civilians killed were armed, and that the Widgery Inquiry was deeply flawed. The Saville Inquiry was established in 1998, as part of the peace process, to investigate Bloody Sunday and was due to report in 2006, but at the time of writing the findings had still not been published. The debate over Bloody Sunday revolves around responsibility: was it the individual soldiers who were responsible for the deaths, officers further up the army's chain of command, or the Conservative government? (On Bloody Sunday, see Pringle and Jacobson 2002; Norton-Taylor 2005.) In March 1972, Heath demanded the transfer of security powers from Stormont to Westminster. Faulkner resigned and, finally, the British government was forced to take direct responsibility for Northern Ireland.

Army practice in Northern Ireland appears neither to have employed 'minimum force' nor to have been designed to win 'hearts and minds', in spite of the prescriptions of counter-insurgency. The use of CS gas, the Falls Road Curfew and internment constituted communal punishment. Following internment, in August 1971, the army's operations were designed primarily to facilitate the collection of intelligence on IRA activity in the main centres of Catholic population and thus to enable IRA activists to be arrested and put behind bars. The army set out to compile intelligence dossiers on all the inhabitants of a suspect area so that the IRA could be rooted out. These were compiled by regular house searches, person stop-and-searches, arrests and 'the interrogation in depth' (torture) of selected suspects. Paddy Hillyard has argued: 'It has not been simply a matter of the widespread curtailment of basic rights through the widespread abuse of the powers of stop, arrest and search, but the constant and systematic harassment of thousands of people within clearly defined areas.' The number of house searches escalated as shown below:

1970	3,107
1971	17,262
1973	74,556
1974	74,914
1975	30,002

Hillyard estimated that the impact of such tactics on the Catholic community resulted in one in four Catholic men between the ages of 16 and 44 being arrested at least once between 1972 and 1977. On average, every Catholic household in Northern Ireland had been searched twice, but since many homes would not be under suspicion, some houses in certain districts would have been searched 'perhaps as many as ten or more times' (Hillyard 1988, pp. 169, 197). Robin Evelegh, Commanding Officer of the 3rd Battalion Royal Green Jackets in Belfast, complained that the army's 'widespread search, arrest and screening operations' 'strongly alienated' the non-terrorist population: 'Nothing could have been more calculated to drive the non-committed part of the population into the arms of the terrorists from a sense of personal outrage and humiliation' (Evelegh 1978, p. 29). The employment of such tactics, by alienating the local population, was likely to lead to a more restricted flow of vital intelligence to the security forces.

Political Will? The Loyalist Backlash and Army Discontent

British counter-insurgency strategy required the political elite to be determined and uncompromising in their resolve to defeat insurgency. Following internment, however, bipartisanship appeared to be weakening, and leading politicians in both the Conservative government and the Labour opposition were becoming more sympathetic to the goal of Irish unity (Patterson 1986; Dixon 1993; Bew *et al.* 1995, pp. 168–9). In his Guildhall Speech to the City of London, Heath declared that the nationalists' aspiration for Irish unity by democratic and constitutional means was legitimate, and that if a majority in Northern Ireland wanted Irish unity 'I do not believe any British government would stand in the way.' There were also reports of an emerging bipartisan consensus in favour of Irish unity (*Guardian*, 29 November 1971; *The Economist*, 11 December 1971; Heath 1998, pp. 432, 436). The former Conservative prime minister, Alec Douglas-Home, objected to direct rule, arguing that Northern Ireland was not like Scotland or Wales, 'The real British interest would I think be served best by pushing them towards a United Ireland rather than tying them closer to the United Kingdom' (PREM 15/1004, 13 March 1972). At a cabinet meeting on 4 February 1972, the Conservative government considered repartition and population exchange with the South to resolve the conflict. As Eamonn McCann points out, 'The minutes suggest that the British Government was far from dogmatic about the constitutional future of the North. None of the ministers is recorded expressing a straightforward defence-of-the-realm position' (*Sunday Tribune*, 26 September 1999). The Minister of Defence, Lord Carrington, even argued that expecting nationalists to wait twenty years for a united Ireland was asking too much, which may suggest that he considered that there was no overriding defence objection to Irish unity (Bew *et al*. 1995, p. 169).

The conflict, particularly on the left, was seen increasingly by the political elite as a colonial one rather than an internal UK problem. The logical corollary of this position was British withdrawal and Irish unity. In November 1971, Harold Wilson put Irish unity, albeit by consent, on the agenda in his 15-point plan. In March 1971, James Callaghan had raised the proposal for an all-Ireland council. Senior Labour politicians began to discuss British withdrawal under the code-name 'Algeria'. The alternative party of government – and a credible one at that – was not displaying the political will and determination required by British counter-insurgency doctrine. The response from the Conservative government to Wilson's plan was not hostile (Dixon 1993, p. 292). In March 1972, Wilson went to Dublin to meet the IRA. This was followed by the introduction of direct rule, a key IRA demand that alienated unionists. Following the introduction of direct rule, William Whitelaw, the newly-appointed Secretary of State for Northern Ireland ordered the army to take a 'low-profile' approach in nationalist areas to create the political space for a constitutional initiative. In June 1972, the Provisionals announced a ceasefire and in July Gerry Adams was among the IRA leaders who were flown to London to take part in talks with the Conservative government.

British 'determination' was further undermined by an apparent shift in British public opinion. A poll by the market research company NOP published by the *Daily Mail* in September 1971 suggested that 59 per cent of people in Britain wanted the immediate withdrawal of the army from Northern Ireland. The British media found itself under attack from Conservative politicians, who felt their reporting of Northern Ireland was undermining the morale of the British people and their army (Dixon 2000). Even before internment, the Home Secretary had warned of the danger of a populist movement for British withdrawal gaining momentum if soldiers continued to be killed. After Bloody Sunday, ministers in the Conservative cabinet expressed their concerns about the rise of 'troops out' sentiment in Britain. Heath argued that 'there was a growing feeling that they could not go on indefinitely doing a horrible job with no sign of an improvement' (*Sunday Tribune*, 26 September 1999). The Conservative cabinet feared that threatening to withdraw would demonstrate a weakening of the government's resolve, and carrying out withdrawal 'could only result in extensive bloodshed in Northern Ireland, in which the Roman Catholic element of the population might well be the main sufferers'. In order to sustain domestic public support for the deployment of the army in Northern Ireland 'it was desirable that movement towards some political solution of the conflict should be seen to be in prospect' (Cabinet, Confidential Annex, Cab 128 (48) 3 February 1972). There was a belief in the IRA that if sufficient British soldiers were killed this would precipitate withdrawal. From the IRA's perspective they were riding a post-war tide of victories for 'liberation movements' and, even by the end of 1971, the IRA was sufficiently encouraged for its paper to declare 1972 'The Year of Victory' (Hamill 1985, p. 22; Smith 1995, p. 101).

The apparent gains of the IRA and the ambiguity of British policy towards Northern Ireland provoked unease among loyalists, who feared their position within the Union was becoming undermined and mobilized to defend it. In late 1971 and early 1972, the DUP, the UDA and Vanguard were established, Vanguard was a hardline faction principally within the UUP which later (in 1973) established itself as the Vanguard Unionist Progressive Party. A vicious loyalist murder campaign got under way, which was probably partly a response to increasing republican violence and directed towards pushing the state to adopt a more repressive security policy (Patterson 1986; Loughlin 1995, ch. 9; Bruce 1999, p. 191). During 1971–73 a loyalist backlash developed, raising the prospect of the British army facing the 'nightmare scenario' of a war against both loyalist and republican paramilitaries.

Whitelaw's new 'hearts and minds' approach to security involved the adoption by the army of a 'low profile', no re-occupation of republican 'no-go' areas, the introduction of 'special category' (that is, political) status for republican prisoners, and the release of detainees. In March 1972, 913 republican detainees had been interned; by June 1972 this was down to 372 and by August 1972 to 243. The government's general policy was 'to exploit the introduction of direct rule in the hope of creating a better "hearts and minds" climate among the Catholics without thereby provoking Protestant reaction' (Carver 1989, pp. 421–2). These concessions and the subsequent negotiations with the IRA recognized the political nature of the republican struggle and contradicted the message that was being promoted in the propaganda war, where the IRA were portrayed as mindless psychopaths, thugs and criminals.

In reaching out to republicans, Whitelaw risked provoking unionists. By June 1972, an opinion poll found that 74 per cent of Catholics (but just 21 per cent of Protestants) thought Whitelaw was doing a good job (McAllister 1977b, p. 116). Loyalists, fearing that the truce with the IRA was the prelude to a sell-out by the British government, began to establish their own barricades. On 3 July, a stand-off between 8,000 members of the UDA and the outnumbered army threatened to lead to heavy bloodshed if soldiers were forced to fire on the advancing loyalists. The IRA was also escalating its campaign after the end of the ceasefire. The Army negotiated and averted a clash with the UDA that could have resulted in the army fighting a war on two fronts: 'an unenviable and probably impossible position' (Hamill 1986, p. 110).

The army was unhappy with the government's new strategy as it was felt that the release of detainees would lead to greater violence, and the 'low profile' approach of the army gave the IRA a chance to regroup (Hamill 1986, p. 103; Carver 1989, p. 427). The 'weakness' being displayed by the army, it was argued, resulted in the drying-up of intelligence. Army morale suffered and officers complained 'that the low profile restrictions were causing casualties and [they] felt that the policy had nothing to do with their jobs' (Hamill 1986, pp. 106–7). There was also dissatisfaction that the politicians, by negotiating with the IRA and being ambiguous on the constitutional future of Northern Ireland, were not demonstrating the determination necessary to win and were thus provoking a backlash among the loyalists. The army suffered rising casualties and the 'nightmare scenario' of a 'war on two fronts' appeared to be approaching. Army officers were 'convinced that the army had a better understanding of what was going on and they rated the Government as being politically naive' (Hamill 1986, p. 107). The former Chief of General Staff, Michael Carver, argued that the army faced a dilemma. They could fight the UDA to prevent them fighting the IRA, or else they could take the offensive against the IRA as a way of preventing the UDA from fighting them. Either way, the army had to act and show that violence did not pay. A less repressive approach towards nationalists might help to draw support away from the IRA, but this might reduce the pressure on the IRA and could encourage loyalist paramilitary activity to move into the vacuum (Carver 1989, pp. 424–5, 423). Since 1969, the British political and military elite had striven to avoid confrontation with Protestants (Bew *et al.* 1995, p. 167). By concentrating their efforts against the republicans, the security forces were dealing with their principal threat but also soothing unionist discontent, probably running with the grain of the locally recruited security forces' attitudes and preventing a 'war on two fronts' (Urban 1992, pp. 238–9).

The decision of the British, on 31 July 1972, to launch 'Operation Motorman' to remove the republican 'no-go' areas was in keeping with the structural, anti-republican, bias of British policy. It was a massive and successful operation, employing 12,000 troops, and marked a 'decisive blow' against the IRA and a major step in the reduction of violence (Smith 1995, p. 110). Advocates of a more repressive, 'militarist' strategy of counter-insurgency might argue that signs of political concessions by the British political elite aggravated the conflict in Ireland to the heights of the summer of 1972, and that it took the biggest British military operation since Suez to clear the no-go areas, a 'tough' measure that was long overdue. Consequently, this produced the desired decrease in violence. Those with a more 'political approach' to counter-insurgency would argue that Motorman succeeded because the government had created the political space in which it could be successful. The introduction of direct rule and Whitelaw's 'softly, softly' security policy had divided the nationalist community. The IRA's 'Bloody Friday' bombing atrocity (killing eleven and injuring 130) and war-weariness were also taking their toll on republican support for violence (Smith 1995, p. 104).

The loyalists were not pacified by Operation Motorman. In October 1972, the UDA briefly declared war on the British army, and unionist politicians adopted a more militant rhetoric. Former unionist minister, John Taylor, said: 'Enjoy this Christmas, it may well be your last in peace. After New Year you will probably have to organise to resist an imposed solution by the British Government.' William Craig, leader of Vanguard, declared his willingness 'to come out and shoot and kill'. In late 1972 and early 1973 the army did crack down on loyalist areas. In February 1973, the first loyalists were interned and in response loyalists called a strike that brought Northern Ireland to a standstill and resulted in widespread violence. One of the loyalist leaders of the strike claimed that 'the power of the grass roots' can no longer be ignored (Bew and Gillespie 1993, p. 59).

The Security Dilemma

The events of the summer of 1972 illustrate Britain's security dilemma in Northern Ireland and the constraints operating on its power. The British had two, not necessarily compatible, principal objectives as far as the local security forces were concerned:

1. To create forces which implemented the law impartially and which enjoyed the confidence and consent of the people of Northern Ireland. This was seen to require that the personnel of such forces be drawn widely from across all communities in Northern Ireland.
2. To create such forces swiftly and in sufficient strength to control and bear the brunt of the conflict so that the British army could be either withdrawn or its commitment significantly reduced.

Catholic recruitment to the part-time UDR was, initially, favourable. Moderate nationalist politicians (including the SDLP) and church leaders encouraged their followers to join. By March 1970, Catholics constituted 39 per cent of the recruits for the new organization (Ryder 1992, p. 39). However, the murder by the IRA of Catholic members of the security forces, and the repressive policy of Stormont – which alienated many in the Catholic community – and perhaps also sectarianism within the force, contributed towards a decline in Catholic recruitment to both the UDR and RUC. The apparent shift in British policy during 1972 and the resulting 'Protestant backlash' began to undermine Protestant recruitment to the local forces and therefore also to undermine British hopes of extricating the army from the conflict. The RUC was still weak, its intelligence and morale were poor and it could not hope to take on the burden of primacy in the struggle against the IRA.

The dependence of the British government and military on the Protestant community for the recruitment of the local security forces in effect constrained the ability of the British to police that community. If the army 'took on' the Protestants too forcefully they ran the risk that Protestants would not join the UDR and the RUC. The consequences for British security policy were dire: the advantages of police primacy would be lost and the British army would be unable to give up the burden of policing. While General Harry Tuzo, the GOC 1971–3, denied that the army dealt more leniently with loyalist extremists than the IRA, he 'made it clear that he was reluctant

Table 4.1   Army recruitment figures and deaths, 1969–76

Year	Army recruitment	Year	Army deaths
1969–70	21,411	**1970**	0
1970–71	24,337	**1971**	44
1972–73	31,298	**1972**	108
1973–74	26,484	**1973**	59
1974–75	15,310	**1974**	44
1975–76	22,041	**1975**	15
1976–77	27,238	**1976**	14

Sources: Dixon 2000 p. 111; McKittrick *et al.* 2004, p. 1473.

to find himself fighting two different wars at the same time' (Carver 1989, p. 428). Similar dilemmas of policing a communally divided society such as Northern Ireland had also been apparent in Britain's withdrawal from the Empire (Dixon 1997c, pp. 199–200).

The army's reliance on the local security forces was compounded during the years 1972–74 by a crisis within its own ranks. In 1972, no fewer than 103 soldiers were killed, and the following year the army experienced a recruitment crisis that was attributed to its role in Northern Ireland. The recruitment of men into the army from civilian life is shown in Table 4.1.

Lord Carrington, Minister of Defence, commented in June 1973: 'Northern Ireland has had some effect, not among serving soldiers so much, but parents who may have discouraged their sons from going into the Service' (*The Times*, 20 June 1973). An army survey found that: 'After four years of trying to keep the peace in Ulster, however, there is no little doubt that the army's role there is bad for recruiting. Surveys among potential recruits show that early in 1973, although the overwhelming majority thought it should remain there, 46 per cent of them were put off joining by the prospect of serving there.' The problems of recruitment and the retention of currently serving soldiers was compounded by the widespread opposition of many army relatives to their sons serving in Northern Ireland, and their agitation for withdrawal. British politicians feared a populist campaign to 'bring our boys home', like the one that had developed in Britain over Palestine in the late 1940s (Dixon 2000). The army was overstretched by its involvement in Northern Ireland and this threatened its ability to contribute fully to NATO. The recruitment crisis underscored the importance of police primacy in Northern Ireland

and the need to increase recruitment to the local, and by now over-whelmingly Protestant, security forces. Antagonizing unionism was unlikely to produce the necessary flow of recruits to implement police primacy, and threatened the army with a 'war on two fronts' (Hamill 1986, p. 149). The dependence of security policy on the need to recruit Protestants into the security forces is the context against which the British government's failure to order the army to take stronger action against the Protestant community can be comprehended more fully, and in particular its reluctance to take on the loyalist Ulster Workers' Council (UWC) strike in May 1974 that brought down the British-backed power-sharing executive.

Conclusion

The 'structuralist' argument that the outbreak of conflict in Northern Ireland was inevitable has been deployed by Labour politicians and civil servants to absolve themselves from responsibility for the crisis in Northern Ireland. Just as structuralist modernization theory let politicians off the hook by predicting the inevitability of Irish unity, the assumption that the English had failed, and always would fail, to do anything positive in Ireland was a self-fulfilling prophecy. Nevertheless, considerable constraints do seem to have operated on the Labour government's room for manoeuvre, and the fear that British 'interference' might provoke a civil war was a real one. The assumptions of British political ideology were inadequate to understand the communal pattern of politics in Northern Ireland. The 'modern', 'progressive' British political model was imposed through a programme of reforms, but there was little understanding of the impact of these reforms and the fears they aroused. When the reforms failed to stop the violence it was 'the natives' (nationalists and unionists) and 'irrational, sinister forces' who were increasingly blamed for their own plight, with little responsibility being attached to British political or military elites. The emphasis of policy shifted from reform to security, resulting in the disaster of internment. In both the Labour and the Conservative parties; increasingly Northern Ireland was no longer seen as being 'British', and the easiest way out appeared to be Irish unity.

The lack of determination displayed by British politicians in the propaganda war was undermining the army in its fight with the IRA, and threatening also to involve it in a 'war' with loyalists. This was apparent in the failure to introduce direct rule earlier; the premature introduction of internment; the negotiations and truce with the IRA; the release of detainees and 'disastrous' low-profile approach of Whitelaw; and Labour's support and Conservative sympathy for Irish unity. From the perspective of British counter-insurgency strategy, by raising uncertainty about the constitutional future of Northern Ireland, the politicians were losing the propaganda war and encouraging the IRA to believe they were winning and that they should continue to intensify their 'armed struggle'. In addition, this approach also raised the hackles of unionists who, believing they were to be driven into a united Ireland, mobilized to put pressure on the British to act against the IRA. The imperative to Ulsterize security was only likely to be realized by recruiting from among unionists, who might not join the security forces if they felt they were implementing a policy that was destroying the Union. This resulted in a bias against confrontation with unionists, and towards confrontation with republicans, which is perceptible throughout 'the Troubles'. If the government alienated both republicans and loyalists, this might lead to the army's 'nightmare scenario' of an unwinnable 'war on two fronts', against both the IRA and loyalist paramilitaries, in which their position could become untenable. From this counter-insurgency perspective, the consequence of the politicians' weakness was the heavy casualties and recruitment crisis suffered by the army, as well as the growing disillusionment and support for withdrawal among British public opinion. The strain this produced on civil–military relations manifested itself in calls from some quarters for a stronger military role in British politics, and raises questions about the extent of political control over security policy (Foot 1989; Dixon 1997b; pp. 201–3).

5

The First Peace Process, 1972–4: The Power-Sharing Experiment and Its Failure

After the introduction of direct rule in 1972, the British government tried again to construct an accommodation on the moderate, centre ground of Northern Irish politics where, it was assumed, there existed a 'moderate silent majority' for peace. The 'power-sharing experiment' attempted to deal with both unionist and nationalist claims and to find a compromise to which the Northern Irish political elites could bring their parties and voters. If a deal was struck that was 'too favourable' to either nationalism or unionism, then it was less likely that the party leaders who had the rough end of the deal would be able to persuade their supporters and voters to endorse that agreement. Furthermore, the ability of political leaders to lead their parties and voters was likely to vary from party to party, and be influenced by the wider political environment. Power-sharing with some kind of Irish dimension was always likely to be the only settlement that could attract significant cross-community support. After the violence of the previous four years, was it possible for nationalist and unionist political elites to reach a settlement that could bridge the gap between their parties and voters? What kind of power-sharing, and what kind of Irish dimension could maximize support for accommodation? How could the governments, if not the parties themselves, create the conditions in which support for a centrist settlement would be maximized? Alternatively, what constitutional arrangement might minimize nationalist and unionist alienation, and contain the conflict?

British Colonial Policy: Building up the Moderates

British attempts to build up a 'moderate centre' in Northern Ireland were reminiscent of its imperial policy. In the Empire, the British had intervened and attempted to engineer constitutional settlements based on the 'centre', 'an amorphous mass of responsible, tolerant, silent and simple people ready to be mobilized in defence of compromise. The aim was to elicit and organize this "centre" ' (Utley 1975, p. 25; Darwin 1988, p. 168; Furedi 1994).

Frank Furedi's discussion of Malaya, Kenya and British Guiana in *Colonial Wars and the Politics of Third World Nationalism* bears comparison with British policy towards Northern Ireland. He argues that, in these cases, 'radical nationalists' were susceptible to influence from the 'grassroots', which made it difficult for them to cut deals with the British colonial power. The British attempted 'to restore order' which was in effect 'about curbing or deactivating mass politics' (Furedi 1994, p. 189).

British imperial officials attempted to establish political structures that distanced nationalist politicians from mass pressure. The British became adept at detaching and strengthening moderates from anti-colonial movements and isolating the extremists, who tended to be more popular and plebeian (Furedi 1994, p. 240). British administrators could not influence the masses directly but could do so by influencing their political leaders. However, those moderate nationalists who wished to 'collaborate' with the British faced the difficulty of doing so while at the same time retaining credibility and popularity with the masses (Furedi 1994, pp. 247, 250). Nationalist, anti-colonial leaders had to be responsive to their own activists and the masses or face being outflanked by rival elites. Simultaneously, they had to try to lead their movement towards what appeared to be a 'realistic' settlement.

Extreme activists would put pressure on anti-colonial leaders and so 'London was sensitive to the need of anti-colonial leaders to retain a radical public image' (Furedi 1994, p. 255). Furedi suggests there is some limited evidence that the British would manufacture martyrs out of their nationalist 'collaborators'/moderates, by arresting them, in order to bolster their image among the masses (Furedi 1994, p. 251).

The Moderate Silent Majority?

British strategy combined elements of both a top-down and a bottom-up approach to conflict resolution (Dixon 1997a, 1997c, 1997d). On the one hand the political elites were to be coerced and cajoled into agreement (top-down), while on the other initiatives were taken to promote reconciliation at the grassroots level (bottom-up). The initial tranche of reforms instituted after troops were deployed on the streets of Northern Ireland in August 1969, for example, were aimed at dealing with what were perceived to be the roots of the conflict: economic, social and security reforms were implemented. The Community Relations Commission was among proposals to encourage 'harmonious community relations'. Politicians of both major British parties publicly subscribed to the assumption that the electorate was more 'moderate' than its political representatives, either because this belief was genuine or as part of the propaganda war to encourage and mobilize moderation.

The faith of both major British political parties in the moderates appeared to be borne out by the success of the trade union movement, the women's peace movement and moderate political parties in challenging communal polarization. The revitalization of the NILP was seen, particularly in Labour circles, as an important step for uniting Catholic and Protestant workers along class rather than sectarian lines. The NILP's apparently strong showing at the June 1970 General Election (98, 194 votes) suggested that it was a major player in the conflict and demonstrated a potential to transcend communal divisions (its strong showing was probably related partly to the absence of a nationalist alternative, as the SDLP was only established in August 1970). The apparent success of the trade union movement in uniting Protestant and Catholic workers within their ranks also reinforced the moderate assumptions of *both* British Labour and Conservative politicians. During 'the Troubles' the trade union movement has been largely successful in preventing violence spilling over on to the shop floor. Its leaders, both Protestant and Catholic, were leading figures calling for calm and 'moderation'.

Following the introduction of direct rule in March 1972, a peace movement developed and took to the streets in nationalist West Belfast, which was 'assiduously cultivated by both Whitelaw and the SDLP' (McAllister 1977b, p. 116). Some Catholics called for a ceasefire, since many were tired of the conflict and the levels of violence. In April 1972, the Official IRA murdered Catholic Ranger William Best of the Royal Irish Rangers, home on leave in Derry. There followed angry protests from the women of the Bogside and the Creggan, and calls for the OIRA to leave these areas. In May 1972, the OIRA declared a ceasefire, recognizing that 'the overwhelming desire of the great majority of all the people . . . is for an end to military actions by all sides'.

It is often claimed that the difference between the first and second peace process is that the second was inclusive while the first excluded loyalist and republican paramilitaries. The question as to whether the British government pursued an 'inclusive' or 'exclusive' approach to peacemaking in Northern Ireland is too crude. The question is *under what circumstances* was the British government prepared to bring paramilitaries into a political process (and the British had considerable experience of talking to 'terrorists' in the retreat from Empire)? To bring paramilitaries into a political process prematurely could undermine democracy and encourage violence by giving legitimacy to those with guns rather than those with votes. More pragmatically, bringing in paramilitaries ran the risk of alienating both moderate unionist *and nationalist* opinion, and driving it away from negotiation and the possibility of a power-sharing settlement built on the centre ground. In June 1972, the Provisional IRA called a short truce and shortly afterwards secret talks were held with the British government. Willie Whitelaw attempted to build on the opportunity opened up by the introduction of direct rule to win over nationalists to an accommodation with unionism (see Chapter 4).

The British Conservative government appeared to have been investigating the prospects of bringing the IRA into a peace process but was rebutted by intransigent IRA leaders (O'Doherty 2007). During this period the Provisionals believed they were on the verge of defeating the British, and so their uncompromising stance in talks with the British government and opposition is not so surprising. From the IRA's anti-colonial perspective they were riding the tide of post-war decolonization, because, if the British had retreated from the rest of the Empire, why not also from Northern Ireland? They hoped to kill as many British soldiers as were killed in Aden, believing, with some reason, that this might precipitate a withdrawal (Dixon 2000). The republicans' unwillingness to negotiate ruled them out of any peace process, though the British continued to try to draw them into democratic politics. Sinn Féin was encouraged to contest the British General Election of February 1974, and after that election Sinn Féin and the loyalist UVF were legalized (Taylor 1997, p. 170). The PIRA worked to undermine any power-sharing settlement: in September 1973 it bombed a London hotel to coincide with power-sharing negotiations, and during the period of the power-sharing executive it stepped up its bombing campaign to bring the executive down (Smith 1995, p. 125). The PIRA's intransigence left the government little alternative but to build peace on the moderate centre ground of Northern Irish politics, attempting to boost moderates while marginalizing the PIRA and loyalist extremists. A security crackdown could be implemented with the support and endorsement of constitutional nationalism from both North and South.

The success of the 'moderates' fuelled hopes that it was these members of civil society who were more representative of the people than were the 'intransigent' and 'bigoted' politicians. 'Moderates' claimed the existence of 'a silent moderate majority', and some favoured a referendum to test this sentiment. The *Belfast Telegraph* was an influential propagandist for the moderate cause, applauding 'the triumph of commonsense from below' (Bromley 1989, p. 218). David Bleakley, of the NILP, and former Minister for Community Relations, claimed in his book *Peace in Ulster* (1972): 'Fortunately the evidence indicates that the mass of Ulster people are on the side of reconciliation.' Their presence is not often obvious because 'they speak a language which too often goes unnoticed in an age which gives pride of place to news framed in a context of violence' (Bleakley 1972, p. 67). At the British army headquarters in Lisburn, briefing officers spoke of the 'mass of moderate opinion about to be mobilised', and 'the great white snowball of peace' that was rolling out of Derry (Hamill 1985, p. 106). Opinion polls seemed to bear out the optimism of the government and the 'moderates'. In August 1972, *Fortnight* magazine published opinion poll results concluding that 'after four years of violence in Northern Ireland there has been a substantial swing towards non-sectarian voting'.

The 'moderate centre' of Northern Ireland politics, apart from the SDLP, met at the Darlington Conference in September 1972. Whitelaw hoped to split off the liberal wing of the Ulster Unionist Party, and shepherd the hardliner Brian Faulkner from centre stage (*The Times*, 2 June 1973), in order to build up the moderate middle ground of the SDLP, NILP and APNI. The inclusion of the SDLP among the 'moderate' parties was open to question. It drew its support more or less exclusively from Catholics, supported Irish unity and refused to participate at Darlington because of the continuation of internment. Including the SDLP in a 'moderate' coalition with unionists was likely to severely test its stability. A less diverse coalition of moderates might have a greater chance of success, and hence the British Conservative government's hope that the 'socialist' NILP would perform well at forthcoming elections and prove to be 'a more compromising representative of moderate opinion', or perhaps put pressure on the SDLP to adopt a more accommodating stance.

The British government's problem was that it was two years since elections had been held in Northern Ireland and it was difficult to assess what kind of support each of the parties commanded. The violence of the intervening period had allowed the people to look into the abyss of communal violence and, it was argued, they would surely not vote for those 'extremists' who had generated that violence and stood in the way of fair compromise. Opinion polls reinforced the government's hopes of a strong 'centre'. British politicians, from both major parties, attempted to shore up the centre ground by threatening the people of Northern Ireland with the 'consequences' of rejecting Britain's power-sharing approach. Again, there were overtones of chauvinistic British nationalism, as 'we', the British people, demanded that 'they', the people of Northern Ireland, accept the settlement 'we' were developing to settle 'their' conflict. Heath warned that people would 'get very fed up' if the people in Northern Ireland did not take this opportunity to get together (*The Times*, 24 March 1973). Supporting the government's 1972 Green Paper (see below), Merlyn Rees argued:

> If we were rejected, that of itself would mean that there was no moderate majority in both communities, in both camps, which is the basis on which we have been working for four years. If it were proved wrong, it would mean needing to face up to a complete reappraisal of policy by any British Government, because the basis on which that Government had been working would have been shown to be false. (House of Commons Debates, vol. 846, col. 57, 13 November 1972)

Since it was felt that the current political elites did not represent the moderate majority, Harold Wilson spoke of the election of 'genuinely representative' politicians at the polls. British threats against the people of Northern Ireland proved to be counter-productive; rather than boosting moderates they helped to produce precisely those conditions of constitutional insecurity that historically had undermined moderate forces (Lawrence *et al*. 1975, pp. 68, 85).

The Settlement: Power-sharing and an Irish Dimension

The British government's wooing of the nationalist community after direct rule and the PIRA's 'Bloody Friday' outrage opened up the political space for the SDLP, urged on by the Irish government, to lift its ban on discussions with Whitelaw. Although the SDLP did not take part in the Darlington Conference it did produce a policy document, *Towards a United Ireland*, which reflected the assumptions of modernization theory and adopted a greener stance than any of the nationalist parties in the Republic. This hardline position may have been adopted in anticipation of a peace process in which concessions would have to be made. Northern Ireland, it argued, was 'inherently unstable' and any settlement would have to take place in an all-Ireland context. The British government was urged to declare itself in favour of Irish unity, and a power-sharing executive was proposed, but with control of security policy remaining at Westminster. A National Senate of Ireland would integrate the whole island 'by preparing the harmonization of the structures, laws and services of both parts of Ireland and ... agree[ing] on an acceptable constitution for a New Ireland and its relationships with Britain'. The British and Irish governments should accept joint sovereignty as an interim system of government. The SDLP's policy document was ambiguous on consent and did not state state specifically that Irish unity required the consent of a majority in Northern Ireland, unlike the party's constitution.

The British government's Green (discussion) Paper was published on 31 October 1972 against a background of continuing violence from both loyalist and republican paramilitaries. The Green Paper laid down minimum requirements and parameters for a political settlement and introduced the idea of power-sharing, suggesting that any devolved assembly would have to receive cross-community support and that there were strong arguments for the minority to exercise a share of executive power. The constitutional guarantee was emphasized and would be tested by periodic border plebiscites. It was hoped that clear-cut constitutional guarantees might calm unionist fears and help to pull Northern Ireland back from the brink of civil war (*Guardian*, 11 October 1972). The Border Poll, held in March 1973, produced a 57.5 per cent vote of the electorate for the Union, with 0.6 per cent against (nationalists and republicans boycotted the poll).

Disconcertingly for unionists, British guarantees came with threats. While the Green Paper guaranteed the position of unionists within the UK there was also a veiled threat that membership of the UK carried obligations as well as rights, and it was not for Northern Ireland alone to decide how it was to be governed as part of the UK. Furthermore, the British also claimed 'neutrality' on the constitutional future of Northern Ireland: 'No UK government for many years has had any wish to impede the realization of Irish unity, if it were to come about by genuine and freely given mutual agreement and on conditions acceptable to the distinctive communities.' Britain would not impede Irish unity but its priorities in Northern Ireland were, first, peace and stability; second, prosperity; and, third, that the region should not offer a base for any external threat to the UK (Northern Ireland Office, *The Future of Northern Ireland: A Paper for Discussion*, Belfast, 1972, paras 52, 74). The legitimacy of the Republic's interest in the North was recognized; economic and security interdependence, along with Ireland's membership of the EEC, pointed towards a closer relationship between the North and South of Ireland; and it was 'clearly desirable that any new arrangements for Northern Ireland should, whilst meeting the wishes of Northern Ireland and Great Britain, be, so far as possible, acceptable to and accepted by the Republic of Ireland'. But it was for the people of Northern Ireland to decide what their relationship should be to the UK and the Republic (para. 78).

The government's White Paper, *Northern Ireland Constitutional Proposals*, was published in March 1973 and closely resembled the Green Paper. After consultations, the government had found four 'very significant areas of agreement', concerning: a devolved assembly; a single-chamber elected legislative assembly of 80–100 members; a structure of powerful committees within the assembly; and the protection of fundamental human rights and freedoms. The Northern Ireland Assembly and its power-sharing executive would have responsibility for social security, education, industry, agriculture and planning, with the prospect of security being devolved at a future date. The White Paper recognized that the problems in Northern Ireland required bottom-up community initiatives, economic prosperity and reconciliation as well as constitutional structures. The UK favoured the establishment of a Council of Ireland, which would cover areas of mutual interest such as tourism, regional development, electricity and transport (para. 110). If the Council was to be 'a useful working mechanism in North–South relations, it must operate with the consent of both majority and minority opinion in Northern Ireland, who have a right to prior consultation and involvement in the process of determining its form, functions and procedures' (para. 111). After elections to a new Assembly the British government would consult with the representatives of Northern Ireland opinion and the government of the Republic to discuss three interrelated objectives: the principle of consent and acceptance of the status of Northern Ireland; 'effective consultation and co-operation in Ireland'; and security co-operation against terrorists (para. 116).

The recognition of the importance of the Irish dimension by the British government accompanied a growing acknowledgement of the legitimacy of the Republic's role in resolving the conflict in Northern Ireland. By mid-1971, Heath could not accept that 'anyone from outside the UK can participate in meetings to promote political development of any part of the United Kingdom' (*Irish Times*, 6 April 1998). After the introduction of internment, Heath criticized the Irish prime minister's call for an end to internment 'as unwarranted interference in the internal affairs of the UK'. But on 6–7 September 1971, Heath met Lynch in a meeting that symbolized Britain's recognition that the Republic had a legitimate interest in Northern affairs (Fitzgerald 1991, p. 99). Consultation with the Irish government, according to Heath, 'was essential if we were to convince moderate opinion in Northern Ireland that we were acting in good faith', because 'Until we could establish a productive working relationship with the Irish government, the political deadlock could not be broken' (Heath 1998, p. 424).

During 1972, the nature of the loyalist backlash was becoming apparent, and the impatience of British politicians was beginning to concern Irish legislators. The emphasis of Irish policy correspondingly shifted from the rhetoric of Irish unity towards the prerequisite of reconciliation, and the Irish government encouraged the SDLP to enter talks with the British. On 24 November 1972, Heath and Lynch met, and the Irish Taoiseach described 'a closer meeting of minds than he had ever experienced before'. The London correspondent of the *Irish Times* reported that the Irish 'entered enthusiastically into negotiations, and from this point onwards the British kept them very closely informed, usually in advance, of their proposals. Relations, recently so chilly, soon became warm, even excessively cosy' (Downey 1983, p. 125). The importance of the Anglo-Irish process was indicated by Heath's visit to Dublin in September 1973, the first visit by a British prime minister since 1921. The advantages to the British of a closer relationship with the Irish government were that it increased the likelihood of achieving a settlement with nationalist support; it held out the prospect of more effective cross-border security co-operation against the IRA (which, for some, was the key to defeating the IRA); and it also helped to reduce any international pressure, particularly from the USA.

The White Paper warned the people of Northern Ireland of their obligations (para. 12b) but also looked to the law-abiding majority 'to stand together against those small but dangerous minorities which would seek to impose their views by violence and coercion, and which cannot, therefore, be allowed to participate in working institutions they wish to destroy' (para. 118). The Paper concluded, 'The Government believes . . . that the majority of the people of Northern Ireland have an overwhelming desire for peace and that they will accept the opportunity which these proposals offer' (para. 122).

The problem for the British of pushing the Irish dimension and courting the Irish government was that it tended to further alienate the unionists, who were already highly suspicious of British intentions. The ruling Ulster Unionist Council (UUC) voted not to reject the government's White Paper on 27 March 1973 by 381 votes to 231. On 30 March, a faction broke away from the UUP to found the Vanguard Unionist Progressive Party (VUPP), a party with overt paramilitary connections, which opposed the White Paper proposals along with Paisley's DUP (which then favoured direct rule). Vanguard counted among its members David Trimble, future leader of the UUP (1995–2005) and signatory of the power-sharing Good Friday Agreement 1998. The VUPP was relatively ambivalent about the Union and favoured a powerful Northern Ireland assembly, but there were those who also supported independence. A coalition of loyalists opposed to the White Paper (including the DUP, VUPP, anti-White Paper UUP, representatives of loyalist workers, the Orange Order and the UDA) agreed on four points: the defeat of the IRA; the utter rejection of the Council of Ireland; full parliamentary representation (at Westminster); and control of the RUC by Northern Ireland's elected representatives.

The Failure of the Moderates

The illusion of a 'moderate silent majority' was shattered by the result of elections to the local councils in May, and to the Assembly in June 1973 (see Table 5.1). A *Fortnight/Sunday Times* poll had predicted success for moderate parties and purported to show 'a clear shift to the centre parties and almost total support for making the White Paper proposals work'. The polls' prediction of the number of Assembly seats to be won by the 'moderate parties' are followed by the number actually won: NILP predicted 9 seats (actual 1); the APNI 11 (8); and

Table 5.1   Assembly election results, June 1973

Party	Percentage of vote	Number of seats
Pro-White Paper UUP	29.3	24
SDLP	22.1	19
APNI	9.2	8
NILP	2.6	1
Total pro-White Paper	**63.2**	**52**
Anti-White Paper UUP	8.5	8
DUP	10.8	8
VUPP	10.5	7
West Belfast Loyalists	2.3	3
Total anti-White Paper	**32.1**	**26**

the SDLP 12 (19). The NILP was almost obliterated, winning just 2.6 per cent of the first preference votes, while the APNI took only 9.2 per cent of the vote, well short of the 19 per cent predicted by the *Fortnight* poll. The election was held using the Single Transferable Vote, which, it was hoped, would encourage voters to transfer their preferences to the moderate parties. It was estimated, however, that less than 0.25 per cent of the transferred vote crossed the sectarian divide and lower preferences votes were transferred away from moderates (Cunningham 1991, p. 53). The 'unofficial view' from Whitelaw's office hoped for substantial Alliance success and agreed with the *Fortnight* poll in its assessment of APNI support (*Guardian*, 31 May 1973). The Assembly elections had produced the very outcome the British had tried to prevent, namely a dramatic upsurge for loyalist and anti-White Paper unionists resulting in a 'tribal confrontation' (*Sunday Telegraph*, 1 July 1973). The contrast between opinion poll predictions and electoral outcomes in this election lends credence to the generalization that opinion polls tend to overestimate moderate opinion in Northern Ireland (Whyte 1990, p. 82).

   The outcome of the Assembly elections in June 1973 dashed British hopes of a moderate power-sharing executive composed of the NILP, APNI and liberal unionists. Any power-sharing executive would have to include both the 'hardline' UUP leader Brian Faulkner and the nationalist SDLP in order to achieve sufficient Catholic representation on an executive. This relative diversity of parties meant that unionists would have to be part of an executive with people who favoured Irish unity. Faulkner had only the support of a minority of unionist seats in the assembly if the 'centrist' NILP and APNI were not counted as being unionist. The strong showing of the hard-line VUPP and the DUP was likely to constrain Faulkner's room for manoeuvre.

Crucially, Faulkner did not have a clear mandate for entering a power-sharing executive with the SDLP. The UUP's manifesto had stated: 'We are not opposed to power-sharing in government, but we will not be prepared to participate in government with those whose *primary aim* is to break the union with Great Britain' (my emphasis). According to McAllister, 'the Protestant electorate interpreted the manifesto as explicitly excluding the possibility of power-sharing with the SDLP, while Faulkner's shrewd use of words included it' (McAllister 1977b, p. 129). Two of Faulkner's power-sharing assembly members opposed the White Paper, another supporter was killed in a car accident, and another was elected to be speaker of the Assembly. When the Assembly met, Faulkner enjoyed the support of only a minority of unionists – 21 votes, compared to 27 opposed to the White Paper proposals. Faulkner's problem was to attempt to lead the UUP into an accommodation with nationalism without further splitting his party or losing support to the 'hardline' unionist parties that lurked on his flank. British politicians had already attempted to coerce the Northern Ireland electorate to vote for moderate politicians; with elections out of the way the government now attempted to coerce the parties towards the centre ground.

Bipartisanship and Agreement over Northern Ireland

The British Labour Party had used its influence on behalf of national-ists to delay the introduction of a border poll in 1973 and to oppose the Conservative government's proposals to increase Northern Ireland's representation at Westminster by bringing it into line with the region's population (Dixon 1995a, p. 166). After the Assembly elections, the British parties united to drive unionists and nationalists swiftly towards a settlement. The unity of the British parties would help to persuade the political parties in Northern Ireland, particularly the SDLP, that there was no advantage to be had by holding out on a power-sharing settlement with the Conservative government, since this was also supported by the Labour Party. The Conservative prime minister, Edward Heath, threatened Northern Ireland with integration into the UK if agreement was not reached. Heath's threat (of Northern Ireland being ruled like any other part of the UK) may have undermined Faulkner's position, since many unionists would have preferred integration to power-sharing with an Irish dimension. Whatever Heath's intentions, this outburst helped to propel the SDLP towards talks (Dixon 1995a, p. 168).

The Irish government had also moved into line with the British to impress on nationalists in the North the importance of a settlement. The Irish Taoiseach, Liam Cosgrave, told a meeting of British Conservatives that while he wanted a united Ireland, to press for this goal in the prevailing climate (of loyalist unrest) would 'dangerously exacerbate tensions and fears' (*The Times*, 3 July 1973). Nevertheless, the SDLP went to work on the Irish coalition government and over the summer of 1973 succeeded in winning its support for a strong Irish dimension. It could be that 'the irredentism of the Republic's official ideology made it difficult for a southern government to be in open disagreement with the elected representatives of the "beleaguered minority" in the north' (Bew and Patterson 1985, p. 58). The hardening of the SDLP's position occurred in spite of that party's success in being elected the representatives of the overwhelming majority of Catholic opinion which voted. Although the party leadership may have had difficulty in maintaining party unity, 'the other anti-partitionist groups posed no serious challenge to them' (White 1984, p. 141; see also McAllister 1977b, p. 126) and, following direct rule and Operation Motorman, the IRA's campaign appeared to be waning in popularity among nationalists (Kelley 1988, pp. 199–200).

On 5 October 1973, representatives of the APNI, UUP and SDLP met at Stormont for talks on the formation of a power-sharing executive. They agreed an economic and social programme but came into conflict over whether the RUC should change its name. On 21 November, the SDLP agreed with the UUP and APNI on the principle of a Council of Ireland and the composition of a power-sharing executive. The UUP was to receive the majority of the seats – six – with the SDLP taking four and the APNI one. Four non-voting members were also included: two SDLP, one unionist and one APNI. This allowed Brian Faulkner to claim a UUP majority on the executive, which was an important concession if the UUP leader was to fight off growing dissent within his party. On 23 October, the UUP's Standing Committee supported the policy of allowing UUP Assembly members to join a power-sharing executive, by 132 votes to 105 (Gillespie 1998, p. 103). On 20 November, the day before agreement on the composition of the power-sharing executive, the UUC voted only narrowly against a proposal to reject power-sharing, by 379 votes to 369, and supported the party leadership in a further vote, by 374 votes to 362.

Sunningdale: The Deal

Agreement on the executive opened the way for talks between the three Northern Irish pro-power-sharing parties and the British and Irish governments at Sunningdale, in Berkshire, on 6–9 December. Holding the conference outside Northern Ireland insulated the party leaders from their parties and electoral grassroots. The loyalist parties were excluded from participation in spite of their substantial representation for fear that they would disrupt negotiations. The Sunningdale Conference represented a high point in Anglo-Irish relations: it was largely an 'intergovernmental conference' (White 1984, p. 150) and the Irish government 'had the feeling that they were "working in parallel" with the British Government' (Kyle 1975, p. 439). The talks were held to decide the nature of the Irish dimension that had been outlined in the White Paper and establish the political framework in which power-sharing would operate. The unionists were looking for: recognition of Northern Ireland's constitutional position within the UK; improved security co-operation with the Republic against terrorism, including moves on extradition; and a weak cross-border body. The nationalists, in contrast, wanted a strong, all-Ireland body with executive and harmonizing functions; reform of the RUC; and movement on the release of detainees. The negotiations and controversy revolved around three main areas: Articles 2 and three, and majority consent; the Council of Ireland; and security and extradition.

Articles 2 and 3 and majority consent.   Faulkner needed concessions from nationalists on Articles 2 and 3 of the Irish Constitution and recognition of Northern Ireland's place within the Union if he was to be able to deliver a settlement to Northern unionists. The Irish government felt it would not be able to deliver support for a referendum, required by the Irish Constitution, to change Articles 2 and 3 in the face of strong opposition by the more republican Fianna Fáil party. On only one occasion has an amendment to the Constitution been passed without the support of the principal Opposition party, and that was on the establishment of the Constitution itself. The Irish government offered a solemn declaration 'that there could be no change in the status of Northern Ireland until a majority of the people of Northern Ireland desired a change in that status'. The British government declared that it would support the wishes of the majority of the people in Northern Ireland, and that the present status of Northern Ireland was as part of the UK. If in the future the majority of people indicated a wish to become part of a united Ireland, the British government would support that wish. John Hume saw this 'as an important weapon to use against his republican opponents. If it could be established that the British interest was to ensure that there was peace and stability, it would mean that the solution relied totally on a process of persuasion, undermining the argument for violence' (White 1984, p. 149). The Irish government did not endorse Britain's interpretation of the present status of Northern Ireland, since this would have conflicted with the territorial claim.

The Council of Ireland.   The Council of Ireland was to comprise a Council of Ministers and a Consultative Assembly. The Council of Ministers would have fourteen members, seven from the Northern Ireland executive and seven members of the Irish government, but would only be able to take decisions by a unanimous vote (thus giving unionists a veto). It was to enjoy 'executive and harmonising functions and a consultative role'. The executive functions of the Council of Ireland were not defined; instead 'studies would at once be set in hand to identify and, prior to the formal stage of the conference, report on areas of common interest in relation to which a Council of Ireland would take executive decisions and, in appropriate cases, be responsible for carrying those decisions into effect'. The studies would investigate areas of policy suitable for executive action by the Council of Ireland in the fields of: exploitation, conservation and development of natural resources and the environment; agricultural matters; co-operative ventures in the fields of trade and industry; electricity generation; tourism; roads and transport; advisory services connected with public health; sport; culture and the arts. There was no limit to the array of functions that could be devolved to the Council of Ireland with the agreement of the NI Assembly and the Oireachtas (Irish Parliament). In the New Year, a conference would be held between the executive and the two governments to consider reports on the studies commissioned and to sign the agreement reached. Alongside the Council of Ministers was to be a Consultative Assembly of sixty members, half to be elected by proportional representation from the North and half from the Republic; this was to have 'advisory and review' functions. A Secretariat to the Council would 'service the institutions of the Council and ... supervise the carrying out of the executive and harmonising functions and the consultative role of the Council'.

Security and extradition.   'It was broadly accepted that the two parts of Ireland are to a considerable extent inter-dependent in the whole field of law and order, and that the problems of political violence and identification with the police service cannot be solved without taking account of that fact.' A Joint Law Commission was established to look into the legal issues. The unionists wanted the Republic to deliver on extradition even though the Irish constitution did not allow extradition for political offences; by 1975, none had taken place. It was agreed that people committing crimes of violence in Ireland, however motivated, should be brought to trial wherever they were arrested, allowing members of the IRA to be tried in the Republic for offences committed in the North. The British government indicated a willingness to devolve responsibility for policing to the executive and to end internment as soon as the security situation permitted. There was also a vague hint in the Sunningdale communiqué that policing might become the responsibility of the Council of Ireland.

The Unionists Pushed Too Far?

With the benefit of hindsight, it is clear that the unionists were out-manoeuvred at Sunningdale and pushed 'too far' towards a settlement. Garret Fitzgerald, the Irish foreign affairs minister, noted at the time, 'On any objective assessment the Irish government and the SDLP have gained most and the Unionists least' (Fitzgerald 1991, p. 220). The Irish government and the SDLP, after the event, 'began to confess ruefully that they had had too easy a victory. But after all, they had fought their own corner and had expected others to do likewise' (Kyle 1975, p. 441). It should have been clear to the participants at Sunningdale that Faulkner was already coming under serious pressure both from within his own party and from loyalist rivals to the UUP over his participation in power-sharing. His ability to deliver sufficient unionists to an accommodation was therefore highly constrained. The Irish government threw its weight behind the

SDLP at Sunningdale, whereas the British government attempted to play the role of 'honest broker' between nationalists and unionists. The UUP delegation appeared ill-prepared for the talks and came under considerable pressure not only from nationalists but also from Edward Heath, the British prime minister. The *Irish Times*' correspondent later commented that Heath's 'desire to rid himself of his Irish incubus' led him to bully Faulkner. He 'sided, again and again, with the SDLP; he ensured that the outcome was precisely what was sought by the representatives of the Northern Ireland Catholics' (*Irish Times*, 13 August 1974; Faulkner 1978, p. 234; Downey 1983, p. 126; White 1984, pp. 145–6; 153 Bew and Patterson 1985, p. 64).

The contrast between the behaviour of the British and Irish governments was a strong one. The Republic, together with the SDLP, declared its support for Irish unity, while the British declared that it would implement the will of the majority, not favour the Union. This was a position Heath had taken up since at least 1971 and restated at Sunningdale. Both the British and Irish governments assumed that if Faulkner accepted something then he could sell it (White 1984, pp. 146, 152). However, both Paddy Devlin of the SDLP, and Conor Cruise O'Brien of the Irish government's delegation, were concerned that Faulkner was being pushed too hard. Paddy Devlin told O'Brien and the Alliance party delegates, 'Look, we've got to catch ourselves on here. Brian Faulkner is being nailed to a cross. There is no way Faulkner can sell this' (White 1984, p. 152). Garret Fitzgerald later recalled that Devlin 'was not going to have his friends . . . hung from lamp-posts on their return to Belfast, as they assuredly would be if the list of executive functions we had agreed were published' (Fitzgerald 1991, p. 215; see also White 1984, p. 159). The list of powers was subsequently reduced, but British and Irish governments were dismissive of the dangers to Faulkner's position. Whitelaw later told Conservative commentator T. E. Utley, 'you always told me that I was driving Faulkner too far. My goodness, you were right! But what a damned fool he was to allow himself to be driven' (*The Times*, 7 May 2005).

There was plenty of scope for loyalists to exploit the detail of Sunningdale to rally unionists against the agreement. The British position on the Council of Ireland had shifted from giving it 'some executive functions and a consultative role' to having 'executive and harmonisation' functions (Bew and Patterson 1985, p. 60). The Council of Ireland could be interpreted as having the makings of an all-Ireland Parliament. The Council of Ministers was to be a free-standing, executive body with what were likely to be extensive powers and without a need to have its decisions ratified by the NI Assembly. The Consultative Assembly also had the potential to develop from a consultative role into a legislative all-Ireland Parliament. The British failed to move significantly over internment or on reform of the RUC, in spite of strong pressure from the Irish government. This probably led the SDLP to focus on and play up its gains on the Council of Ireland (Bew and Patterson 1985, p. 59; Bew and Gillespie 1993, p. 74).

If the British had conceded on the security agenda then Faulkner's position might have been undermined as much by changes in security policy as by the Council of Ireland. Some opinion polls indicate that security issues are probably more divisive in Northern Ireland than the constitutional question. Faulkner perhaps calculated that he could more easily deliver a *symbolic* Council of Ireland, on which unionists had a veto, than tamper with the RUC (a powerful guarantor of the Union and unionist power). In this Faulkner underestimated the symbolic importance of the Council to unionists (Faulkner 1978, pp. 229, 237). For many unionists the detail of the Sunningdale Agreement was likely to be obscured by the aim of Irish nationalists, through modernization, to bring about a united Ireland and widespread suspicion of British intentions and guarantees. For many unionists, their perceptions of the track record of the parties and governments involved in Sunningdale was probably a better guide to their disposition and the outcome of any agreement than the rhetoric and ambiguity of the Sunningdale communiqué. Loyalists were overwhelmingly opposed to Sunningdale. But even the moderate 'unionists' of the Alliance Party were concerned at the power of the Council of Ireland (White 1984, pp. 155–6).

The Irish government largely failed to deliver its share of the Sunningdale Agreement to the Faulkner unionists. This may have been because of its vulnerability to nationalist pressure from the opposition Fianna Fáil Party. The Irish government's recognition of Northern Ireland was one of the few gains for unionism, but this became devalued by the Boland case in the Republic, which contested the Irish government's decision to endorse the Agreement claiming that Sunningdale was contrary to the Irish Constitution. In defending itself against Boland's charges, the Irish government denied that any part of Ireland was part of the UK, denied that majority consent was necessary for Irish unity, and claimed that Sunningdale was merely a statement of policy and represented only de facto recognition of Northern Ireland. The Irish government attempted to retrieve the situation by reassuring unionists and claiming that the factual position was that Northern Ireland was part of the UK and could not be changed without majority consent (Bew and Gillespie 1993, pp. 78–9, 81). The Irish government also failed to deliver on extradition, and the Joint Law Enforcement Commission later recommended that, instead of extradition, the courts in the Republic could try people for offences committed in the North (Gillespie 1998, pp. 104–5).

Leading figures in the SDLP clearly saw the Council of Ireland, modelled on the 'modernizing' institutions of the EEC, as a step down the road to a united Ireland (White 1984, p. 145; Devlin 1975, p. 32; see also Chapter 3 above). Public declarations of this boosted the argument of the anti-power-sharing loyalists. In December 1974, the SDLP's Austin Currie claimed that Sunningdale 'fulfilled Wolfe Tone's desires to break the connection with England and substitute the common name of Irishman for Catholic, Protestant and Dissenter' (*Irish Times*, 17 December 1973, quoted in Gillespie 1998, p. 107). The Irish prime minister, Liam Cosgrave, gave an interview, arguing that Sunningdale meant that a united Ireland was on the way (White 1984, p. 156). The following month, Hugh Logue of the SDLP infamously told a heckler in Dublin that the Council of Ireland was 'the vehicle which will trundle Unionists into a United Ireland'. This statement confirmed unionists' worst fears about Sunningdale and, coupled with the Boland case and the failure to deliver on extradition, severely damaged what chances Faulkner had of selling the settlement to unionism. The fragility of the power-sharing experiment was not apparent to the British public, who were being led to assume that, based on a 'moderate majority', the Northern Ireland conflict had been resolved, at least for a generation.

Selling Sunningdale

Power-sharing unionism's grip on the UUP was disintegrating, and in December the United Ulster Unionist Council (UUUC) was founded to unite anti-Sunningdale unionism (Gillespie 1998, pp. 105–8). The power-sharing experiment got under way on 1 January 1974, but three days later the UUC voted against the Sunningdale settlement by 454 votes to 374 and Faulkner resigned as UUP leader. According to Gillespie, 'Faulkner's resignation as leader of the Ulster Unionists ended the moral legitimacy of the Sunningdale deal and killed

Sunningdale as an effective political package.' Faulkner had been invited to participate in the executive as leader of the UUP but, since he was no longer leader, on what basis was he included in the executive (Gillespie 1998, p. 108)? Although the power-sharing parties had represented a majority of the people of Northern Ireland, Faulkner only represented a minority of the unionist population. The agreement reached by Faulkner on the composition of the executive and at Sunningdale was not to be submitted by the elites for the endorsement of the electorate. The insulation of the power-sharing executive until the next Assembly elections, due in 1977, would, it was hoped, give power-sharing a chance to work and prove its worth to the people of Northern Ireland.

The British General Election of February 1974 was called for domestic reasons and gave opponents of power-sharing the opportunity to hold a referendum on Sunningdale. The result further dispelled hopes in the moderate silent majority as power-sharing unionists were decimated at the polls. The SDLP retained its share of the vote but the APNI share dropped from 9.2 per cent to 3.1 per cent, and Faulkner's unionists (13.1 per cent) were heavily defeated. The anti-Sunningdale parties, who had joined together in the UUUC, won a majority (51.1 per cent) of the vote under the slogan 'Dublin is only a Sunningdale away'. The *Belfast Telegraph* revised its 'moderate' analysis and, after anti-Sunningdale unionism's 'sweeping victory' at the polls, dropped its criticism of 'loyalist populism' as being unrepresentative and undemocratic. The executive lacked 'representation of the loyalist masses' and, to save power-sharing, loyalists would now have to be appeased (Bromley 1989, pp. 220–1).

The newly elected Labour government refused to hold fresh elections to the Assembly to take into account the shift in mood of the unionist population, and announced that there would be no elections to the Assembly for four years. The new Secretary of State for Northern Ireland, Merlyn Rees, was pessimistic about the prospects for power-sharing and made contingency plans in the event of its collapse (Rees 1985, p. 60; Donoughue 1987, pp. 128–9; Whitelaw 1989, p. 122). He described power-sharing as 'a remarkable achievement' which was 'almost unbelievable' given the history and strong pressures on elected representatives in the region (Rees 1974). By April 1974, Rees did not believe the executive could last much longer and shared Faulkner's view that there should be a watering down or abandonment of the Council of Ireland, but he was overruled in the cabinet by Wilson and Callaghan (Devlin 1975, pp. 16–17; Downey

1983, p. 134; Bew and Patterson 1985, p. 66; Benn 1989, p. 137; Fitzgerald 1991, p. 232).

The Labour government's announcement of a security strategy of normalization reinforced unionist fears of a British withdrawal. Normalization combined an attempt to Ulsterize the burden of security, putting the locally recruited UDR and RUC in the frontline as far as possible and reducing the exposure of the British Army, with criminalization, treating paramilitary violence as a criminal rather than a political act (*Hansard*, vol. 871, col. 1466, 4 April 1974; Dixon 1997b). With fewer soldiers on the streets, and paramilitaries being treated like common criminals, the conflict would appear to the outside world as a 'normal' issue of law and order. Complementing normalization was the legalisation of Sinn Féin and the UVF to encourage their participation in the political process. The unionist *Newsletter* argued: 'Little wonder anger is growing. Little wonder the majority, particularly, are more convinced than ever that the real British design must be to scuttle, or . . . get out at the earliest possible opportunity through the offices of the Council of Ireland' (*Newsletter*, 15 April 1974).

Unionists complained, with some reason, that the Sunningdale settlement was being imposed over the heads of the people of Northern Ireland (*Newsletter*, 25 and 28 February 1974). Following the election, Faulkner attempted to shore up his diminishing support by taking a more hardline stance; he opposed the Council of Ireland unless the Republic repealed its territorial claim. Unionists and the Alliance preferred a gradual approach to the ratification of Sunningdale, to allow unionism to become accustomed to the operation of the executive and to prevent further antagonism. Faulkner and the British government heightened unionist insecurities by using the threat of British withdrawal in an attempt to scare unionists into supporting the executive as a least-worst alternative. There was also some evidence of unrest among the SDLP. Paddy Duffy, the SDLP's Treasurer, spoke of the possibility of a reassessment of party policy in favour of joint British and Irish rule for ten to fifteen years before Irish unity if Sunningdale was not ratified (*Newsletter*, 7 May 1974).

Opinion polls continued to indicate considerable support among Catholics for power-sharing and a Council of Ireland, but much less so among Protestants. An NOP poll conducted between 31 March and 7 April 1974 found 69 per cent of the people of Northern Ireland favoured giving the executive and Sunningdale a chance. However, while 72 per cent (against 4 per cent) of Catholics thought the Sunningdale proposal for a Council of Ireland was a good rather than a bad idea in principle, only 26 per cent of Protestants thought it was good in principle, while 52 per cent thought the Council of Ireland was bad. Around 55 per cent of Catholics said power-sharing was their most favoured solution to the conflict, but only 18 per cent of Protestants did (Rose *et al.* 1978). Reflecting on this period, Rees claims to have been less impressed by opinion polls than by a petition demonstrating the strength of loyalist opposition to Sunningdale (Rees 1985, p. 59).

The Ulster Workers' Council Strike: Politics in the Streets

The power-sharing executive came under pressure from both republicans and loyalists. The IRA escalated its bombing campaign in the spring of 1974 to undermine power-sharing and break the British government's will to remain in Northern Ireland (*The Sunday Times*, 7 April 1974). The power-sharing executive was brought down in May 1974 by the 14-day-long loyalist Ulster Workers' Council strike. This 'general' strike was precipitated by a decision to ratify Sunningdale in the Assembly, by 44 votes to 28. The strike paralysed Northern Ireland, in particular by a series of power-cuts, and brought the power-sharing executive to its knees.

There is considerable controversy over the nature of the UWC strike. There are two main schools of thought: first, a more 'nationalist' view sees the power-sharing experiment as a viable initiative that was beginning to reap dividends for the people of Northern Ireland. It stresses the importance of the loyalist paramilitaries and intimidation in the success of the UWC strike, and argues that the Labour government lacked the nerve to deploy troops early in the strike; if it had, the strike would have collapsed (Anderson 1994, pp. 29, 32). Second, a more 'unionist' perspective emphasizes the spontaneity of the strike and the widespread support it quickly gained among unionist civil society and the masses, frustrated by an unrepresentative political elite. The role of intimidation is acknowledged, particularly at the start of the strike, but the strike's popular appeal among unionists is emphasized. The executive was 'effectively dead' by December 1973 (Gillespie 1998, p. 112), perhaps more apparently following Faulkner's loss of his party's support in January and the rout of power-sharing unionists at the February 1974 election. From this perspective, the executive was likely to collapse in any case, whatever the Labour government or participants in the executive did. In this context, the British government's failure to act against the UWC and risk confrontation with unionism is more understandable, particularly in light of the 'security dilemma' and fear of a war on two fronts.

The decision to call the UWC strike was taken by a new Protestant working-class leadership rather than solely by the traditional elected representatives of the loyalist community. It consisted of paramilitary leaders and factory workers, including several active trade unionists, and was seen by many as an important development in Protestant working-class consciousness (Fisk 1975, pp. 48, 64). The organizers of the strike were non-party loyalists who were suspicious of their political representatives. The loyalist politicians opposed the strike and only threw their full weight behind it once it was apparent that it was gaining increasing public support (Anderson 1994, pp. 71–2). 'The politicians seemed to have been a moderating influence inside the [UWC] Committee, constantly advising against pushing people too far' (Anderson 1994, p. 89; also p. 26). Harry West, a leading anti-power-sharing unionist, argued that the strike was not aimed at democratic government but at an imposed government:

> The Executive is a group of people appointed by an English politician who is not answerable in any way to the assembly or to the Ulster electorate. It is the appointed Executive which is supposed to represent Northern Ireland in any Council of Ireland. The whole Sunningdale project is thus completely dissociated from any kind of control. (Anderson 1994, p. 137)

The *Newsletter* suggested that unionists had, in recent years, been herded by the British government towards the edge of a cliff and had gone along with this until the point at which they were being asked to jump. During the UWC strike they were saying 'No' (*Newsletter* editorial, 27 May 1974). Popular support for the strike gathered pace among unionists as it was seen as the only means by which an imposed system of government could be removed. The *Belfast Telegraph* 'miscalculated the strength of loyalist opposition to the arrangements proposed at Sunningdale and showed little appreciation of the underlying fears of British withdrawal which drew many loyalists into supporting alternative constitutional schemes' (Bromley 1989, p. 228).

The Labour government appealed to the 'moderate silent majority' to assert themselves against these 'Protestant fascists' who were an

'intimidating, bullying minority'. The Northern Ireland labour movement failed to live up to the hopes invested in it, as a 'Back to Work'
march failed and the NILP's vote declined. The official trade union
movement had to fight off challenges to its authority from loyalist
workers' organizations who felt that it was politically unrepresentative of their workers' views. The apparent success of the Northern
Ireland trade union movement in keeping violence off the shop floor
may have misled observers into believing they had more of a 'moderating' influence over their members than was the case. Although
unions did contain both Catholic and Protestant members, 'The situation however has only been reached by carefully avoiding many
of the contentious issues which divided Northern Ireland society,
and indeed almost any hint of political controversy' (Darby 1976,
pp. 150–1; Whyte 1990, p. 39). Belatedly, the SDLP realized
Faulkner's failing popular support and attempted to shore up his
position and reassure unionism by phasing in the Council of Ireland.
Backbench SDLP Assembly members rejected the compromise package and a Labour Minister of State warned them that if they did not
support it they would lose the support of the Labour Party, which
had been so important in giving the SDLP influence at Westminster (Dixon 1995a, p. 169). The SDLP took a further vote, narrowly
endorsing the package.

   The executive did not have any security powers and was reliant
on the Labour government taking a security initiative to break the
strike. The government was reluctant to send the army in against
the strikers, risking a violent confrontation with unionism, but it was
also unable to run essential services. There were real concerns that
deploying the British army, which Rees felt was his 'only firm base'
in Northern Ireland, to break the UWC strike would have precipitated a violent confrontation with loyalists and the dreaded 'war
on two fronts' (Fisk 1975, p. 203; see also Chapter 4 above). Rees
believed that 'in their hearts' the RUC supported the UWC strike
and an adviser to the Labour government claimed that there were
limits to what the RUC would do against their religious brethren.
Rees argued: 'It is one thing to fight the IRA and quite another
to fight a whole community' (Rees 1985, p. 90; see also Fisk 1975,
pp. 203–4; Donoughue 1987, p. 129). Wilson's 'Spongers Speech'
sealed the fate of the executive: the British prime minister attacked
'people who spend their lives sponging on Westminster and British
democracy and then systematically assault democratic methods'.
Faulkner recalled the 'immense damage' done by Wilson's insulting

speech, which 'brought out Provincial feeling against him and vastly increased popular support for the strike' (Faulkner 1978, p. 276). In his resignation statement, Faulkner finally accepted that 'from the extent of support for the present stoppage ... the degree of consent needed to sustain the Executive does not at present exist' (McAllister 1977b, p. 145). British policy towards Northern Ireland since 1972 collapsed with the power-sharing executive.

Blaming 'Them', Not 'Us'

The Labour government's explanation of the UWC strike reversed following the executive's collapse. Initially, Labour had taken the 'Irish nationalist' line that the loyalist strikers were 'Protestant fascists', bullies who had succeeded through intimidation. After the triumph of the strike, Labour shifted towards a more unionist position, suggesting the inevitability of power-sharing's failure and so distancing the Labour government from responsibility for its collapse. In his British nationalist 'Spongers Speech', Wilson had rallied 'us', the 'British' people, against 'them', the people of Northern Ireland, tapping into chauvinist, populist sentiment which manifested itself in opinion polls supporting withdrawal (Dixon 1996a):

> The people on this side of the water, British parents, British taxpayers, have seen their sons vilified and spat upon and murdered. They have seen the taxes they have poured out almost without regard to cost ... going into Northern Ireland. They see property destroyed by evil violence and are asked to pick up the bill for re-building it. Yet people who benefit from this now viciously defy Westminster, purporting to act as though they were an elected government, people who spend their lives sponging on Westminster and British democracy and then systematically assaulting democratic methods. Who do these people think they are?

This speech was a far cry from Wilson's position in September 1971, when he claimed that the Northern Ireland conflict was 'within our house, within our national family' (*Hansard*, vol. 823, col. 22, 22 September 1971).

The Labour government turned its back on the 'moderates' and talked up the importance of a new Protestant nationalism displayed during the strike, which it viewed as a new class awareness that might form the basis for an accommodation among working-class

Protestants and Catholics. For a time, the UWC was seen, along with the loyalist paramilitary groups (the UVF and UDA), as perhaps a more accommodating, and representative, alternative to the sterility and intransigence of unionist politicians (this argument was also heard during the second peace process) (Dixon 1997d). The UVF launched the Volunteer Political Party which rather unsuccessfully contested elections (Nelson 1984, ch. 14). In the Westminster election of October 1974 and the Convention election of May 1975 the 'hardline' trajectory of unionist opinion was confirmed and power-sharing unionists were decimated. However, the nationalist SDLP was not punished by their electorate for their involvement in the power-sharing experiment. Garret Fitzgerald reported that Rees told him: 'much of the trouble in Northern Ireland in the previous five years had derived from taking advice too often from moderates' (Fitzgerald 1991, pp. 244–5).

Lessons?

The power-sharing experiment probably came closer than any other initiative during 'the Troubles' until the second peace process (1994–2007) to managing successfully the conflict in Northern Ireland. Competing interpretations of its collapse can be coupled with different prescriptions for resolving the conflict.

'Power-sharing Collapsed because Unionists Opposed Power-sharing and the Irish Dimension'

This bleak interpretation suggests that unionists were unwilling to share power with Catholics and dressed up their opposition to power-sharing by focusing on the Council of Ireland. This is indicated by Faulkner's lack of a mandate for entering into power-sharing with the SDLP, and therefore his eroding support even before the negotiations at Sunningdale. For republicans, this interpretation underlines the fact that no partitionist accommodation was possible with intransigent unionism; a resolution to the conflict could only come through a military campaign to bring about a united Ireland. For nationalists, however, this argument might imply the need to impose a settlement over the heads of the unionists, such as the Anglo-Irish Agreement 1985. For unionists, the lack of support for power-sharing might imply either a more integrationist settlement treating Northern Ireland like any other part of the UK, or even independence. Some of those unionists who worked to bring down power-sharing, David Trimble and John Taylor, later emerged as champions of the Good Friday Agreement in 1998.

'Power-sharing Collapsed because of the Irish Dimension'

This interpretation suggests that Sunningdale was 'a bridge too far'. Faulkner was pushed too hard in the negotiations at Sunningdale, the Irish government did not deliver its share of the settlement and as a result the Northern Ireland prime minister was unable to sell the package to the unionist community. Evidence is provided – from opinion polls, unionist opinion, newspapers and politicians – which suggests that unionists might well have accepted power-sharing with nationalists if this had not included an Irish dimension, or such a strong Irish dimension. The close result on the UUC in favour of power-sharing, but before Sunningdale, indicates at the least a party finely balanced on the issue and perhaps anxious at the prospect of negotiating the Irish dimension. The implication from this interpretation is that power-sharing is a viable settlement to the conflict in Northern Ireland as long as it is not encumbered with an Irish dimension, or at least with a weaker Irish dimension than that outlined at Sunningdale.

'Power-sharing and the Irish Dimension Collapsed because of the Weakness of the Labour Government'

This view is held by nationalists but also by some power-sharing unionists who blame the British rather than the executive for the collapse of power-sharing. This nationalist interpretation blames the Conservatives for calling the February 1974 election at a vulnerable time for the executive, and the Labour government for not using force to nip the UWC strike in the bud and prevent the paramilitary intimidation that was the key to its success. It suggests that what is required in the future is for the British government to face down any unionist resistance, if necessary by force. This breaking of the 'unionist veto' on constitutional developments would provoke a reassessment within that community of its relationship with Britain and make it more amenable to accommodation. However, the British had attempted and failed to coerce the mass of unionists into the

Sunningdale settlement, indicating the weakness of this approach. Neither did the confrontation between the British government and unionism after the Anglo-Irish Agreement 1985 (AIA) provoke the reassessment among unionism that nationalists had predicted. If anything, confrontation over Sunningdale and the AIA appeared, at least initially, to harden attitudes among unionists.

'Power-sharing Failed because the Political Environment was too Polarized to Sustain it'

This argument suggests that the power-sharing experiment was too far ahead of its time. The intensity of the violence and the rapidly changing and uncertain political environment was not conducive to building an accommodation between unionists and nationalists. The non-participation in the 'peace process' of loyalist and republican paramilitaries and their determination to destabilize the executive, along with the ambiguity of British government policy, were significant factors in the failure of the experiment. The structural constraints were such that it was simply beyond the power of the various agents (politicians, parties, governments) to bridge the gap.

Conclusion

The British government's policy towards Northern Ireland has combined elements of both a bottom-up approach, focusing on reform and reconciliation from below, and a top-down approach, focusing on an elite settlement. The government favoured reconciliation through the promotion of non-sectarian parties, 'integration' and grassroots 'reconciliation' work; and, at least initially, had faith in 'the people' or civil society as a 'moderating' influence. The elections of June 1973 were a severe setback to the hopes of a more voluntary power-sharing accommodation, and the British government took an increasingly coercive and elitist (top-down) approach, as pressure was exerted on the constitutional parties towards the centre ground. With hindsight, it is clear that Faulkner and power-sharing unionists were out-negotiated at Sunningdale by nationalists and pushed 'too far' by the British. The February 1974 General Election demonstrated that unionism was strongly opposed to the deal. The British and Irish governments took little action to shore up power-sharing unionism and it eventually succumbed to the power of unionist civil society and mass protest during the UWC strike.

The British government has to share responsibility for creating the climate of constitutional uncertainty and grievance in which the unbalanced Sunningdale settlement failed. Unionist fears that power-sharing and Sunningdale represented an attempt to manipulate Northern Ireland out of the Union were 'reasonable' (rather than paranoid), given British policy during this period. The British parties were impatient at their inability to resolve the conflict in Northern Ireland and appeared ready to off-load the problem if possible. At this point the easiest route to British extrication appeared to be through Irish unity, with which there was considerable sympathy at Westminster among both the Labour *and* Conservative parties. Harold Wilson later argued in his memoirs that the continuation of Sunningdale and power-sharing was a more radical and speedy way of uniting Ireland than his 15-point plan (Wilson 1979, p. 70; see also Haines 1977, p. 114).

By pushing pro-power-sharing unionists 'too far', the chances of reaching a compromise – whether 'just' or not – that all parties could sell to their supporters were not maximized. The failure of the SDLP to be punished by its electorate for its involvement in power-sharing, in spite of its concessions during the UWC strike, and its lack of an electoral rival, indicates that the SDLP might have been able to move further towards Faulkner's position without jeopardizing its electoral support (although there were problems in managing the party; see Dixon 1997c, 1997d). Yet even if a deal had been cut more 'evenly' between nationalists and unionists there is still doubt as to whether the pro-power-sharing forces had sufficient support or a sufficiently favourable political environment in which to make such a deal work.

The shadow of Sunningdale was apparent during the second peace process. A former Conservative claimed in 1994 that any settlement would be 'Sunningdale plus', which begged the question of why, if Sunningdale failed in 1974, should a similar settlement be more successful? During the negotiations of the Good Friday Agreement 1998, an adviser to the UUP said, referring to Sunningdale, that his party's negotiators could 'see the ghosts of the past in the corridors' (*Irish Times*, 3 April 1998). Seamus Mallon famously argued that the Good Friday Agreement 1998 was 'Sunningdale for slow learners', these were those unionists and republicans who had worked to bring down a similar power-sharing deal twenty-five years before.

6

The Limits of British Policy, 1974–81: From Withdrawal to Integration

The UWC strike and the two Westminster elections of 1974 destroyed the assumption on which British bipartisan policy had rested since at least the introduction of direct rule in 1972. This was that there existed a 'moderate majority' for compromise, and that unionist and nationalist 'extremists' had little popular support within their communities, but relied on intimidation to impose their will. The sweeping success of the loyalist coalition in the February 1974 General Election and the popular support for the UWC strike exploded the myth that, on the loyalist side at least, the 'moderate silent majority' were coerced by a small group of 'extremists' who had no popular support. It was not until the Hunger Strikes of 1981 that the extent of the Provisionals' popular support became obvious. Having defied Britain's attempts to 'impose' a settlement, there was now a widespread expectation in Northern Ireland that the Labour government would live up to its threats and withdraw. This period established the parameters of British policy towards Northern Ireland. Why did Britain not withdraw after the collapse of power-sharing? What explains Britain's 'pro-unionist' policy between 1974 and 1979? Why did Mrs Thatcher abandon the unionism of the Conservatives' 1979 manifesto and sign the Anglo-Irish Agreement in 1985? To what extent has British policy towards Northern Ireland been constrained and therefore characterized by continuity?

The Withdrawal Option

Opinion polls suggested that, in British public opinion, withdrawal from Northern Ireland would have been a popular policy. Merlyn

152

Rees had been preoccupied with the effect that the collapse of the executive might have on British public opinion and its support for withdrawal, particularly since it was those who proclaimed loyalty to the British Crown who had defied the British Parliament and its policy (Rees 1985, pp. 92–3; Fitzgerald 1991, pp. 237–8). In the early 1970s, Labour spokespeople had made public threats of 'consequences' if power-sharing was brought down. Privately, the Labour leadership referred to the option of withdrawal from Northern Ireland by the codename 'Algeria' (Haines 1977, p. 114; Donoughue 1987, p. 128). In April 1974 an Irish government delegation met Wilson and were unhappy with his talk of an 'agonising reappraisal' on the issue of British troops serving in Northern Ireland if the executive fell (Fitzgerald 1991, pp. 233–4). Following the collapse of power-sharing, withdrawal was seriously considered by a cabinet sub-committee of the Labour government. The other main possibilities considered were repartition and the creation of a 'no-man's-land' along the border with the Republic. 'The committee ended up rejecting all three possibilities, arguing that all of them would probably aggravate the problem still further' (Bew and Patterson 1985, p. 77).

The British Labour government rejected the withdrawal option above all because it was thought likely to destabilize Britain and Ireland. According to Rees, 'A declaration of intent to withdraw was not on; the position of the Army would become untenable immediately such a declaration was made, irrespective of the time-scale given' (Rees, quoted in 'Minutes of meeting between the Secretary of State at the NIO [Northern Ireland Office] and a Conservative Deputation led by Mr Neave', 12 December 1975). Following a British withdrawal, it was expected that sectarian conflict between loyalists and republicans would have led to an irresistible demand in the Republic for it to send its army North to protect nationalists. Civil war in Ireland could have destabilized the Southern government and British trade with a key partner. According to a British 'secret military analysis', the regular Irish Army 'would not necessarily be decisive, either militarily or politically' against Northern unionists (Donoughue 1987, p. 133). It was also feared that the civil war would spill over into Britain, particularly those cities in which there was a large Irish community (*Sunday Times*, 26 May 1974). The civil service advised Rees that a unilateral withdrawal would be followed by a 'catastrophic breakdown of control . . . accompanied by major violence'. A gradual withdrawal without power-sharing would result in a loyalist government that would receive no support from the South against republican violence (Rees 1985, p. 99). The pressure of international opinion and the destabilization created by the conflict might have resulted in Britain re-intervening, but this would probably have required the deployment of even greater force.

The debate on Northern Ireland within the higher echelons of the Conservative Party gives a sense of the constraints operating on British policy regardless of which party was in power. In September 1975, Margaret Thatcher's 'Leader's Steering Committee' considered the options on Northern Ireland:

> It was agreed that withdrawal was not a solution to violence in either Northern Ireland or in Britain. It was agreed that a United Ireland was not feasible. Repartition was discussed, and views expressed for and against. The difficulties of a large-scale population movement and of agreeing a new boundary with the Dublin Government were referred to, though it was felt that the idea needed careful examination. Direct Rule was thought inevitable, at least in the short term, if the Convention broke down. ('Leader's Steering Committee', LSC (75) 41 minutes, 10 September 1975)

A draft paper by Airey Neave, the Shadow Secretary of 'State for Northern Ireland, entitled 'Debate on Northern Ireland', considered the long-term options for Northern Ireland. Direct rule had value 'only as a medium-term measure' and 'was not attractive as a medium-term solution'. Integration would end uncertainty over Northern Ireland's constitutional position but 'it would increase the burden at Westminster at a time when devolution for Scotland and Wales is contemplated. It would worsen relations with the minority and the Republic'. Repartition 'is impractical except in a civil war situation, when fear rather than policy would lead to de facto repartition'. A federal Ireland 'has drawn no significant support'. As for independence, 'It can be argued that Northern Ireland is a financial and military burden; that local politicians remain unco-operative; and that the British public are fed up with Northern Ireland: however, without the British Army there would be all-Ireland civil war.' 'National Army morale would suffer a blow from an apparent defeat by terrorists. Britain would face international opprobrium for creating a "Congo" situation, and a militant extremist state could appear on our doorstep, with serious consequences for our social order.' Withdrawal would also conflict with successive pledges made by the

British government ('Debate on NI: January 12th, LCC/76/95, Draft 4, 22 December 1975).

Some leading British politicians may have felt or hoped that Sunningdale would lead gradually to a united Ireland and remove the issue from British politics. After the power of unionism had been demonstrated during the UWC strike, Irish unity was no longer the most convincing means by which the British could extricate themselves from Ireland without leaving a power vacuum, instability and civil war. The transfer of power to an independent, unionist-dominated, Ulster – bolstered by the overwhelmingly Protestant RUC and UDR – was now likely to be a more effective means of complete British withdrawal (Donoughue 1987, p. 128; for NIO officials on independence, see Fitzgerald 1991, p. 279).

This adaptation to the newly apparent 'realities of power' was indicated by the shifting perspectives of Harold Wilson, James Callaghan and Merlyn Rees, who felt Britain had done its best to impose a settlement but now it was up to the Irish to sort out their own mess (Rees 1985, pp. 94–5). Wilson, who had declared in favour of Irish unity in 1971, developed a 'Doomsday Scenario' involving the announcement of dominion status for Northern Ireland and the transfer of sovereignty to a new constitutional authority, which would permit a British withdrawal (Donoughue 1987, p. 129). As Home Secretary in 1969, Callaghan had argued that independence might be preferable to direct rule. In 1973, Callaghan published *A House Divided*, in which he favoured Irish unity; he had also told Fitzgerald that Irish unity would only require the 'acquiescence' of the people in the North (Fitzgerald 1991, p. 131). By 1981, Callaghan was opting for an independent Ulster, arguing 'that Britain was incapable of ever offering a settlement that would satisfy both sides' (House of Commons, vol. 7, col. 1046–53, 2 July 1981). Merlyn Rees also shifted his ground, detecting and encouraging a new Ulster nationalism, particularly among 'extremists', that would transcend sectarian divisions in an independent Ulster. Significantly, integration was felt by both Labour and Conservatives to lead to Westminster being even more dominated by Northern Ireland affairs (*Hansard*, vol. 874, col. 1066–8, 4 June 1974; Wilson 1979, p. 128). The government's White Paper *The Northern Ireland Constitution* (1974) described 'a new awareness in the Protestant and Catholic working class of their real interests' (White Paper, para. 53) and some journalists also detected hope in a new common Northern Ireland identity. The UDA, with its New Ulster Political Research Group, unsuccessfully took up the idea of an independent Ulster. There was also a flirtation with independence among some members of the SDLP.

The parameters of British policy were being tested. Irish unity or Ulster independence appeared to be unrealistic options, although the British government may have encouraged the latter in the hope of winning significant nationalist support. The contemplation of these options by the two principal parties in British politics, and their reasons for rejection, suggests that there was little overriding British interest in Northern Ireland beyond stability. The belief among some in the IRA leadership that the British were about to withdraw was not compatible with an analysis that suggested its interests were inextricably bound up with a military presence in the North.

The British government were faced with three 'hard realities':

(i)   there could be no solely military victory to the conflict, as British counter-insurgency strategy made clear (see Chapter 4);

(ii) unionists could not be coerced into a united Ireland (this had been demonstrated during the power-sharing experiment: see Chapter 5);

(iii) there could be no stable and peaceful Northern Ireland unless there was some accommodation to the legitimate demands of nationalists, probably involving power-sharing, if not also an Irish dimension.

Stalemate: The Constitutional Convention

Following the collapse of power-sharing, the British government proposed a Constitutional Convention of the parties in Northern Ireland to negotiate a settlement. The responsibility for a solution was placed with the people and politicians of Northern Ireland. If they failed, Rees later argued, 'it would at least show the world, and give a message to the South of Ireland, that the blame did not all lie with the British' (Rees 1985, p. 107). According to its White Paper, *The Northern Ireland Constitution* (Cmnd 5675), the government continued:

> to believe that the best and most desirable basis for political progress in Northern Ireland would be the establishment of local institutions enjoying broadly-based support throughout the community ... It has always been recognised that there is no means to

impose such a system upon Northern Ireland if substantial sections of its population are determined to oppose it. (para. 48)

While it was acknowledged that there 'is an Irish dimension' it was only vaguely defined and there was no mention, as there had been in Wilson's 15-point plan, of the goal of Irish unity.

The collapse of power-sharing and subsequent elections made it painfully apparent that the centre ground in Northern Ireland had diminished and the likelihood of a new accommodation was a distant one. The October 1974 British General Election results confirmed the dominance of anti-power-sharing unionists as the UUUC increased its share of the poll from 51 per cent to 58 per cent. The Constitutional Convention elections in May 1975 again produced an anti-power-sharing majority, 54.8 per cent of the vote and 47 out of 78 seats. Between the Assembly elections of June 1973 and the Constitutional Convention elections in May 1975 the vote for the centre parties fell from 38.3 per cent to 17.5 per cent, while the loyalist vote rose from 35.4 per cent to 54.8 per cent. A review of opinion polls found that 'British Government policy is vulnerable because the settlement it recommends – power-sharing – is now a minority taste among all four communities within the British Isles ... The concurring majority accepting direct rule appears to do so by default, because there is nothing else that the two communities can agree about' (Rose *et al.* 1978, pp. 45, 47, 52). Even supposing the SDLP was prepared to accept power-sharing without an Irish dimension, there was no guarantee that this would be acceptable to unionist political leaders. The grounds on which an acceptable compromise might be achievable had shifted towards unionism (Fitzgerald 1991, p. 256).

While an Irish dimension appeared no longer to represent practical politics – since unionists had so strongly opposed it – there remained a possibility that power-sharing could be resurrected. In September 1975, William Craig, the notoriously hardline leader of the VUPP, proposed an emergency voluntary coalition government with nationalists. Craig claimed that coalition government in times of national emergencies, such as war, was part of the British political tradition and he proposed giving the SDLP representatives three seats in a voluntary coalition, backed by a strong committee system, which would last for no longer than five years. Ian Paisley initially favoured Craig's emergency coalition proposals but then reversed his position under grassroots pressure and to avoid a split within the DUP (Moloney and

Pollak 1986, pp. 332–5; Smyth 1987, pp. 101–2). Denounced by other loyalist parties, the one hopeful initiative during the Constitutional Convention collapsed, taking with it Craig's political career and the VUPP. Craig's fate was a reminder of the difficulties unionist leaders faced in bringing unionism towards an accommodation.

The UUUC used its majority in the Convention to monopolize the Convention's report to the Secretary of State. It proposed a virtual return to Stormont except for a committee system that would 'give real and substantial influence to an opposition and to make Parliament more effective', a privy council in which some places would be offered to leading members of opposition parties, and a 'Bill of Rights and Duties to protect the rights of the individual citizen'. The representation of the minority in the executive should not be compulsory, and an institutionalized Irish dimension was rejected in favour of good neighbourly relations. Rees told the Commons that the Convention report did not 'command sufficiently widespread acceptance throughout the community to provide stable and effective government' (*Irish Times*, 13 January 1976). The Convention reconvened but failed to find a wider and more acceptable framework. On 5 March 1976, Merlyn Rees said that the government 'does not contemplate any major new initiative for some time to come'.

The Labour government ruled out the options of Ulster independence and Irish unity. With little prospect of a compromise power-sharing settlement, the government fell back on direct rule, insulation and containment. Harold Wilson's senior policy adviser said that after the 'humiliating capitulation' in May 1974, the British prime minister tried not to get too deeply involved in Northern Ireland: 'Our policy became one of consolidation, trying to contain terrorism and just to get through from year to year' (Donoughue 1987, p. 132; see also Haines 1977, p. 112). Northern Ireland no longer appeared as a routine item on the cabinet agenda (Wilson 1977, pp. 65–6). The Prevention of Terrorism Act (PTA) was introduced by the Labour government in response to the IRA's Birmingham pub bombings in November 1974 (killing 19 and injuring 182). The debate on the PTA was characterized by 'the passionate desire of a British Parliament to batten down the hatches, to shut out the ugly, dangerous infection which threatens us from outside' (*New Statesman*, 6 December 1974). The Act made provision for the exclusion of people entering Britain from Northern Ireland, and for their exile to that region, without any requirement to inform the victim of the reasons for their exclusion. The Labour government continued to pursue 'Ulsterization', heightening concerns that the British were withdrawing, but also further insulating the conflict from British politics.

The IRA Ceasefire, 1975–6, and the Fear of British Withdrawal

After the collapse of the executive, the Labour government did not keep the Irish government informed of its Northern Ireland policy (perhaps for fear of further alienating unionists) and appeared to be deliberately cultivating a belief that it was about to withdraw in order to demoralize and defeat the IRA.

The Irish government was concerned that British withdrawal would destabilize Ireland and pose a threat to democratic government in the Republic (Fitzgerald 1991, p. 271). When the British government became engaged in 'contacts' with the IRA, the Irish government opposed these on the grounds that they lent the republicans legitimacy and undermined constitutional nationalism (Fitzgerald 1991, p. 262). This fear was probably sharpened by the impressive displays of unionist violence and power demonstrated by the Protestant backlash in 1972, the loyalist mobilization around the UWC strike, and the loyalist atrocity in Dublin and Monaghan in May 1974, which killed 27 people and injured 120. There have been allegations that the British security forces were involved in these bombings. The Irish government accepted that unionism had been pushed too far at Sunningdale and hoped for some kind of devolved settlement. There were reports that the Irish coalition government feared that, in the event of a British withdrawal, the loyalty of the Irish army could not be counted on and a coup might result in a right-wing Fianna Fáil takeover (Kyle 1975). The Irish government campaigned in the USA and Europe against withdrawal from Northern Ireland and sought reassurances from the British government on the matter (*Irish Times*, 20 July 1983, 21 July 1983). In January 1975, Garret Fitzgerald, the Irish minister for foreign affairs, asked Henry Kissinger to intervene if the British government decided to withdraw, since it would endanger Ireland and even lead to communist influence, an argument that was likely to draw US interest (Fitzgerald 1991, p. 259). The Irish government also warned its EEC partners that most of the solutions being mooted for Northern Ireland would have violent consequences that would sweep across Ireland (*New Statesman*, 22 November 1974). It also refused the SDLP's request to draw up contingency plans for British withdrawal, since this might give the British an excuse to withdraw (Fitzgerald 1991, p. 255). According to a leaked policy document, the Irish government's policy following the UWC strike was to adopt a low profile and avoid any reference to the Irish dimension (seen as an idea in advance of its time), which might reduce the chances of power-sharing by increasing loyalist strength (*Irish Times*, 26 September 1974; Murray 1998, p. 55). The negotiations and truce between the British government and the IRA, in late 1974 and early 1975, were seen as further evidence of British intent to withdraw.

Both major British parties had warned the people of Northern Ireland of the 'consequences' of rejecting the power-sharing experiment, so it was not surprising that after the UWC strike there was a widespread expectation that the British were about to withdraw, leaving behind an independent Northern Ireland. While the Irish government, the SDLP and unionists feared the consequences of British withdrawal, the republican movement thought their time had finally come. The collapse of power-sharing, the establishment of the Constitutional Convention and acceleration of Ulsterization raised expectations within the IRA that they were on the brink of victory, having 'long since forsaken the notion that Britain had any desire to stay in Ireland' (Bew and Patterson 1985, p. 80). Republican expectations of a British withdrawal had reached such a height that Ó Brádaigh warned the British not to withdraw and leave behind a 'Congo situation' (that is, a bloody civil war).

The Labour government exploited republican expectations by entering into a truce with the IRA and using this pretext to further Ulsterize the conflict and demoralize and defeat the republican movement. Successive British governments had attempted to bring the IRA into the political process in 1972. Rees's legalisation of Sinn Féin and the UVF (the UDA had not been banned) and his announcement of the end of internment also represented an attempt to encourage the Provisionals down a political path and a hope that they might contest the Convention elections. He mentioned that given 'a genuine and sustained cessation of violence', anything might be possible, hinting at withdrawal (Smith 1995, p. 130; Taylor 1997, pp. 170–1).

On 10 December 1974, Protestant clergymen met the IRA at Feakle in the Republic of Ireland. The clergymen had drafted a document which they hoped to clear with the Provisionals and the British government. The IRA leader Ruairí Ó Brádaigh maintains that he received a letter from the British government requesting a meeting to devise structures of British withdrawal from Northern Ireland (Taylor 1997, p. 177). William Arlow, one of the Protestant clergymen at Feakle, claimed that the British had given an undertaking to the IRA that if the Convention collapsed the British would begin the process of withdrawal. This is probably the impression that the British government deliberately attempted to convey to the IRA in an attempt to split and demoralize the movement (*Irish Times*, 9 June 1978; *Sunday Times*, 18 June 1978; Bew and Patterson 1985, pp. 82–3). During the truce, the British government refused to give a public undertaking to withdraw, because of the impact this was likely to have on the unionist population, leading to 'a Congo-type situation which both Brits and the Republican Movement wish to avoid. Grave statements lead to the opposite happening' (Republican Minutes, quoted in Taylor 1997, p. 190). The IRA demanded British withdrawal and self-determination, an amnesty for all 'political' prisoners and an end to detention without trial. The IRA leadership demonstrated their control over their movement by calling an unannounced ceasefire on 27 January 1975. This became official on 9 February.

The truce was to be monitored through a number of 'incident centres' manned by Sinn Féin, to avoid the misunderstandings and confrontations that destroyed the 1972 truce. These incident centres, with their 'hot lines' to the government, 'were a watershed in the public perception of Sinn Féin, giving it a political standing in the nationalist community and, more importantly, a physical presence' (Taylor 1997, p. 186). The clear recognition of the political nature of the republican movement and hope that it would contest elections contrasted starkly with the attempt of the government to criminalize the IRA and normalize the conflict. The SDLP and the Irish government were concerned at the boost these centres gave to Sinn Féin's credibility among nationalists in the North.

The loyalists saw the incident centres as further evidence confirming the widespread expectation that the British were withdrawing. In the expectation that the British were about to pull out, loyalist and republican paramilitaries attempted to assert their predominance by turning to sectarian assassination. The loyalist paramilitaries declared their support for an independent Ulster, and between 1974 and 1976 loyalist paramilitaries killed 452 people – 40 per cent of all their victims throughout the conflict (Fay *et al.* 1999, p. 138). In 1975–6 the IRA killed 85 Protestant civilians, while loyalists and loyalist paramilitaries killed at least 171 Catholic civilians (Sutton 1994, p. 198). The strength of the loyalist backlash 'tied up IRA resources and questioned long-held Republican assumptions about the Loyalist community' (Moloney 1980). The victims of republican paramilitaries were increasingly sectarian, being Protestant civilians and the locally recruited security forces (Sutton 1994, p. 198, 202). The republican leadership, split between moderate and hardline factions, had severe difficulty in maintaining the unity of the IRA during the truce (Bew and Patterson 1985, pp. 84–6; Smith 1995, pp. 122, 130). According to Ó Brádaigh, the bilateral truce broke down in September 1975 because of an unprecedented assassination campaign by loyalists; the failure of the British to give a public declaration of intent to leave Ireland; and the attitude of the Irish government in sabotaging the process by hunting down [Dáithí] Ó Conaill and making representations to the British (Ó Brádaigh, *Sunday Tribune*, letters, 17 October 1993; *Irish Times*, 30 April 1992).

There was evidence that Britain was not about to withdraw. On 4 November 1975, Rees announced the abolition of special category status: all those convicted after 1 March 1976 would be treated as 'ordinary criminals'. The criminalization of republican prisoners marked a further step in Britain's strategy of normalization, and republican resistance to this led to the Hunger Strikes of 1981. On 12 November, Rees announced the closure of the incident centres. IRA hopes of a British withdrawal received a further setback when Harold Wilson declared, on 12 January 1976, that a united Ireland was neither a practical proposition nor a solution that any British party would wish to impose, and announced a raft of security measures (Bew and Gillespie 1993, p. 109). Nevertheless, speculation about British withdrawal continued into 1977 (*Irish Times*, 15 January 1977). The last meeting between the Provisionals and representatives of the British government took place on 10 February 1976 (though one account suggests talks 'persisted intermittently until July 1976': *Sunday Times*, 18 June 1978). The British used the truce 'to increase their surveillance and infiltrate the IRA's ranks, and in the first five months of 1976 over 400 people were charged with violent offences' (Smith 1995, p. 133).

British deception during the 1972 and 1975 ceasefires (and later during the Hunger Strikes of 1980–1) led republicans to be suspicious of declaring any future extended ceasefires. In March 1993, the British government representative cited a letter from Rees to Wilson which stated, 'We set out to con them and we did' (Sinn Féin 1993, pp. 28, 31). The old Provisional leadership now made way for the new, younger, more militant, 'Northern leadership' of Adams and McGuinness, who attempted to restore unity and morale to a shattered organization (Patterson 1997, p. 181). Since 1972 the IRA had believed it was on the brink of victory over the British and regularly declared each year to be the 'Year of Victory'. Even in 1977 the IRA continued to declare that victory was close (Smith 1995, pp. 135, 137), but this may have been seen as necessary 'propaganda' to sustain the morale of the organization. During 1977, the IRA finally accepted that their offensive against the British had failed to produce a withdrawal, and that the Southern leadership's 'Truce' strategy had collapsed. The IRA reorganized itself into a cellular structure to minimize the chances of penetration by the security forces, and settled down for the 'Long War'. Simultaneously, there was an attempt to 'broaden the battlefield' beyond the 'armed struggle', to involve republicans in a political struggle in the 'war' against the British presence. According to a captured IRA document on the reorganization of the republican movement, Sinn Féin was to be radicalized 'under army [IRA] direction ... and should agitate about social and economic issues which attack the welfare of the people' (Clarke 1987, pp. 251–3; Patterson 1997, p. 180).

The British government, in the meantime, continued to develop its strategy of normalization. This involved criminalizing the paramilitaries and creating the appearance of a more 'normal' society by Ulsterizing security and putting the police rather than the army in the front line of the fight against terrorism/criminality. The truce and the increasingly communal nature of the violence reduced the pressure on the British army, and this finally allowed the government to implement its policy of Ulsterization and police primacy. The army resisted its loss of power and there was considerable counterproductive rivalry with the RUC. According to some reports, the army was also running its own propaganda war against Merlyn Rees, unhappy with the government's 'contacts' with the IRA and its policy for the release of detainees. At the end of March 1975, the Labour government asserted its control over the army's 'black propaganda' operation (Curtis 1984, pp. 241–3; Hamill 1985, pp. 177–83; Rees 1985, pp. 225–8, 302; Foot 1989; Mason 1999, p. 166). There has been continuing concern about the lack of political control over the security forces (Urban 1992; Dixon 1997b; Needham 1998).

In 1976 and 1977 over 2,500 people, mainly from the IRA, were convicted of murder, attempted murder, and arms and explosives offences. An internal IRA document admitted that the RUC was having success in breaking down IRA members during interrogation: 'The three-day and seven-day detention orders are breaking volunteers, and it is the Irish Republican Army's fault for not indoctrinating volunteers with the psychological strength to resist interrogation' (Clarke 1987, p. 251). A Provisional leader admitted, 'We were almost defeated' (Moloney 1980; Kelley 1988, pp. 284–5). In August 1978, Amnesty International found that suspects detained in Castlereagh RUC detention centre had been 'ill-treated'. This was confirmed in the subsequent Bennett Report, commissioned by the British government.

Loyalist paramilitary killings and support for independence declined as it became clear that the British government was not going to withdraw. In September 1977, the Secretary of State for Northern Ireland, Roy Mason, declared that 'The myth of British withdrawal is dead forever' (*Irish Times*, 17 September 1977; Loughlin 1995, p. 205). The decline in loyalist paramilitary violence between 1977 and 1985 has been attributed to the effectiveness and increased strength of the RUC against the IRA, reducing the need for para-military organization; the effectiveness of the RUC against the loyalist paramilitaries; and 'the low incidence of dramatic initia-tives and the calming effect this had on unionist perceptions of their precarious position' (Bruce 1999, pp. 191–2).

The battle for leadership of unionism was fought between the UUP and Ian Paisley's DUP. The VUPP had been the third-largest unionist party at the 1975 Convention elections, but by the 1977 local elections its share of the vote was just 1.5 per cent. The UUP managed to establish its dominance in the unionist bloc, increasing its share of the vote from 25.8 per cent in the Convention elections, to 29.6 per cent in the 1977 local elections, and to 36.6 per cent in the 1979 Westminster elections. Ian Paisley's DUP suffered: its share of the vote fell from 14.8 per cent in 1975, to 12.7 per cent in 1977, and to just 10.2 per cent in 1979. In 1977, Paisley entered into a United Unionist Action Council with anti-Craig Vanguard elements, the remnants of the UWC and the UDA. They called a loyalist strike for May 1977 to force the British government to adopt the loyalist Convention Report and more repressive security measures. Roy Mason described the strike as the most dangerous threat to Northern Ireland during his tenure as Secretary of State: 'If Paisley succeeded in unleashing the worst instincts of Ulster loyalism, we probably wouldn't be able to hold the line.' He was concerned that 'civil disobedience could easily spill into open insurrection' (Mason 1999, pp. 173, 185, 190). The UUP opposed the strike, the RUC stood firm and the 10-day strike collapsed. Although Paisley had staked his credibility on a successful outcome, the DUP made significant gains in Council seats in the elections which followed shortly afterwards.

The British Parties and the Ulster Unionists

The close result of the October 1974 Westminster General Election created a strong incentive for both British parties to court Ulster Unionist support in the House of Commons. The Labour government's need to avoid alienating the Ulster Unionists and the pressure from the Conservative Opposition to take a more repressive stand on law and order succeeded in making the period 1976–9 that most fondly remembered by unionists since the outbreak of 'the Troubles' (Dixon 1994b). The election of Mrs Thatcher to the leadership of the Conservative Party in February 1975 led to the appointment of two right-wing, unionist Conservative MPs, Airey Neave and John Biggs-Davison, as respectively opposition Conservative spokesperson and deputy on Northern Ireland. The rhetoric (if not the substance) of bipartisanship was broken as the Conservative front bench became very critical of the Labour government's security policy. Labour's less authoritarian inclinations on security issues did not reflect public opinion and therefore left it vulnerable to Conservative attack. In January 1976, the Labour government united with the Conservative Opposition behind a package of security measures including increased surveillance operations; more checkpoints; more extensive use of personal identity checks; and the official introduction of the Special Air Service (SAS) into Northern Ireland (*Irish Times*, 13 January 1976). On 15 January 1976, Harold Wilson chaired the first all-party security meeting on Northern Ireland. Bipartisanship remained intact because of the parallel shifts in the policy of the Labour government and Conservative opposition, but also because of the strength of 'moderate' or 'wet' Conservatives, who favoured the approach of the Heath government's Irish policy and acted as a check on Neave's unionism. They were resistant to any shift in party policy that abandoned power-sharing and broke the bipartisan approach with the Labour Party (Dixon 1995a, p. 170).

The Labour government, under pressure from the Conservatives and competing with them for the support of the UUP at Westminster, took a more unionist stance on constitutional and security issues. By the end of 1977, Airey Neave had threatened to break bipartisanship on four occasions, but claimed that Labour had now taken over the security policy of the Conservative party (Dixon 1995a, p. 170). The replacement of Rees by the hardliner Roy Mason in September 1976, long demanded by the Conservatives, bolstered bipartisanship and facilitated Labour's attempts to win the support of the Ulster Unionists at Westminster (*Daily Telegraph*, 3 December 1976). The new Labour Secretary of State, accepting the impasse on the constitutional question, took a low-key approach to the constitutional question, emphasizing instead economic and security reforms and concentrating on making direct rule work. But even Mason did not believe a purely military solution was possible (Mason 1999, p. 224). British governments continued to see the promotion of economic prosperity and reducing inequalities as the means by which the conflict could be ameliorated and a climate created in Northern Ireland that would be more conducive to a political settlement. The minority Labour government reached an 'understanding' with the Ulster unionists in 1977. The Labour government's constitutional approach became more unionist, as did the Conservative opposition, moving away from power-sharing and promising to increase Northern Ireland's representation at Westminster in line with its population (Dixon 1994b).

Constitutional Irish Nationalism: The SDLP and the Republic

From the SDLP's perspective, the Labour government had failed to save power-sharing through its inactivity and was now undermining constitutional nationalism by negotiating with the IRA and making concessions to the 'integrationist' unionist agenda. There was debate within the SDLP between, on the one hand, the supporters of Gerry Fitt and the party leadership, who favoured partnership and a strong Irish dimension and, on the other, dissidents in favour of working with loyalists towards British withdrawal and accommodation in an independent Ulster. At its 1976 party conference there was significant support for independence and a complementary motion calling for 'the British government to declare its intentions of withdrawing to give the divided people of Northern Ireland the opportunity to negotiate a final political solution and a lasting peace'. This motion was defeated by only 153 votes to 111, with twelve abstentions and ten out of sixteen of the party's former Convention members voting in favour of a British declaration of intent to withdraw (a key IRA demand). Opponents of a declaration of intent feared this would result in a violent grab for power by republican and loyalist paramilitaries, resulting in civil war and a bloodbath. Ben Caraher, vice chairman of the SDLP, argued, 'The only people who could possibly be considered realistic negotiators would be the paramilitary groups because they would have the power. The SDLP would have no power and little relevance because only those who could enforce their voice would have power.' A British declaration of intent would lead to a collapse of its power and a swift withdrawal: 'The urge to clear out lock, stock and barrel would be overwhelming.' The independence lobby argued that the British were withdrawing in any case, and that the party should be looking to independence as a compromise that would allow loyalists and republican paramilitaries to give up violence and work out alternative constitutional arrangements (*Irish Times*, 6 and 11 December 1976).

The SDLP warned the Labour government that its drift towards integration would result in the alienation of constitutional nationalism to the benefit of the IRA. In September 1977, James Callaghan reassured the SDLP and the Irish government that he was determined to bring about some form of power-sharing (*Irish Times*, 21 September 1977). In October 1977, the Irish Independence Party was founded; it sought British withdrawal from Northern Ireland, following which the people of Northern Ireland might choose independence or a united Ireland (*Guardian*, 8 October 1977). This further increased pressure on the SDLP to adopt a more radically nationalist approach. In 1978, the SDLP party conference passed a carefully worded withdrawal motion with only two dissenters. It called for British disengagement 'as part of an overall political solution' and for a conference of the two governments and the 'two traditions' in the North 'with a view to finding a permanent solution to the Irish problem'. The motion expressed SDLP disaffection without demanding a precipitate or unconditional British withdrawal, which would lend legitimacy to the IRA's political position. This represented an attempt by party leaders to pressurize the British into coercing unionists to deal with nationalists (*Irish Times*, 6 April 1978).

As the prospect of a British withdrawal receded and the Labour government took a more unionist approach to Northern Ireland, so nationalists in the Republic also adopted a more militant stance. In June 1977, the 'greener' Fianna Fáil party replaced the Fine Gael/Labour Coalition as the government of the Republic of Ireland. In 1975, Fianna Fáil published a policy statement arguing for the British government to encourage the unity of Ireland and declare its commitment to implement an ordered withdrawal from Northern Ireland. The Fianna Fáil leader, Jack Lynch, retreated from his party's policy statement. He argued that 'in the present, unstable and emotional atmosphere such a declaration [of intent by the British to withdraw] would be highly dangerous' (Fitzgerald 1991, p. 271). Fianna Fáil's call for a British declaration of intent to withdraw was seen by some as influential in winning the 1977 election. On 11 January 1978, Jack Lynch, the new Taoiseach, called for a British declaration of intent to withdraw, but with no date to be set. Also in that year, the Irish government stated that it would not renew the Sunningdale guarantee given to unionists. Public opinion in the Republic was increasingly supportive of Irish unity: in 1973, 37 per cent indicated that a united Ireland was their preferred solution, and this increased to 42 per cent in 1977, 54 per cent in 1978 and 56 per cent in 1980 (Mair 1987a, p. 90). A 1978 survey of opinion in the Republic found that 75 per cent of respondents endorsed this position (Rose *et al.* 1978, p. 48).

The shift in the position of the SDLP and the Irish government towards a 'greener' withdrawal position may well have been a tactical move to check the unionist drift of British policy. Between 1974 and 1977, for both nationalists and unionists, there was a heightened expectation that the British would pull out. By 1978, withdrawal could be advocated, safe in the knowledge that this policy would not be implemented. This 'greener' stance appeared to provoke a bipartisan British response, with both the Labour government and the Conservative opposition moving to reassure the SDLP on their continuing commitment to power-sharing (Fitzgerald 1991, p. 288). After the Conservative Party's 1979 Westminster election victory, the British government rejected integration and shifted towards devolution. This allowed the SDLP to soften its withdrawal position and, by November 1979, it was calling only for the British to withdraw their constitutional guarantee from unionists (*Guardian*, 5 November 1979). The Irish government also appeared to be shifting its position on the North towards some locally elected devolved administration at Stormont (*Guardian*, 22 November 1979; *Irish Times*, 25 August 1982). However, the election of Charles Haughey to the leadership of Fianna Fáil in December 1979 ended cross-party co-operation in the Republic regarding the North as Haughey took up a more militantly republican stance. He insisted on a British declaration of intent to withdraw, while Fine Gael and Labour preferred Irish unity by consent (Mair 1987a, pp. 98–9).

The US Dimension

During the early 1970s, the US executive did not exert much pressure on the British government over its Irish policy (Wilson 1995; Heath 1998, p. 435). Britain's power-sharing experiment and co-operation with the Republic probably reassured the US government. In 1976, a British junior minister in Northern Ireland reported that the US government would co-operate to stem the flow of funds to republicans so long as the British government acted in an 'even-handed manner': 'there is no alternative to partnership and co-operation in Northern Ireland' (House of Commons, vol. 903, col. 160, 12 January 1976). During the mid-1970s, the SDLP and the Irish government looked to the USA to bring pressure to bear on the British government. The collapse of power-sharing, the truce between the IRA and the British government, the emergence of the 'Peace People' (a cross-community peace movement) and the descent of Northern Ireland into sectarian violence undermined the republican 'anti-imperialist' view of the conflict. This suggested that the British and the IRA were the main protagonists in the conflict and paid little attention to unionist opposition to Irish unity. The process of normalization (criminalization and Ulsterization) allowed the British government to present the violence in Northern Ireland as criminal, anti-terrorist and (even) anti-communist, arguments that were likely to resonate strongly in the 'West'. The British government and constitutional Irish nationalism were united, however, in their attempts to counter Irish-American support for the IRA (Wilson 1995, pp. 109, 119). The rumours about a British withdrawal may have galvanized the Irish government into action against the IRA, which represented a significant threat to the Irish state. The advantage of the Irish government's anti-IRA campaigning in the USA is that it was likely to have more credibility and make a greater impact on an Irish-American audience than the British government might. The Irish government also used arguments about Western security and anti-Marxism to draw the attention of the US audience (Prior 1986, pp. 219–20).

Jimmy Carter, running for the US presidency in 1976, raised the issue of Northern Ireland in his pursuit of the Irish-American vote. Irish republican groups in the USA capitalized on human rights violations in Northern Ireland to galvanize support against the British government. Supporters of constitutional nationalism mobilized to counter republican influence and speak out against the IRA. According to A. J. Wilson, 'Irish-American political leaders had traditionally been reluctant to issue outright condemnations of the republican tradition because they typically supported Irish unity and strategically adopted an ambiguous position on the use of violence.' The 'Four Horsemen' – leading Irish-American figures: Thomas 'Tip' O'Neill, Speaker of the House of Representatives, Senator Ted Kennedy, Senator Daniel Moynihan, and Governor Hugh Carey of New York – issued a statement on 16 March 1977 opposing the use of violence in Northern Ireland. Governor Carey attacked the Provisionals as 'Irish killers' and the OIRA as 'Irish Marxists', and these sentiments were echoed by the liberal Democrat, Senator George McGovern (Wilson 1995, pp. 130, 133). This may have had an effect on the flow of funds to the US-based Irish Northern Aid Committee (NORAID), which is pro-republican, from hard-core republicans, which reached its low point in the second half of 1977 after the Carter initiative and the statement of the 'Four Horsemen' (Guelke 1988, p. 132; Wilson 1995, p. 139). US politicians may have reassessed their attitude to Northern Ireland as the more communal nature of the conflict became apparent after the collapse of power-sharing and the Irish government lobbied to avoid a British withdrawal. The Irish ambassador to Washington, Sean Donlon, has described the way he sought to move Irish-America away from support for violence and a view that Britain was the cause of all the problems, to an Irish nationalist position (Mallie and McKittrick 2001, p. 38–9). The US ambassador to Ireland, William Shannon, explained in 1977:

> Senator Kennedy is typical of most Irish Americans, and myself, in his change of views about the problem in Northern Ireland. When it started in 1969 the civil rights issue burst into flames, and Irish Americans tended to think of it as the final act of the drama which began in 1916. There was an instinctive desire to rally behind the Irish, kick the British out, and reunite the country ... But as the guerrilla war dragged on, people have become much more conversant with the realities and complexities of the situation. Now Irish Americans realise that if the British withdraw it would be nothing like the withdrawal from Dublin in 1922. On the contrary, if Britain was to withdraw now, there would be more violence. (*The Times*, 27 September 1977, quoted in Wilson 1995, p. 140)

The 'Four Horsemen' later called on the British government to launch a new political initiative, envisaging talks between the UUP and the SDLP. They pressured President Carter to issue a state-ment on Northern Ireland, a draft of which, it was reported, 'stressed that the Irish government would have to be represented at any polit-ical discussions' (Wilson 1995, p. 135). A statement on Northern Ireland was issued by President Carter on 30 August 1977, signalling a significant departure in US policy and establishing a precedent for future interventions. It attacked republican supporters in the USA and offered economic aid in the event of a solution to the conflict.

There is a strong argument that constitutional Irish nationalism succeeded in bringing US pressure to bear on the British govern-ment to shift its policy on Northern Ireland. The involvement of the Foreign Office in Northern Ireland affairs from the late 1970s onwards suggests a recognition of the importance of the international dimension of the conflict (Donoughue 1987, p. 135). The British government was attacked for human rights abuses and political inac-tivity by US politicians (Wilson 1995, pp. 156–7), and in 1979 the US State Department suspended the sale of arms to the RUC after pres-sure in Congress. The British government's 'Atkins Initiative' on 25 October 1979 is often attributed to pressure from the USA (Guelke 1988, p. 117; Wilson 1995, pp. 164–5). When the initiative did not make much progress, 'The Four Horsemen were somewhat disap-pointed that the British did not force the unionists into some form of cooperation' (Wilson 1995, p. 164).

Undoubtedly US pressure has been a significant constraint on British policy during 'the Troubles'; the difficulty lies in attempting to assess the extent of US influence. The shift of British policy from integrationism to the 1972–4 policy of power-sharing with an Irish dimension could be attributable to pressures other than US influ-ence. After all, the Sunningdale settlement of 1973 had been agreed at a time when US influence was not thought to be particularly sig-nificant. The impact of US pressure on the Atkins Initiative is largely circumstantial, as there is evidence that British policy was likely to shift away from the integrationism of the Conservative Party's 1979 manifesto even before the British General Election and before the US ban on the sale of guns to the RUC. In any case, the Initiative was not such a departure in British policy since Mason had held talks with the parties. US influence may have been exaggerated; with or without US pressure there were strong, long-term structural constraints oper-ating on British policy which explain the pursuit of power-sharing and an Irish dimension in 1979–80.

Back on Track: The Atkins Talks, 1979, and the Dublin Summit, 1980

The Conservative Party's 'unionist' 1979 General Election manifesto promised on Northern Ireland that 'In the absence of devolved
government we seek to establish one or more elected regional councils with a wide range of powers over local services.' The election
of a Conservative government with a large majority freed both
Labour and Conservative parties from the need to win the support of
Ulster Unionist MPs at Westminster and therefore gave the British
government more room to manoeuvre. The Conservatives disap-
pointed unionists by failing to implement its 'integrationist' manifesto
promise and instead launched an initiative to promote power-sharing
devolution and in 1980 an Anglo-Irish process. Humphrey Atkins
told the Northern Ireland Committee (NIC) of the Conservative
Parliamentary Party 'that he did not intend to go ahead with it
[the regional council scheme] at present since its only supporters
in Northern Ireland were the Official Unionists' (NIC, 31 October
1979). The rapid retreat of Labour and Conservatives from their
more unionist stance after the 1979 election suggests that their previous attitude was a tactical adjustment to win UUP support at
Westminster, as well as a reaction to the polarization of politics in
Northern Ireland.

Airey Neave seems to have been shifting from his integrationist
stance *before* the 1979 election, and the Conservatives were unlikely
to implement their integrationist manifesto.(*Guardian*, 27 March
1979, 31 March 1979; *Daily Telegraph*, 31 March 1979; Prior 1986,
p. 193; Dixon 1998). The integrationism of the Conservative Party's
1979 election manifesto was soon jettisoned and the Conservative
government picked up from where the power-sharing experiment
left off in 1974, pursuing a twin-track strategy. First, power-sharing
and devolution were promoted through the 'Atkins Talks' of 1979–80
and subsequently through Prior's 1982 'Rolling Devolution' initiative.
Second, an Irish dimension was considered by the Atkins Initiative
and promoted through the Anglo-Irish process from 1980 onwards.
Originally, the Atkins Initiative ruled out discussion of the 'Irish
Dimension', but this was forced on to the agenda by the SDLP,
who refused to participate without its inclusion (Bew and Patterson
1985, p. 114). Gerry Fitt resigned from the SDLP over its refusal to
engage in the Atkins Initiative without discussing the Irish dimension
when, he argued, the British had significantly qualified the unionists'

constitutional guarantee (*Guardian*, 22 November 1979). Like Paddy Devlin, who had been expelled in 1977, Fitt was on the more socialist wing of the SDLP and prioritized an accommodation with unionism over the all-Ireland dimension.

The relative continuity of British constitutional policy – in spite of Thatcher's personal unionist sympathies – can be explained in terms of the internal and external constraints operating on it (Dixon 2001b; Dixon 2008). During the 1975–9 period, Thatcher was constrained in her attitude towards Northern Ireland by the threat of intra-party opposition from 'moderate' Conservatives and the importance of bipartisanship. Geoffrey Howe, future foreign secretary involved in the negotiation of the Anglo-Irish Agreement 1985, returned from a visit to Northern Ireland in 1977 arguing that 'the facts of Ulster life virtually compel both major parties to proceed on similar lines on the constitutional questions' ('Report by Geoffrey Howe on visit to Northern Ireland 3rd and 4th July 1977'). After 1979, Margaret Thatcher argues, she realized that to defeat terrorism she had to undermine support for republicanism. This would not be achieved by implementing the Conservative manifesto's integrationist policy, since this would alienate nationalists in the North, the government of the Republic of Ireland (who Thatcher hoped would co-operate in fighting the IRA and pacifying the region) and international opinion (Thatcher 1993, pp. 384–7; Goodall 1993, p. 128; and Prior 1986, p. 194 make similar points). The continuity of Conservative government policy was facilitated by the presence in the policy-making elite of ministers and civil servants who had been intimately involved with the 1973 policy. Thatcher's ignorance of Northern Ireland affairs may suggest a heightened vulnerability to the influence of such experience (Prior 1986, p. 239).

Thatcher warned, in a *New York Times* interview, 'We will listen for a while. We hope we will get agreement. But then the government will have to make some decisions and say, having listened to everyone, we are going to try this or that, whichever we get most support for' (Bew and Patterson 1985, p. 112). This was hardly the statement of a politician with strong convictions over Northern Ireland. On 21 May 1980, Thatcher and the Irish Taoiseach, Charles Haughey, met and recorded the importance of the 'unique relationship between the peoples of the United Kingdom of Great Britain and Northern Ireland and the Republic and ... the need to further this relationship in the interests of peace and reconciliation'. There were reports that the Irish government was prepared to enter a defence agreement with the UK in return for Irish unity (*Sunday Times*, 18 May 1980). In November 1980 the 'Atkins talks' collapsed without agreement. The following month, the British prime minister led an impressive delegation of British politicians to Dublin for an Anglo-Irish summit. The two governments agreed to establish 'joint studies to consider citizens' rights, security matters, economic co-operation and possible new institutional arrangements'. These studies 'explored possible forms for new Anglo-Irish institutions at various levels', were pursued at an official level during 1981, and presented to both Parliaments on 11 November 1981. This co-operation was cemented in the Anglo-Irish Intergovernmental Council established in November 1981 and heralded regular meetings at ministerial and official level between the two governments.

At the Dublin summit, Thatcher acknowledged Britain's unique relationship with Ireland and said that at future meetings there would be 'special consideration of the totality of relationships within these islands'. Don Concannon, who had been a Labour Minister of State at the NIO for five years, commented on the study groups set up by the Dublin Summit 1980: 'My own view of the study groups is that they represent the old, unofficial governmental co-operation on a formalised basis and improved status' (Don Concannon, 'Report on the Visit to the Irish Republic 31/3/81 to 2/4/81 presented to M. Foot', Labour Party Archive). The Irish Taoiseach, Charles Haughey, claimed that the December summit had significance for the unity of Ireland. This angered Thatcher and alienated unionism. Paisley took to the 'Carson Trail' to prevent the betrayal of the Union by perfidious Albion through the extension of the Anglo-Irish process.

The Propaganda War and the Hunger Strikes, 1980–1

As the IRA's hopes of a quick victory against the British evaporated, the 'Long War' between the British government and the IRA was likely to place an even greater premium on the 'propaganda war'. Publicly, the British condemned the IRA as criminal 'godfathers', terrorists or even Marxists, who prevailed only through intimidation. It was a propaganda strategy also deployed in the withdrawal from the Empire (Carruthers 1995). The process of 'normalization', 'criminalization' and 'Ulsterization', was designed by the British (and followed to some extent by the Irish government) partly to win the propaganda war in Britain, Ireland and internationally. Privately, successive British Labour and Conservative governments had treated the republican movement as being politically motivated, continued to have 'contacts' with the IRA, and had granted their prisoners 'Special Category' status. It was thought that to accept publicly that the IRA were not psychopaths or criminals would give the IRA a propaganda boost.

A secret report by Brigadier Glover, 'Northern Ireland Future Terrorist Trends' (1978), implied that the IRA's violence was 'politically inspired' by 'an inward looking Celtic nationalism' rather than Marxism, and there were no indications of a 'substantial link' between these organizations and the Soviet Union. Glover argued that 'Our evidence of the calibre of rank and file terrorists does not support the view that they are merely mindless hooligans drawn from the unemployed and unemployable.' The report noted a recent trend away from 'cowboy' shootings and sectarian attacks 'which, by alienating public opinion, both within the Catholic community and outside the Province, is politically damaging'. Propaganda was important to the IRA and the leadership was becoming 'increasingly sensitive of the need to avoid alienating support not only in the Roman Catholic areas of the Province but also in the Republic and among those of Irish extraction'. Glover went on to become Commander-in-Chief UK Land Forces, and after his retirement in 1987 stated publicly that 'In no way can or will the Provisional IRA ever be defeated militarily. The army's role has been now for some time . . . to help create the conditions whereby a full democratic, peaceful, political solution can be achieved' (*The Times*, 6 June 2000).

The Hunger Strikes were the site of a 'propaganda battle' fought between the British government and the republican movement. The British government wanted to portray the paramilitary prisoners as criminals and/or terrorists instead of granting them political, 'prisoner of war', status which might legitimize their 'armed struggle' in the eyes of the world. Roy Mason was particularly sensitive to the importance of the propaganda war against the IRA (Mason 1999). The Catholic Primate of All-Ireland, Tomas Ó Fiaich, claimed that conditions in the Maze Prison were 'unfit for animals', and that the paramilitaries were not ordinary prisoners. According to Mason:

> In a few emotive and grossly biased sentences he seemed to be undermining the legitimacy of our entire struggle against terrorism . . . His partisan words had far more impact than I could possibly say. From that point on, publicity began to move decisively

against us, particularly in the United States. As John Hume of the SDLP told us in September, the Provisional IRA was 'winning the propaganda battle hands down'. (Mason 1999, pp. 210–11)

Mason states that an intercepted message from a republican prisoner said: 'It is no longer a status issue. Whoever wins this has the war won' (Mason 1999, p. 212).

The republicans resisted Britain's criminalization strategy and sought 'political status' for their 'prisoners of war'. Both prisoners and the British government 'chose terms that would have the most appeal to the broader public they were trying to manipulate, that would appear to make them more reasonable and their positions more tenable'. The 'truth' of these statements mattered less than their effectiveness in the propaganda war. The Sinn Féin spokesperson argued: 'Balanced statements . . . which seek to temper criticism of one side with criticisms of the other help no one.' While the British 'won the contest of wills' with the prisoners over political status they 'lost the propaganda war, resuscitated an ailing IRA, and politicized militant Republicanism' (O'Malley 1990, pp. 206–8, 211).

The Hunger Strikes were the result of the British policy of criminalization. In June 1972, those interned or imprisoned were granted 'Special Category' status giving certain privileges to those convicted of scheduled offences, but this was phased out from 1 March 1976. The republican movement resisted criminalization – at first republican prisoners refused to wear prison uniforms and instead wrapped themselves in blankets. A 'no-wash' protest became a dirty protest in April 1978, when prisoners were denied permission to use toilets unless they wore prison uniform, and refused buckets to slop out (O'Malley 1990, p. 22). Prisoners smeared excrement over their cells and refused to shave or bath. The IRA began a campaign of assassination against prison officers and eighteen had been killed by the end of the dispute. In 1980, the prisoners resorted to a traditional form of republican protest, the hunger strike. They made five demands:

(i)   to wear their own clothes;
(ii) to refrain from prison work;
(iii) to associate freely with one another;
(iv) to organize recreational facilities and have one letter, visit and parcel a week; and
(v)   to have lost remission fully restored.

The British government felt that these demands amounted to granting the prisoners political status and, as Margaret Thatcher argued, 'a kind of respectability, even nobility' which could not be allowed (Thatcher 1993, pp. 389–90). For Thatcher, there was no political crime: 'Murder is murder is murder'. James Prior told Conservative backbenchers:

> The central demand of the hunger strikers – for political status – could not be conceded for three reasons: (a) it would be morally wrong to accept that crimes committed for political reasons were different from other crimes; (b) the claim for political status had been rejected by the European Commission on Human Rights in June; and (c) because it would produce a violent Protestant backlash, and give encouragement to terrorists everywhere. (NIC, 6 November 1980)

The IRA sought, in the words of Bobby Sands, the leader of the Provisionals in the H-Blocks, to 'broaden the battlefield' of the prison campaign beyond friends and relatives of the prisoners. In order to 'stir people's emotions[,] to arouse ... and activate them'. Sands argued for an 'army of propagandists' to put their views across:

> Now to tackle this broad spectrum of people in which we'll be plunging we must create our own mass media. The Brit mass media being unreliable but we can use it wherever possible and through time they'll be forced to cover us, through what we are going to stir up ... personally I envisage creating an atmosphere of mass emotion trying to use it as best we can and as soon as we can. To assert pressure from all angles on the Brits. (Smuggled prison communication from Bobby Sands, August 1980, quoted in Clarke 1987, pp. 242–3, 245)

The IRA's 'Long War' strategy, developed in the late 1970s, had advocated such a political mobilization.

The first Hunger Strike fizzled out in December 1980 when the strikers believed that the British government had made concessions on the substance of their demands. Publicly, Thatcher took a resolute stand against the Hunger Strikers; but privately the government 'encouraged dialogue' inside the prison and urged the Foreign Office to make contact with the prisoners (O'Malley 1990, pp. 30, 31–5). When British concessions were not forthcoming, the Provisionals thought they had been duped by the British government and this experience was to inform their handling of the second Hunger Strike.

A second Hunger Strike was launched in March 1981, led by Bobby Sands. He was unexpectedly elected to Westminster at a by-election on 9 April 1981, which brought the Hunger Strikers great publicity. During the campaign, voters were urged to vote for Sands to save his life. Controversially, the SDLP withdrew from the by-election contest to avoid splitting the nationalist vote, and this allowed Sands to defeat the UUP candidate by 30,492 votes to 29,046, on a very high turnout of 86.9 per cent. The DUP did not stand, to avoid splitting the unionist vote. After 66 days on hunger strike, Sands died on 5 May 1981; over 100,000 people attended his funeral. Nine other republican prisoners followed Sands to their deaths. O'Malley argues that both the British government and the IRA leadership in the Maze 'were impervious to the pleas for compromise, obsessed with the manipulation of the propaganda war, determined to prevail no matter what the cost. Each mimicked the other's behaviour' (O'Malley 1990, p. 64).

Richard O'Rawe was a senior IRA prisoner in the H-Blocks in 1981 and has alleged that the Sinn Féin leadership rejected a deal to end the Hunger Strikes in order to reap the electoral gain of the deaths of the Hunger Strikers. In *Blanketmen: The Untold Story of the H-Block Hunger Strike*, O'Rawe claims that he accepted a deal that would have granted the substance of the demands apart from free association, but Gerry Adams turned it down because of the propaganda advantages of the Hunger Strike. Denis Bradley, a link between MI5 and the IRA for over twenty years, has also claimed that the IRA were offered a deal that was later accepted but only after six more hunger strikers had starved themselves to death (30 April 2006).

The diminishing publicity gained by the Hunger Strike and the apparent futility of further deaths increased pressure for the strike to be called off. On 3 October 1981, the Hunger Strike was ended, 217 days after it had begun. By the end of 1981, 'the prisoners had been granted the substance of their demands'. Concessions would only be granted once the hunger strikers had been defeated and 'the concessions had ceased to be non-negotiable demands' (O'Malley 1990, pp. 200, 211).

The British government faced down the Hunger Strikers, partly to prevent a backlash from among unionists and British public opinion, 92 per cent of whom opposed the granting of political status to the IRA (O'Malley 1990, pp. 198–9, 201; Prior, NIC, 6 November 1980).

The effect of the Hunger Strikes on unionists was disastrous. Nationalists argued that the republican prisoners were political, and this was indicated by the way in which they had been sentenced in non-jury courts, their non-criminal family backgrounds and the huge increase in the prison population. Unionists tended to interpret the election of Sands and the turnout at his funeral as implying widespread Catholic support for terrorists who had murdered members of their community. They were not soldiers but terrorists who did not wear uniforms, targeted civilians and when they did take prisoners tortured and killed them. For unionists, the publicity and interest surrounding the deaths of the hunger strikers contrasted painfully with the funerals of twenty-two UDR and RUC men who had been killed by the IRA during the Hunger Strikes (O'Malley 1990, pp. 181–2).

After the Hunger Strikes and Sinn Féin's subsequent success at the ballot box, it was no longer possible to argue convincingly that there was no substantial Catholic support for the IRA and their 'armed struggle' that had killed so many Protestants. The SDLP, which had contributed to Sands' victory by declining to stand in the by-election, was condemned by unionists, who said that: 'its repeated denunciations of violence and the IRA were a charade concealing the murderous intent behind the conciliatory words of Catholics. All Catholics were Republicans, enemies of the state' (O'Malley 1990, p. 165).

The alienation of unionists was reflected in the electoral support given to the hardline DUP. In the local government elections of May 1981, the DUP narrowly out-polled the UUP by 26.6 per cent to 26.5 per cent, illustrating the polarization of opinion in Northern Ireland engendered by the Dublin Summit and the Hunger Strikes. In the local government election of 1977, the UUP had established a 16.9 per cent lead over the DUP. The centrist Alliance Party also lost ground between 1977 and 1981: its vote fell from 14.4 per cent to 8.9 per cent. At the European election of 1979, the DUP's Ian Paisley had easily beaten the UUP candidate by 29.8 per cent to 21.9 per cent, and this pattern in European elections was to be repeated. The DUP challenge to the UUP only eased in 1985. There was even speculation that Paisley might adopt a more 'moderate' approach towards negotiations with nationalists now that he appeared to be winning the battle for leadership of the unionist bloc. In this atmosphere of polarization, a political accommodation between nationalists and unionists appeared less likely.

Publicly, Thatcher and the Labour Opposition were resolute against the hunger strikers. Privately, the government was negotiating with them, prepared to show some flexibility but not to lose face. Under Secretary to the Northern Ireland Office, Sir Kenneth Stowe, said, 'Northern Ireland is not a place to grow martyrs if you can avoid it. We were anxious to try to find some way of enabling the hunger strikers to get off the hook' (*Guardian*, 4 March 2006). Much later, even Thatcher admitted to admiring the courage of the hunger strikers, if not their cause (Mallie and McKittrick 2001, pp. 34–5). The Foreign Office was more concerned than the NIO with the impact of the Hunger Strikes on international opinion, and opened up direct contact with the prisoners. The NIO was in touch with the prisoners through priest intermediaries (O'Malley 1990, p. 197). Gerry Adams later commented on the public/private contrast in the British government's position:

> The fact is ... that the British government in their general demeanour and general public position were telling lies because on the one hand while Margaret Thatcher was saying the hunger strikers were the IRA playing its last card, on the other hand [a governmental official] was relaying to the IRA prisoners involved exactly what Mrs Thatcher's position was ... The private position was a considerable bit apart from their public position in terms of the content as well as in the substance of what they were saying. (O'Malley 1990, p. 100, also, p. 197)

Publicly, the British Labour Party gave full, bipartisan support to Thatcher's non-concession policy, and its spokesperson visited Bobby Sands in prison to express this position. Privately, the Labour Party leader, Michael Foot, urged Thatcher to make concessions (Thatcher 1993, p. 391). The Irish government did not grant its IRA prisoners political status, and the political position adopted by the Irish parties towards the Hunger Strikers shifted depending on whether the party was in government or opposition. With the 'responsibility' of government, both major Irish parties pursued similar policies (O'Malley 1990, pp. 149, 152–3).

The republicans won a huge propaganda victory during the Hunger Strikes. They were able to portray the political nature of the conflict in Northern Ireland to the outside world (criminals tend not to kill themselves on hunger strike) and also to demonstrate a significant base of popular support (*Sunday Times*, 31 May 1981). This represented a blow to the British government's attempts to normalize the conflict and criminalize the IRA. The Hunger Strikes of 1981 unexpectedly led Sinn Féin into electoral politics, although it may have been a logical next step in the IRA's 'Long War' strategy. However, Sinn Féin's entry into the electoral arena was likely to place constraints on the IRA's violence: the Sinn Féin 'fish' needed a supportive nationalist 'sea' if they were to be electorally successful. The IRA curtailed its violence to maximize the mobilization of support for the Hunger Strikers (Smith 1995, pp. 160–1). At Sinn Féin's Ard Fheis (conference) in 1981, Danny Morrison asked, 'Who here really believes we can win the war through the ballot box? But will anyone here object if, with a ballot paper in one hand and the Armalite in the other, we take power in Ireland?' The Ard Fheis voted to contest the local elections and to take their seats if they won. Sinn Féin performed strongly, electing two candidates to Westminster and two to the Dáil. They reached their electoral peak at the Westminster General Election in 1983, winning 13.4 per cent of the vote but failing to dislodge the SDLP (17.9 per cent) as the main nationalist party. There appeared to be a real danger that Sinn Féin might overtake the SDLP and become the dominant nationalist party. This threatened to reduce the chances of any accommodation between nationalism and unionism, worsening the security situation and destabilizing Ireland. Although there was evidence in the European elections of 1984 and the local government elections of 1985 that Sinn Féin's vote had peaked, the Irish government exploited the republican threat to put pressure on the British government to sign the Anglo-Irish Agreement in 1985 (Fitzgerald 1991, p. 529). Fitzgerald argued, 'The Anglo-Irish Agreement is the result of the IRA's performance on the hunger strike' (O'Malley 1990, p. 221).

Conclusion

Since partition British governments had attempted to avoid re-opening the 'Irish Question'. Troops were reluctantly deployed on the streets of Northern Ireland in 1969 and only when disaster threatened was direct rule finally introduced in 1972. Between 1972 and 1974, some movement towards Irish unity seemed to be the most promising way of extricating Britain from the conflict. But the Protestant backlash and unionist resistance defeated power-sharing and closed off this option. The limit of the British government's power to impose a solution on the conflict was exposed. The British government's best chance of withdrawing from Northern Ireland now appeared to be an independent Ulster rather than Irish unity, which reflected a new awareness of unionist power. The British government deliberately encouraged withdrawal speculation in order to engage the IRA in a truce and demoralize the republican movement. Nationalists, and even republicans, in Ireland responded to the prospect of a British withdrawal with consternation, since it was most likely to lead to a destabilizing civil war. Anticipating a withdrawal, the violence became more communal between republican and loyalist paramilitaries. In the meantime, the British government was able to reduce the burden of the conflict on the army and finally implement a policy of Ulsterization. Britain settled down for the 'Long War' with its strategy for both the 'real' and 'propaganda' wars against the IRA in place. As unionist constitutional insecurity decreased and the security forces secured greater success against the IRA, loyalist paramilitary violence dropped away. The IRA reorganized itself into a cellular structure for the 'real' war and prepared its resistance to Britain in the propaganda war, resulting in the confrontation over the Hunger Strikes.

In the propaganda war between 1974 and 1981, the British attempted to underline the (not altogether compatible) image of the conflict as communal (unionists versus nationalists), terrorist (state versus international, possibly Marxist, subversion) or criminal (police versus psychopaths/'godfathers'), while the republicans countered with their view of the conflict as a historically resonant, colonial one between British 'imperialists' and the 'freedom fighters' of the IRA. The republican movement effectively resisted Britain's 'normalization' strategy, scoring a 'victory' in the propaganda war over the Hunger Strikes. The confrontation between the British government and the Hunger Strikers portrayed a simple, colonial picture of haughty British imperialism against brave 'freedom fighters' that had been so familiar in the British retreat from the Empire. The position of unionists is lost in this image of British–IRA confrontation, though the views of unionists probably constrained the British response to the Hunger Strikes. The lack of an overriding British interest in Northern Ireland beyond stability and the autonomy of unionist resistance to Irish unity undermines the credibility of republican ideology.

The public, high-profile, propaganda war played out between the parties to the conflict had disguised various political realities that have often been acknowledged only privately. The British government maintained its propaganda offensive against republicans through criminalization and Ulsterization, while privately (and implicitly during the Truce) accepting that the republicans were largely politically motivated. Publicly, British governments refused to deal with terrorists, while privately they investigated the possibility of a negotiated settlement. The Irish government publicly maintained its commitment to Irish unity while privately was anxious to prevent British withdrawal and also co-operated with its traditional enemy against the IRA.

British policy appeared to swing from one extreme (speculation about withdrawal) to another (proposals for integration). The prospects for power-sharing had plummeted after the electoral collapse of 'moderates' and the failure of the Constitutional Convention. The Labour government and Conservative opposition sought UUP support in a finely balanced House of Commons by offering a more unionist approach to policy. The Irish government and the SDLP responded to the unionist drift of British policy by adopting a more militantly nationalist negotiating stance and attempting to bring international, mainly US, pressure to bear on the British government. Integration, by further alienating nationalists and republicans, offered the British little prospect of a stable settlement. After 1979, when Unionist MPs did not occupy such a pivotal position in the House of Commons, both the Labour Party and the new Conservative government swiftly retreated from their prior, more integrationist position. The Conservative government rejected the integrationist promise of its election manifesto and pursued the twin-track approach of power-sharing and an Irish dimension. The constraints operating on British governments of whatever political conviction have ensured a broad, underlying continuity of policy (Dixon 2001b). This explains why Margaret Thatcher – purportedly a champion of unionism – was to develop a process that resulted in the Anglo-Irish Agreement of 1985, seen by most unionists as a terrible betrayal of the Union.

7

The Anglo-Irish Agreement: Origins and Impact

The Anglo-Irish Agreement (AIA) was signed by the British and Irish governments on 15 November 1985. The 'Conservative and Unionist' prime minister, Margaret Thatcher, stout defender of British sovereignty against the European Union, had signed an Agreement that gave a foreign government a consultative role in British policy towards Northern Ireland. What had brought about the shift in Conservative policy from the integrationism of its 1979 election manifesto to the Anglo-Irish Agreement? Did the AIA represent a 'remarkable *volte face*' in Anglo-Irish relations, or was there more evolution and continuity in British policy? Did the British sign the AIA primarily in order to improve the security situation in Northern Ireland, by addressing nationalist alienation and winning the Republic's co-operation in the fight against terrorism? Was the AIA designed to coerce unionists and nationalists into power-sharing? Or was it just a step towards accommodation?

Negotiating the Anglo-Irish Agreement, 1981–5

By the end of 1981, Northern Ireland had been polarized by the experience of the Hunger Strike and the murder of the Unionist MP Robert Bradford by the IRA. James Prior, who succeeded Humphrey Atkins as Secretary of State for Northern Ireland in September 1981, said privately that 'the province was "closer to civil war than is generally recognised"'. In January 1982, Prior outlined his thinking on Northern Ireland to the important Conservative Backbench Northern Ireland Committee: 'The involvement of the minority was essential for the defeat of terrorism.' 'Mr Prior said political advance was the vital prerequisite for improved security: since it would lead the Roman Catholic community to give their firm support to the security forces' (NIC, 28 January 1982). Integration was not a possibility, since discussion with the local parties revealed 'a complete lack of interest'. Inactivity 'made it very difficult for the government to defend its Irish policy in times of grave crisis' and cope with the political burden of dealing with Northern Ireland (Goodall 1993, p. 127). The British government was concerned both at the plight of the SDLP (Prior, NIC 24 May 1984) and the gains made by the DUP at the expense of the UUP. Prior had 'deliberately ignored' Paisley 'so as to strengthen the hands of the Official Unionists (though so far that tactic had not had the desired effect)' (NIC, 28 January 1982). Prior also expressed concern at the size of the subsidy to Northern Ireland.

In 1982, Prior launched his 'Rolling Devolution' initiative. Elections were held for a Northern Ireland Assembly. Powers would increasingly be devolved to the Assembly if 70 per cent voted for them, demonstrating cross-community support. Although the 'vast majority' of the cabinet supported Prior's plan, Thatcher was opposed and encouraged Conservative backbench opposition (Prior 1986, p. 199). According to Prior, Thatcher watered down his proposals on the Irish dimension and 'was worried about any form of, or even any suggestion of, devolution, for fear that this would give an opportunity once more to the advocates of devolution in Scotland and Wales to revive their campaigns' (Prior 1986, p. 197). The SDLP and Sinn Féin (SF) took part in the elections to the Assembly but the SDLP – under electoral pressure from Sinn Féin – refused to participate on the grounds that it ignored the Irish dimension. Sinn Féin also boycotted the Assembly.

The Conservative triumph at the British General Election of 1983 and Fine Gael/Labour's victory in the December 1982 Irish election opened up a window of opportunity for a significant British–Irish initiative on Northern Ireland. The Irish had pushed for an initiative in the second part of 1983, and discussions were started between officials (Dermot Nally for the Irish, and David Goodall for the British). As Goodall pointed out, the two prime ministers were coming to the initiative with 'widely differing positions', but both shared concern about the threat of Sinn Féin to security and political stability. Thatcher 'was determined not to compromise the Union' and 'was interested primarily in finding ways of improving the security situation, and in particular of improving cross border cooperation against terrorism between the British and Irish security forces' (Goodall 1993, p. 129). The 'acid test' of any British–Irish deal was security, and particularly cross-border co-operation (Young 1989, pp. 472–4; Goodall 1993, p. 129; Thatcher 1993, pp. 385, 397, 415; ICBH 1997, pp. 51–3). Thatcher sought an agreement 'which would acknowledge in a public way the Republic's interest in the affairs of the North, while keeping decision-making out of its hands and firmly in ours' (Thatcher 1993, p. 398). Geoffrey Howe, the foreign secretary, later recalled that in return for 'more effective cross-border security co-operation from the Irish government' (favoured particularly by Thatcher) the Irish had to be able to demonstrate an enhancement of their political role in Northern Ireland (Howe 1994, p. 417). The British government proposed a Joint Security Commission to consider joint policing on both sides of the border, and Thatcher also requested a study of the feasibility of repartition (which she had considered in the mid-1970s), as this might produce political and security gains (Fitzgerald 1991, pp. 517–18; Thatcher 1993, p. 398; Howe 1994, p. 420). Repartition was raised again and again by Thatcher (Hurd 2003, p. 302).

The Irish government was alarmed at the growth in political support for Sinn Féin and feared this would spread to the Republic and undermine its stability (Goodall 1993, p. 129). An initiative that addressed nationalist alienation could demonstrate to nationalists the advantages of constitutional politics and cut off Sinn Féin's advance. Fitzgerald would 'drastically lower nationalist sights on Irish unification' in return for an institutionalized role for the Republic in Northern Ireland, which would promote reform and address nationalist alienation. The Irish argued that a role for the Republic in law and order in Northern Ireland, perhaps a mixed British–Irish police force operating in nationalist areas, and British and Irish judges sitting in the Northern Ireland courts, would make the Union more acceptable to nationalists. The Irish government also hoped that the British government would concede joint authority in return for the repeal of the territorial claim (Goodall 1993, p. 130; Howe 1994, p. 416).

The ambition of the AIA was toned down because of British misgivings. The British doubted the capacity of the Irish government to deliver a referendum in the Republic on Articles 2 and 3, which was necessary to change the constitution. The British also feared that the attempt might provoke a republican backlash in the South, thus wrecking the initiative (Fitzgerald 1991, p. 511). In addition, Thatcher felt the price that the Republic was asking for the repeal of Articles 2 and 3 was too high (Thatcher 1993, pp. 395, 399). Howe favoured the option of joint authority together with a system of strong devolution (Hurd 2003, p. 303). This was strongly opposed by unionists and ruled out by the British government, but the 'central concept' of the AIA was established:

> firm and formal Irish acceptance of the Union (though without the repeal of Articles 2 and 3 of the constitution) as a basis from which the Irish Government, on behalf of the nationalist minority in Northern Ireland, could be given a systematic and institutionalised influence on British decision-making there without any diminution of British sovereignty. (Goodall 1993, p. 130; Hurd 2003, pp. 303–4)

Prior argued the case for a fresh Anglo-Irish initiative if the political and security situation was not to get out of hand. He told the Conservative backbench Northern Ireland Committee in November 1983: 'The Irish Republic now had as stable a government as it was ever likely to get, and so a great opportunity existed to move forward; it should be taken during the next year (or two, at the outside)' (NIC, 10 November 1983). Prior was frustrated by the negativity of the Ulster unionists who 'were making no overtures whatsoever to the SDLP. The Unionists' "retraction of their commitment to the minority" – coming at a time of great SDLP weakness – had the most serious implications. It would be disastrous if Provisional Sinn Féin overtook the SDLP' (NIC, 10 November 1983). If this happened, Prior could foresee the whole of Ireland being taken over by Sinn Féin, a Marxist organization, and this could result in the whole of Ireland becoming 'a Cuba off our western coast' (*Irish Times*, 11 November 1983; Prior 1986, p. 235).

Constitutional Irish nationalism launched the New Ireland Forum 1983–4 to develop a common nationalist approach to Northern Ireland and bolster the SDLP against Sinn Féin. All the major parties in the Republic participated, along with the SDLP. The electoral challenge of Sinn Féin shifted Fitzgerald's priorities from attempting to reach out to unionists to bolstering constitutional nationalism in the North. There were differences among nationalists over whether Irish unity required the consent of a majority of people in Northern Ireland. Fine Gael accepted consent, while Fianna Fáil's leader, Charles Haughey, argued that unionist consent could result from pressure and coercion (Kenny 1986, pp. 44–5, 67, 108). Nevertheless, the New Ireland Forum Report was issued, recommending three options: a unitary Irish state; a federal state; and joint authority. The latter implied a continuing role for the British in Northern Ireland and represented a step away from the other traditional national-ist options, which Fitzgerald claims were necessary to defend his nationalist flank from Fianna Fáil.

Thatcher's 'dismissal' of the three recommendations in the Forum Report, in what became known as her 'Out! Out! Out!' statement in November 1984, may have disguised a privately more sympathetic approach. The reaction was spontaneous and not diplomatic, and the press and the Irish reaction suggested that the British–Irish sum-mit had not gone well. However, there had been 'a great deal of common ground' between the two governments and, according to the Secretary of State for Northern Ireland, Douglas Hurd, 'The importance of the [Forum] document was fully appreciated on our side: Garret Fitzgerald was correct in saying that the analysis of the problem contained in the Report marked a step forward' (NIC, 22 November 1984; Fitzgerald in ICBH 1997, p. 18; Needham 1998, p. 39). Thatcher's unwise outburst was counterproductive in that it attracted strong pressure from within the cabinet, her advisers and US opinion to modify what was publicly perceived to be her negative stance towards the Republic. The US president, Ronald Reagan, told Thatcher that making progress on Northern Ireland was important and that there was great congressional interest in the matter (Dixon 2006a, p. 80; Campbell 2004, pp. 434–5).

British ministers referred to the government's 'twin-track' strat-egy in Northern Ireland. This was 'designed on the one hand to involve the constitutional nationalists in the institutions of Northern Ireland, and on the other to make progress on the Anglo-Irish front' (Hurd quoted in the *Observer*, 31 March 1985; Scott in NIC, 28 March 1985). Chris Patten was investigating by shuttle diplomacy whether a model of internal government could be constructed 'capable of winning [the] "reluctant acquiescence" of both communities (it was unrealistic to expect enthusiastic approval)' (NIC, 28 March 1985). Nationalist alienation and the Sinn Féin threat to the SDLP could be offset by giving the Irish government a say in the affairs of Northern Ireland. By June 1985 Patten announced that the government was not going to be able 'to bring both the internal train and the Anglo-Irish train into the station at the same time' (NIC, 13 June 1985). The Anglo-Irish train was coming in and it was hoped the SDLP might be prepared to enter a devolved internal arrangement in its wake. Patten underestimated unionist reaction to this proposal: he thought there was only a 'risk' that unionists would be too alienated to talk about progress on devolution. According to Patten, 'The SDLP wanted as much influence in an internal arrangement as they received in 1974 or at the very least influence commensurate with their share of the total vote' (NIC, 13 June 1985). The British government's overtures to the Irish government may have been offset by a more repressive stance on security policy to reassure unionism (*The Observer*, 31 March 1985).

Moderating Unionists?

On the one hand unionists could be reassured by Thatcher's 'Iron Lady' resolution during the Hunger Strike and 'unionist' reputation. On the other, the Conservative government's abandonment of its integrationist policy, the 1980 Dublin Summit, Rolling Devolution and suggestions of an Anglo-Irish initiative concerned unionists. The UUP's improved performance against the DUP in the British General Election of 1983 gave it some room for manoeuvre towards a more accommodating stance. In April 1984, the UUP launched *The Way Forward* policy document which proposed that the Northern Ireland Assembly should be given a greater administrative function, and committees composed in proportion to the parties in the Assembly would take responsibility for health and education from unelected area boards. Prior welcomed the document as 'a considerable step forward' (NIC, 24 May 1984). The DUP document, *The Future Assured*, was also relatively accommodating, proposing that any bill rejected by a proportionally representative departmental committee would require a weighted majority of 60 per cent in the assembly before it became law. In early 1985, the unionist leaders were trying to encourage the SDLP to participate in and shore up the Northern Ireland Assembly, in the optimistic belief that the tide was going their way (Aughey 1989, pp. 67, 69).

Douglas Hurd found Northern Ireland politicians to be privately courteous but publicly aggressive, 'All the constitutional parties had constituencies to answer to, and were wary of breaking free from the tired old rhetoric' (Stuart 1998, p. 146). Shortly before the Anglo-Irish Agreement was signed, the Northern Ireland Assembly Devolution Report Committee published the 'Catherwood proposals' in September 1985, offering for discussion a proposal giving the minority some checks and balances in a devolved assembly. In correspondence between Thatcher and the leaders of the two unionist parties in August and September 1985, Molyneaux and Paisley 'accepted the need for a cooperative and formalised relationship between Dublin and London' but opposed an Anglo-Irish Secretariat that would give the Republic 'a direct influence in the internal affairs of Northern Ireland'. While unionists would accept protection for minority interests, they would not accept power-sharing 'as of right' at the executive level (Aughey 1989, p. 187).

Unionists were excluded from the negotiation of the AIA because it was felt that they would not reach agreement and would disrupt negotiations. While Dublin kept the SDLP informed, the unionists were kept in the dark (Hurd 2003, p. 307). There is some question as to whether the UUP's apparently more accommodating stance in the run-up to the signing of the AIA in November 1985 was a genuine shift of stance or a tactical manoeuvre to undermine the inter-governmental negotiations and capture the moral high ground in the wake of any agreement. Conservative ministers were sceptical of the more moderate developments in unionist thinking (Chris Patten, NIC, 13 June 1985). In November 1984 the Secretary of State for Northern Ireland, Douglas Hurd, said 'In private, political leaders are reasonably responsive to the government's ideas: but in public they were difficult. Therefore, the moderate elements in the Official Unionist documents had not been fully tested' (NIC, 22 November 1984). Hurd later concluded that Paisley, 'was never a man with whom a senior British government minister could do serious business' (Hurd 2003, p. 298). Even Conservative allies of the Ulster Unionists were frustrated by their apparent intransigence. John Biggs-Davison argued that if the Official Unionists continued to be difficult the logical thing might be for the Conservatives to organize in Northern Ireland (NIC, 20 June 1985). T. E. Utley, a leading Conservative unionist, confidant of Margaret Thatcher and leader writer for the *Daily Telegraph*, argued:

Our interest lay in obtaining greater cross-border co-operation on security where huge scope existed for improvement. It was necessary to face the fact that although the Irish Republic regards the IRA as a great threat, co-operation with Britain will remain a sensitive political issue in the South. Thus gestures should be made towards them as long as they did not create panic among Unionists in the North. The gestures would not lead to unity, but should be designed to produce a more favourable disposition to increased co-operation on security. The attainment of that aim was surrounded by considerable difficulty. It must not be obtained at the price of an injudicious concession.

Utley favoured integration, but argued that 'it would be difficult to restore efficient local government if Sinn Féin obtained a large representation, and thus received a degree of legitimacy which it could exploit in ways that would make security worse' (NIC, 21 February 1985).

Explaining the Anglo-Irish Agreement, 1985

The Anglo-Irish Agreement was signed on 15 November 1985, giving the Republic a consultative role in the running of Northern Ireland. Both governments 'affirmed that any change in the status of Northern Ireland would only come about with the consent of a majority of the people of Northern Ireland'. The Agreement set up a British–Irish Intergovernmental Conference (IGC) which would meet regularly, and on which the Irish government delegation would represent northern nationalist interests on issues of politics, security, legal/justice issues, cross-border co-operation, identities and cultural traditions, and discrimination. The British and Irish governments would make 'determined efforts ... to resolve any differences' between them. Cross-border co-operation was to be promoted in security, economic, social and cultural matters. Provision was also made for a devolved, power-sharing assembly to takeover some of the functions of the IGC. A permanent secretariat made up of British and Irish civil servants was established at Maryfield, outside Belfast. The International Fund for Ireland was established to promote economic and social advance and encourage contact, dialogue and reconciliation throughout Ireland.

There are contending explanations for the signing of the AIA, which tend to place different weights on one or a combination of the following, often interrelated and overlapping, arguments.

Fear of Sinn Féin

Constitutional nationalists in Ireland and the British government were fearful that Sinn Féin might overtake the SDLP and become the principal party of nationalists in the North. This would make the chances of accommodation within the North a more distant prospect, could worsen the security situation and threaten the stability of Ireland (Thatcher 1993, p. 401). The Irish government attempted to shore up the SDLP against Sinn Féin, while the British government attempted to deal with the IRA's threat to security and simultaneously pacify unionism. The Irish and British governments both had an interest in redressing nationalist alienation and improving security co-operation in order to deal with the republican electoral and security threat (Fitzgerald 1991, p. 475). In negotiations, the Republic wanted Northern nationalist alienation dealt with by a reform of the security system. Proposals for this included reform of the RUC (possibly a separate Catholic police force in nationalist areas); Irish judges involved in joint courts; three judge courts; and the police patrolling with the British army. By the time it was realized that Sinn Féin's vote had peaked, a momentum had developed in the negotiations, 'and the joint fear of Sinn Féin electoral success had gradually been replaced on both sides by a positive hope of seriously undermining its existing support within the nationalist community' (Fitzgerald 1991, p. 532). For the British, the AIA could address nationalist alienation, strike at the base of Sinn Féin's support, and improve security co-operation with the Republic against the IRA.

Security Policy

Several key sources confirm that Thatcher's principal motivation for signing the Anglo-Irish Agreement was security (Young 1989, pp. 472–4; Lawson 1992, p. 670; Goodall 1993, p. 129; Thatcher 1993, pp. 385, 397–8, 413; Howe 1994, p. 415; Hurd 2003, p. 302). As Charles Powell, Thatcher's senior aide, remarked, 'it was security first, second and third' (Mallie and McKittrick 2001, pp. 18–19, 43–5). Thatcher realized that unless she took a 'wider political approach' which dealt with nationalist alienation in Northern Ireland, she would not be able to improve the security situation. To defeat the IRA, first, they had to be rejected by the nationalist community; second, they had to be deprived of international support; and third, relations between Britain and the Republic had to be carefully managed (Thatcher 1993, pp. 383–4). David Goodall, who was in the cabinet office and helped to negotiate the AIA, emphasizes the importance

Thatcher placed on the importance of security. She had wanted an agreement limited to security co-operation:

> And one of the tasks, certainly of Geoffrey Howe and also of officials, was to try and convey to the Prime Minister, get her to understand, that it was suicide for an Irish Government to enter into a security arrangement with the British which had no political content, which would simply make the Irish Government in the eyes of their own electorate appear to be supporting British military and security activity in Northern Ireland, without any political benefit for it. (ICBH, 1997)

The Republic would accept the legitimacy of the Union while gaining an Irish dimension that would end nationalist alienation (ICBH 1997, pp. 51–3). Fitzgerald hoped that reduced nationalist alienation and reform of the security forces in Northern Ireland would undermine the minority's toleration of the IRA (Fitzgerald 1991, p. 496). Mrs Thatcher later complained about the Irish government's failure to deliver security improvements. This did not necessarily relate to a rise in the statistics of violence but to 'the real danger that Sinn Féin would replace the SDLP as the main voice of nationalist opinion – with the inevitable consequence that violence and terrorism would increase' (Howe 1994, p. 415). The assumption was that greater electoral support for Sinn Féin would permit the IRA to extend its campaign and list of 'legitimate targets' rather than act as a restraint on IRA activity. Thatcher claimed that the AIA failed to deliver any significant improvement in the security situation, and its alienation of unionism led her to regret signing the Agreement.

External Pressure

The Anglo-Irish Agreement was signed to contain external pressure from the Republic, the USA and Europe on the British government (Fitzgerald 1991, pp. 468, 535). Irish government sources claim that their lobbying for US pressure played a decisive role in persuading Thatcher to modify her position (Wilson 1995, p. 245) while Guelke argues that US pressure probably played a significant role (Guelke 1988, p. 147). Others play down US influence: the British foreign secretary during this period, Geoffrey Howe, wrote, 'Only rarely were we under direct pressure from the other side of the Atlantic specifically to change our policies' (Howe 1994, p. 422). However,

Thatcher also mentions international opinion as a constraining factor on British policy and the advantages of the AIA in dealing with it (Thatcher 1993, pp. 403, 413; Dixon 2006a).

Bureaucratic Conflict

It has been suggested that the AIA was driven by bureaucrats, and that they actually sought to circumvent Thatcher's instinctive opposition to the Agreement (Fitzgerald 1991, p. 334; Howe 1994, p. 414). There is considerable evidence of bureaucratic conflict over the negotiation of the AIA between the cabinet office, foreign office and the Northern Ireland office. Robert Armstrong and David Goodall were responsible for negotiating much of the AIA on behalf of the British government and favoured a more ambitious settlement. The British and Irish civil services were involved in negotiating the AIA and probably had some impact in shaping the attitudes of their political leaders. Robert Armstrong and Dermot Nally (the leading Irish civil servant) had both been involved in negotiating Sunningdale. At one point Margaret Thatcher accused David Goodall of being too 'green', or pro-Irish (Mallie and McKittrick 2001, pp. 49–50). The foreign office was concerned at the damage Northern Ireland did to the UK's international image, particularly in the USA. There is some evidence that foreign office officials believed that Irish unity was in Britain's long-term interests (Hurd 2003, p. 304). The foreign office contrasted with the 'narrow contributions' (Donoughue 1987, p. 135) from the 'traditionalists' (Howe 1994, p. 420) in the Northern Ireland office. The NIO was closer to conditions on the ground and 'more realistic' than the English-based civil service about the impact of policy changes on Northern Ireland, particularly, perhaps, on how far the unionists could be pushed (see Fitzgerald 1991, p. 510). Although they warned Thatcher of a backlash against the AIA, even the NIO did not anticipate its extent (Howe 1994, p. 420; Stuart 1998, pp. 138–9, 150). Robert Andrew, the Permanent Secretary at the NIO from 1984 to 1988, argued: 'We were very conscious of what had happened at Sunningdale . . . and we were conscious that if this agreement was pushed too far and was too radical, there would be a very strong reaction from the Unionist majority' (ICBH, 1997, pp. 21, 40). Tom King, who succeeded Hurd as Secretary of State for Northern Ireland in September 1985, probably reflected the influence of the NIO when he raised 'serious concerns' about the AIA just after he took office (Fitzgerald 1991, pp. 557–8; Howe 1994, p. 425).

British Withdrawal

Unionists argued that the Anglo-Irish Agreement was yet another turn of the ratchet in Britain's long-term goal of withdrawal from Northern Ireland, in which the Union was by stages being destroyed. The British were being driven by the bombing campaign of the IRA and the foreign office's need to appease US opinion and bring the Republic into NATO. *The Times* commented that the three men primarily responsible for the AIA – Armstrong, Howe and Hurd – saw Northern Ireland as an encumbrance, 'a drain on the economy and an obstacle in foreign relations', and did not have any enthusiasm for the Union (*The Times*, 5 December 1985, quoted in Cochrane 1997, p. 16). This account is plausible but lacks evidence and underestimates the difficulties that would face the British government in trying to manipulate Northern Ireland out of the Union, which had emerged so starkly in the early to mid-1970s.

Coercive Power-Sharing

This nationalist argument suggests that unionists were blocking any progress towards power-sharing devolution in Northern Ireland. The Anglo-Irish Agreement was therefore a rational, Machiavellian masterplan which, by establishing a stronger Irish dimension, coerced the unionists into seriously negotiating a power-sharing settlement with nationalists (O'Leary and McGarry 1996, pp. 234, 238; Hume also used this argument, *The Observer*, 27 April 1986). David Goodall, who worked in the cabinet office and was involved with the negotiation of the AIA, argues that it was intended to introduce an Irish dimension without ending the Union, but also contained an incentive designed 'to push the people of the Province in the direction of devolution and power-sharing' (Goodall 1993, pp. 129, 131). Yet the evidence overwhelmingly supports Goodall's view, along with all the other key sources, that Thatcher's primary motivation in negotiating the AIA was to undermine the IRA and win the co-operation of the Republic against terrorism.

The Irish government may have felt that the AIA would shoehorn the unionists into power-sharing, but there is little evidence and considerable doubt as to whether this loomed large in the calculations of Thatcher, although others in the government and bureaucracy may have nursed this hope. Thatcher's doubts about power-sharing devolution were apparent in her hostility to Prior's Rolling Devolution initiative, which she felt was unrealistic and might set a dangerous precedent for devolution in Scotland and Wales (Thatcher 1993, p. 400, but see, p. 387). One report suggests that Thatcher favoured an Irish dimension over devolution as a way of calming nationalist alienation (*Irish Times*, 2 March 1982). Nick Scott told Conservative backbenchers before the signing of the AIA that full power-sharing 'was ruled out by the opposition of some of the parties in the province' (NIC, 28 March 1985; Hurd was also pessimistic – see Fitzgerald 1991, p. 512). Neither was the coercive element in the AIA novel, as the British had brought considerable coercive pressure to bear on the parties during the first peace process in 1973.

Thatcher: English Unionist, English Nationalist?

Thatcher claims her 'own instincts are profoundly unionist' and felt that 'given my own known attitude towards Irish terrorism they [unionists] would have confidence in my intentions' (Thatcher 1993, p. 385; see also Prior 1986, p. 196; Powell in Mallie and McKittrick 2001, p. 59). The British prime minister and other leading Conservatives were shocked and bewildered by the outraged reaction of Ulster unionism to the AIA, indicating a considerable gap in perception and understanding between Ulster unionists and their English or 'British' Conservative allies. Thatcher's sympathy for Ulster Unionism in Northern Ireland was highly qualified. She was, according to Hurd, 'an anti-Unionist Unionist' (Stuart 1998, p. 140) who supported the Union but found Unionists difficult to deal with, was critical of the Unionist record of discrimination against Catholics and had some sympathy with the minority's plight (Fitzgerald 1991, p. 527; Thatcher 1993, p. 386; Loughlin 1995, p. 210; Campbell 2004, p. 428). By contrast, she agreed that the SDLP 'were a moderate party in comparison with the Unionists, adding that they were very courageous' (Fitzgerald 1991, p. 381).

Thatcher's attitude towards the AIA is probably best understood as that of an English Unionist (or English Nationalist, as she once argued: see the *Guardian*, 16 November 1985). Her sympathy for unionism, and unionism's enthusiasm for Thatcher, was based on her hardline security stance, but this served to disguise her 'weakness' on the constitutional position of Northern Ireland. Her antipathy to multiculturalism and 'homogeneous' view of the English/British nation may have spilled over into her sceptical view of the prospects for power-sharing and sympathy for repartition (Hurd 2003, p. 302). Thatcher's English nationalism is illustrated by her concern for the plight of 'our boys' in the British army and Northern Ireland's financial drain on the rest of the UK (Needham 1998, p. 217; see also Loughlin 1995, p. 210; Hurd 2003, p. 302). Her sympathy for the soldiers can partly explain her determination to improve security through the negotiation of the AIA and acceleration of the policy of Ulsterization, which kept the British army out of the front line against terrorism (Hamill 1985, p. 257). Robert Andrew, Permanent Secretary to the NIO, reported that the reason for the government's initiative on Northern Ireland was the economic drain on the UK, and 'she was concerned about casualties among "our boys", and "our boys" actually meant the ones on the mainland rather than the RUC, but it was concern about "our boys"' (ICBH 1997, pp. 21–2). David Goodall reports Thatcher's determination to 'do something about Ireland', 'if only to stop the drain on British lives and treasure', by implication excluding Northern Ireland from the definition of 'British' (Goodall 1993, p. 127; see also Prior 1986, p. 204; Fitzgerald 1991; Howe 1994, p. 412; on Andrew see ICBH 1997, p. 22; Fitzgerald see ICBH 1997, p. 61).

Why Was the Anglo-Irish Agreement Signed?

The Anglo-Irish Agreement was the product of competing agendas and priorities. The weight of evidence of politicians and civil servants involved in the negotiation of the Anglo-Irish Agreement is overwhelmingly supportive of the argument that the Agreement was signed by Thatcher to improve security co-operation with the Republic and contribute to the defeat of the IRA. The rise of Sinn Féin alarmed both governments and led to a political response designed to meet the republican challenge. The considerable bureaucratic rivalry, coupled with Thatcher's apparently poor English unionist understanding of Northern Ireland, resulted in an Agreement that was the product of differing agendas. For others within the British government and bureaucracy it may have represented a step towards accommodation along the lines of Sunningdale, but they had to 'get around' Thatcher's misgivings (Fitzgerald 1991, p. 334). 'It took a gigantic struggle by many far-sighted people to persuade her [to sign the AIA]; but, although her head was persuaded, her heart was not' (Howe 1994, p. 427). Howe (who favoured joint authority, Hurd 2003, p. 303) thought the Agreement was the start of an evolving situation of historic importance (Fitzgerald 1991, p. 542) and 'as much as could be achieved in one generation' (Goodall 1993, p. 131). For Goodall, the AIA was not a definitive solution but 'a step in the right direction, improving mutual confidence and understanding of the problems of Northern Ireland between Dublin and London, and creating a new framework within which a solution might gradually evolve' (Goodall 1993, p. 131). Hurd, Secretary of State for Northern Ireland 1984–5, favoured the Union but was irritated by the unionists and believed the rights of nationalists had to be respected (Hurd 2003, p. 304). The Irish government was also motivated by concern at the rise of Sinn Féin and the continuing threat the republican movement posed to the stability of the Republic. The AIA would address nationalist alienation to stem the political success of Sinn Féin. Its pursuit of joint authority may have been an attempt at a final British–Irish settlement.

The AIA did not represent, as Brendan O'Leary has argued, a 'remarkable *volte face*' or 'a decisive turning point in Anglo-Irish relations' (O'Leary 1997). Many of the terms of Sunningdale 'may be seen as direct precedents for those of the 1985 Agreement' (Hadden and Boyle 1989, p. 20). The former prime minister, Edward Heath, said there was nothing in the AIA that was not in the Sunningdale Agreement of twelve years earlier. Hurd, who served both Heath and Thatcher, also favoured a settlement along the lines of Sunningdale (Stuart 1998, p. 138). The former cabinet secretary, Robert Armstrong – who had also been involved with Irish policy under Heath, Wilson and Thatcher, and was a leading negotiator of the Anglo-Irish Agreement – argued that it was part of a process that could be traced back to the Sunningdale Agreement and the idea of a Council of Ireland (Armstrong 1993, p. 204). The Conservative government's clear majorities at Westminster in 1979 and 1983 allowed it to revive the twin-track policy previously pursued by Heath's government. The advantage of the AIA was that by dealing only with the 'external track' it could not be brought down as easily as the Sunningdale Agreement had been.

The Reaction to the Anglo-Irish Agreement

Both Thatcher and Fitzgerald 'had the same problem in mirror-image. Each was worried that they had gone too far [in the negotiations] and would lose support' (Howe 1994, p. 423). Not surprisingly, the two governments tailored their contrasting interpretation of the Agreement to reduce domestic opposition: Fitzgerald addressed his republican flank by arguing that the AIA was 'as near to Joint Authority as one can get', while Thatcher soothed unionists by claiming the Irish role was merely consultative and Northern Ireland's place in the Union was actually reinforced.

Nationalists generally welcomed the AIA, The SDLP had been a leading force behind the Agreement and welcomed the British government's decision to face down the 'unionist veto' on political progress. Hume claimed that the AIA, 'Implicitly declared Britain to be neutral or agnostic on the question of a united Ireland'. The SDLP was not willing to suspend the AIA to enter serious talks with unionists, and John Hume predicted that the unionists would be forced to negotiate by the end of 1986. The Irish Dáil endorsed the Agreement by 88 votes to 75, and the Seanad (Irish Senate) by 37 to 16. All the parties except Fianna Fáil supported the AIA: its leader, Charles Haughey, argued that the deal was unconstitutional and copper-fastened (or further entrenched) partition, but was later forced to qualify his opposition to the Agreement and committed his party to making it work (Mair 1987a, p. 108).

The republican movement publicly opposed the AIA as a security-driven agreement designed to defeat the IRA. Privately, there is evidence that leading members of Sinn Féin welcomed it (Mallie and McKittrick 1997, pp. 35–6; *Guardian*, 21 July 1997). One of the unintended consequences of the Agreement may have been to demonstrate to republicans that unionists were not simply the dupes of the British state, and that republicans may be able to 'do business' with the British government. In the USA, the House of Representatives supported the Anglo-Irish Agreement by 380 votes to 1. The British government encountered fierce opposition from unionists in Northern Ireland, but little from British politicians, who illustrated again their lack of sympathy for Ulster Unionism by passing the AIA by 473 votes to 47.

The Unionists Revolt: Violence and the Union

Unionists saw the AIA as a step towards a united Ireland and their reaction was overwhelmingly hostile, even threatening to split the moderate Alliance Party. There were three principal unionist objections to the Agreement:

1. *While the Agreement recognized that there could be no change in the 'current status' of Northern Ireland without the consent of a majority, nowhere was the 'current status' defined.* In the 1973 Sunningdale Agreement the British government had stated that 'The present status of Northern Ireland is that it is part of the United Kingdom.' To demonstrate the weakness of the Republic's guarantee, two unionist politicians took a case to the Irish High Court claiming the AIA contradicted Articles 2 and 3 of the Republic's constitution. Echoing the Boland case of 1974, the Irish High Court rejected this claim but ruled that the Articles were a 'claim of legal right', a 'constitutional imperative' and Northern Ireland was not recognized as part of the UK.
2. *The AIA represented a complete capitulation to the nationalist agenda and gave the SDLP no incentive to enter into a power-sharing administration with the unionists.* Even if an assembly had been set up, the British–Irish Intergovernmental Conference would still retain considerable powers. If the AIA was merely consultative, why did Article 2 state that 'determined efforts will be made through the conference to resolve any differences'?
3. *Unionists complained because they had not been consulted by the British over the Agreement.* By contrast, the SDLP, through their close relationship with the Irish government, had been kept informed of the negotiations.

The strength of unionist opposition to the AIA was underestimated by British and Irish politicians. On 23 November there was a huge demonstration against the AIA. Although the NIO claimed the demonstration numbered only 30,000, probably to discourage further protest, there were in fact 250,000 demonstrators (out of a total unionist population of about a million), 'the biggest rally of the Protestant people since ... 1912' (Needham 1998, pp. 76–7). On the anniversary of the signing of the AIA in 1986 there was a protest of 200,000 people and rioting in loyalist areas. A petition in January/February 1987 raised 400,000 signatures. A *Sunday Times*/MORI opinion poll published on 24 November 1985 found that 83 per cent of Protestants did not think the AIA would improve the prospects for peace, while just 7 per cent thought it would. The poll asked those opposed to the AIA to indicate their support for different ways of protesting: 53 per cent favoured signing a petition; 44 per cent a mini-General Election; 39 per cent mass demonstrations; 27 per cent strikes; 15 per cent rent and rate strikes; 14 per cent refusal to pay water/electricity charges; 14 per cent a declaration of independence; and 10 per cent armed revolt (*Sunday Times*, 24 November 1985). The unionist MPs at Westminster resigned their seats so that a poll could be taken in Northern Ireland on the Anglo-Irish Agreement. In the following by-elections, 418,230 votes were cast for anti-AIA candidates, representing 43 per cent of the electorate as a whole, though one unionist lost his seat to Seamus Mallon of the SDLP. The vote for the centrist Alliance Party slumped. Unionist councils refused to set rates and were fined.

The British government anticipated unionist violence and hostility but was surprised at its extent. Thatcher called for immediate progress on the security front to placate unionists, and with Tom King 'agreed that the political priority was to win over the support of at least some Unionist leaders and that wider Unionist opinion which I [Thatcher] felt was probably more understanding of what we were trying to achieve' (Thatcher 1993, p. 403). The British government's need to placate unionist opinion is the context in which Thatcher and King made inaccurate statements that exaggerated the advantages of the Agreement to unionists. The Secretary of State for Northern Ireland, Tom King, argued that the Irish prime minister 'has in fact accepted that for all practical purposes and unto perpetuity there will never be a united Ireland because he has accepted the principle of consent that the will of the majority in Northern Ireland must predominate and that Northern Ireland, which is our fervent wish, remains part of the United Kingdom' (*Irish Times*, 4 December 1985). Thatcher wrongly claimed that 'the people of Northern Ireland can get rid of the intergovernmental conference by agreeing to devolved government' (*Belfast Telegraph*, 17 December 1985).

The Conservative government had demonstrated again to unionists their English nationalist 'weakness' on the Union. Without the threat of unionist violence and civil war, the British government probably had no overriding interest in remaining in Northern Ireland. Constitutional politics could not guarantee the Union, the unionist MPs could easily be outvoted in the House of Commons and, as the Anglo-Irish Agreement appeared again to demonstrate, the unionism of their Conservative allies was suspect. To prevent Northern

Ireland being rolled out of the Union, 'constitutional' unionists took politics into the streets and used the threat of violence to demonstrate to the British and Irish governments (and perhaps also the nationalists) the limits to which unionists could be pushed, thus underlining the parameters of British policy. Had constitutional unionists failed to mobilize and show the strength of their opposition to the Agreement then the two governments might have taken that as a signal that the British–Irish process could be accelerated towards joint authority (Seldon 1997, p. 432). Hurd later argued that the failure of unionists to destroy the Agreement was a measure of the progress made since Sunningdale (Hurd 2003, p. 308). The unionist dilemma was that constitutional unionists, by threatening violence, could encourage and legitimize the position of those who actually *used* violence (Dixon 2004b).

The leaders of the constitutional unionist parties, Molyneaux and Paisley, were operating in a grey area in which it was difficult to discern whether their intention was to incite or contain violence. Unionist politicians were not only expressing the outrage of unionist opinion but also attempting to mobilize unionist power and threatening violence in order to set limits on British policy. At the same time, unionists ran the risk of inciting and escalating violence which would split unionism, worsen relations with nationalists and further damage the Union. The uneasy relationship between constitutional politics and the threat of violence was something the VUPP had attempted to straddle in the 1970s. Shortly before the AIA was signed, the Ulster Clubs were formed and they occupied this political ground between constitutional politics and violence, including a place on the steering committee for John McMichael of the UDA (Bruce 1994, p. 104). David Trimble, future leader of the UUP, was a member of both organizations and he described the 'unionist dilemma':

> If you have a situation where there is a serious attack on your constitutional position and liberties – and I regard the Anglo-Irish Agreement as being just that – and where the Government tells you constitutional action is ineffective, you are left in a very awkward situation ... do you sit back and do nothing, or move outside constitutional forms of protest? I don't think you can deal with the situation without the risk of an extra-parliamentary campaign ... I would personally draw the line at terrorism and serious violence. But if we are talking about a campaign that involves demonstrations and so on, then a certain element of violence may

be inescapable. (*Newsletter*, 6 November 1986, quoted in Cochrane 1997, pp. 157–8; see also Aughey 1989, p. 72)

Unionist Politicians: Leading or Following?

At the end of February 1986, Molyneaux and Paisley appeared willing to try to reach agreement with Thatcher. At a meeting in Downing Street the leaders of the DUP and UUP were assured that the AIA would be operated sensitively and were offered concessions on new arrangements for enabling unionists to make their views known to the government; on consultations about the handling of Northern Ireland business at Westminster; and on the need for discussions on devolved government. Molyneaux and Paisley agreed to reflect on the British government's proposals, and the UUP leader expressed the hope that a forthcoming loyalist strike might not go ahead. The unionist leaders had shifted from saying initially that they would accept no part of the AIA to agreeing to discuss devolution if the AIA was suspended. The British government wanted to be seen to be meeting unionist demands and calming their misgivings about the AIA. Tom King claimed that after devolution only cross-border security and economic co-operation would be dealt with by the IGC. When the unionist leaders returned to Belfast their supporters forced them to retreat, and they subsequently announced that they would hold no further talks with the prime minister unless the AIA were scrapped. Thatcher continued to oppose suspending the AIA and it was 'a gap' in the meeting of the Intergovernmental Conference that allowed the all-party Brooke Talks to get under way in 1991 (*Irish Times*, 26 February 1986, 27 February 1986).

The significance of this episode is that it illustrates the constraints operating on the unionist political elites and the problems they were to have in managing unionist opposition to the AIA. Molyneaux and Paisley had worked hard to find a compromise with the government and 'This was almost their undoing' (Aughey 1989, p. 89; Bruce 1994, p. 113) According to the *Sunday Times* it was obvious that Molyneaux and Paisley had been 'running to keep up with the pace of events in Ulster' and it would require some effort for the constitutional politicians to reassert their leadership (*Sunday Times*, 2 March 1986, quoted in Owen 1994, pp. 61 and 75–6). The British prime minister recognized the dilemma of unionist leaders: 'Ian Paisley was in the forefront of the campaign against the Agreement. But far more worrying was the fact that behind him stood harder and more sinister figures who might all too easily cross the line from civil disobedience to violence' (Thatcher 1993, p. 403).

The unionist party leaders struggled to contain and control unionist protest against the AIA. On 3 March 1986, the loyalist strike against the AIA was accompanied by intimidation and rioting in which police were shot at twenty times, and forty-seven RUC officers were injured. Attacks followed on police homes (see below). The UUP leader, James Molyneaux, roundly condemned the violence and declared that future strikes would not be supported by his party. He was criticized by the DUP for giving up at least the threat of another day of action and the leverage this gave unionists against the British government. The DUP argued that the level of violence had been exaggerated, and that unconstitutional action had to be 'bold and unapologetic' if it was to be effective against the British. In April, a young Protestant, Keith White, was killed by a plastic bullet during rioting in Portadown. In the wake of this incident, Paisley hardened his rhetorical stance against rioting, risking the opposition of radicals within his own party (Cochrane 1997, pp. 149–50, 153). Unionist leaders were concerned that protest might escalate beyond their ability to control it. Molyneaux commented, 'the reality is that Mr Paisley and I ... have been overtaken by the people of Northern Ireland' (*The Times*, 11 April 1996, quoted in Owen 1994). On 23 April 1986 a programme of protest and civil disobedience was launched to assert the control of politicians rather than paramilitaries over the anti-Agreement campaign. On 10 November 1986, a paramilitary-style militant loyalist group, Ulster Resistance, was formed. Ian Paisley participated in this group, although it has been argued that he played a moderating role within the organization by attempting to keep control of the protest and ensure that it did not turn into a revolt (Aughey 1989, pp. 76–7; see also Cochrane 1997, pp. 159–60, 162).

Whether unionist leaders exerted a moderating influence over their parties or not depends on your assessment of whether the people they led within their party and their electorate tended to be more 'extreme' or 'moderate' than their party leaders. In other words, to what extent do the structures in which politicians operate constrain their ability to lead their parties? The 'orthodox nationalist view' would condemn the unionist party leaders for stirring up loyalist opposition to the Agreement and encouraging it on to the streets, with the resulting violence and intimidation. This view would suggest that the unionists are more 'moderate' than their unrepresentative politicians and that, generally, it is the politicians who cynically stoke up and exploit communal sentiment to further their own political ambitions. The constitutional pretences of unionist politicians are contrasted with the violence that is incited by their political rhetoric.

An alternative perspective would recognize the roles that Paisley and Molyneaux played in attempting to avert confrontation in February 1986. Finding the Unionist Party and (perhaps) also public opinion opposed to negotiation, the two party leaders attempted to restrain and control unionist protest by leading that protest and channelling it, to some extent, into non-violent tactics. This view would emphasize the importance of unionist leaders being seen to represent and articulate unionist grievance, in order to maintain their leadership positions, but at the same time attempting to control and restrain the political expression of that grievance. In this view, the unionist electorate at this point were more 'extreme' than their political leaders. Molyneaux took 'the long view' that the existence of a united unionist front on the AIA was an end in itself, maintaining unionist morale and allowing the letting-off of steam 'which had it not been released, may have been used for more destructive purposes' (Cochrane 1997, p. 193). Protest would continue until the British realized the AIA was not working. An indication that there was more extreme loyalist opinion than that being expressed by DUP leaders is apparent in the emergence and relative electoral success of the 'extremist' Protestant unionist, George Seawright. Seawright was expelled from the DUP for anti-Catholic remarks, but subsequently succeeded in winning significant support as a 'Protestant unionist' and was elected to Belfast City Council (Bruce 1994, pp. 143–5). It is difficult to assess the constraints operating on politicians, who often have a particular interest in emphasizing those constraints and their own powerlessness, but it is worth considering that at times they may act in ways that are either more 'extreme' or more 'moderate' than their supporters.

Security, Polarization and Reform

The difficulty with which the RUC policed unionist demonstrations against the AIA illustrated again Northern Ireland's 'security dilemma': the limited ability of the RUC to police the community from which it was principally drawn. Demonstrating loyalists clashed repeatedly with the RUC during the long, hot summer of 1986, and some police officers were driven from their homes in loyalist areas. Between March and December 1986 there were 600 reported incidents of intimidation of police and their families; 120 police families had to abandon their homes, and 111 families were attacked or threatened on one or more occasions. Meanwhile, the IRA continued its campaign of violence against the RUC. This placed considerable pressure on the overwhelmingly Protestant RUC, many of whom may have sympathized with the unionist demonstrators they were deployed to police. An above-average number of applications from RUC officers for jobs outside the force suggests strain and unrest (Owen 1994; Ryder 1997).

The RUC's willingness and ability to police Northern Ireland was once again called into question. According to Ryder, British ministers and their officials demonstrated 'a dangerous complacency ... about feelings within the RUC'; 'the integrity of the force was recklessly taken for granted and the strength of emotional turmoil inside the ranks was dangerously underestimated' (Ryder 1997, p. 328). In April 1986, RUC officers were discussing mutiny, and one was quoted as saying that 'many of his colleagues were considering mutiny and resignations on a large scale' (*Irish Times*, 7 April 1986, quoted in Owen 1994, p. 73). The leaders of the DUP and UUP had placed carefully worded advertisements calling on the RUC to stage a 'Curragh style revolt' (Ryder 1997, p. 330). The Police Federation's representative in Parliament, Sir Eldon Griffiths, claimed that 'intolerable burdens were being placed on the RUC' (*Newsletter*, 11 April 1986, quoted in Owen 1994, p. 74). In a letter to *The Times* he argued, 'I adhere to the view that it is impossible in a free society for a civilian police force to police for long against the majority' (Ryder 1997, p. 329, quoting *The Times*, 30 April 1986). According to Richard Needham, the Intergovernmental Conference:

> did start to give Southern politicians and Southern policy makers a much better feel for the intractable division between the two communities in the North. They began to appreciate the limits to British power in either coercing the unionists or defeating the IRA. However much Southern ministers complained about the abuses of the security forces, they began to acknowledge in private the limits of control that could be exercised on the young men and women who were fighting terror in the hedgerows of south Armagh and in the alleyways of the Ardoyne. (Needham 1998, p. 78)

The prospects for power-sharing, already poor, appeared to recede even further as public and political opinion polarized. According to the polls, nationalist alienation did not appear to have been substantially reduced, but the AIA may have had a more subtle, favourable impact on Catholic opinion (O Connor 1993). Some have claimed that the Brooke Talks in 1991 were a product of the AIA (Goodall 1993, p. 133). Alternatively, it could be argued that there was already movement towards power-sharing within unionism before the AIA, and that the Agreement, coupled with its subsequent polarizing effects in Northern Ireland on public and political opinion, delayed rather than accelerated the start of meaningful inter-party talks on power-sharing. The all-party Brooke Talks followed the announcement of a ten-week gap in the meeting of the IGC. Such a compromise might have been reached in the wake of the AIA in February/March 1986 had the Conservative government been serious about pursuing devolution and addressing unionist grievances.

Violence increased after the AIA. Thatcher was disappointed that her restraint in developing security policies that might alienate nationalist opinion had not produced better security co-operation from the Republic against the IRA (Thatcher 1993, p. 415), although Goodall argues that cross-border security co-operation had 'significantly improved' (Goodall 1993, p. 132; Needham 1998, p. 79). Charles Powell suggested that there was a strange situation where, just as unionists realized that the AIA wasn't a threat to them, Thatcher was starting to lose faith because it hadn't delivered (Powell, Brook Lapping interview).

It is difficult to assess the AIA's impact in accelerating a process of reform in Northern Ireland. The strength of unionist opposition to the AIA led to the British government 'adopting an extremely cautious position' on implementing reforms that would improve equality of opportunity and esteem or the improvement of administration and justice. A 'tacit agreement' between the British and Irish governments to minimize the contribution of the AIA to reform, and the British emphasis on its own policy, 'was intended to minimize unionist reaction to the establishment and operation of the new arrangements' (Hadden and Boyle 1989, pp. 73, 77). Therefore, Northern nationalists tended not to be aware of the benefits that the AIA had provided for them (Fitzgerald ICBH 1997, p. 64). One Irish diplomat argued that the Agreement was busy 'below the water' because the Unionists would 'go crazy altogether if they knew its full practical detail'. The Irish government had great ambitions for the Agreement as a major step towards Irish unity (Delaney 2001, p. 289). It is also possible that some of the post-Agreement reforms would have been implemented by the British government in any case, and that the negotiation of the AIA delayed British reforms so that they could be used as a bargaining chip in negotiations. According to the Northern Ireland Minister, Nick Scott, 'it was difficult for the government to decide whether measures designed to reassure Catholics (such as the repeal of the Flags and Emblems Act) should be undertaken as a separate exercise or as part of the hoped for agreement with Dublin' (NIC, 28 March 1985). By 1989, a review of the AIA reported that 'disappointing progress' had been made, and that 'it cannot seriously be argued that the Agreement has resulted in any marked improvement in the general security situation or in better intercommunal relations' (Boyle and Hadden 1989, pp. 77, 73).

By 1988, the unionist protest against the AIA was running out of steam, and the third anniversary demonstration was marked by only minor unionist protests. The UUP performed well against the DUP in elections held after the AIA. But this was not necessarily a vote for a more accommodating party, since unionist opinion was moving in an increasingly integrationist direction and the share of the unionist vote was down. Within the UUP there was a majority of integrationists against a minority in favour of power-sharing (Bew *et al.* 1997, p. 72). There was also some talk of movement towards independence in the DUP and the UDA after the signing of the AIA. The SDLP had been the big winner from the AIA but increasingly appeared to be turning its back on devolution and power-sharing with unionists, favouring instead the development of the AIA into joint authority. The SDLP also looked to build common ground with Sinn Féin in the 1988 SDLP/SF talks. This dialogue was part of a chain of events that resulted in the IRA ceasefire of August 1994 and the 'peace process'.

Conclusion: An Even-Handed Settlement?

The AIA was signed by Thatcher principally to improve security, but others sought movement towards a historic accommodation between unionism and nationalism along the lines of the Sunningdale Agreement (Goodall 1993, p. 129; see also Needham 1998, p. 88). The British were out-negotiated by the Irish government over the AIA, as they had been at Sunningdale, and this was a cause of serious concern for unionism (Dixon 2004b). Thatcher's English unionism did not appreciate the impact the Agreement would have on Ulster unionism. Unionists mobilized and demonstrated again their power to bring Northern Ireland to the brink of civil war. The thrust of this power came from below, and unionist politicians struggled to assert control over it. Without such a strong unionist reaction the British and Irish governments may have calculated that they could push unionists even further in the future.

The limits of British power and its ability to impose its will on the conflicting parties was once again exposed. Both Margaret Thatcher and her successor, John Major, believed that the AIA had been a failure. For Major, the AIA 'had provoked years of Unionist disenchantment for meagre benefits' (Major 1999, p. 433). The unionist veto on Irish unity lay not just in the democratic principle of consent but also in the ability of unionism to make Northern Ireland ungovernable. There could be no British imposed settlement (Major 1999, pp. 433, 441–2, 492). The AIA may have resulted in some in the Irish government having a greater appreciation of the limits of British power, in particular its ability to police unionism. The belief that the British government could simply deliver unionists to a deal persisted among other Irish nationalists into the peace process (Dixon 2009).

The AIA is possibly more significant for its unintended than its intended consequences. An unintended consequence of the AIA and the British government's subsequent 'facing down' of unionism is that it might have helped to further undermine the republican ideological position that unionism was just a tool of British imperialism. This growing realization might have contributed towards the developing debate within republicanism, encouraged by nationalists, on whether Britain had any selfish strategic or economic interest in Northern Ireland. Sinn Féin was to shift its ideological position to the point where in 1994 it was able to justify an IRA ceasefire.

8

Endgame? The Origins of the Second Peace Process, 1988–94

There are strongly divergent ideological explanations of the 'peace process' from the contending parties and governments in Britain and Ireland (for a detailed account of the peace process, see Dixon 2008a). These competing explanations are deployed to win political support and sympathy in the propaganda war and put pressure on other parties to the conflict to make concessions or compromises in negotiations. Nevertheless, based on the evidence available, we can cast doubt on key partisan accounts of the peace process and its evolution. In particular, two influential perspectives, one unionist and one nationalist, are singled out for criticism. A more convincing explanation of the peace process, it is argued, lies in understanding the problems of attempting to achieve a 'balanced' settlement that brings both republicans and unionists to a historic accommodation along the lines of the Sunningdale settlement. During the recent conflict, both the 'real war' and the propaganda war resulted in the development of a considerable gap between public rhetoric and underlying, sometimes privately acknowledged, political 'realities'. The key problem of the peace process was to bridge the ideological gap between unionists and republicans, and bring sufficient cross-community elites, parties and voters to an agreement that would be sustainable. Leading participants in the peace process have attempted to choreograph its public presentation and wind down the propaganda war in order to maximize support for the process from diverse constituencies of public and party opinion. Privately, there has been at least some recognition, even among 'enemies', of the problems and constraints facing the various parties to the conflict in building peace (Dixon 2002a).

This chapter reviews the events and controversies leading up to the IRA ceasefire of 1994, while the following chapter covers

1994–8. They should be read together, and an assessment and critique of an influential unionist and nationalist view can be found at the end of the next chapter while an analysis of the peace process is carried out in the final chapter of the book. Some of the key questions of the peace process include: What are the origins of the peace process? How has the peace process been managed? Did the British government obstruct the peace process by artificially raising the issue of decommissioning? How has the Sinn Féin leadership managed to sign up to the Good Friday Agreement, which falls short of Irish unity and includes a regional assembly? How has the UUP leadership been sold an agreement that includes an Irish dimension and a place for 'terrorists' in government?

Two Perspectives on the Peace Process

A Pro-Peace Process Nationalist View

An influential nationalist account tends to portray the *Irish* peace process as a unilateral Irish initiative coming from John Hume and Gerry Adams, supported by nationalist politicians in the North of Ireland and the Republic (O'Leary and McGarry 1996; Mallie and McKittrick 1997; Ruane and Todd 1999; Mallie and McKittrick 2001): Gerry Adams and John Hume enter into dialogue in 1988 and attempts are made to find common ground among nationalists in Ireland; in 1993 a 'Hume–Adams' document emerges around which Hume, Adams and the Republic's prime minister, Albert Reynolds, are united; and this opens the way for the IRA's ceasefire in August 1994.

The British government fails to appreciate the importance of the Hume–Adams dialogue and has to be pushed, persuaded and cajoled by the 'pan-nationalist front' (the SDLP, Sinn Féin, the Irish government and the US president) to shift its intransigent position on the peace process. However, the British remain wedded to an exclusive approach and the failed path of all-party talks among the constitutional political parties, building peace from the centre outwards and excluding Sinn Féin. 'Pan-nationalism' succeeds in provoking a reassessment in British policy, which moves slowly and reluctantly to bring the republican movement into the political process. The IRA ceasefire represents a triumph rather than a defeat for nationalism and republicanism. The British government refuses to accept the sincerity of the ceasefire and then erects decommissioning as a further artificial barrier to IRA participation in all-party talks. This impasse over decommissioning leads to the breakdown of the IRA ceasefire in February 1996. The obstructionism of British policy is explained as being the result of the Conservative government's precarious majority at Westminster and its dependence on the Ulster unionist MPs at Westminster; the ideological affinity between Conservatives and unionists; the influence of the security establishment; and the stupidity and incompetence of the Conservative government.

The Labour government elected in April 1997 with a clear majority in the House of Commons accelerates the Peace Process and brings Sinn Féin to the negotiating table in spite of unionist objections. Their bluff called, the UUP sits down in all-party talks with Sinn Féin in September 1997. The Good Friday Agreement (GFA) is signed in April 1998 and supported as paving the way to Irish unity. This trend is reinforced by the growing Catholic proportion of the population of Northern Ireland. Unionists fail to fulfil their commitment to the GFA and, along with the British, insist on an IRA surrender through decommissioning. When devolution does take place it is ended in February 2000 by the British government taking sides with the unionists over their demand for decommissioning. When devolution is restored, the British continue to support the unionist agenda.

This account allows the Sinn Féin leadership an honourable, face-saving explanation for its involvement in the peace process, which could be used to persuade the republican movement to accept its peace strategy. They could argue that it was the power of pan-nationalism, of which they were now a part, that was the driving force behind the *Irish* peace process. The war had not reached stalemate and neither were the IRA defeated; rather, the 'struggle' had been taken on to a new, unarmed level, where the might of pan-nationalism had demonstrated its worth by forcing the British government into a series of reversals. The Good Friday Agreement was presented as a further step towards the ultimate goal of Irish unity.

An Anti-Peace Process Unionist View

An influential unionist view (championed by Robert McCartney of the UK Unionist Party and the DUP) sees the peace process as a 'surrender process' that is just the latest British attempt since 1921 to disengage from Ulster and bring about a united Ireland. The end of the Cold War in 1989 removed Britain's strategic interest in Northern

Ireland and the IRA's city bombings of 1992, 1993 and 1996 created a powerful economic incentive for Britain to withdraw. The IRA's 1994 ceasefire was merely a tactical move to exploit the opportunities that a peace process gave them. Suspicions that a secret deal had been done between the British government and the IRA/Sinn Féin were reinforced when, in November 1993, the government admitted having secret 'links' with Sinn Féin. During the 'surrender process', the British government has capitulated again and again to the terrorism of IRA/Sinn Féin, who banked any political advantage and keep their guns ready to restart their terrorist campaign. The peace process corrupted democracy by appeasing the power of the gun and the terrorist rather than respecting the people and the verdict of the ballot box. The IRA demonstrated in February 1996 that their ceasefire, contrary to pan-nationalist assurances, was not permanent but tactical.

Since 1997, the new Labour government has capitulated to republican demands and Sinn Féin has been admitted to all-party talks without any IRA decommissioning. The UUP sold out unionists by negotiating with Sinn Féin and then signing the Good Friday Agreement, which represents a further step in Britain's manipulation of Northern Ireland out of the union. Since the GFA, the British have continued to concede ground to the republicans. Terrorist prisoners have been released and the RUC destroyed, while the IRA seeks to re-arm and carry out punishment beatings and shootings. The IRA have not decommissioned a single weapon, yet Sinn Féin terrorists sit as ministers for health and education in the new government of Northern Ireland. This unionist perspective would tend to favour the exclusion of unreconstructed terrorists from all-party talks and government. It would see the way forward as devolution resulting from talks among the constitutional parties or (for others) the closer integration of Northern Ireland with the rest of the UK.

Paradoxically, these pro-peace process nationalist accounts and anti-peace process unionist accounts reinforce each other, both agreeing that the peace process is leading towards Irish unity. The nationalist account welcomes this prospect, while the unionist one hopes to rally unionists to prevent this outcome.

'Balancing' Unionism and Nationalism

The account of the peace process presented here underlines the difficulties that the British and Irish governments had in bringing both republicans and unionists *simultaneously* to the negotiating table in order to achieve a 'balanced settlement'. This explains many of the apparent contradictions and inconsistencies in British policy during this period, and leads to a more convincing explanation of the peace process than that offered by the nationalist or unionist views displayed above (but perhaps at the risk of presenting an over-benevolent view of British policy). The problems of bringing unionist and nationalist political elites to the negotiating table and delivering their constituencies to a deal were apparent during the negotiation and failure of power-sharing in 1973–4. Then the Sunningdale Agreement was so unfavourable to unionism that Brian Faulkner was unable to maintain the support of his party or its adherents, a recurrent problem among unionist politicians (Seldon 1997, p. 423; see also Chapter 5 above). During the second peace process, the Sinn Féin leadership experienced difficulty in bringing the republican movement along with the peace process, while the UUP leadership had problems with both its party and the electorate.

After twenty-five years of violence and a propaganda war in which opponents were demonized and expectations of victory raised, there was a polarization among the people of Northern Ireland. Those political elites who wanted a settlement were going to have to manage the winding down of the propaganda war and prepare their respective supporters and voters for the compromises necessary for peace. This was perceived as requiring some choreography between the participants of the peace process in order to reassure different constituencies and bring them towards a settlement. The British government had to balance the claims of both republican and unionist political leaders in order to create an environment that would maximize the chances of the political elites bringing their parties, supporters and voters to the negotiating table simultaneously and selling an agreement to them. It found itself in the contradictory position of having to declare itself first as a neutral arbiter between unionism and nationalism – in order to attract republicans into the process – as well as a champion of unionism, in order to reassure unionists of their place in the Union (Dixon 1998, 2001b, 2002a; Major 1999, pp. 435–6, 440–2).

The British government's attempts to investigate, through secret talks and public overtures, whether Sinn Féin would or could end their 'armed struggle' and enter the political process threatened to upset unionism, particularly as the IRA continued to bomb and kill in Britain and Northern Ireland. The unionists who had been the victims of so much IRA violence were suspicious that the British government's overtures to the republican movement involved a surrender to terrorism. The British government's courting of republicanism risked destroying any prospect of agreement among the 'constitutional' parties and alienating unionism to the extent where loyalist and republican violence was escalating uncontrollably. John Major was also operating under considerable domestic pressure, since his governing majority was not secure and domestic opinion might not understand his dealings with terrorists (Duignan 1995, pp. 127, 147).

Ironically, while the British government was publicly hostile to the republican movement, privately it had every interest in seeing that Gerry Adams and the Sinn Féin leadership, if they were genuinely intent on ending the violence, were supported in turning a united republican movement into a democratic political process. The British prime minister had information that at least a faction within the republican movement wanted to find a way out of the violence (Major 1999, pp. 433, 436). In April 1992, Richard Needham, the Northern Ireland minister, argued that the IRA knew that they could not win, but did not know how to give up the 'armed struggle' without creating a major split in the organization. Adams had to be able to show his followers that the fight had been worthwhile and had to get the prisoners released (Needham 1998, p. 322, p. 126).

While the republican leadership might have been convinced of the futility of the 'armed struggle', there was likely to be a transition period during which the leadership would have to espouse the old, violent 'politics of illusion' while they attempted gradually to shift the wider republican movement towards democratic politics (Dixon 1997d, pp. 14–15). To maximize the ability of the Sinn Féin leadership to commit the republican movement to an unarmed strategy, they would need an 'honourable' way out of the conflict. The republican grassroots would have to be convinced that, through 'unarmed struggle' and the 'pan-nationalist front' (Sinn Féin, SDLP, the Republic of Ireland, the USA), republicans could wield more power than by continuing with the 'armed struggle'. The peace process would therefore have to be presented as a solely Irish (pan-nationalist) initiative that demonstrated its power by securing a series of apparent victories over the British government. The Irish government might publicly take a more hardline republican stance than it privately favoured, in order to show the republican movement that it was part of a wider 'pan-nationalist' movement that would champion its cause, use its influence to achieve some republican goals and not leave the movement isolated. This presentation of the Irish peace process might have appeased republicans, but it also raised unionist anxieties for their future in the Union. The British government's role was therefore to reassure unionists and champion their concerns, as well as to encourage republicans to enter a peace process.

Unionist and republican political leaders attempted simultaneously to represent their parties and electorates while at the same time leading them towards the centre ground. This could involve contradictory actions, with hardline statements disguising fractionally more accommodating positions. Along with the contradictory messages being sent out by the British and Irish governments (and the USA), this makes interpreting the peace process difficult. An official at the Northern Ireland Office said: 'You have to remember . . . in these negotiations no one says anything necessarily because they believe what they are saying, but because they know someone else on their side expects them to say it' (*Observer*, 5 April 1998; Dixon 2002a, 2008a).

Rethinking the 'Armed Struggle'?

While the 'nationalist view' suggests that the peace process was brought about as a result of Irish pressure for a change in British policy, the Provisionals were already rethinking the 'armed struggle' by at least the mid- to late 1980s. The problems for republicans in contemplating a ceasefire had been intensified by British duplicity in 1975–6 (see Chapter 6). The confrontation between the British state and unionism over the Anglo-Irish Agreement could not be reconciled easily with a republican ideology that considered the unionists to be the tools and dupes of British imperialism. Publicly, republicans attacked the AIA; but privately there is evidence that leading figures welcomed it (see Chapter 8). A reassessment by republicans of both British interests and Ulster unionism was a logical development (Mallie and McKittrick 1997, pp. 33–4). The problem for observers was that, while there may have been some developments in republican thinking and in Sinn Féin rhetoric, the brutal reality of the IRA's continuing violence overshadowed this and seemed to be a better indication of the republican movement's intentions.

The SDLP–Sinn Féin talks in 1988 brought out into the open the ideological gulf between republicanism and constitutional nationalism, a gulf that by 1993–4 had been bridged, and paved the way for pan-nationalist unity. During these talks, Sinn Féin declared there would not be an end to IRA violence before its participation in any talks. They argued that the British should relinquish sovereignty over Northern Ireland and persuade the unionists to accept Irish unity, though Republicans also began to take more seriously unionist fears and concerns about a united Ireland. Sinn Féin's 1987 document, *A Scenario for Peace*, indicated a persistent vein of republican thought that saw unionists as illegitimate, temporary settlers in Ireland and declared that 'Anyone unwilling to accept a united Ireland and wishing to leave would be offered re-settlement grants to permit them to move to Britain' (Bean 1995, pp. 18–22).

The SDLP's principal argument was that, far from having key strategic and economic interests in Northern Ireland, as the AIA demonstrated, British policy towards Ireland was *'now* neutral and agnostic' (*Irish Times*, 19 September 1988; in fact, it had deployed this argument since the early 1970s). The British had no military or economic interest in Ireland; it was the opposition of one million unionists that prevented Irish unity. In the event of a British withdrawal there was likely to be a bloody civil war. The SDLP made clear its opposition to the IRA's armed struggle but conceded that it was a political rather than a criminal movement, but this was not to be interpreted as lending any legitimacy to IRA actions. The SDLP favoured a strategy that welded together a 'pan-nationalist front' bringing national and international pressure to bear on the British government to persuade unionists into a united Ireland.

There is evidence to suggest that, by the mid- to late 1980s, the republican movement had fought itself, both politically and militarily, into a stalemate with the British government (O'Brien 1993, p. 198; Bean 1995; Smith 1995, p. 196; Patterson 1997). While the IRA escalated its campaign of violence in order to 'sicken the British', by deliberately targeting the British army rather than the locally recruited security forces, reports from British security sources suggested that there was a sense of war-weariness among the IRA leadership that was despairing of the futility of the 'armed struggle' (O'Brien 1993, ch. 8). On Remembrance Day in November 1987 the IRA detonated a bomb in Enniskillen that killed eleven and injured over sixty more. It was a damaging 'own goal' for the republicans in the propaganda war. The contradictions of the 'Armalite and ballot box strategy' generated debate within the republican movement and ideological developments. In *The Politics of Irish Freedom* (1986), Gerry Adams argued that the armed struggle was still of 'primary importance because it provides a vital cutting edge', but there was a realization in republican circles that violence 'on its own is inadequate and that non-armed forms of political struggle are at least as important'. The 'armed struggle becomes armed propaganda' (Adams 1986, p. 64). Sinn Féin's involvement in electoral politics drew to the party many of the republican movement's brightest activists: 'The elitist, conspiratorial assumptions of the armed struggle were constantly undermined by the changes in republican political culture necessitated by community activism' (Bean 1995, p. 8). Sinn Féin's document, *Towards a Lasting Peace in Ireland* (1992), recognized both Northern Ireland's economic dependence on Britain and the possibility of a Protestant backlash following British withdrawal. A leading member of Sinn Féin told the annual Wolfe Tone commemoration in June 1992 that British withdrawal 'must be preceded by a sustained period of peace and will arise out of negotiations', and Adams started to indicate a sympathy for joint authority (Patterson 1997, p. 240). In hindsight, these ideological developments within republicanism might have helped to 'educate' republicans and prepare them for the compromises of the peace process.

The key question about the republican movement is whether the Sinn Féin leadership's rhetorical shift during the late 1980s and 1990s was merely a device to maximize its electoral appeal, or did it represent a genuine, sincere movement in the attitudes of leading republicans towards the 'armed struggle'? The clandestine nature of the republican movement makes this question difficult to resolve. Nationalists have tended to accept the sincerity of Sinn Féin's shift, while unionists, who faced the brunt of republican violence, have been highly sceptical.

There is evidence that, while the Sinn Féin leadership might have been convinced of a new, unarmed struggle, the middle and lower ranks, and South Armagh and Tyrone were less enthusiastic (O'Brien 1993, pp. 204–8; Dixon 1997d, pp. 14–15). In February 1992, Gerry Adams reportedly said that 'he feared the emergence of an undisciplined, breakaway group from the IRA if a premature ceasefire is called in Northern Ireland' after failing to win sufficient backing for his new strategy at Sinn Féin's annual conference (*Daily Telegraph*, 24 February 1992). Hugh Annesley, the Chief Constable of the RUC, later described the IRA ceasefire as 'a very considerable achievement for the leadership. I have no doubt that if Adams and Co. had tried it in 1989, '90, '91, then they would have been unable to carry the leadership with them' (*Guardian*, 6 September 1995). This

struggle between the Sinn Féin leadership and grassroots republicanism may help to explain the slow and contradictory shifts in Sinn
Féin's rhetoric during this period, as the Adams leadership strained
to sell a new strategy to the wider movement (Moloney 2002). It was
not only unionists who tended to see the shifts in republican ideology
and the ceasefire as a tactic to maximize its effectiveness in the propaganda war, and to destabilize Northern Ireland and pursue Irish
unity. Rhetorical shifts were accompanied by an escalation of IRA
violence and the reassertion of fundamentalist positions: 'The IRA
leadership had their own perverted logic. For them, an offer of peace
needed to be accompanied by violence to show their volunteers that
they were not surrendering' (Major 1999, p. 433).

The Secularization of the Republic?

During the early 1990s, Irish politics appeared to be undergoing a
process of secularization in which old cleavages over nationalism and
partition were being replaced by more 'modern' divisions based on
economics and class. The formation of the Progressive Democrats
in 1985, a split from the traditionally nationalist Fianna Fáil, combined a free market ideology with liberalism on social issues and
moderately nationalist views on the North. In 1990, Mary Robinson,
a secularizing, socialist feminist, was elected president of the Republic in spite of her sympathies for Northern unionism. The McGimpsey
case in March 1990 upheld the view that Articles 2 and 3 of the Irish
Constitution constituted a claim of legal right over Northern Ireland
and a constitutional imperative. Following this, in December 1990, a
bill was introduced aimed at unilaterally amending Articles 2 and 3
and was supported by the Workers' Party, Labour and Fine Gael but
defeated by 74 votes to 66 (Bew and Gillespie 1993, p. 242). By 1993,
a poll suggested that 51 per cent in the Republic of Ireland favoured
rewriting Articles 2 and 3 to make Irish unity an aspiration, while just
28 per cent favoured their retention (*Irish Times*, 27 November 1993).
Gerry Adams was alarmed that the Republic might trade Articles 2
and 3 for a settlement (Sharrock and Devenport 1997, p. 286). There
were also strong movements for peace in the South, particularly after
the Warrington bombing in March 1993, and unionists seemed to be
receiving a more sympathetic hearing. It has been argued that the
secularization of politics in the South and an accompanying 'social
and cultural transformation' 'have fundamentally blocked off the

militant Catholic communalism that underlies much of the republican movement's northern success from any substantial echo in the
south' (Hazelkorn and Patterson 1994, p. 60; see also Mair 1987b).
The apparent rise of secularization and 26-county nationalism, coupled with Sinn Féin's electoral marginalization in both North and
South, 'propelled Adams towards a political alliance with the greener
elements' in the South (Patterson 1997, p. 279).

A Departure in British Policy?

In response to political developments within Sinn Féin, Peter Brooke,
the Secretary of State for Northern Ireland (1989–92), through public
speeches and secret contacts attempted to investigate the possibility
of ending the stalemate and bringing the republican movement into
the political process. In November 1989, Brooke gave an important
interview which claimed that, while the security forces could contain
the IRA he found it 'difficult to envisage' their military defeat. Neither would devolved government or economic development 'cause
terrorism to falter'. If the terrorists decided 'that the game had ceased
to be worth the candle' then it would be possible that the British government could sit down and talk with Sinn Féin. Significantly, Brooke
also used the colonial Cyprus analogy when asked whether he would
consider speaking to Sinn Féin: 'Let me remind you of the move
towards independence in Cyprus and a British minister stood up in
the House of Commons and used the word "never" in a way which
within two years there had been a retreat from that word.' Brooke
said he hoped the government would be 'flexible' and imaginative if
the IRA stopped its violence (*Irish Times*, 4 November 1989). This
speech was made days before the fall of the Berlin Wall and a year
before the revival of the back channel between the British government and Sinn Féin, and represents an important overture to the
republican movement. On 9 November 1990, Brooke's Whitbread
speech reinforced this by arguing that 'The British Government has
no selfish strategic or economic interest in Northern Ireland; our role
is to help, enable and encourage.' Margaret Thatcher had approved
Brooke's speech (whereas before the end of the Cold War she had
had reservations), and gave her personal approval to secret talks with
Sinn Féin in October 1990 in order to find out what was happening in
the republican movement (Seldon 1997; *Guardian*, 16 October 1999).
In addition to these public overtures, the British army developed a

'peace plan' in 1992 and 1993 and, for the first year since 'the Troubles' began, the security forces did not kill anyone (*Irish Times*, 31 December 1993; Bew and Gillespie 1996, p. 15).

The nationalist view presents Brooke's initiatives as a radical departure in British policy yet there are considerable continuities between British policy in the early to mid-1970s (see Chapters 4–6). Britain had made statements on British neutrality in the past; politicians had spoken of the possibility of Irish unity by consent, had a history of dealing with the IRA (in contrast to the Irish government) and had long believed that there was no military solution. The British government's rhetorical invitations to Sinn Féin were reminiscent of previous overtures: 'It was almost as if Sir Patrick had dusted down and slightly rephrased what Merlyn Rees had said in the run-up to the 1975 truce. What was to follow had much in common with that process' (Taylor 1997, pp. 328–9).

The International Dimension

The international dimension plays an important part in the nationalist account of the peace process. Nationalists and republicans argue that the end of the Cold War changed the international climate and precipitated moves to end anti-imperialist conflicts in South Africa and the Middle East. These developments made it far more difficult for the IRA to continue its anti-imperialist military campaign and facilitated the IRA's 1994 ceasefire. The end of the Cold War also prompted the British government to moderate significantly its attitude towards Northern Ireland, making possible an accommodation with republicans. The end of superpower rivalry allowed the USA to ignore its 'Special Relationship' with the UK and interfere in the internal affairs of its closest ally. The USA was able to overcome British intransigence and push the process forward. The acceleration of European integration broke down distrust between the British and Irish governments and provided models for overcoming conflict. Northern Ireland could not escape the 'irresistible logic of globalization' (Cox 1997, 1998, 2006).

The continuity of British policy towards Northern Ireland suggest that the international dimension is not as significant as nationalists have claimed (Dixon 2002b, 2006a). British governments had previously claimed that they had no selfish strategic interest in Northern Ireland and would accept a united Ireland if that was with the consent of the people of the North (Dixon 2001b). This had been argued by the SDLP since the early 1970s and was accepted by some leading Provisionals in the mid-1970s (see Chapters 5 and 6). The end of the Cold War and the restatement by Brooke of British policy in 1989–90 may have been more important for precipitating an ideological rethink among republican activists. The later development of peace processes in South Africa (1990) and Israel/Palestine (1993) were also, no doubt, useful to the Sinn Féin leadership for legitimizing the unarmed strategy, by pointing to the example of other liberation movements. The apparent upsurge of 'ethnic conflict' following the end of the Cold War provided an alternative explanation of the conflict in Northern Ireland, although it was less flattering to the republican movement, since comparisons with the former Yugoslavia and other 'ethnic conflicts' suggested Sinn Féin/IRA were engaged in a 'tribal' conflict rather than a war for national liberation.

The peace process is the result of an unfolding dynamic that cannot be separated from previous developments, and the search for a single point of origin is probably misleading. Nevertheless, there are strong arguments that developments that resulted in the peace process were already under way well before the end of the Cold War. These include:

- Sinn Féin's shift to the 'long war' in the late 1970s, setting the republican movement down a more political path.
- The further emphasis on political and electoral struggle during and after the Hunger Strikes (1981), leading to the 'ballot box and Armalite' strategy.
- An informed commentator, Ed Moloney, dates Gerry Adams' commitment to the peace process from 1982 (Moloney 2002, ch. 7).
- The Anglo-Irish Agreement (1985), which gave the Irish government a say in the running of Northern Ireland. The British government's determination to face down unionist resistance to the Agreement suggested to republicans that the British were prepared to act against unionism, and that unionists were not simply the dupes and puppets of British imperialism.
- There is evidence of British contacts with Sinn Féin from 1986 (Moloney 2002).
- In terms of republican ideology, Sinn Féin's decision to end abstentionism in 1986 was a major development, provoking a split in the movement and the formation of republican Sinn Féin.

- Irish government contacts with Sinn Féin (1988).
- By the mid- to late 1980s there was evidence that the republican movement had fought itself, both politically and militarily, into a stalemate with the British government.
- The Hume–Adams talks (1988) initiated a debate within nationalism, with the SDLP arguing that the British had no military or economic interest in Northern Ireland and were effectively neutral. They proposed a 'pan-nationalist front' to bring national and international pressure to bear on the British to persuade unionists into a united Ireland.

The impact of the end of the Cold War on republican opinion is exaggerated, because there were major developments in republican thinking *before* 1989.

The international dimension has played a significant role in the Northern Ireland conflict, not so much in the way described by the pan-nationalist script but rather in the performance of that script. The impact of the international on the Northern Ireland peace process has been exaggerated deliberately in the performances of pan-nationalist actors in order to persuade key republican actors and audiences to abandon the armed struggle for an unarmed one. The British government recognized the importance of this script for persuading the IRA into a peace process, and, to some extent, it acquiesced and played its role as villain in the pan-nationalist drama. If the British government believed that leading actors in the republican movement wanted to enter a peace process then it had every interest in encouraging such a favourable development. However, the pan-nationalist performance on the world stage dramatized the apparent weakness of British pan-unionism, the international isolation of unionism and undermined pro-Agreement unionism. The unionist audience received the presidency of George W. Bush more favourably, but this has not resulted in the 'Oranging' of the White House. After the signing of the GFA, pan-nationalism, which paid a price for bringing the republican movement in from the cold, has turned on Sinn Féin and demanded that it should now complete decommissioning and disband the IRA (Dixon 2006a).

All-Party Talks versus 'Irish Peace Initiative'?

The attempt to reach an all-party agreement among the constitutional parties proceeded – through the Brooke (1991) and then

Mayhew (1992) talks – while the British government both publicly and privately investigated the possibilities of an IRA ceasefire and negotiations. The two processes, the Brooke/Mayhew talks and the IRA ceasefire initiative, were proceeding in parallel. These were not necessarily contradictory or competing processes, as the nationalist view suggests, but complementary (Duignan 1995, pp. 103, 119). The prospect of an agreement among the constitutional parties at the centre could further marginalize the republican movement in Britain and Ireland, and continue to undermine its violent campaign. Sinn Féin leaders were concerned at the progress of the Brooke/Mayhew talks and feared that they might succeed (Smith 1995, p. 197; Patterson 1997, pp. 231–2, 234). The prospect of bringing Sinn Féin into the political process might have acted as an incentive to unionists, but not the SDLP, to negotiate more earnestly in the Brooke/Mayhew talks. The establishment of an accommodation with the SDLP would allow unionists to avoid the distasteful prospect of having to negotiate with Sinn Féin.

If the British government had only pursued the Irish peace process it would have had no fall-back position if it had turned out that the Sinn Féin leadership was not sincere in its desire to enter the political process. The unionists could be pacified by continuing with the talks process. If agreement was reached among the constitutional parties, Sinn Féin could always join the political process after a ceasefire. Periodically through 1993 and 1994, both British and Irish governments were able to threaten to revive the talks process, with the implicit threat to Sinn Féin that if it did not co-operate they would go down the talks route (Major 1999, p. 463). Albert Reynolds made this threat shortly before the IRA's 1994 ceasefire, saying that if the IRA did not call a permanent ceasefire then they can 'shag off' and detour away for another twenty-five years of killing. He would go down the all-party talks route with the British government (Duignan 1995, p. 147). As late as February 2005, the Irish government was threatening to exclude Sinn Féin and revive all-party talks in order to put further pressure on the IRA to fully decommission and get Sinn Féin to commit to purely peaceful means.

The SDLP was in a position to play a pivotal role in influencing which process, the 'talks' or 'ceasefire initiative', was to be advanced. It could opt to push the talks process through enthusiastic and active engagement in the Brooke/Mayhew talks, or the SDLP could push the 'Irish peace process', pursuing its talks with Sinn Féin and the Irish government, and play a blocking role in all-party talks. The strength of the British and Irish governments' threats to Sinn Féin that they would push the talks process were in part dependent on the willingness of the SDLP to participate actively in that alternative. Without the SDLP, any settlement emerging from the 'talks process' would not have sufficient nationalist support.

The British government, Irish government and the SDLP were all crossing the line from attempting to marginalize Sinn Féin in the propaganda war to attempting to bring them into the democratic political process. In crossing the line from marginalization to engagement there was a real risk of lending legitimacy and credibility to the republican movement, which they might convert into increased electoral support. Engagement suggested that republicanism was a political movement with legitimate grievances and concerns that would have to be accommodated. For republicans, engagement would allow their position to be seen as 'reasonable' and one for which the electorate might consider voting (Mallie and McKittrick 1997, p. 422). A further by-product of attempting to bring republicans into the political process was that it appeared to increase their influence, and this risked upsetting the 'balance' and destabilizing unionism. The British government's public overtures to Sinn Féin and later revelations of private contacts intensified unionist fears that 'perfidious Albion' was again doing a deal behind their back to force Northern Ireland out of the Union.

The Brooke–Mayhew Talks (1991–2): Worth a 'Penny Candle'?

The polarization following the AIA in 1985 prevented attempts to bring all parties into talks. In 1988, implicitly accepting the failure of their anti-Agreement campaign, the unionist leaders requested that the Secretary of State, Tom King, begin a process of 'talks about talks' to end the deadlock. In February 1989, representatives of the constitutional parties met in Duisberg: 'Discussion centred on ways of accommodating the Unionist demand that the workings of the AIA should first be suspended and the insistence of the SDLP that there should be no suspension and that discussions should be held outside the agreement' (Flackes and Elliott 1999, p. 241). In a speech on 9 January 1990, Brooke referred to the 'three relationships': relationships within Northern Ireland; the North/South dimension; and the East–West Anglo-Irish relationship. These relationships were to be considered during the Brooke/Mayhew talks, with nothing being 'finally agreed in any strand until everything is agreed in the talks as a whole'. The acceptance by unionists of the three strands implied that a wholly internal settlement was not possible. The Combined Loyalist Military Command, the umbrella body of the loyalist paramilitaries, announced a ceasefire to coincide with the start of the talks. In March 1991, a ten-week gap in the meetings of the IGC was announced, which allowed the all-party 'Brooke' talks to proceed the following month. The talks ended on 3 July 1991 having not moved beyond the procedural level or reached strands two and three. From leader writers in Britain and Ireland , it appears that the unionists generally took the blame for the talks' collapse. The talks were reconvened by the new Secretary of State, Patrick Mayhew, after the 1992 General Election.

Sinn Féin's hopes for the election of a more sympathetic Labour government at the 1992 election were shattered by the Conservatives' fourth victory in a row (Bew and Dixon 1995). However, John Major's majority in the House of Commons was reduced to 21 and was likely to be eroded through by-election defeats. One actuary predicted that 10.73 Conservative MPs could be expected to die in the course of a full five-year term of Parliament. This enhanced the leverage of the nine Ulster Unionist MPs and their sympathizers on the Conservative backbenches. In Northern Ireland, Gerry Adams lost his seat in West Belfast to Joe Hendron of the SDLP. Shortly after the election, the IRA bombed the Baltic Exchange in the City of London, killing three and inflicting damage worth £800 million, thus causing more damage with one bomb than all the IRA's other bombings since 1969. Further City bombings were carried out in the years that followed, posing an economic cost to the British government and a significant threat to the City of London as the world's financial centre. This prompted unionist claims that Britain's promotion of the peace process was driven by IRA bombs.

All-party talks among the constitutional political parties were reconvened under the new Secretary of State for Northern Ireland, Sir Patrick Mayhew, in April 1992. The pro-Union parties (APNI, UUP, DUP) entered the talks to devolve power to Northern Ireland and limit the impact of the AIA and the role of the Republic in Northern Ireland's affairs. The SDLP, on the other hand, wanted to extend the AIA and the role of the Republic. Strand Two of the talks on the North/South dimension took place in London in July 1992 and, remarkably, included both the participation of the Irish government and the loyalist DUP. This was the first time in seventy years that all the constitutional parties had reached the negotiating table. However, the DUP leadership was suffering some internal party pressure over its decision to go to London and negotiate with the Irish government (*The Times*, 8 July 1992; *Irish News* editorial, 1 October 1992). Paisley and Robinson later stormed out of the talks, since Articles 2 and 3 were not to be discussed, though significantly they did leave behind 'observers'. James Molyneaux led his team to Dublin, in an important symbolic move, to discuss the North–South dimension. Shortly before the Mayhew talks were suspended, on 10 November 1992, the UUP tabled important new proposals for the future of Northern Ireland. These:

(a) proposed a Bill of Rights;
(b) gave nationalists a 'meaningful role' in the Northern Ireland administration;
(c) proposed a North–South 'Inter-Irish Relations Committee', operating within the context of a Council of the British Isles, which would, where there was a common interest, facilitate business and better understanding between the Belfast and Dublin administrations; and
(d) proposed the removal of Articles 2 and 3 of the Republic's constitution.

The unionists found themselves blamed for the lack of progress during the Brooke talks, but came out of the Mayhew talks with credit. Unionist flexibility later came back to haunt the party when the Northern Ireland Office used the documents submitted by the Unionist Party as its benchmark for drawing up the Framework Documents of February 1995 (this was supposed to summarize the area of agreement between nationalism and unionism). This resulted in a document which, arguably, leaned towards the nationalist position.

Loyalists and Republicans: Playing to Different Audiences

In the early 1990s, loyalist paramilitary violence escalated to the point where the paramilitary were killing more people than the IRA. Two factors are usually cited to explain this: first, increases in loyalist violence have been linked to unionist insecurity about their constitutional future. The second factor was the removal of a generation of UDA leaders and their replacement by a younger, more violent, leadership (Bruce 1999). There have also been allegations of collusion between elements of the security forces and loyalist paramilitaries which, during the course of the peace process, have been substantiated. The outstanding issue is the extent of this collusion, and how far up the chain of command it goes, rather than its existence (see, for example, Tonge 2006, ch. 4; O'Brien 2005). The UDA was banned in August 1992. Some argue that the increasing 'effectiveness' of loyalist terrorism in nationalist areas was putting pressure on the republican movement to go for a settlement (Rowan 1995, p. 100).

The British government's attempt to pursue all-party talks while at the same time encouraging the republican movement into the political process probably exacerbated unionist insecurities and increased loyalist violence. Mayhew attempted simultaneously to make overtures to republicans and reassure unionists. On 16 December 1992, Mayhew criticised Britain's historical record in Ireland and argued that the government would not stand in the way of a united Ireland if that was the will of the majority, and pursued by democratic and peaceful means. Any new structures for Northern Ireland would have to be acceptable to both major traditions and have an all-Ireland dimension. But there was no question of dealings with the IRA while its members espoused violence (*Guardian*, 17 December 1992). Unionists reacted with outrage to the speech, and even the moderate Alliance Party leader, John Alderdice, implied that the British government was extricating itself gradually from Northern Ireland (*Irish Times*, 18 January 1993). On 2 March 1993, Mayhew attempted to reassure unionism by expressing his desire to restart all-party talks and denying that the government was neutral on Northern Ireland (*Guardian*, 3 March 1993). Alderdice was not convinced and insisted that the Conservatives were looking to take Northern Ireland out of the union 'through the back door' (*Newsletter*, 4 March 1993; *Irish Times*, 11 March 1993).

In April 1993 it was revealed that Hume had been engaged in secret talks with Gerry Adams. In June 1993, the Sinn Féin leader shook hands with the Irish president. This outraged unionists, since it appeared to lend the republican movement legitimacy and represented a retreat in the propaganda war. Furthermore, the Secretary of State for Northern Ireland told a German newspaper, *Die Zeit*, in April 1993, 'Many people believe that we would not want to release Northern Ireland from the United Kingdom. To be entirely honest, we would, with pleasure. No, not with pleasure. I take that back. But we would not stand in the way of Northern Ireland, if that were the will of the majority' (*Guardian*, 1 May 1993). On 23 April Mayhew again attempted to reassure unionists and shore up support for the UUP against the DUP by raising key unionist demands; he declared there would be no joint authority, proposed a Northern Ireland select committee, suggested devolution to local councils, and made no mention of the Irish dimension. The rising tide of loyalist terrorism caused great concern among nationalists. The nationalist *Irish News* commented, 'The British government has succeeded in alienating nationalists and unionists alike. Sir Patrick Mayhew has achieved the remarkable feat of having simultaneously stoked unionist fears without having placated nationalists' (*Irish News*, 26 March 1993, quoted in Bew and Gillespie 1993, p. 294). In the summer of 1993 the *Shankill People*, a local unionist newspaper, described 'A community in retreat which feels itself being squeezed physically, territorially and culturally'.

Hume–Adams

Following the collapse of the Mayhew talks in 1992, the British stepped up their secret contacts with Sinn Féin and investigated the possibility of a face-to-face meeting to persuade them there was no longer any need for an armed struggle (Sinn Féin 1993, p. 13). On 24 April, the IRA detonated a bomb at the NatWest tower in the City of London. The British government subsequently sent a message to Sinn Féin: 'Events on the ground are crucial, as we have consistently made clear. We cannot conceivably disregard them. We gave advice in good faith taking what we were told at face value. It is difficult to reconcile that with recent events' (Sinn Féin 1993, p. 30). There were IRA bombings on 20 May in Belfast, 22 May in Portadown, 23 May in Belfast and Magherafelt, and on 26 May a soldier was shot and injured (*Daily Telegraph*, 30 November 1993). On 3 June the British government representative gave a coded account to Sinn Féin of the British cabinet's deliberations. Translated, this message suggested that recent bombings by the IRA had made a meeting with Sinn Féin much more politically risky for John Major, and gave support to those in the cabinet who opposed the initiative (Sinn Féin 1993, p. 36).

Contacts between Hume and Adams were publicly acknowledged during the SDLP/Sinn Féin talks of 1988, but continued off and on after that (Mallie and McKittrick 1997, p. 118). On 6 October 1991,

Hume sketched out the first draft of a joint declaration to be made by the British and Irish governments which, it was hoped, would succeed in winning an IRA ceasefire. On 10 April 1993, it was revealed publicly that John Hume and Gerry Adams had been engaging in secret talks. This revelation ruled out further progress in the Mayhew talks, since the unionists would not sit down with John Hume while he was involved in talks with Gerry Adams. In June 1993, a secret 'Hume–Adams' document was agreed by Hume, Adams and the Irish government, which was then put to the British government. Publicly there appeared to be an emerging public consensus among Irish nationalists and the British Labour Party around a policy of joint authority, which proposed that the British and Irish governments would jointly govern Northern Ireland. The Irish Foreign Minister, Dick Spring, argued that the British and Irish governments might have to consider an agreement over the heads of the Northern Ireland politicians and put it directly to the people in a referendum, if the unionists refused to reconvene the Mayhew talks (*Guardian*, 8 July 1993).

On 25 September, Hume and Adams stated publicly that they had released a report to the two governments. The British and Irish governments were furious that the Hume–Adams process was being linked publicly to the joint initiative by the British and Irish governments. The British government was interested in the Hume–Adams initiative but it could not bring the unionists into negotiations if this was seen to be on republican terms. The British prime minister would suffer politically from both unionist and domestic British public opinion if he was seen to be condoning a process linked to a leading figure in a terrorist organization. Hume–Adams would have to be declared dead in order to avoid the impression that it had any relevance to the forthcoming British–Irish governmental initiative (Duignan 1995, p. 106; Mallie and McKittrick 1997; Dixon 2002a, pp. 733–4; O'Kane 2007). A process with Gerry Adams's fingerprints on it risked further alienating unionists. In October 1993, loyalists carried out their 'most sustained assault on the nationalist community in Belfast since the early Seventies'. They made nearly thirty attacks in nationalist areas of Belfast, killing three Catholics (*Observer*, 24 October 1993). On 23 October, the IRA attempted to bomb a meeting of loyalist paramilitaries on the Shankill Road, the heart of loyalist West Belfast, but the bomb exploded prematurely, killing the bomber, Thomas Begley, and nine Protestant civilians. In retaliation for the Shankill bombing, on 30 October loyalist gunmen burst into a pub in Greysteel and murdered five Catholics and injured eight. In these conditions of heightened insecurity and increased violence, elements in both the British and Irish governments acknowledged the importance of choreography and trying to bring republicans into the political process, while at the same time reassuring unionists.

Both the British and Irish governments were unhappy with the high-profile nature of Hume's dialogue with Gerry Adams. The Irish government attempted twice to put distance between itself and Hume–Adams, but was forced to retreat on both occasions. The SDLP leader had considerable influence over public opinion in the South, and this constrained the Irish government's ability to distance itself from Hume. Unionists did not have a comparable influence on the British (Dixon 1995b, p. 500; Duignan 1995, p. 120). John Major was also experiencing difficulty managing domestic public opinion over the IRA's bombing campaign in England.

In addition, Major had problems with his diminishing majority at Westminster (particularly with Conservative 'Eurosceptics') and unrest among unionist (or 'law and order') inclined Conservative backbenchers, who could exploit anti-terrorist sentiment among public opinion (these MPs often turned out to be the same people). Since the 1992 British General Election, the Ulster Unionists had increased pressure on the Conservatives by abstaining or voting against the government in the Commons.

In July 1993, the Conservative government, facing a problem with its own rebels over the Maastricht Treaty, arrived at an 'understanding' with the Ulster Unionist MPs at Westminster. Both unionists and the government insisted no deal had been done, while reports emerged in the papers of unionist demands for more accountable and better governance. The Conservative government's need for UUP support in the Commons increased that party's influence, and Molyneaux was regularly consulted by the government. This gave the UUP leader the confidence not to oppose the Downing Street Declaration in December 1993, and forced the British government to play something more like the supporting role for Ulster Unionists that the Irish government has traditionally played for Northern Ireland nationalists (Dixon 1994b, pp. 36–9).

Talking to Terrorists

Both British and Irish governments were reluctant to engage in public contact with republicans for fear this would lend the republicans legitimacy and translate into increased political support and a growth of IRA violence. Irish governments perceived that the IRA was a threat to the Republic, and leading nationalists, such as John Hume and Garret Fitzgerald, were critical of the record of the British governments' contacts with republicans. The British had a back channel to republicans from at least the mid-1970s, and this had been active during 1975–6, in 1981, and again from 1990. In 1972, both the Conservative government and the Labour opposition had had meetings with the IRA. While publicly the British government was trying to reassure unionists, in private its contacts with Sinn Féin were intensifying. Up to February 1993 London actively courted the republicans by sending nineteen messages, but receiving only one reply (Mallie and McKittrick 1997, p. 246). This suggests that the British, contrary to the 'pan-nationalist' view, were keen to explore the republican movement's willingness to declare a ceasefire. The government kept the republicans informed of the Mayhew talks, passing on a detailed government report and assessment of the discussions in October 1992. This document also provided an outline of what kind of agreement the British thought it was 'possible to achieve, rather than its own sense of priorities in individual areas' (Sinn Féin 1993, p. 20). It anticipated closely proposals later published in the Framework Documents in 1995, and states that the two governments were contemplating imposing a settlement over the heads of the parties.

A joint statement by the British and Irish governments in Brussels on 29 October had specifically ruled out talks with 'those who threaten or support political violence', and claimed there 'can be no secret agreements or understandings between the governments and organisations that support violence "as a price for its cessation"'. On 28 November 1993, the British government's 'back-channel' links with Sinn Féin were revealed in the *Observer* newspaper. Only a week earlier, John Major had told the House of Commons that '[If he thinks] we should sit down and talk with Mr Adams and the Provisional IRA, I can say only that that would turn my stomach. We will not do it'. After leaving government, Major justified his deceit: 'When I was certain that someone was genuinely seeking a peace I'd have spoken to Beelzebub, if it would have delivered peace, because that was my objective' (*Belfast Telegraph*, 14 October 1997). The Irish government also had secret contacts with the Sinn Féin/IRA.

The British government and Sinn Féin published differing accounts of their contacts. This is not surprising, since they each had contrasting audiences to reassure. The British government needed to convince unionists that its 'contacts' with Sinn Féin were not intended to secretly sell out the Union. There was also a risk that domestic British public opinion would not understand why the government was talking with the terrorists who were bombing English cities. The Sinn Féin leadership had to reassure the republican rank and file that it had not been 'colluding' with the British government or betraying the struggle. Both Sinn Féin and the British government released documents giving their account of the 'back-channel' contacts. The British version issued by Mayhew contained twenty-two errors. It was later withdrawn and revised in a way that brought it closer into line with Sinn Féin's version. The British version claimed contacts had been initiated in 1993, although Peter Brooke subsequently confirmed Sinn Féin's version that the 'contacts' dated back to 1990, and this has been confirmed by other well-placed sources (Mallie and McKittrick 1997, p. 244; Seldon 1997, p. 415; Major also casts doubt on Mayhew's account in Major 1999, p. 442). For these reasons, Sinn Féin's account of the back-channel contacts (although incomplete) is thought to be a more accurate account of events.

Sinn Féin's account of the contacts allowed it to claim that all the running was made by the British and thus avoid charges from republican hardliners that there had been any surrender. The Sinn Féin leadership was working to its own agenda, which appeared to be advanced by British willingness to talk face-to-face with only a temporary ceasefire, and the British representatives' talk of the inevitability of Irish unity through European integration. In Sinn Féin's account, the British had initiated contact in 1990 and had driven the process by sending representatives, messages, advance copies of speeches, confidential documents, and ultimately initiated a proposal for face-to-face meetings. The British government was to attempt to persuade the republican movement that there was 'no longer' any need for the armed struggle. This implied recent developments had changed the situation in Northern Ireland, and that it was not Sinn Féin that had changed its position or principles, but rather external conditions. Sinn Féin's account, however, which stressed the active role played by the British government in the contacts, did not fit with the nationalist account of the peace process, which suggested that it was a unilateral Irish initiative.

The British government's incentive was to produce an account of its dealings with Sinn Féin that limited the effects of the revelations on the unionist community, and to some extent on British public opinion. Increased loyalist insecurity might result in a further escalation of loyalist violence: 'What concerned the RUC was the possible reaction of the North's loyalist paramilitaries if they thought a deal was being done between the British government and the IRA. All hell could break loose' (Holland and Phoenix 1997, p. 8). Mayhew also expressed concern that revelations of British–republican contacts would boost the more 'hardline' DUP at the cost of its more accommodating UUP rival (Mallie and McKittrick 1997, p. 250). The British also wanted to avoid bringing the republicans into a 'peace process' only to lose the unionists.

In Northern Ireland, opinions on talks with paramilitaries were polarized along communal lines. Protestants tended to oppose British talks with the IRA or even loyalist paramilitaries, while Catholics were in favour. Before the revelation of contacts in July 1993, a poll found 74 per cent of Protestants opposed to the opening of informal channels of communication with Sinn Féin, while 70 per cent of Catholics were in favour (*Irish Political Studies* 1994, p. 221).

The British account of the contacts claimed that they had been initiated by Sinn Féin in February 1993 with a message claiming that the war was over. Unionists were more likely to accept that the British government should enter into contacts with the IRA if it was to manage their surrender. The British account of the contacts was altered to conceal the fact that the British had initiated a more intensive stage of contact with Sinn Féin in 1990 and sustained it over the years. Such prolonged, secret contacts were likely to fuel unionist suspicions over British motivation and lead to questions as to why these contacts continued while IRA violence had not stopped. The tone of the Sinn Féin account also suggests a closer and warmer relationship between the British representatives and republicans than does the British version.

There is some evidence of an attempt by the British government and Sinn Féin to choreograph the Provisionals' ceasefire and its entry into a peace process during the 'back-channel contacts' (Dixon 2002a). The use of intermediaries allowed both sides to blame these for 'misunderstandings' and to distance themselves from hostile interpretations of their actions (*Observer*, 5 December 1993). There were public overtures between the British government and Sinn Féin, while 'behind the scenes' they passed each other advance copies of speeches and continued their dialogue (Miller and McLaughlin 1996, pp. 125–6).

In 1975, the British had offered the IRA advice on media issues, and again in 1993 the British government offered Sinn Féin advice on how best to manage public opinion and criticize the British government. Sinn Féin should emphasize that the British government was foot-dragging on the peace process: 'Sinn Féin should comment in as major a way as possible on the PLO/Rabin deal ... Sinn Féin should be saying "If they can come to an agreement in Israel, why not here? We are standing at the altar, why won't you come and join us".' It also said that a full frontal publicity offensive from Sinn Féin was expected, pointing out that various contingencies and defensive positions were already in place (Sinn Féin 1993, p. 41).

The Downing Street Declaration

The British and Irish governments were working on a joint declaration which, drawing on Hume–Adams, it was hoped would lead to an IRA ceasefire. However, the British government sought to rewrite the Irish government's draft because Major judged that it was too closely associated with Hume–Adams and therefore 'had no chance of being accepted by Unionist opinion' (Mallie and McKittrick 1997, pp. 228, 264). On 25 November, Major wrote to Reynolds, arguing that there was no point in proceeding with the Joint Declaration because the text would be seen by the unionist mainstream as being the product of negotiations with Sinn Féin, which the statements of Hume–Adams had reinforced: 'As we've agreed all along, association with Hume–Adams is a kiss of death for any text intended to secure acceptance on both sides of the community'. While the British government was investigating developments within the republican movement, it also needed to ensure that in the process of doing this the government did not alienate unionists to the point where the Mayhew talks might not be revived (Mallie and McKittrick 1997, p. 229).

The Joint Declaration (also known as the Downing Street Declaration or DSD), published on 15 December 1993, attempted to attract Sinn Féin into a 'peace process' without alienating unionism. It was therefore 'constructively ambiguous', capable of being favourably or unfavourably interpreted by both nationalists and unionists. The rhetoric of the document was nationalist, acknowledging the importance of overcoming the 'legacy of history', promising to promote co-operation at all levels between North and South, and seeking 'to create institutions and structures which, while respecting the diversity of the people of Ireland, would enable them to work together in all areas of common interest. This will help over a period to build the trust necessary to end past divisions, leading to an agreed and peaceful future.' This hinted at the possibility of unity through co-operation and European integration (modernization theory: see Chapter 3). The British government restated that it 'had no selfish strategic or economic interest in Northern Ireland'. The document was welcomed by the SDLP and widely among opinion in the Republic. Nationalists claimed that Hume–Adams was the basis for the Joint Declaration and this illustrated the power of the pan-nationalist front. The Taoiseach, apparently in preparation for Irish unity, undertook to examine Southern political life for any elements that might be seen as a threat to unionism's way of life or ethos.

The unionists received a reaffirmation of the principle of consent, and the Irish government promised to change its constitution to fully reflect the principle of consent in Northern Ireland. At the crux of the document was an attempt to reconcile self-determination with the consent of the people of Northern Ireland:

> The British government agree that it is for the people of the island of Ireland alone, by agreement between the two parts respectively, to exercise their right of self-determination on the basis of consent, freely and concurrently given, North and South, to bring about a united Ireland, if that is their wish.

The UUP's reaction was muted; Molyneaux did not endorse the document but did not oppose it, and argued it was not a sell-out of the Union. The loyalist paramilitary groups, the UVF and UDA, paralleled the UUP's position by neither accepting nor rejecting the Joint Declaration. They had been consulted behind the scenes and were able to influence the document (Dixon 2009; Spencer 2008). Ian Paisley's DUP rejected the Joint Declaration and criticized UUP acquiescence in it. An opinion poll suggested that the DUP might be more in tune with unionist opinion in Northern Ireland. According to this, 56 per cent of the people of Northern Ireland supported the Joint Declaration, and 87 per cent of nationalists – but just 43 per cent of unionists. Given the tendency of opinion polls to overestimate moderation, the UUP's position appeared to be out of step with its voters (*Guardian*, 22 December 1993). A leadership initiative to explain the Declaration to the membership, and a hardening of the UUP's stance on the resumption of the talks process was designed to pacify rising dissent and talk of mutiny in the party (Cochrane 1997, pp. 320–3). The British government attempted to soften the impact of the

Downing Street Declaration on unionism by declaring its intention of setting up a Northern Ireland Select Committee and claiming that there would be no amnesty for republican prisoners. Of great significance for the subsequent history of the peace process, the government also insisted that the IRA would have to decommission its weapons before taking part in all-party talks (*Guardian*, 17 December 1993). The Irish deputy prime minister, Dick Spring, also announced that the IRA would have to hand over their guns (Duignan 1995, p. 136). The UUP's lack of opposition to the Joint Declaration was 'pivotal' in helping to limit adverse unionist reaction in Northern Ireland as well as right-wing, pro-unionist dissent within the Conservative party, which had been antagonized by the Declaration (*Independent*, 18 December 1993; Seldon 1997, pp. 429, 539; Major 1999, p. 450).

Republicans were surprised that Major had signed up to the Joint Declaration in spite of his apparent dependence on Unionists for support at Westminster (Mallie and McKittrick 1997, pp. 271–2). Gerry Adams argued that, in the Joint Declaration the British government recognized, albeit in a heavily qualified manner, the right of the Irish people to self-determination, and later claimed that it marked 'a stage in the slow and painful process of England's disengagement from her first and last colony' (Patterson 1997, p. 253). The republican movement did not endorse the Declaration; indeed, it called for its 'clarification' by the British government and set up a peace commission to consult the republican movement. Galvanizing republican discontent with the declaration, Bernadette McAliskey argued, 'It cannot be sold, that's the difficulty Gerry Adams is in . . . Gerry Adams cannot sell this thing, that's the beginning of the story and the end of the story in reality' (Sharrock and Devenport 1997, p. 316).

'Pan-Nationalism' and the 'Tactical Use of the Unarmed Struggle'

The British government refused to 'clarify' but did 'explain' the Joint Declaration for Sinn Féin. The likely parameters of a settlement had already been indicated in the leaking of an Irish government document in November 1993; Reynolds suggested that the consent principle might result in reform of the government of Ireland Act, and changes to Articles 2 and 3 of the Irish Constitution would be conditional on cross-border institutions with executive powers (Patterson 1997, p. 253). During the summer of 1994, the republican movement considered an IRA ceasefire and debated a document called TUAS, a 'constructively ambiguous' acronym that allowed it to be presented as different things to different audiences. TUAS was presented as the 'Tactical Use of the Armed Struggle' for traditional republicans, but as the 'Totally UnArmed Strategy' to audiences in England, the Republic and the USA (Moloney, *Sunday Tribune*, 30 January 2000).

The debate within the republican movement was not so much about the morality of the 'armed struggle' but rather its effectiveness in bringing about the goal of a 32-county democratic socialist Repub-lic. For the republican leadership to win the widespread support of the republican movement for an IRA ceasefire they had to demon-strate that the 'pan-nationalist front' (Sinn Féin, SDLP, Republic of Ireland, USA, EU?, British Labour Party?) could be a power-ful and effective alternative to violence. The substantial contributing factors which pointed towards the launching of the unarmed struggle were:

(a) Hume's leadership of the SDLP;
(b) the strength of the coalition government in Dublin;
(c) Reynolds' lack of historical baggage and his knowledge of how popular a nationalist consensus would be among the grassroots;
(d) the power of the Irish-American lobby;
(e) the Irish-American lobby's ability to influence President Clinton; and
(f) Britain's lack of popularity within the EU.

The TUAS document stated: 'It is the first time in 25 years that all the major Irish nationalist parties are rowing in roughly the same direc-tion. These combined circumstances are unlikely to gel again in the foreseeable future.' (The TUAS document is reproduced in Mallie and McKittrick 1997, pp. 421–4.) The (contested) expectation that Catholics would be a majority in Northern Ireland within a generation and vote themselves into a united Ireland may also have played an influential role in persuading republicans to end the 'armed struggle'.

According to security sources, the IRA ceasefire required 'massive planning, massive consultation – a massive show of democracy on their part to keep their people behind them'. The internal debate was divided: the leadership favoured peace; the middle and higher levels did not think a ceasefire would work but were prepared to give it a chance, whereas the grassroots favoured war (Rowan 1995).

Conclusion

With the benefit of hindsight, it is tempting to reinterpret history to suggest that political developments within the republican movement during the 1980s led inexorably and inevitably towards the IRA's ceasefire of 1994. From this vantage point, the nationalist view castigates those who ever doubted the sincerity of the IRA's conversion to a 'Totally UnArmed Strategy' (Mallie and McKittrick 1997). There are two main problems with this perspective: first, the upsurge of appalling republican violence suggested that IRA actions were a stronger indicator of republican intentions than Sinn Fin rhetoric about peace. The IRA increased violence so that they could demonstrate that their ceasefire was not a surrender.

Second, those convinced of the sincerity of the republican movement's shift towards peace and the permanence of the subsequent IRA ceasefire announced on 31 August 1994 were under the impression that the TUAS document stood for 'Totally UnArmed Strategy'. Later the weight of evidence – not least the end of the IRA's supposedly permanent ceasefire in February 1996 – shifted and it appeared more likely that the IRA's ceasefire was not permanent, and that TUAS stood for the 'Tactical Use of the Armed Struggle' (Moloney 2002). There was a very real fear that the IRA, after exploiting the benefits of an unarmed strategy (in terms of legitimacy and electoral support), would then return to violence stronger than ever before and better placed to destabilize Northern Ireland.

9

Bridging the Gap? The Peace Process, 1994–8

Introduction

On 31 August 1994, the IRA declared a 'complete cessation of military operations'. Prior to this ceasefire there appeared to have been little convergence in the public positions of any of the parties to the conflict, and no obvious convergence in public opinion (see Table 1.2 on p. 23 for some Northern Irish opinion poll data over time). Both unionists and republicans could believe they had won. In this climate, it was difficult to see what kind of agreement might 'bridge the gap' and win the acquiescence, if not the consent, of both republicans and unionists. The Irish government concentrated on soothing republican fears and demonstrating to the republican movement the effectiveness of the political path by championing the nationalist cause. The British government had to perform a 'dual role': to deliver concessions to nationalists to underpin the IRA's ceasefire and reassure them they would be dealt with fairly in any negotiations, and at the same time reassure unionists by championing the Union and bring them to the negotiating table with republicans. As a 'senior British source' argued: 'It is the job of the British Government to push the Unionists to a line beyond which they will not go; it is the job of the Irish Government to pull the Republicans to a line beyond which they will not come. What was left in the middle, the limits of potential agreement, would be left for discussion between the parties' (*Observer*, 5 February 1995).

Ceasefire Reactions

The roles assumed by the British and Irish governments during the peace process are illustrated by the contrast in the reception the IRA's ceasefire received in Dublin and London. The Irish government's task was to keep the republican movement on board and demonstrate to it the benefits of the non-violent, political path it was apparently taking. They therefore quickly accepted the IRA's ceasefire as permanent, and within days Gerry Adams was received into the pan-nationalist family through a public three-way handshake in Dublin. Sinn Féin was also swiftly admitted to the Republic's all-Ireland 'Forum for Peace and Reconciliation'. In November, the Republic released some republican prisoners.

Paralleling Irish support for the republicans, the British government expressed unionist scepticism of the IRA's intentions. The UUP leader, James Molyneaux, assured unionists that no secret deals had been done, and shared the British government's concerns that the IRA's ceasefire declaration had not stated that it was 'permanent'. A significant body of unionist opinion felt that the British government had done a secret deal with the IRA in return for the ceasefire. The loyalist *Newsletter* was wary about 'the real intent of the republican leadership' (*Newsletter*, 1 September 1994). For the DUP, the ceasefire was a tactical ploy by the IRA to win concessions from the British government, part of a British strategy to push Northern Ireland out of the Union. NIO officials met with loyalist paramilitaries to let them know that the Union was safe, and no secret deals had been done with republicans to bring about the ceasefire (Rowan 1995, pp. 117–18). On 16 September, the British government took steps to reassure unionists by declaring its commitment to a referendum on any package for the constitutional future of Northern Ireland. Six weeks after the IRA's cessation, on 13 October 1994, the Combined Loyalist Military Command (CLMC), comprising the UDA, UVF and Red Hand Commando, declared a ceasefire.

Permanence and Decommissioning

Following the signing of the DSD, the British insisted that the IRA's handing-over of explosives would figure high on the agenda of the 'exploratory talks', and would have to take place before all-party talks (*Guardian*, 17 December 1993). There would be three principal, and highly symbolic, steps for Sinn Féin on the way to all-party talks:

  (i)   exploratory dialogue with civil servants;
 (ii)   direct contact between ministers of the British government and Sinn Féin; and
(iii)   an invitation to all party-talks with unionists.

Public opinion polls confirmed the difficulties of bringing republican and unionist parties into all-party talks. Protestants were sceptical of the IRA's ceasefire, believing that the IRA had called a cease-fire because they had cut a deal. or had an ulterior motive. They were keen to see tangible evidence of the IRA's intentions and over-whelmingly (92 per cent to 5 per cent) favoured decommissioning (of both loyalists and republicans) as a precondition to Sinn Féin's entry into all-party talks (*Irish Political Studies* 1995, p. 309). The loyalist paramilitaries refused to decommission unilaterally but agreed to do so if the IRA also began decommissioning, and in the meantime the loyalists would not strike first. Catholics were more convinced of the sincerity and permanence of the IRA ceasefire than were Protestants, although a plurality of Catholics (46 per cent to 37 per cent) also wanted to see decommissioning by the paramilitary organizations (*Irish Political Studies* 1995, p. 309). However, as decommissioning became a more hotly contested issue between nationalists and union-ists in the peace process, Catholics began to fall into line with their political leaders, who opposed decommissioning.

The importance of the permanence of the IRA ceasefire was that, if sincere, it prevented Sinn Féin from using the threat of a return to violence at the negotiating table with the constitutional parties. The implicit threat of a return to violence would bolster Sinn Féin's bar-gaining position in all-party talks (its political support was only 10–12 per cent). The republican movement, given its scepticism of British governments and their intentions (particularly in view of its perfidy during the 1975 ceasefire), was opposed to declaring a 'permanent' ceasefire that robbed the movement of its bargaining power and could be interpreted as a surrender. Towards the end of September, Adams implied that the ceasefire was not necessarily permanent but contin-gent: 'None of us can say two or three years up the road that if the causes of conflict aren't resolved that another IRA leadership won't come along because this has always happened' (Bew and Gillespie 1996, p. 70). The Sinn Féin leadership may have been unable to deliver a 'permanent' cessation, but the wording of the ceasefire was more than even the RUC Chief Constable had expected (*Guardian*, 22 May 1996).

The British Army had long argued that there was no purely military solution to the conflict in Northern Ireland (see Chapter 5). There were reports that senior British army officers 'have long believed that the IRA really does mean to abandon its military campaign' (*The Economist*, 27 January 1996). This judgement of IRA intentions may have led to the pragmatic approach adopted by leading figures in the security forces – the RUC, the British army and MI5 – towards decommissioning. The army and RUC placed no importance on the handover of weapons, since the paramilitaries could rapidly re-arm; they were more concerned with the will and intention of those with weapons (*Guardian*, 16 November 1995). Indeed, senior soldiers and policemen suggested privately that pressing the IRA or the loyalists on the issue of disarmament could be counterproductive, since it might lead to increased pressure on the republican leadership and the breakdown of discipline (*The Economist*, 11 March 1995; see also the *Observer*, 1 January 1995). The RUC Chief Constable argued – as did his top officials and the Irish police, the Gardai – that Adams could not persuade the IRA to decommission before negotiations: 'He doesn't have that much control over them' (Mitchell 1999, p. 30). Michael Oatley, a former MI6 officer who had been involved in secret talks with the IRA, also acknowledged the leadership's problems with its grassroots. Weapons were dispersed under the control of local cells: 'Volunteers are not sheep. All joined to pursue an armed campaign for agreed objectives which have now been modified. Discipline in the face of such changes has been remarkable. Leaders can but lead; confidence in new policies takes time to spread' (*Sunday Times*, 31 October 1999).

The republican movement had been notorious for its splits. The chances of a permanent end to violence and a workable settlement would be reduced if significant numbers left the Provisional movement for more hardline paramilitary groups, such as the Irish National Liberation Army or the Continuity IRA, or established new breakaway groups, such as the Real IRA (founded 1997). The British government and the security forces therefore had a vested interest in seeing that the Sinn Féin leadership retained control of a united, disciplined movement and that splitters and dissenters were dissuaded. It was probably essential, in the short term at any rate, for the Provisionals to retain at least some of their weapons not only in order to maintain their own discipline but also to 'police' the extremist factions who might try to usurp the IRA's position and exploit difficulties within its ranks (Rowan 1995, p. 101; Mallie and McKittrick 1997, pp. 400, 405). There were reports that, in the run-up to the ceasefire, the Provisionals had established a team to deal with dissent and to ensure that the INLA and the Continuity IRA did nothing to endanger the peace process. If the Sinn Féin leadership was pushed 'too far' for concessions (for example, on decommissioning) during the peace process then the danger was that the Sinn Féin leadership would not be able to maintain unity.

There is evidence that the Conservative government shared to some extent the RUC's analysis of the republican movement, the conditionality of the ceasefire and the problems facing the leadership. As John Major recalled, 'Adams and many in the Provisional leadership seemed committed to a political process, but the IRA remained in full and active readiness' (Major 1999, pp. 461, 470, 477, 478). In January 1995, Patrick Mayhew told a group of sixth formers, in what he thought was a private meeting, that Gerry Adams' ability to control the 'hard men' in the republican movement was vital to maintain the IRA ceasefire, and that it 'would be a disadvantage to everybody' if he was replaced:

> To some extent we have got to help Mr Adams carry with him the people who are reluctant to see a ceasefire, who believe they might be betrayed by the British Government. If the hard men say, 'What did Gerry Adams do? We have called a ceasefire but got nothing sufficient in return', then Mr Adams will take a long walk on a short plank and be replaced by someone much harder. (*Irish Times*, 9 January 1995)

Also, in the same month, Peter Brooke praised Adams as a 'brave' and 'courageous' man (Mallie and McKittrick 1997, pp. 408–9).

Decommissioning and Demilitarization

The British government probably did not expect the IRA to declare a permanent ceasefire, and the security forces advised it that the IRA would not decommission. But there was also evidence that the IRA might well contemplate '*demilitarization*'. This 'constructively ambiguous' phrase could be interpreted to mean all-round demilitarization of paramilitaries and security forces or else the reduction of the British military presence. Prior to the ceasefire, Martin McGuinness had spoken of a 'total demilitarization' of Northern Ireland involving the IRA, loyalist paramilitaries and the British Army, which may have encouraged the British government to believe there could be movement on this issue (*Sunday Tribune*, 31 July 1994). He reportedly told Reynolds and Spring, 'We know the guns will have to be banjaxed' (Duignan 1995, p. 151).

The question of permanence and decommissioning was of symbolic importance to both republicans and unionists. Republicans saw a permanent ceasefire and decommissioning as being tantamount to surrender, leaving the nationalist community defenceless and themselves vulnerable to British treachery. For unionists, decommissioning represented a tangible symbol of the republican movement's intention to end the violence, and evidence of its commitment to the democratic process. If the republicans did surrender weapons it would be an indication of the leadership's ability to deliver its movement. Decommissioning also represented a test of the resolve of the British government to defend the Union. The unionists had little reason to trust the word of the Conservative government: it had negotiated secretly with Sinn Féin while publicly denying contacts, conceded to Sinn Féin demands for the clarification of the DSD and then retreated from its insistence on the permanence of the IRA's ceasefire. The British government had insisted publicly on decommissioning and the permanence of the IRA ceasefire; if it reneged on these pledges, what price its guarantees over consent and constitutional change?

Nationalists and republicans have claimed that the British government introduced the decommissioning issue only after the IRA's ceasefire in order to deadlock the 'peace process' (see, for example, O'Leary and McGarry 1996, p. 358). However, there is considerable evidence that the decommissioning issue was raised by both British and Irish governments *before* the IRA's ceasefire, and John Major claims that, if anything, the Irish government made the running (Major 1999, pp. 470–2). In October and December 1993, Patrick Mayhew stated the British government's demand for decommissioning. Again, as after the Downing Street Declaration, the British argued that the handing over of guns and explosives would be dealt with in exploratory talks after the IRA had declared a permanent ceasefire, and full negotiations would start once the IRA had handed over 'all its arms and proved that it had permanently renounced violence' (*Guardian*, 17 December 1993; see also Bew and Gillespie 1996). In an interview on 8 January, Adams criticized Mayhew, Hurd and Major for repeating their demand for an IRA weapons handover (*Irish News*, 8 January 1994; further recognition of the decommissioning demand by Adams came in the *Irish News*, 14 January 1994 and 26 February 1994; see also Bew and Gillespie 1996, p. 46). The Irish government also demanded the decommissioning of IRA weapons well before the IRA ceasefire (*Irish Times*, 16 December 1993; Bew and Gillespie 1996, pp. 35, 54).

The Irish government supported decommissioning prior to and immediately after the IRA ceasefire, but then shifted its position. Contemporary newspaper reports suggest that Albert Reynolds believed IRA decommissioning would not reach the agenda until sectarian murder had been brought to an end, and that paramilitaries would have to be disarmed soon: 'Both governments should be shortly in a position to organise and implement a full demilitarisation which will require the co-operation and participation of the paramilitary organisations' (*Irish Press*, 22 September 1994; *Irish Times*, 22 September 1994; *Independent*, 1 September 1994 on sectarian murder and IRA decommissioning; see also Bew and Gillespie 1996, p. 74).

By October 1994, both governments had plans for decommissioning, though the Irish were arguing that decommissioning could only be achieved when all-party talks were well under way (*Irish Times*, 22 and 25 October 1994). On 17 November 1994, Reynolds resigned as Taoiseach in a storm of domestic controversy. He was replaced by a Fine Gael/Labour Coalition led by John Bruton, who had a reputation for being more sympathetic to unionism than his Fianna Fáil predecessor.

So why did the Irish government shift its position on decommissioning after the IRA ceasefire? This is most convincingly explained as arising out of the dual role the Irish government was expected to play during the 'peace process'. Like the British government, which had to champion unionist interests while pushing that community towards accommodation, the Irish government had a responsibility to push republicans towards the 'centre ground' but also to champion their interests (Duignan 1995, pp. 125, 138; O'Kane 2007). In the wake of the ceasefire, pan-nationalism moved to shore up the Sinn Féin leadership and demonstrate the benefits flowing from the 'unarmed struggle'. If the Irish government had broken ranks with the 'pan-nationalist front' and aligned itself with the British government against Sinn Féin over decommissioning, this would have represented a severe blow to the credibility of the republican leadership's unarmed, pan-nationalist strategy, and undermined the IRA's ceasefire.

The British government claimed that it had to deliver on decommissioning to have any prospect of bringing about all-party talks (*The Times*, 16 December 1994). But Major attempted to avoid turning the surrender of guns into a precondition for progress and in October

1994 a distinction was drawn between the decommissioning of explosives (Semtex), which were not used for defensive purposes, and guns. In January 1995 it was suggested that the IRA might decommission their offensive weaponry and that this might be linked to prisoner releases and the withdrawal of troops to barracks during daylight hours. The gap between the British government's public insistence on decommissioning and its private view of decommissioning's futility was 'every day wider'. What the government was seeking was a gesture from the Provisionals, the sudden 'discovery' of Armalites in the Republic, 'Something to calm the increasingly fragile nerves of its Ulster Unionist allies that this peace process isn't leading them inexorably down a path to somewhere they would rather not go' (*Guardian*, 17 January 1995). The new Irish Taoiseach, John Bruton, said both governments were agreed that the decommissioning of weapons was 'not a pre-condition' to all-party talks and rejected suggestions that the British were deliberately stalling and attempting to keep Sinn Féin out of any talks.

The Framework Documents: 'Overbalancing'?

The Framework Documents were published on 22 February 1995. They are composed of two sections: the first contains the British government's understanding of where agreement might be found among the parties on new institutions for Northern Ireland, while in the second section the British and Irish governments present their best assessment of where agreement could be found concerning new political arrangements between Northern Ireland and the Republic, and between the two governments. The proposals were 'strongly commended' to the parties (Framework Documents, p. vi). They suggested the establishment of a power-sharing Northern Ireland Assembly and executive, with a system of checks and balances to protect minorities alongside a North–South body with considerable 'executive, consultative and harmonising functions'. Separate referendums in Northern Ireland and the Republic would be called to endorse any settlement. There was also an implicit threat to unionists that if they attempted to collapse any settlement, North–South co-operation would continue.

The Framework Documents were laced with the rhetoric of 'harmonisation' and North–South co-operation, which nationalists had long interpreted as paving the way to Irish unity (see Chapter 3).

The Irish government and opposition were 'well-satisfied' with their achievement. The republican leadership's response to the documents was 'enthusiastic', and Adams commended its 'all-Ireland character' (*Irish Times*, 23 February 1995; Delaney 2001: 377).

The principal unionist parties were united in their condemnation of the Framework Documents, which they felt were another step down the slippery slope to Irish unity (Cochrane 1997, p. 334). Unionists feared that 'harmonisation' and the all-Ireland focus of the documents would lead 'inexorably to joint authority between Belfast and Dublin', with the North–South body acquiring more and more powers, thus becoming an 'embryonic all-Ireland government' leading ultimately to Irish unity ('Response to Frameworks for the Future', UUP, 10 March 1995). The policy areas for harmonization suggested to unionists an ideological project of constitutional engineering to produce Irish unity rather than pragmatic co-operation. Furthermore, the Assembly was so hamstrung with checks and balances that it would be deadlocked, leaving the North–South institution and the Anglo-Irish process to dominate. Unionists were looking for a final settlement, not an interim step towards Irish unity. Protestants and Catholics, like their political representatives, reacted very differently to the publication of the Framework Documents. A narrow majority in one poll believed the Framework Documents 'form the basis for a lasting peace'. While 73 per cent of Catholics agreed with this statement, only 36 per cent of Protestants did, and 58 per cent of Protestants and 49 per cent of Catholics thought the documents 'will eventually lead to a united Ireland' (*Irish Political Studies* 1996, pp. 257–8).

Why did the governments produce such an apparently one-sided document? It has been claimed that the British government simply miscalculated, and using the papers from the Mayhew talks they attempted to construct a balanced document without taking into account the changing political context between 1992 and 1995 (NIO source). This account appears less than convincing. Major had consulted Molyneaux over the Joint Declaration but did not do so over the Framework Documents, even though he was aware by October 1994 of the UUP leader's increasingly difficult position within his own party (Major 1999, p. 465). A more likely explanation of the 'one-sidedness' of the Framework Documents is the British and Irish governments' need to deliver concessions to the nationalist community in order to underpin the Sinn Féin leadership's position and entrench the IRA ceasefire. All-party negotiations would then allow some dilution by unionists (Bew *et al.* 1997, p. 211). Major later argued that unionists misunderstood the Framework Documents, but in his memoirs he appeared to accept that they were tilted towards nationalism. In negotiating peace in Northern Ireland, 'balance' was important: 'If one side was happy I knew I had probably got it wrong. If my proposals attracted no more than grumbling and grudging acquiescence from both sides, I was perhaps on the right track' (Major 1999, pp. 469, 492).

The consequence of entrenching Adams' position was the discrediting of Molyneaux's 'inside track' strategy and the end of his leadership of the UUP. In March 1995, the UUP rejected the Framework Documents, and Molyneaux was faced with a damaging 'stalking horse' challenger for the leadership. His challenger claimed that the UUP leadership since 1984 had 'totally miscalculated the government's intentions and misled the pro-Union majority as to the security of the Union'. In August 1995, Molyneaux resigned the leadership.

The alienation of unionists after the publication of the Framework Documents and the plight of James Molyneaux suggested that the British government would have to work harder to keep unionists on board the peace process. In May 1995, the North Down by-election was won by the UK Unionist Robert McCartney, whose campaign was based on opposition to the Framework Documents. In July, there was a confrontation at Drumcree between Orange marchers and nationalist residents in Portadown, which crystallized unionist alienation and resentment at the course of the peace process. David Trimble, the MP for Upper Bann, played an important role in the Drumcree dispute and was subsequently elected, to the dismay of the British and Irish governments, to replace James Molyneaux as party leader. He was supported by the grassroots of his party, as the most 'hardline' of the candidates, but not by the party hierarchy or fellow MPs.

The British government's pursuit of the peace process, in spite of its 'understanding' with the Ulster unionists in July 1993, suggested that the unionist MPs at Westminster did not have a veto on British policy. Since July 1993, the British government had continued its secret contacts with Sinn Féin; concealed these contacts; negotiated the nationalist-sounding Downing Street Declaration; 'clarified' the DSD for Sinn Féin after refusing to do so; accepted the 'permanence' of the IRA's ceasefire; watered down its commitments on decommissioning; and finally signed up to the nationalist-orientated Framework Documents. These were published *after* Major's support had fallen so low that he needed UUP support to command an overall Commons majority.

The US Charade: Adams' Visa and 'Washington 3'

The US government played its part in the pan-nationalist front. President Clinton had taken his cue to enter the stage from key Irish nationalist actors, and secured Adams' first visa to the USA in 1994 and forced the British to drop their exclusion of Sinn Féin from an investment conference in Belfast. In 1995, Adams wanted to visit the USA again and to raise funds for Sinn Féin. The British had little answer to Sinn Féin's argument that if they could raise money in the UK why should they not be allowed to raise funds in the USA? The British *publicly* opposed Sinn Féin fundraising and wanted the US government to use its leverage with Sinn Féin to make progress on the decommissioning of IRA weapons before all-party talks could take place. In *private*, however, Mayhew told US officials that he wanted Sinn Féin to 'seriously discuss decommissioning' rather than just the handover of weapons before entering talks (see Dixon 2006a). Nancy Soderberg, Deputy National Security Adviser, described 'a complete disconnect' between what Mayhew asked of the US government in private and his stronger public statements for decommissioning later the same day, when he announced 'Washington 3' (O'Clery 1996, p. 191; and see below).

Patrick Mayhew's behaviour in not emphasizing to the USA the importance of an arms handover could be interpreted as a complete blunder; or else the British government, perhaps convinced of the moderation of the unionist electorate, may have believed that, in spite of the publication of the Framework Documents, it had room to push unionists further by taking steps to water down the conditions necessary to bring Sinn Féin into talks. Again, privately, the British government might not have been too distressed at the decision by the US president to lift the ban on Adams and allow him to raise funds in the USA. This decision would also bolster the credibility of the Sinn Féin leadership's unarmed strategy by demonstrating its influence in the USA. The British government's publication of the Framework Documents and its weakening of the decommissioning conditions in Washington 3 resulted in rising unionist and Conservative backbench dissent. The British prime minister made a public show of his fury at Clinton's decision over the Adams visa and refused to take the US president's telephone calls for five days (*Irish Times*, 15 March 1995;

O'Clery 1996, p. 195). Later, Clinton praised Major for taking 'brave risks' in making peace 'within the context in which he must operate' (*Daily Telegraph*, 18 April 1995). According to a source close to Clinton, by April 'the President had developed a genuine respect for Major and figured he was trying to do the right thing and understood why Major might need to make a gesture by not taking a phone call' (O'Clery 1996, p. 219).

Mayhew's announcement of the 'Washington 3' conditions for Sinn Féin's inclusion in all-party talks represented a further softening rather than a hardening of the British government's position on decommissioning. For Sinn Féin *to join all party talks*:

(a) republicans must demonstrate a willingness in principle to disarm progressively;
(b) there should be agreement on the practical modalities of decommissioning; and
(c) there should be actual decommissioning of *some* arms as a tangible confidence-building measure and to signal the start of a process. (my emphasis)

The British government's line on decommissioning had been cloaked in ambiguity. Initially, the British government had demanded 'substantive progress' on IRA decommissioning before they could enter into talks with *ministers*, let alone all-party talks. In Washington, Mayhew was arguing that British ministers would meet Sinn Féin if there was a 'willingness in principle' to disarm progressively (*Irish Times*, 8 March 1995). In May 1995, Michael Ancram met a Sinn Féin delegation, which prompted the UUP to refuse to meet the minister while he was engaged in such talks (*Independent*, 11 May 1995).

Explaining the Decommissioning Deadlock

John Major's principal interest was to see a successful peace process resulting in a stable accommodation between unionism and nationalism, which could only improve his re-election chances. The security forces had long held the view that there could be no purely military victory over the IRA. In spite of his dwindling support at Westminster and problems with his backbenchers, Major had advanced the peace process, suggesting he was not the prisoner either of his own backbenchers or the Ulster unionists. The UUP's influence at Westminster was limited; they could bring the Conservatives down but opinion polls suggested the result would be a Labour government with a large majority and without the need for UUP support. A former adviser to Patrick Mayhew argued that Major's ability to help unionists was 'severely limited': 'Mr Trimble . . . cannot compel the Government to adopt a Unionist agenda and Mr Major is unable to find the means of delivering it without risking the central achievement of his period in office – peace in Northern Ireland.' The most that Trimble 'could expect to achieve is to exert a negative influence on events' (*Guardian*, 18 January 1996).

The demand for decommissioning had been made jointly by the British and Irish governments prior to the ceasefire, and was not a post-cessation invention. The British government was under pressure from unionists to maintain their position on decommissioning. The difficulties of unionists in negotiating directly with republicans had been signalled prior to the ceasefire. At the UUP's party conference in October 1993 the party reacted angrily to suggestions that it would engage in talks with Sinn Féin even after decommissioning (*Sunday Tribune*, 17 October 1993; Bew and Gillespie 1996, p. 21). Ulster unionist MPs insisted that decommissioning take place, while Major 'has had little or nothing to say on this subject, and it does not appear to be of over-riding concern in the Republic' (*Irish Times*, 1 September 1994; *Guardian*, 1 September 1994). Pro-unionist Conservative cabinet members and backbenchers appeared more motivated by security issues (for example, decommissioning) than the Framework Documents, and tended to take their cue from the UUP (Mallie and McKittrick 1997, pp. 351, 352). This suggests that the primary influence on decommissioning was coming from the Ulster unionists rather than from Conservative unionists (Seldon 1997, p. 484), although it is difficult to disentangle the two factors. Newspaper reports suggest that there were 'significant ministerial and inter-departmental differences of opinion' on the handling of the peace process. While Major was determined to push the process forward, he was constrained by Michael Howard, the home secretary, and other right-wingers on the Conservative backbenches (*Independent*, 3 August 1995). Gerry Adams acknowledged the constraints on Major, but the peace process was 'the only positive thing he has going for him' and could put him in the history books (*New York Times*, 25 April 1995).

The British were 'demilitarizing' and had retreated from their demand for IRA decommissioning before Sinn Féin representatives met ministers. The Irish and US governments were both urging a gesture by the IRA on decommissioning in order to secure entry into all-party talks with unionists (*Irish Times*, 24 June 1995). In May, Bruton and Major had described such a gesture as 'not so much a requirement from both governments, but a necessary step for Sinn Féin in talks with other political parties in Northern Ireland' (*Irish Times*, 24 June 1995). In June 1995, the British and Irish governments agreed on a joint effort to break the deadlock over decommissioning. Dick Spring, the Irish foreign minister, wrote to Bruton, setting out the reasons for the deadlock:

> The essential difficulty as I see it is that the British Government, already in a vulnerable position, is afraid of movement away from its Washington tests, because there is nothing to protect its flank. On the other hand, those who believe that the British Government has the power to persuade the Unionists to engage in dialogue in the absence of progress on decommissioning are suffering from a delusion. And our own best assessment suggests that the Sinn Féin leadership is powerless to force the issue with their hardliners, even assuming they want to. (Quoted in Mallie and McKittrick 1997, p. 356)

There was some recognition even within Sinn Féin that it was the pressure from unionists and their reluctance to sit down to negotiate with Sinn Féin without any gesture on decommissioning that underpinned the decommissioning demand from Britain. In January 1995, Sinn Féin's newspaper argued: 'Today the Dublin government, the RUC and Garda chiefs, and many political parties agree that the issue of arms should not be pushed forward as an obstacle to the peace process. One suspects that even John Major does not believe that this should happen' (Patterson 1997, p. 275).

While the Irish understood the British government's problems with unionists, Spring's best assessment was that the Sinn Féin leadership also had little room for manoeuvre and that the republican grassroots were getting restless (Mallie and McKittrick 1997, p. 356). The difficulties encountered by the Sinn Féin leadership with its dissidents may explain why by September the Irish government had moved more into line with the republican position on decommissioning. According to Major, 'In private Adams and McGuinness were reasonable. They had boxed themselves in, and seemed to want help in getting out' (Major 1999, p. 477).

On 5 September the Irish government pulled out of an Anglo-Irish summit scheduled for the following day. The Irish prime minister, John Bruton, had been coming under pressure from Sinn Féin, John Hume, Dick Spring and the Fianna Fáil opposition 'not to be seen to be embracing London's insistence on some form of IRA disarmament as a pre-condition to all-party constitutional talks' (*Guardian*, 6 September 1995). The summit also looked set to embrace the option of an international disarmament commission to which Sinn Féin also objected (*The Economist*, 2 December 1995). 'Senior republicans' later warned that Britain was close to its goal of splitting the pan-nationalist consensus by winning Bruton's support for decommissioning: 'It's going to be very difficult for Mr Bruton as Taoiseach. By seeming to echo Major the whole image going out is that the nationalist consensus is gone. It was on that basis that the IRA gave their ceasefire' (*Guardian*, 25 September 1995). One report suggested Sinn Féin warned Bruton there would be 'blood on the streets' if he met John Major at their scheduled summit and agreed a 'twin-track' process: decommissioning and talks (*Guardian*, 21 February 1996).

In order to preserve the IRA ceasefire, the US and Irish governments had to make sure 'the whole image going out' was of a pan-nationalist consensus driving the British back. According to Major, 'The Irish were clearing every step they took with the Provisionals; and the Provisionals kept upping the ante' (Major 1999, p. 478). Days after the cancellation of the Anglo-Irish summit. Spring moved to restore the image of pan-nationalist unity when he argued against any decommissioning before all-party talks (Bew and Gillespie 1996, p. 118). In October, Spring was claiming that 'The crucial point is that the guns are silent.' Both the British and Irish governments believed that their respective 'clients' – the unionists and the republicans – could be pushed no further (*Independent*, 7 September 1995). British ministers reportedly believed the IRA should decommission out of conviction, but also because the government believed it should reflect unionist concerns, in parallel with the way the Irish government reflected nationalist interests (*Independent*, 6 September 1995).

The Mitchell Report and the End of the IRA Ceasefire

On 28 November, the British and Irish governments announced a 'twin-track process to make progress in parallel on the decommissioning issue and on all-party negotiations'. The two governments had 'the firm aim' of achieving all-party negotiations by the end of February. The governments would 'invite the parties to intensive preparatory talks to reach widespread agreement on the basis, participation, structure, format and agenda to bring all parties together for substantive negotiations'. These matters for discussion would include 'whether and how an elected body could play a part'. An international body, chaired by US Senator George Mitchell, was to be established to 'provide an independent assessment of the decommissioning issue'. The governments would not be bound to accept its recommendations, which were advisory, but 'will consider carefully any recommendations it makes and give them due weight on their merits'.

George Mitchell's report on decommissioning was published on 24 January 1996. It concluded that 'the paramilitary organizations will not decommission any arms prior to all-party negotiations'. However, there 'is a clear commitment on the part of those in possession of such arms to work constructively to achieve full and verifiable decommissioning as part of the process of all-party negotiations'. Major claims that Mitchell privately admitted that 'he was stretching a point for tactical reasons': that is, there was little evidence that the IRA would decommission during negotiations, but this optimistic interpretation helped to push the peace process forward (Major 1999, p. 486). The Commission recommended that 'some decommissioning take place during the process of all-party negotiations rather than before or after'. Those involved in negotiations should affirm their total and absolute commitment to what became known as the 'Mitchell Principles' of democracy and non-violence.

The British government struck a compromise between unionist and republican positions: the unionists would get an 'elected body' (rather than an assembly). while the republicans would be allowed into all-party talks without *prior* decommissioning. Decommissioning would take place during all-party talks, as envisaged by Mitchell. John Major told the Commons, 'The government believe that such an elective process offers a viable alternative direct route to the confidence necessary to bring about all-party negotiations. In that context, it is possible to imagine decommissioning and such negotiations being taken forward in parallel' (House of Commons, vol. 270, col. 354, 24 January 1996). Patrick Mayhew, according to the *Guardian*, 'publicly insists the IRA and loyalists must hand in some weapons before talks, but in private is prepared to accept whatever proposals will ensure that Unionists will talk to Sinn Féin. Interested in an assembly if it will bring David Trimble along' (*Guardian*, 20 January 1996).

The UUP, though critical of Mitchell's failure to insist on decommissioning, were relatively content. They endorsed the elected body but their position was ambiguous. This was sufficient to indicate that they might well take part in all-party talks without prior decommissioning. But it also allowed them to defend their flank from Paisley by insisting that the need for decommissioning had not been removed. The DUP was also prepared to join an elected body that contained Sinn Féin members.

Nationalists reacted with outrage over the British government's decision, as they saw it, to 'bin' the report, though this compromise had long been trailed and was winning support with the US government, the British Labour opposition and even the Irish government (Mitchell 1999, pp. 33–8, 40). Publicly, nationalism had to remain united against the British to persuade republican hardliners that the pan-nationalist front was still united, powerful and could deliver through the unarmed struggle. Privately, however, the Irish government had reacted positively to Trimble's suggestion of an elected assembly and probably realized this was the most likely basis for a compromise that would bring both unionists and republicans into all-party talks (*Guardian*, 16 November 1995; Major 1999, p. 480).

On 9 February 1996, the IRA ended its 18-month ceasefire by detonating a bomb in the Canary Wharf area of London's Docklands, killing two and injuring over 100 others. The IRA's operation had been planned from the previous October or November, even before the Mitchell Commission was established (Patterson 1997, p. 285). Unionists argued that the IRA bomb demonstrated that the ceasefire had not been permanent, and vindicated its view of the ceasefire as a tactic. Nationalists and republicans, on the other hand, tended to blame the British government's intransigence and its interpretation of the Mitchell Report for bringing about the end of the ceasefire. Peter Hain, later Secretary of State for Northern Ireland, 2005–7, was reported to be one of five Labour MPs who sent greetings to Sinn Féin's 1996 Ard Fheis (annual conference) just six weeks after the Canary Wharf bomb (*Independent* 25 March 1996; Dixon 2006b).

During the first IRA ceasefire, the balance of power had shifted radically against the republicans. In 1994, the 'pan-nationalist front', which was to be the driving force behind the republican movement's unarmed strategy, consisted of Reynolds, Clinton, Hume and, arguably, also Kevin McNamara, keeper of the British Labour Party's pro-nationalist Irish policy. By February 1996, John Bruton had replaced Reynolds, and Mo Mowlam had shifted Labour's policy towards the centre. Clinton was supportive of Major's compromise on elections to get round the deadlock on decommissioning and may have drawn closer to the British government as the two deployed troops in Bosnia (O'Clery 1996, p. 227, p. 232, Seldon 1997, pp. 621–2). John Major later acknowledged the constraints on Adams, the intelligence he was receiving had shown that 'much of the Provisional movement' opposed Adams's unarmed strategy and saw the ceasefire as tactical (Major 1999, p. 488).

Reviving the Peace Process

The British and Irish governments accelerated the pace of the peace process through a joint communiqué released on 28 February. This prompted accusations that the governments had moved in response to renewed IRA violence. The two governments demanded a restoration of the ceasefire and agreed 'that an elective process would have to be broadly acceptable and lead immediately and without further preconditions to the convening of all-party negotiations with a comprehensive agenda'. At the beginning of negotiations all parties with an electoral mandate would have to make clear their total and absolute commitment to the Mitchell principles of democracy and non-violence. The participants 'would also need to *address . . .* its proposals on decommissioning' but this implied that actual decommissioning would not have to take place before the talks, to include Sinn Féin, started (my emphasis). Sinn Féin could take part in negotiations if the IRA reinstated its ceasefire and signed up to the Mitchell principles of democracy and non-violence.

The Forum elections on 30 May 1996 were the first elections to be held since the 1994 IRA ceasefire and were an important indicator of how the peace process had affected public opinion in Northern Ireland. The assumption of those in the British government and others that there existed a 'moderate silent majority' in Northern Ireland to sweep away the region's 'intransigent politicians' is comparable to the hopes of 1972–4 (see Chapter 5 above, and Dixon 1997b) and was severely shaken by both the Forum elections and the second confrontation at Drumcree in July 1996.

Although one in four people in Northern Ireland had voted for a party with a paramilitary wing, some of these votes could be interpreted as votes for the 'peace strategy' being pursued by those parties and, in Sinn Féin's case, as a vote for the reinstatement of the ceasefire. Sinn Féin, in spite of the end of the IRA's ceasefire and criticism from nationalist politicians, did better than expected, achieving its best-ever result in a Northern Ireland election. The disastrous performance of the UUP against the DUP was of considerable importance for the fate of the peace process. The UUP, which had taken a more conciliatory approach towards the peace process, crashed to its worst-ever electoral performance (apart from in European elections), while the DUP's hardline stance appeared to be reaping rewards and put pressure on David Trimble not to be seen to be 'too compromising' by softening his stance on Sinn Féin's entry into talks. The IRA failed to restore its ceasefire, and its bombing of Manchester's city centre (injuring 200 people) and its murder of Garda Jerry McCabe in the Irish Republic, hardened opinion in both Britain and Ireland. Sinn Féin members were prevented from taking their seats when all-party talks started on 10 June 1996.

Drumcree and the Security Dilemma

The confrontation between Orange marchers returning along their 'traditional' route from a service at Drumcree church through the nationalist Garvaghy Road area of Portadown increased tension in Northern Ireland and led to an annual confrontation during the peace process. The Orange marchers saw themselves exerting their democratic and cultural right to march on the 'Queen's highway' along traditional routes they had walked for over 100 years. At the time of the Anglo-Irish Agreement, unionists marched through the nationalist 'Tunnel' area of Portadown in spite of government bans. This led to violent clashes with the RUC, and the march was subsequently re-routed along the mixed Garvaghy Road area. In recent years, the Garvaghy area had become overwhelmingly Catholic, and the residents more resistant to the parade. Marchers argued that nationalist protest was IRA-inspired, since the newly-formed Garvaghy Road residents' association was led by Brendan Mac Cionnaith, a former republican prisoner, whom they refused to meet.

The nationalist residents of the Garvaghy Road objected to what they saw as a 'triumphalist', intimidating, sectarian parade passing through an overwhelmingly nationalist area. The nationalists demanded 'parity of esteem' and called for the marchers to return along the same route they had come by. Dick Walsh argued: 'The right to march, now loudly proclaimed by the unionists and resisted by their opponents, was once among the demands of the civil rights movement. A right often officially denied by ministers of home affairs and unofficially by Mr Paisley's friends' (*Irish Times*, 20 July 1996).

The Drumcree march, like the decommissioning issue, was seen by nationalists and unionists as an indicator of the power of nationalism and unionism to influence developments in the peace process. After reaching an agreement in July 1995, Paisley and Trimble headed the march and 'danced a jig' when they entered the town centre. This was seen by nationalists as triumphalist and breaking the spirit of the agreement; consequently, relations were soured between nationalists and unionists. David Trimble's 'hardline' credentials were boosted at Drumcree and this probably contributed to his election to the leadership of the UUP the following September. The confrontations at Drumcree, which became annual events, took many observers by surprise, particularly those, such as the British government, who had detected a gap between the moderation of the masses compared with the intransigence of the political elites (Dixon 1997d).

The conflict over Drumcree probably reflected polarization within Northern Ireland, but also added to it. It represented an alternative indicator of public opinion to elections and opinion polls. The confrontation at Drumcree in July 1996 resulted in appalling violence and shocked observers and public opinion. Unionists tended, with some reason, to see the conflict as being engineered by republicans (*Irish Times*, 5 March 1997; O'Doherty 1998). Nationalists were more likely to portray the confrontation as an upsurge of community feeling aggravated by Paisley's and Trimble's 'triumphant dance' the previous year. This time the RUC re-routed the Orange Order's traditional march away from the Garvaghy Road and there were fears that up to 100,000 Orangemen would converge on Drumcree to push the march through. This stand-off resulted in three days of rioting and sympathy protests across Northern Ireland which brought the region to a standstill. On 8 July, Michael McGoldrick, a Catholic taxi driver, was murdered by members of the UVF in neighbouring Lurgan. The reaction to Drumcree was symptomatic of unionist alienation from a peace process in which the British government appeared to be weakening the Union by making concession after concession to republican and nationalist demands. The decision to re-route the Orange march was seen by unionists as a threat to their identity and an attempt to appease republicans who had engineered the confrontation.

The mobilization of unionists exposed the vulnerability of the security forces in ways similar to those of 1972, 1974 and 1986. The RUC were stretched by widespread rioting and the army was eventually deployed. The *Independent* reported:

> substantial parts of the country seem to be largely in the grip of men in balaclavas who, through a mixture of menace and force of numbers, are posing a serious challenge to lawful authority. The security forces have made it clear that, with thousands of loyalist protesters active at spots all over Northern Ireland, they cannot guarantee free passage – even on major roads. The RUC is plainly almost at full stretch and more British troops are being sent in . . . almost elemental forces which periodically spring to the surface of Northern Ireland, are being unleashed. The current crisis . . . could let loose elements that no one will be able to control. (*Independent*, 11 July 1996)

Trimble met the leader of the hardline paramilitary organization, the Loyalist Volunteer Force, highlighting the 'grey area' between constitutional and unconstitutional politics (Dixon 2004b). On 11 July, after a five-day stand-off between the RUC and unionists at Drumcree, as well as trouble across Northern Ireland, the RUC Chief Constable allowed the march to go ahead. He feared that the confrontation planned for the following day would have brought thousands of Orangemen on to the streets and led to a widespread breakdown of law and order. He indicated that 3,000 soldiers and police could not have contained 60–70,000 loyalist demonstrators and the security forces might have had to use live ammunition to stop the crowd (*Sunday Times*, 14 July 1996; *The Times*, 15 July 1996). Following the RUC's decision to allow the Orange march to go ahead, there was serious rioting in republican areas which Sinn Féin struggled to restrain.

During and after Drumcree 1996 there was low-level conflict across Northern Ireland. The RUC estimated that over 600 Protestant and Catholic families moved during the week of the 'Siege of Drumcree' because of 'ethnic cleansing', resulting in 'probably the biggest single episode of demographic realignment in 25 years'. Up to £50 million of damage was done to property (*Irish Times*, 28 December 1996). In the aftermath of Drumcree, nationalists boycotted Protestant shops, putting some out of business. Sinn Féin supported the boycott but denied they were orchestrating it. There were also incidents of attacks on churches, Orange Halls and civilian homes. Loyalists picketed a Catholic church at Harryville for 20 months in protest against a ban on an Orange march at nearby Dunloy (*Irish Times*, 4 December 1996; *Irish News*, 1 June 1998). *The Economist* commented: 'Intimidation and boycott are the stuff of Irish history. They are hard to prove and harder still to quantify, but their effects are poisonous and lingering' (*The Economist*, 3 August 1996).

The confrontation at Drumcree in 1996 highlighted, once again, the 'security dilemma': the limited ability of the security forces to cope with a mass uprising among unionists. There were fears that Northern Ireland could descend into all-out civil war. The new RUC Chief Constable, Ronnie Flanagan, later said: 'Northern Ireland cannot withstand another summer like this one. The intensity of the violence which our officers withstood was of a scale that I hadn't seen over 25 years. The country stared into the face of great difficulty and crept right to the edge of the abyss' (*Independent*, 31 August 1996). Patrick Mayhew issued a statement after the Anglo-Irish Conference meeting on 18 July 1996 claiming 'that he could not guarantee the RUC would be able to stand up to another Drumcree-type show of force'. Mark Durkan, SDLP chairman, said Mayhew was sending out a dangerous signal: 'People are getting a cue now from the Secretary of State that the way in which you impose or secure the outcome you want on a contentious march is to use local geography and mobilise numbers' (*Irish Times*, 20 July 1996).

The peace process had again reached deadlock. The polarization of society in Northern Ireland indicated at the Forum elections and as a result of Drumcree constrained the possibility of movement towards the centre ground among nationalist and unionist political elites. British hopes in the 'moderate silent majority' – as with the first peace process 1972–4 – were again dashed. For Major, the centre ground 'barely existed' (Seldon 1997, p. 662). In the wake of Drumcree, Major appealed to the people of Northern Ireland to reject the extremes and look to the centre (even though the 'extremists' had just been 'rewarded' at Drumcree: see the *Independent*, 17 July 1996). Mayhew accepted the faults in his own analysis: 'For my own part, and I think for a great many people, the wish had been father to the thought that on each side ancient fires of hostility and fear had greatly diminished. They had not' (Mayhew speech to the British–Irish Association, 7 September 1996).

New Labour, New Peace Process?

On 1 May 1997, a 'new' Labour government was elected with a 177-seat majority. Those who accepted the nationalist view of the peace process believed that the Conservative government had been deliberately obstructive of the peace process, and that a Labour government, with its large majority and traditional sympathies for Irish unity, would (and did) easily succeed where the Conservatives had failed. Sceptics tended to interpret the breakdown of the first IRA ceasefire as arising out of the problem, which would face any government, of bringing republicans and unionists simultaneously to the negotiating table. The Labour Party in opposition had maintained bipartisanship and supported the Conservative government's Northern Irish policy. The new Secretary of State for Northern Ireland, Mo Mowlam, later wrote:

> The Major government had been unable to stand apart from mainstream unionism on decommissioning or parades or on many other issues. We could. We had a clear, principled position and we stuck to it. We were in a position to take a lead. I often sympathized with Major or Mayhew during Prime Minister's or N. Ireland Questions in the House of Commons when they were desperate to make progress, going through questions, giving answers designed not to offend the unionists in the House or the nationalists either in the House or across the water. At times we had to do much the same, but never to the same extent as John Major and Paddy. We were able to make statements and progress in a way that had just not been possible for them. (Mowlam 2002, pp. 116–17)

The Labour government's success in steering the peace process to the Good Friday Agreement in April 1998 could be taken as evidence that the Conservatives were dragging their feet. Yet, in many respects, the Labour government's policy towards Northern Ireland followed that of the previous Conservative government. In opposition Labour had given bipartisan support to Conservative policy and in government it attempted to deliver the Conservatives' 'Mitchell Report compromise'. The unionists already had their Forum and the Labour government offered Sinn Féin certain procedural guarantees, including an end date to all-party talks. Labour's fudge on decommissioning was not far from the Conservatives' aspiration that it should be dealt with in parallel, but not at the start of talks. Labour's task was made easier by the political credit that comes to a newly-elected government with such a large mandate. The relatively good showing for the UUP against the DUP in the General Election eased the electoral pressure on Trimble and facilitated his decision to enter all-party talks that included Sinn Féin.

The Labour government attempted to give constitutional reassurances to unionism while making concessions to republicans to restore the IRA's ceasefire. Prime Minister Tony Blair delivered a speech that reaffirmed his belief in the UK. Northern Ireland would remain in the Union so long as that was the wish of the majority expressed formally through a referendum and endorsed by the British Parliament: 'This principle of consent is and will be at the heart of my government's policies on Northern Ireland. It is the key principle.' Given Labour's adherence to this principle Blair argued, 'none of us in this hall today, even the youngest, is likely to see Northern Ireland as anything but a part of the United Kingdom. That is the reality, because the consent principle is now almost universally accepted.' Having sought to reassure unionism, Blair turned to Sinn Féin: 'The settlement train is leaving. I want you on that train. But it is leaving anyway, and I will not allow it to wait for you. You cannot hold the process to ransom any longer. So end the violence. Now.'

On 16 June 1997 two RUC men on patrol in Lurgan were murdered by the IRA. Publicly, Mowlam cut off dialogue with Sinn Féin but behind the scenes exchanges continued. After assuring residents that the Drumcree parade would not go through the Garvaghy Road, she reversed her decision, to the fury of nationalists. There were concerns, as in 1996, that the police would be overwhelmed if the Drumcree stand-off continued for too long (Mowlam 2002, p. 95).

The Labour government gambled that in their 'honeymoon period' after the election they could concede to Sinn Féin's demands, win an IRA ceasefire, and bring the unionists into all-party talks. If the IRA refused to declare a ceasefire then the peace process was effectively dead and the two governments could fall back on the all-party talks process, knowing they had made all reasonable attempts to restore the ceasefire. The IRA restored its 'complete cessation' on 20 July, but its second ceasefire was met with more caution and scepticism than the scenes of celebration that accompanied the first one.

Following the IRA ceasefire, attention now focused on the Unionist Party leader, David Trimble. If the UUP walked away from talks there would be no prospect of an agreed settlement. The fear of unionists was that a settlement might then be imposed over their heads by the British and Irish governments and submitted to a referendum. Although the British government had denied this in the past, they had been sufficiently ambiguous to leave room for doubt. Trimble carried out a wide-ranging consultation exercise within his party. Ian Paisley warned Trimble that if he entered all-party negotiations he 'could find himself . . . a chief without Indians'. Although the UUP did not attend the start of talks on 9 September 1997, the UUP (along with the UDP and PUP) took their seats on 17 September in what many commentators agreed was a brave gamble. On 23 September, the Ulster Unionists sat down at the negotiating table with Sinn Féin for the first time in 75 years. A leaked document later revealed Blair's appreciation of the risks Trimble had taken for peace. He told the US 'Congressional Irish Lobby' that Trimble 'had come a good deal further than many Unionists wanted him to . . . It was important to remember that Trimble was under constant attack from Paisley and McCartney, so that giving comfort to the Ulster Unionists was vital' (*Irish Times*, 17 February 1998).

The talks process lasted from September 1997 until April 1998. The British government attempted to pacify both republican and unionist audiences. Violence spilled over and both the UDP – the political wing of the UDA – and Sinn Féin were temporarily kicked out of the talks after violence by their military wings. The Heads of Agreement document in January 1998, as well as visits to loyalist prisoners by Mowlam and Trimble, helped to steady loyalist nerves about the direction of the peace process, and clarification a few weeks later of this document reassured republicans. The republican leadership had sent out mixed messages, launching a 'no return to Stormont' campaign while at the same time talking about the process producing a renegotiation of the Union. In the autumn of 1997 a splinter group of republicans balked at signing up to the 'Mitchell principles' and broke away to form the 'Real IRA'. Trimble was criticized for failing to prepare his party and supporters for the compromises necessary in any settlement.

The Good Friday Agreement

The outline of the Good Friday Agreement (or Belfast Agreement), signed on 10 April 1998, was widely anticipated, and to a considerable extent dictated by what was deemed to be 'politically possible'. What was remarkable about the Agreement was that it won the support of the leadership of both Sinn Féin and the UUP when it fell so far short of their publicly stated positions. The GFA was, to some extent, choreographed by the British and Irish governments to maximize support among public opinion for the deal. There was an attempt to manage the presentation of the negotiations so that all the pro-Agreement parties and governments could appear to their audiences to have 'won' from the negotiations. This, it was hoped, would help to secure the endorsement of the people in the subsequent referendum. The most dramatic, probably 'unscripted', scene of the talks involved the walking out of Jeffrey Donaldson of the UUP, from the nego-tiations because he felt that the GFA did not make explicit enough the link between the release of prisoners and IRA decommissioning and Sinn Féin's participation in government. A side letter from Blair reassured Trimble on decommissioning, who then agreed to sign the GFA. The Agreement's 'constructive ambiguity' on decommissioning allowed Sinn Féin and the UUP to interpret its decommission-ing section very differently, but this stored up problems for the future when it became clear what was the dominant interpretation (Dixon 2009).

The Agreement comprised several elements.

A Northern Ireland Assembly

This is a 108-member assembly, elected by proportional represen-tation (single transferable vote), to have legislative and executive power over those matters formerly the responsibility of the Northern Ireland departments. The Assembly is constrained by checks and balances to prevent majority domination. Members of the Legisla-tive Assembly (MLAs) have to indicate whether they are unionists or nationalists (or 'other') for the purpose of cross-community vot-ing. There are two alternative special voting procedures that can be triggered for key decisions. First, *parallel consent*, in which a majority of both unionists and nationalists present, and voting must support, a proposal. Second, *weighted majority,* where 60 per cent of MLAs, including 40 per cent of both nationalists and unionists, must be in support. This element of the GFA has been criticized for entrenching and legitimizing communal division rather than attempting to tran-scend it. A consultative 'Civic Forum' has been formed, comprising representatives of business, trade unions, the voluntary sector and others with expertise.

An Executive

The First Minister (Trimble, UUP) and Deputy First Minister (Mallon, SDLP) were elected by a procedure that required cross-community support. The rest of the 10-member executive (3 UUP, 3 SDLP, 2 SF, 2 DUP) was appointed by the d'Hondt formula and reflects party strengths in the Assembly, guaranteeing executive positions for all parties with sufficient popular support.

The North–South Ministerial Council

This brings together those with executive responsibilities in Northern Ireland and the Republic, and covers twelve subject areas. There are six areas of co-operation (Transport, Agriculture, Education, Health, Environment and Tourism) and six implementation bodies (Inland Waterways, Food Safety, Trade and Business Development, Special EU Programmes, Language, Aquacultural and Marine Matters). Decisions on the Council are taken by agreement on both sides, with each side being accountable to their respective parliaments.

The 'British–Irish Council and Intergovernmental Conference'

The aim of this is to bring together representatives of the assemblies in Britain and Ireland to promote 'the totality of relationships among the peoples of these islands'.

Equality, Human Rights, Victims

The European Convention on Human Rights has been incorporated into UK law. In addition, there will be a Bill of Rights for Northern Ireland. A Human Rights Commission and an Equality Commission have been established. The Northern Ireland Victims Commission is part of a programme of reconciliation work.

Reform of Policing and Criminal Justice

There was to be a wide-ranging review of the criminal justice system and an independent commission was to be established to make recommendations for policing so that it would 'deliver a fair and impartial system of justice'.

Decommissioning and Prisoners

The GFA said little about decommissioning, committing the participants to use 'any influence they may have, to achieve the decommissioning of all paramilitary arms within two years'. Those paramilitary groups who had not established or maintained a 'complete and unequivocal ceasefire' would not qualify for early release of their prisoners, who would all be released within two years.

Sunningdale for Slow Learners?

Sunningdale cast a long shadow over the negotiations. A 'senior SDLP representative' said that his party was conscious of Trimble's difficulties and of the danger of a 'dramatic scenario with echoes of 1974' if unionists were pushed too far (*Sunday Business Post*, 5 April 1998). If the British and unionists had pushed the nationalists and republicans 'too far', then the Provisionals would probably have ended their ceasefire, while the alienation of the SDLP would have made any accommodation a distant prospect.

Seamus Mallon called the second peace process 'Sunningdale for slow learners', a criticism directed at both Sinn Féin/IRA and David Trimble and the UUP leadership, who had all rejected power-sharing in 1974. There were considerable similarities in the first (1972–4) and second (1994–8) peace processes:

(a) faith in 'the people' and the 'moderate silent majority';
(b) the British government attempted to include paramilitaries in both peace processes. The IRA refused to participate in the first peace process, but both republican and loyalist paramilitaries agreed to participate in the second peace process;
(c) a British declaration that it would accept the will of the majority in Northern Ireland if it favoured Irish unity and effectively that Britain had 'no selfish strategic or economic interest' (these declarations, it was hoped, would undermine the republican rationale for violence);
(d) British declarations of neutrality accompanied by statements of support for the Union;
(e) close co-operation between the British and Irish governments;
(f) an attempt to 'balance' unionist and nationalist claims; and

(g) a settlement at Sunningdale 1973 and the Good Friday Agreement 1998 on broadly the same ground: power-sharing and an Irish dimension.

There were some important differences between the Sunningdale Agreement and the Good Friday Agreement. The GFA is a more sophisticated and ambitious document which, for example, includes an East–West dimension that Sunningdale didn't have. The d'Hondt method of forming the Executive gives parties with sufficient support a *guarantee* of some Executive power if they choose to take it. In a voluntary, power-sharing coalition it is possible for nationalist and unionist parties to share power while excluding other significant parties from the Executive, which would have formed an Opposition. In 1974, republicans and loyalists could have been excluded from a power-sharing Executive, while the Good Friday Agreement, by contrast, ensured that republicans would have a share of power.

A 'Balanced' Settlement?

The Good Friday Agreement was designed to be presented in different ways to different audiences, like other key documents in the peace process. As Mo Mowlam points out:

> Fortunately the Agreement had space built in for each side to argue its merits in their own way. So for Trimble it 'secured the union' while for Adams it 'severely weakened' it. Both could point to different bits in the text to justify their views. That the Good Friday Agreement was open to multiple interpretations proved to be both a strength and a weakness – but it was the only way to get an agreement between all the different parties. (Mowlam 2002, p. 231)

The UUP leadership (and republican dissidents) presented the GFA as a disaster for republicans because it entrenched the Union, while for republicans it was transitional to Irish unity.

Nationalist and Republican Reactions

The North–South bodies were a key concession for pro-GFA nationalists and republicans. It could be argued that they formed the embryo for a government of a united Ireland that would gradually develop through a process of modernization and harmonization (see Chapter 3). Nationalists and republicans also gained from a strong commitment to the equality agenda, security, justice and language reform. Republicans could also take comfort from proposals for the swift release of paramilitary prisoners. A Sinn Féin Ard Fheis endorsed the Agreement and the leadership called for a 'Yes' vote, North and South, in the referendum.

Republicans opposing the GFA – the 32 County Sovereignty Committee and the Real IRA, Republican Sinn Féin and the Continuity IRA – argued that it represented the defeat of the republican movement. The 'armed struggle' had not been fought to see the legitimation of British rule in Ireland, the restoration of 'Stormont', the end of Sinn Féin abstentionism, acceptance of the principle of consent and the repeal of Articles 2 and 3. The all-Ireland referendum endorsing the GFA overturned the result of the all-Ireland 1918 General Election from which republicans claimed a democratic mandate for armed struggle. The Commissions on equality, human rights and policing were all British-appointed (Tonge 2004).

Unionist and Loyalist Reactions

The pro-GFA unionists argued that they had stood and fought for the Union while the rejectionist unionists had run away. The GFA had strengthened the Union, removed the Anglo-Irish Agreement and restored power and democracy to Northern Ireland. The East–West 'British–Irish Council and Intergovernmental Conference' was also an important recognition of the British dimension of the settlement and a counter-weight to the North–South body. The repeal by the Irish government of Articles 2 and 3, and their replacement endorsing unity by consent, strengthened and entrenched the Union. Prisoner releases and other aspects of the GFA, such as policing reform, would happen regardless of the GFA, and it was expected that decommissioning would take place before Sinn Féin sat in an Executive. It was argued that the anti-GFA unionists had no alternative to the Agreement, and unionist intransigence would result in an acceleration of the Anglo-Irish process under direct rule.

Unionist misgivings about the GFA were reinforced by the strong republican embrace of the Agreement. Anti-GFA unionists attacked the GFA for undermining democracy and making concessions to terrorists. It was not so much the constitutional issues, such as the

North–South bodies set up by the GFA, but the 'law and order' issues of prisoner releases, Sinn Féin getting into government without IRA decommissioning, and the reform of the RUC that most antagonized anti-Agreement unionists.

Six out of ten UUP MPs at Westminster, the Loyalist Volunteer Force and the Orange Order opposed the GFA. The mainstream loyalist paramilitaries and their political wings (UVF, UDA and UFF) supported the GFA. David Trimble managed to win over the UUP executive (53 votes to 23), and the Ulster Unionist Council, which consists of grassroots activists, voted by 72 per cent to 28 per cent (540 votes to 210) in favour of the Agreement.

The Good Friday Agreement: Segregation or Integration?

There are two contrasting approaches to conflict management in the academic literature on Northern Ireland: consociationalism, which is segregationist; and the civil society approach, which is integrationist. At the heart of consociationalism is a pessimistic, primordial view of communal identity which suggests that, for example, unionist and nationalist identities are an essential and 'natural' part of human beings that are not susceptible to change. Those who want to manage conflict must therefore work around these antagonistic communal identities rather than engage in futile or dangerous attempts to challenge or reconstruct them. Consociationalists aim to consolidate and reinforce these national and unionist identities in order to make them into the stable pillars of a very limited democracy. Contact between communal groups leads to conflict, so consociationalists favour segregation as a way of avoiding conflict and demobilizing people so that the benign elites have the freedom to lead the way to a power-sharing accommodation (Dixon 1997a, 2005). They claim the Good Friday Agreement is a consociational settlement, and they argue that negotiators were either following a consociational blueprint or else unconsciously drawn towards consociationalism by its compelling logic.

The civil society approach to conflict management is optimistic that communal identities can be remade into less antagonistic forms, partly by promoting contact and integration between people. By contrast with consociationalism, they favour the extension of democracy and the empowerment of civil society (groups that exist between the family and the state) because they argue that it is the people who are more accommodating than their malign elites. Civil society (integrationist) critics have accepted that the GFA is consociational and criticize it for reinforcing communalism, particular the requirement for MLAs to register as 'nationalist', 'unionist' or 'other'. They also criticize the d'Hondt system for Executive formation, which leads to ministerial 'fiefdoms' and no effective opposition to the Executive.

The Good Friday Agreement is best characterized as an integrationist variant of power-sharing. The Agreement bears some superficial, resemblance to consociationalism because integrationist power-sharing bears a superficial resemblance to segregationist power-sharing. *It is the (conservative) theory behind consociationalism's prescriptions that make those prescriptions consociational, not just the prescriptions themselves.* Consociationalists support power-sharing as a means of entrenching communal divisions in order to build an elitist and segregationist settlement on these primordial, communal pillars. Integrationists support power-sharing as a way of attempting to shift Northern Ireland from violent to non-violent conflict, to find a political means of dealing with the underlying causes of conflict and ameliorating antagonistic communal identities. There are numerous non-consociational aspects of the Agreement; for example, the core of consociationalism is supposed to be elite co-operation and consensus, but this has been absent from the devolved executives. The GFA is also explicit about encouraging integrated education and mixed housing (Dixon 2005).

The Referendum: An 'Honourable' Deception?

The Good Friday Agreement attempted – like previous British–Irish agreements – to be all things to all people. During the negotiations, Trimble told his executive that his bottom line was that before Sinn Féin had got into the executive it would have to drop its abstentionist line and begin decommissioning. The UUP leader believed he had reassurances from Blair that the process of decommissioning would begin immediately after the assembly came into being in June 1998 (*Sunday Tribune*, 12 April 1998). The Sinn Féin leadership were able to win republican support for the GFA by pointing to the difficulties that unionists were having in endorsing the Agreement. The Irish government released the 'Balcombe Street Gang' from prison to bolster the republicans' 'Yes' campaign, but this had a disastrous impact on unionism. Public and private opinion polls showed a haemorrhaging of Protestant support for a 'Yes' vote. A poll conducted for the *Irish Times* shortly after the prisoner releases suggested that while 56 per cent supported the GFA, 45 per cent of unionists would now vote 'No'. Just 35 per cent would vote 'Yes' and 20 per cent were undecided (*Irish Times*, 15 May 1998). This represented a major shift from a similar poll taken just after the GFA, which suggested that 62 per cent supported the Agreement (*Irish Times*, 16 April 1998).

Tony Blair went on the offensive to win over the support of unionists for a 'Yes' vote in the referendum. He encouraged the belief among unionists that Sinn Féin would not get into any Executive without decommissioning, but did not state this unambiguously. The *letter* of the Agreement did not insist on IRA decommissioning before Sinn Féin participated in the executive, but the British prime minister cultivated the impression among unionists that this was the *spirit* of the Agreement. On 20 May, Blair issued five handwritten, personal pledges to the people of Northern Ireland based on 'emotional triggers' revealed in polling and designed to address the fears of sceptical unionists (*Sunday Times*, 24 May 1998). The five pledges were:

1. No change in the status of Northern Ireland without the express consent of the people of Northern Ireland;
2. Power to take decisions returned to the Northern Ireland Assembly, with accountable North–South co-operation;
3. Fairness and equality guaranteed for all;
4. Those who use or threaten violence to be excluded from the government of Northern Ireland; and
5. Prisoners kept in jail unless violence is given up for good.

The prime minister 'was putting his credibility very much on the line, and putting things in his own handwriting was his way of showing people that he was sincere' (Mowlam 2002, p. 251). Rawnsley commented on the 'five pledges' that Blair made to unionists: '. . . The actual text of the Good Friday Agreement was stretched as far as it could go, and perhaps a little beyond, with the pledge: 'Prisoners kept in unless violence given up for good' (Rawnsley 2000, p. 141). These reassurances, like those given to Trimble during the negotiations of the GFA, were carefully worded to give the public impression of support for the unionist position, but were sufficiently ambiguous to avoid a cast-iron commitment and allow Blair to wriggle out of them after the referendum had been passed.

The referendum was passed by 71.1 per cent to 28.8 per cent on a high 81 per cent turnout in Northern Ireland. It was calculated that the referendum passed with the support of a bare majority of Protestants and an overwhelming majority of Catholics. An exit poll for RTE, the Irish television company, suggested that 51 per cent of Protestants and 99 per cent of Catholics supported the Agreement (*Independent on Sunday*, 24 May 1998) while a *Sunday Times* poll found 96 per cent of Catholics and 55 per cent of Protestants in favour. The 'Yes' campaign had the support of the media, the British and Irish governments, most of Northern Ireland's politicians and several influential figures, including the former RUC Chief Constable and 'policeman's policeman', Sir John Hermon. Analysis of the referendum result suggested that the 'Yes' vote in the unionist camp was bolstered by 140–160,000 new voters, most of them Protestants, who came out to support the Good Friday Agreement (*Sunday Tribune*, 25 May 1998). In the Republic, the referendum was passed by 94 per cent to 6 per cent on a low 56 per cent turnout.

In the wake of the referendum result, Blair backed down on the spirit of the commitments made during the campaign. The British government refused to enact legislation which linked the release of paramilitary prisoners to decommissioning. Neither did it insist that the IRA decommission before Sinn Féin entered the executive. At the Assembly elections in June 1998, the UUP suffered their worst-ever result (apart from the European elections), coming second to the SDLP in first preference votes. The DUP came within 3 per cent of the UUP vote and the anti-GFA unionists won a total of 27 seats, just three short of the 30 seats needed to deadlock the Assembly. The high turnout for the referendum campaign, which was thought to have brought out 'Yes' voting unionists, was not repeated for the Assembly elections. After the Assembly election the UUP (28 seats) needed the support of the PUP (2 seats) to give them a majority over the 27 MLAs for the anti-Agreement unionists (20 DUP, 5 UKUP, 3 Independent Unionists). Even among the 28 UUP MLAs there were rumblings of discontent (McDonald 2000, p. 268). The Alliance Party won 6 seats and the Women's Coalition 2, SDLP 24 and Sinn Féin 18 seats.

Tony Blair deceived unionists and the Northern Irish people into believing that Sinn Féin would not get into government without decommissioning. He also allowed unionists to believe that paramilitary prisoners would not be released until decommissioning had taken place or some other indication that their 'war was over'. Language was chosen very carefully so that the prime minister could avoid telling an obvious, 'outright' lie while at the same time deceiving the audience over the implications of the Good Friday Agreement. There is opinion poll evidence suggesting that there was a common perception among both 'Protestants' and 'Catholics' that participation in government and prisoner releases were linked to decommissioning (Dixon 2009). This 'honourable' deception probably helped the British government to win over a bare majority of Protestants to vote 'Yes' in the referendum on the Agreement and allow the peace process to move forward. The cost of this was that, as the deception was uncovered, unionists became increasingly aware that they had been duped by Tony Blair and became increasingly cynical about future assurances from the British government about the peace process. This was reflected in declining support for the pro-Agreement Ulster Unionist Party and its leader, David Trimble. The deception perpetrated by Blair on the people of Northern Ireland in May 1998 may have emboldened him to perpetrate similar deceptions in the run-up to the disastrous Iraq war in March 2003.

Conclusion

The problem for the British government in defending its position in a high-profile way against both nationalist and unionist critics is that these defences can be used in the propaganda war against it. For example, emphasizing the positive and long-term role the British have played in the peace process is likely to antagonize some sections of unionist opinion. On the other hand, emphasizing the continuity of British policy and the impracticality of Irish unity is unlikely to convince republicans to enter a peace process that they believe will result in Irish unity. The account of the peace process presented here casts serious doubt on the influential nationalist and unionist views of the peace process described at the beginning of Chapter 8 (an analysis of the peace process is presented in the Conclusion to this book).

A Critique of the Pro-Peace Process Nationalist View

The nationalist view can be critiqued on several grounds.

1. *There was no radical shift in British policy under Brooke that opened the way for the IRA ceasefire.* Since the early 1970s, the British had

tried to bring the IRA into the political process but the republican movement, believing it was winning, rejected these overtures. The British government's dilemma was to try to bring republicans to all-party talks without driving unionists away. The British position on its strategic or economic interests and Irish unity had changed little since the early 1970s, and successive British governments had kept the lines of communication open to the republican movement.

2. *The British government played a pivotal role in driving the peace process and it was not principally an Irish affair.* There has been a 'back channel' between the British government and the IRA since the mid-1970s, and this channel was activated on several occasions. There had been secret exchanges between the British government and Sinn Féin in the mid-1980s. In 1989 and 1990, Peter Brooke had made speeches that encouraged republicans to enter the political process, and this was continued by Patrick Mayhew. The renewal of the 'back channel' in 1990 and the subsequent secret exchanges with Sinn Féin indicated a commitment to bringing Sinn Féin into the political process even while the IRA bombed English cities and the Conservative government's majority was diminishing in the House of Commons.

3. *All-party talks without Sinn Féin were 'worth a penny candle'*, since they represented an important incentive for Sinn Féin to end IRA violence, and a viable process that could be revived if the republicans did not deliver a ceasefire and commit themselves to the peace process.

4. *The British did not deliberately obstruct the peace process or artificially establish decommissioning as a barrier for Sinn Féin.* The British government's interests in Northern Ireland were for stability and an agreed settlement (see the Conclusion to this book). John Major was more likely to benefit electorally and secure his place in history if he could pursue the peace process to a successful conclusion. There is evidence of British determination to push the 'peace process' in speeches dating from 1989; in contacts with Sinn Féin dating back to 1990; its efforts at confidence-building; negotiation of the 'nationalist-orientated' Downing Street Declaration and Framework Documents; and its watering down of commitments on decommissioning. Major advanced the peace process even though he was operating under significant constraints from domestic public opinion; a precarious parliamentary majority and then minority; Conservative backbenchers; and the need to keep unionists 'on board'. The impasse over decommissioning

arose more from the need to reassure unionists and bring them into the peace process than to secure his parliamentary majority, as the Irish government acknowledges in its private correspondence. This problem was exacerbated by the apparent polarization of opinion within Northern Ireland. The Labour government, even with a large parliamentary majority, struggled to overcome unionist insistence on decommissioning.

A Critique of the Anti-Peace Process Unionist View

There are several key problems with the unionist view of the peace process:

1. *The peace process is not a 'surrender process'.* Britain's primary interest in Northern Ireland lies in stability and this is most likely to be achieved by reaching a historic accommodation between nationalism and unionism (see the Conclusion to this book). If the British have been trying to disengage from Northern Ireland since 1921 why has it – having succeeded in withdrawing from the biggest Empire the world has ever known – failed to pull out? If Britain has been trying to disengage since 1921, this would suggest that Britain has had no selfish strategic interest in Northern Ireland not only since the end of the Cold War in 1989, but even before the Cold War started in the 1940s. Presumably, the end of Britain's economic interest in Northern Ireland also dates from the 1920s. If this is the case, then surely the British have had better opportunities to quietly slip Northern Ireland out of the Union during the past seventy-five years rather than going through the current, high-profile, peace process? Britain had considerable incentive to coerce Irish unity during the Second World War, but this was impracticable. During the recent conflict the most likely occasion for British withdrawal was the mid-1970s, following the collapse of power-sharing, but this course of action was seen as disastrous by both the British and Irish governments. Britain's primary interest in Northern Ireland is stability and this is unlikely to be achieved through withdrawal, though these interests could change (see Chapter 6).

2. *The peace process is not motivated by the economic effect of the bombing of the City of London in 1992, 1993 and 1996.* The government's public overtures to Sinn Féin date back to the Brooke

Speech in 1989, and the secret, 'back channel' contacts were renewed in 1990 well before the City of London bombings. For a long time Britain has not had any economic benefit from remaining in Northern Ireland. The Baltic Exchange bombing may have increased the economic incentive for Britain to reach a settlement, but this was more likely to be achieved by reaching a stable accommodation than through a withdrawal resulting in destabilization.

3. *British public opinion would probably support the expulsion of Northern Ireland from the Union.* The vulnerability of unionism is that it tends not to be seen in Britain as part of the nation. Opinion polls have consistently shown support for withdrawal from Northern Ireland and any solution that would rid Britain of this issue. However, withdrawal would probably not result in a stable resolution to the conflict because of the strength of unionist resistance to a united Ireland, as illustrated throughout the conflict.

4. *Harmonization and North–South structures are unlikely to erode unionist opposition to Irish unity.* The problem with this is that all the evidence (see Chapter 3) suggests that economic integration does not necessarily lead to political integration or the erosion of national identities. In spite of the harmonizing institution of the EU and the alleged onset of globalization, unionists have, if anything, become more opposed to Irish unity and an Irish identity than they were thirty years ago.

10

The End of the Peace Process? The Implementation of the Good Friday Agreement, 1998–2007

Introduction

The signing of the Good Friday Agreement (GFA) in 1998 was a remarkable achievement. The shape of the deal had been anticipated by: the Brooke–Mayhew talks of 1991–2; the Downing Street Declaration in December 1993; the Framework Documents of 1995; and the 'Heads of Agreement' document in 1998. What was impressive was the willingness of Sinn Féin and the Ulster Unionist Party to support an agreement that represented such a shift from their previous negotiating positions. The British and Irish governments intended that the GFA would be built on the moderate centre-ground of Northern Irish politics, with the SDLP and UUP marginalizing their hardline Sinn Féin and DUP rivals. There was, as in 1994, no obvious convergence in nationalist and unionist public opinion propelling this accommodation from below. This lack of convergence meant that the GFA was designed so that 'each protagonist could interpret it as a victory for his tradition' (Rawnsley 2000, p. 138). Sinn Féin leaders presented the GFA as part of a *process* towards Irish unity, while pro-Agreement unionist leaders claimed it was a *settlement* that involved the strengthening of the Union. The rough parameters of the GFA had been outlined, but the implementation of the Agreement was part of ongoing negotiations and some issues, including criminal law, policing, local government, a bill of rights and decommissioning were left open to interpretation and negotiation in order to provide political elites with the 'creative ambiguity' and 'wriggle room' to allow the Agreement and peace process to survive and evolve.

This chapter will argue that pro-Agreement unionism was under severe pressure as soon as Trimble signed the Agreement. During the referendum campaign, as we have seen (Chapter 9), Tony Blair deceived the public over the implications of the GFA for the release of prisoners and decommissioning in order to win the vote. The deception perpetrated by the British prime minister became more obvious as the Agreement was implemented, prisoners were released and terrorists found their way into government without any decommissioning. According to opinion polls, the public perceived that if anyone had benefited from the GFA it was nationalists rather than unionists. Sinn Féin/IRA got into government twice without giving up any guns (December 1999–February 2000, and May 2000–October 2001), a third time after an unspecified amount of IRA arms had been put beyond use (November 2001–October 2002), and a fourth time, with the DUP, after 'complete' decommissioning (May 2007–).

Anti-Agreement unionists exploited unionist disaffection, and by 2003 the DUP had become the dominant party of unionism. Sinn Féin/IRA had also triumphed over their moderate rivals, the SDLP, but threatened to lose IRA activists to violent republican dissidents in the RIRA and CIRA, who wanted to continue the 'armed struggle'. There was a widespread belief that the triumph of these hardliners represented the failure of the Northern Ireland peace process. The DUP had campaigned for a 'No' vote in the referendum and argued, like Sinn Féin, that the GFA was transitional to a united Ireland. While their opposition to the GFA appeared strong, this smokescreen concealed a more nuanced and tactical approach that allowed them, eventually, to reach a power-sharing deal with Sinn Féin. Sinn Féin did not object to sharing power with the DUP but they were unwilling to settle for anything less than the GFA. It was difficult to see the ground on which compromise could be achieved, particularly since opinion polls appeared to show the polarization of public opinion in the period after the GFA. In December 2004 there was a failed attempt at a 'mother of all deals' between Sinn Féin and the DUP, but this suggested that power-sharing might be on the cards. On 13 October 2006, the St Andrews Agreement laid the groundwork for the restoration of devolution on 8 May 2007.

This chapter describes several different perspectives on the implementation of the GFA and considers why the moderate parties failed to dominate politics after it. It describes how the hardline parties managed to overtake their moderate rivals and agree to share power. Were the hardline parties triumphant because they had moderated their position and stolen the clothes of their moderate rivals? Has the 'mother of all deals' been constructed in spite of growing communal polarization?

Perspectives on the Good Friday Agreement

Seven views on the Good Friday Agreement and its implementation are described below, and will be returned to at the end of this chapter. The first five perspectives are more 'party political' and should not obscure the fact that there were debates going on *within* these parties:

1. *Anti-Agreement republicans.* These included those who advocated a return to the 'armed struggle' (the Continuity IRA, Real IRA) and those who did not, but shared a similar, highly critical analysis of the Provisional republican movement (see *The Blanket* at www.phoblacht.net). They argued that Sinn Féin had betrayed republicanism by ending the 'war', accepting the 'partitionist' Good Friday Agreement (a deal that had been on offer at Sunningdale in 1973) and 'surrendering' to the British state. The CIRA and RIRA fought a violent campaign to try to destabilize power-sharing.
2. *Sinn Féin/IRA.* The Sinn Féin leadership embraced the GFA as a transition to a united Ireland and therefore demanded that its interpretation of the Agreement be implemented in full. The leadership argued that the GFA did not insist on decommissioning before either the devolution of power or the release of prisoners. Sinn Féin may have envisaged participating in devolution for a considerable period of time before having to 'use any influence they may have' to achieve the decommissioning of all paramilitary arms by May 2000. Sinn Féin opposed any attempt to retreat from the GFA but endorsed the St Andrews Agreement in 2006 and decided to share power with the DUP in May 2007.
3. *The SDLP* also favoured the full implementation of the GFA. They wanted unionists to enter government with Sinn Féin before any decommissioning, and criticized Trimble for failing to sell the Agreement adequately to unionism. But they also favoured decommissioning by the IRA, and a strand within the SDLP expressed some sympathy for the plight of pro-Agreement unionism. The party criticized the way the two governments

marginalized their party during the period after the signing of the GFA, but endorsed the St Andrews Agreement in 2006.

4. *Pro-Agreement unionists in the UUP.* argued that the Union was strengthened by the GFA. They argued that IRA decommissioning was part of the GFA and explicitly linked to the requirement that those in office must be committed to democratic non-violent means. The UUP were critical of the failure of the SDLP to share power with the UUP and exclude Sinn Féin after the IRA failed to decommission. The UUP criticized the DUP for failing to sign up to the GFA and argued that the St Andrews Agreement 2006 and devolution 2007 was essentially a remodelled GFA.

5. *Anti-Agreement unionists.* Moderate opponents of the Agreement, like Jeffrey Donaldson, argued that the UUP leader had not got sufficient guarantees on decommissioning and prisoner releases to support the GFA, but would work to make the deal a success if there was a 'Yes' majority. The DUP appeared to reject the GFA completely, but took a more subtle stance, which allowed them to take up their ministerial posts while not participating in the Executive when power was devolved. The party also left open the possibility that it would participate in a reformed GFA, which it did in May 2007. Robert McCartney of the UKUP not only rejected the GFA and the DUPs taking up ministerial posts but he also campaigned unsuccessfully against the St Andrews Agreement in 2006.

The final two perspectives have echoes within the party political debate but are more academic in orientation (see Chapter 9, pp. 270–1).

6. *The Civil Society approach* – this approach to conflict resolution argues that public opinion is more moderate than the extreme political elites. By mobilizing 'the people' and civil society, and through democratization, the extreme elites could be brought into line with the moderates. The people wanted consensus, 'government' and 'bread and butter' issues, not 'tribalism' and constitutional or identity politics. Advocates of the Civil Society approach argued that the Good Friday Agreement was flawed because it was consociational and therefore resulted in polarization after the signing of the GFA (Wilson 2003). This Civil Society position was echoed in the arguments of British and US politicians, the Alliance Party, the Women's Coalition and some in the SDLP.

7. *Consociationalists* claimed that the GFA was consociational and therefore that it should be implemented along consociational lines by reinforcing the communal pillars and creating separate provisions for each community. These pro-nationalist consociationalists insisted that their particular, rigid interpretation of the Agreement be implemented regardless of the consequences of this for pro-Agreement unionists.

Interpreting and Implementing the Good Friday Agreement

The Good Friday Agreement established a constitution for Northern Ireland but there have been important differences over to what degree that constitution is open to interpretation. 'Constitutional Traditionalists' argue that they have the single correct interpretation of the Agreement, while 'New Constitutionalists' argue that the Agreement is necessarily more ambiguous, dynamic and open to interpretation to allow politicians to make peace.

'Constitutional Traditionalists' argue that constitutions deal with conflict and political flux through the creation of a final, clear constitutional *settlement*. This is a single event at which an agreed document sets out and entrenches the political outcome after a conflict has been resolved (Hart 2001, p. 154). The constitution is a 'higher' law interpreted by legal 'experts' who decide the 'correct' interpretation and this is separated from party politics and policy-making. Pro-nationalist consociationalists have claimed to have the 'correct' interpretation of the GFA and demanded that this be implemented, with little regard to the impact this would have on the survival of pro-Agreement politicians in the UUP. For example, they declared the British government's suspension of devolution in February 2000 to be in contravention of the Agreement, even though a failure to suspend was likely to result in the end of Trimble's political career (Dixon 2009). By contrast, these nationalist consociationalists were less pedantic when it was decided that Seamus Mallon's resignation as deputy first minister had not taken place, or the IRA's violence did not constitute a breach of its ceasefire. Those who support a peace process insincerely have used rigid interpretations of agreements as a tactic for destroying them, by treating any contravention of rules as 'criminal acts'. Ian Lustick has argued that a peace process should be strategic, dynamic and ambiguous in order to create the scope for politicians who are committed to the principles underlying the agreement to be flexible and manoeuvre against anti-peace process rivals (Lustick 1997, p. 61, 62).

'New Constitutionalism' describes the practice of politicians during the peace process better than 'Traditionalist Constitutionalism'. 'New Constitutionalists' do not see a constitution as an end point closing down debate but rather as a process or an ongoing conversation in which the constitution is not seen in isolation from the wider social structure and political culture. Constitutions are 'a continuing conversation, or a forum for negotiation amid conflict and division', in which agreement is sought on the principles and practices of governance (Hart 2001, p. 154). Hart argues that the recent history of constitution-making suggests that it must be responsive and flexible in order to deal with uncertainty about the identity and inclusiveness of a 'nation' or a 'people', and to demands for 'participatory constitutionalism' from active citizens. The dilemma is to conduct government on agreed principles and with predictability but to 'avoid freezing into place the voices of one moment' (Hart 2001, p. 156). Constitutions are therefore landmarks in the transformation of conflict, rather than a completed map of conflict resolution (Hart 2001, p. 157). The 'New Constitutionalism' embraces constructive ambiguities – for example, over the timing of decommissioning and devolution – because of the room for manoeuvre that they create for pro-agreement politicians (Hart 2001, p. 164; see also Little 2004, pp. 8, 28, 81). This approach can also account for the fact that the GFA only produced an outline and the implementation of the Agreement was part of ongoing negotiations as the 'broad-sweep provisions of the Belfast Agreement' were turned into 'the detailed provisions of . . . the Northern Ireland Act 1998'. This Act would then have to be subjected to the judicial process and judicial interpretation (Hadfield 2001).

The British government took a pragmatic approach to the GFA, which sought to give politicians the flexibility they needed to manage and bring along key audiences. 'Political skills', or 'lies and manipulation', were used in an attempt to manage and choreograph the peace process to win over key audiences (Dixon 2002a). The law was stretched to take into account the political problems that pro-Agreement politicians were facing. For example, the British government turned a blind eye to IRA and loyalist breaches of their ceasefires. The decommissioning issue was dealt with pragmatically, the dispute being not so much over which politician *should* make concessions on the issue, but rather which politician *could* move without losing the support of key audiences and thereby endangering the peace process.

The Civil Society Approach and the 'People's Peace Process'

The assumptions of the Civil Society approach underpinned the idea of a 'People's Peace Process,' which suggested that 'the people' wanted the peace process to work and public opinion polls could be used to give them a seat at the negotiating table and a voice in 'their' peace process (Irwin 2002, p. 1). It was 'intransigent politicians' and not 'the people' who were the problem, and the peace polls would be used to pressurize the politicians towards accommodation. On the successful devolution of power in May 2007, Tony Blair claimed, 'The leaders played their part. But, ultimately, the people gave the leadership. They set the terms. They held us all to them. They gave the final imprimatur.'

There are several problems with the 'People's Peace Process' and its Civil Society assumptions. There were different groups among 'the people' who saw the peace process in very different terms and were increasingly voting for the more antagonistic, communal parties: the DUP and Sinn Féin. There were also other opinion polls which showed a bleeding of support for the GFA among Protestants. It is also clear from the 'peace polls' themselves that there was little popular support for a compromise such as the GFA prior to the Agreement (Irwin 2002, p. 115). Curtice and Dowds, reviewing opinion poll data, found a worsening of community relations in the two-year period running up to the signing of the GFA, and in the period after the Agreement they found traditional political loyalties were strengthened rather than weakened (Curtice and Dowds 1999). The GFA had been achieved in spite of the fact that Northern Ireland appeared to be more divided in 1998 than it had been in 1989 (see Table 1.2 on p. 23 for some Northern Irish opinion poll data over time). Crucially, they found that the public believed Tony Blair's promises that decommissioning would take place before prisoners were released or an Executive was formed. It was therefore not surprising that these issues continued to dog the peace process (Curtice and Dowds 1999).

Opinion polls do not suggest public convergence driving the Good Friday Agreement, yet even these polls probably overestimate the degree of public moderation. Since the early 1970s, opinion polls

Table 10.1   The tendency for surveys to underestimate support for hardline political parties and overestimate it for the more moderate parties

	Assembly election 26 November 2003 (%)	NILT survey October 2003– February 2004	Under/ overestimation (%)	Milward Brown, poll conducted 6–8 November 2003	Under/ overestimation (%)
DUP	25.6	15	−10.6	20	−13.7
UUP	22.7	19	+3.7	26	+8.3
Alliance	3.7	4	+0.3	6	+2.1
SDLP	17	17	0	22	+1
Sinn Féin	23.5	10	−13.5	20	−4.3

Source: www.ark.ac.uk.

and surveys have been notorious for overestimating the moderation of the people and underestimating support for hardline parties (Whyte 1990; Dixon 1997d). This is illustrated by the result of the Assembly elections in 2003. Although the polls were not taken on the day of the election itself, they do give a good idea of the way polls underestimate support for hardline parties (see Table 10.1). The 2005 NILT Survey also found that respondents would not own up to having voted 'No' in the referendum – only 10 per cent claimed to have voted 'No', while in 2000 only 20 per cent of the poll claimed to have voted 'No' (28.8 per cent had voted 'No' in the 1998 referendum) (www.ark.ac.uk/nilt, June 2006). If moderation is exaggerated in terms of party preference and voting preference, the same may be true of voters on other issues.

Civil Society assumptions informed the judgments of important political actors, particularly in the British government, during the first and second peace processes (see Dixon 1997d; Mowlam 2002; Dixon 2009). By acting on these assumptions, these actors underestimated the challenge facing key moderate politicians in bringing their supporters towards a power-sharing settlement. This was important, because the ability of the British government, in particular, to make realistic judgements of who could, and therefore *should*, make concessions in negotiations was vital in order to maximize the chances of sustaining moderate politicians and the peace process. It will be argued that the British government and others underestimated the difficulties facing David Trimble, and because of this did not support him sufficiently to improve his chances of survival.

'Saving Dave'

There is a perception that Northern Irish politics is a 'zero-sum game' or a 'balance', in which a gain for one 'side' is seen to be at the cost of the 'other.' Pro-Agreement governments and parties had to weigh up the degree of support they would give to Trimble and Adams, and this was important to the survival of those leaders. If Adams' position was undermined there was a fear that the IRA might go back to 'war'. It appeared that the peace process would collapse without Trimble, because during the post-Agreement period, 1998–2003, the DUP did not look as though it would contemplate power-sharing with Sinn Féin. The demise of Trimble and the UUP during this period, and the prosperity of Sinn Féin, raises questions about whether the two governments struck the right attitude in negotiations between the two parties. It may be useful to consider three, overlapping, explanations for the behaviour of the two governments in the post-Agreement period:

1. They may have calculated that Trimble could be saved, but from the signing of the Agreement they decided that it was more important for them to preserve the Adams leadership, and prevent the IRA going back to violence.
2. The two governments might have decided that Trimble's demise was inevitable, so it was more important to preserve Adams' position and await the arrival of the DUP at the negotiating table.
3. The British and Irish governments may simply have miscalculated the acute problems facing Trimble. British governments in the past did not have a great record – either during the first peace process or the Anglo-Irish Agreement – of correctly anticipating the mood of the unionist audience.

Pro-Agreement unionism was in difficulty as soon as the Agreement was signed, and this was suggested by the need Blair felt to deceive the unionist audience in order to win a 'Yes' vote in the referendum and save the Agreement. Critics have argued that it was Trimble's lack of leadership and his failure to 'sell' the deal actively that led to his failure to win-over the unionist audience to the GFA (Dixon 2004a). Many of these critics, however, fail to acknowledge the deception perpetrated by Blair during the referendum campaign. If republican and nationalist critics had recognized Blair's deception, this would have made clear the precarious position of the UUP leader and increased pressure on them to make concessions to shore up Trimble. Nationalists and republicans were critical of, what the latter 'cynically labelled', the 'Save Dave' process (Purdy 2005, p. 68). They argued that Trimble was exploiting his own weakness to gain further concessions from the two governments. It would be surprising if Trimble did not, like other parties, exploit perceptions of his weakness to exact concessions. The downside of this strategy was that if he was seen to be too damaged, then other politicians might conclude that he was mortally wounded and not deal with him, preferring to wait and 'do business' with his successor or the DUP. By signing the Agreement, Trimble had, to a considerable extent, placed his fate in the hands of other actors. The British government, the Irish government, the SDLP, Sinn Féin/IRA and the US president were all in a position to make concessions in ways that would ease Trimble's difficulties in managing his party and supporters. For example, decommissioning by the IRA would have vindicated Trimble's leadership and helped him to fight off the challenge from the DUP.

The recent history of unionist leaders who tried to 'moderate' their position, in particular the fate of Brian Faulkner during the first peace process, suggested that Trimble was likely to have problems delivering the unionist audience to a power-sharing accommodation (Dixon 1997d; Chapter 5). After the GFA was signed, the referendum result, electoral results (see Table 10.2) and opinion polls and surveys should have made it clear that unionist support for the Agreement was already seeping away. Elections did not reveal the extent of the plight of the UUP (and the SDLP) in an obvious way until the Westminster election of 2001, though it could be argued that the full extent could be ignored until the Assembly elections of 2003.

There was, however, clear evidence from opinion polls and surveys of the problems facing the UUP leader (although different polls indicate different degrees of disaffection). The declining support of Protestants for the Good Friday Agreement is most clearly apparent in a series of polls for BBC Northern Ireland (see Table 10.3).

There was a growing perception among Protestants that nationalists had benefited more from the Good Friday Agreement than had unionists (see Table 10.4) and this illustrates the increasingly difficult job Trimble was facing in sustaining his support for the Agreement. Catholics tended to believe that nationalists and unionists had benefited equally, though more Catholics believed that nationalists had benefited more than unionists.

Table 10.2   UUP/DUP electoral rivalry, 1996–2007

Election	UUP (%)	DUP (%)	DUP–UUP (%)
May 1996, Forum	24.2	18.8	−5.4
May 1997, Westminster	32.7	13.6	−19.1
May 1997, Local	27.8	15.9	−11.9
June 1998, Assembly	21.3	18.1	−3.2
June 1999, European	17.6	28.4	+10.8
May 2001, Westminster	26.8	22.5	−4.3
May 2001, Local	22.9	21.4	−1.5
November 2003, Assembly	22.7	25.7	+3
June 2004, European	16.5	31.9	+15.4
May 2005, Westminster	17.7	33.7	+16
May 2005, Local	18	29.6	+11.6
March 2007, Assembly	14.9	30.1	+15.2

Source: ark.ac.uk/elections.

The rapid disillusionment of Protestants with the Good Friday Agreement – even before the institutions were up and running – suggests that it was not so much the institutional aspects of the Agreement that caused unionists the most problems but rather the 'law and democracy' issues of:

(a) prisoner releases;
(b) reform of the police; and
(c) decommissioning or 'guns and government'.

These issues seemed to dominate the political agenda during the Referendum campaign, the 1998 Assembly elections and the following period. Surveys and opinion polls had, in the past, suggested that

Table 10.3   Declining support of Protestants for the Good Friday Agreement

If the referendum was held again today, how would you vote? (Protestant responses)

	Yes (%)	No (%)
1998 May, Referendum result	55.0	45.0
1999 March	45.6	54.4
2000 May	42.8	57.2
2001 September	42.3	57.7
2002 October	32.9	67.1

Source: BBC Hearts and Minds Poll, 17 October 2002.

Table 10.4   Who benefited more from the Good Friday Agreement? Perceptions among Protestants in Northern Ireland, 1998–2005 (percentages)

Thinking back to the Good Friday Agreement now, would you say that it has benefited unionists more than nationalists, nationalists more than unionists, or that unionists and nationalists have benefited equally?

	Unionists benefited a little/lot more (%)	Unionists and nationalists benefited equally (%)	Nationalists have benefited a little more than unionists (%)	Nationalists have benefited a lot more than unionists (%)	Nationalists have benefited a little/lot more than unionists (%)	Neither side (from 2001) has benefited; Don't know (%)
1998	2	41	19	31	50	8
1999	1	32	13	46	59	8
2000	1	29	14	42	56	13
2001	2	19	11	52	63	17
2002	2	19	12	55	67	13
2003	0	18	17	53	70	12
2004						
2005	1	20	15	53	68	12

Source: http://www.ark.ac.uk/nilt/results/polatt.html#gfa

these 'law and democracy' or 'security' issues were even more a bone of contention between nationalists and unionists than the constitutional question (Whyte 1990, p. 88). Unionists tended to oppose the early release of prisoners, Sinn Féin in government without decommissioning, and reform of the police, while nationalists tended to be more favourable (though Catholics also favoured decommissioning but not as strongly as Protestants).

Tony Blair probably believed during the Referendum period that it was the question of 'guns and government' that most concerned unionist voters, and therefore tried, by deception, to reassure them on that issue. The Northern Ireland Referendum and Election Study 1998 suggested that Blair had been successful in creating the misleading impression that decommissioning was linked to both the release of prisoners and the formation of an Executive (see Table 10.5). There was a common perception among Protestants (51% to 29%) *and* Catholics (45% to 27%) that decommissioning was linked to paramilitaries joining an Executive (see Table 10.5). In addition, Protestants (52% to 29%) and Catholics (41% to 31%) also believed that the release of paramilitary prisoners was linked to decommissioning. Catholics (53% to 11%) more than Protestants (42% to 32%) were

Table 10.5   Perceptions of the Good Friday Agreement

Here are some statements about the Good Friday Agreement. For each one, please tell me if you think it is a true statement of what the Agreement says or false.

		Catholic (%)	Protestant (%)	No religion (%)	All (%)
Prisoners will not be released if the paramilitary organizations to which they belong have not decommissioned their weapons	True	41	52	51	47
	False	31	29	35	30
	Don't know	28	19	14	22
Parties with links to paramilitary organizations that have not decommissioned their weapons are not allowed a place on the Northern Ireland Executive	True	45	51	42	47
	False	27	29	33	29
	Don't know	28	20	26	24
The commission on policing could recommend the creation of a new police force to replace the RUC	True	53	42	35	46
	False	11	32	27	23
	Don't know	36	26	38	31

Note: Percentages do not add upto 100% due to rounding.
Source: Northern Ireland Referendum and Election Study 1998: www.ark.ac.uk/sol.

correct in believing that the commission on policing could recommend the replacement of the RUC. Protestants were more disillusioned with the political system than Catholics, and this may reflect the deception perpetrated by Blair during the Referendum campaign. This survey was taken after the Assembly elections, so could underestimate the degree to which Protestants were deceived. After the Referendum it become clear that the British prime minister's guarantees were not as robust as unionists had been led to believe.

Significantly, not only did Protestants and Catholics *perceive* that there was a link between decommissioning and the release of prisoners and the formation of an Executive, but they thought that there *should* be such a link. Protestants believed this more intensely than Catholics. Both Protestants (94%, including 62% strongly supporting) and Catholics (83%, with 32% strongly supporting) were in favour of the decommissioning of paramilitary weapons, but Protestants were more intensely in favour. Catholics marginally supported by 35% to 33% the early release of paramilitary prisoners, while Protestants opposed their release by 77% (with 48% strongly opposed to release) to 7%. However, the poll found cross-community support for the proposition that 'Prisoners should not be released until the paramilitaries have handed in their weapons.' Fifty-seven per cent of Catholics agreed with this proposition (just 12% strongly), while 84% of Protestants agreed with it, 49% of these strongly. Again, Protestants agreed (88%, 54% strongly agree) more intensely than Catholics (54%, 11% strongly agree) with the proposition that 'Nobody with links to paramilitaries that still have weapons should be allowed to be a government minister.' The biggest gap between Protestant and Catholic attitudes was on the issue of the reform of the RUC. Seventy-four per cent of Catholics favoured reform (19% strongly supported, 55% supported) while just 34% of Protestants favoured it (4% strongly, 30% supported) while 28% opposed and 12% strongly opposed a commission into the future of the RUC. Other polls confirmed the gulf between Protestant and Catholic attitudes on police reform. In one poll, 74% of Catholics favoured reform against just 17% of Protestants (Fahey *et al.* 2005; see also Irwin 2002, p. 12). The Patten Commission on policing reported in September 1999 and the issue continued to divide nationalists and unionists.

The Referendum campaign, Assembly election, opinion polls and surveys suggested that David Trimble and pro-Agreement unionism were in trouble from the signing of the Good Friday Agreement. This could have led to strenuous efforts by other pro-Agreement governments and parties to shore up his increasingly precarious position. Unlike nationalism, unionism was divided over whether or not to support the Agreement. Rival politicians in Ian Paisley's Democratic Unionist Party, but also Robert McCartney's more 'respectable' UK Unionist Party, attacked Trimble. More damagingly perhaps, these external assaults were also echoed by leading politicians within the Ulster Unionist Party. The 'hyper-democratic' nature of the party meant that these internal conflicts were also played out in front of an audience, to the embarrassment of the UUP. The regular meetings of the UUC, the ruling body of the Ulster Unionist Party, to vote on participation in the peace process publicly demonstrated the plight of Trimble in trying to sustain his party's and the electorate's support for the GFA.

Republicans and the 'Imperfect Peace'

Although the intention of the British and Irish governments seems to have been to build the Agreement on an alliance of the UUP and SDLP, the pro-Agreement governments and parties were keen to keep Sinn Féin on board. If Sinn Féin became alienated from the peace process this would reinforce the arguments of hardline republicans within Sinn Féin/IRA and from dissident elements for the return to 'armed struggle.' While David Trimble's problems with his 'hyper-democratic' party and the electorate were played out publicly, the tensions within the republican movement were less obvious. Like Trimble, Adams and the Sinn Féin/IRA leadership had an interest in playing up the possibility of an IRA split and the threat from violent, dissident republicans in order to put pressure on others to make concessions in the ongoing negotiations of the peace process. Indeed, one close observer of the republican movement claimed that Adams had misled the two governments into believing that the IRA hard men would not allow him room to manoeuvre (Moloney in *Sunday Tribune*, 7 October 2001). The republican dissidents did not pose a credible electoral threat to Sinn Féin, but they did have a capacity for violence, illustrated most graphically by the Omagh bombing. The GFA sought the decommissioning of all paramilitary arms by May 2000, but republicans envisaged that this was more likely to take place following a prolonged period of devolved rule, which did not materialize because unionists insisted on decommissioning prior to or during devolution (MacIntyre 2000, p. 566).

The Secretary of State's flexible and pragmatic interpretation of the GFA was illustrated by the British government's response to paramilitary violence. The Secretary of State had the power to decide that a paramilitary organization was in breach of their ceasefire and stop the release of prisoners and other benefits of the Agreement (such as participation in the Executive and the release of prisoners). The British government, and other actors, had throughout the peace process turned a blind eye to what was euphemistically known as 'domestic housekeeping' by the IRA, which included so-called 'punishment' beatings and murder. The government's argument was that unless the IRA was left to keep its 'house in order' then there would be a greater chance of a significant split within the IRA or else a strong challenge from a dissident republican organization. Mo Mowlam explained the British government's pragmatic response to the IRA's violence:

> The Agreement was clear: the prisoner releases and other benefits of the Agreement – like a seat in government – were dependent on the maintenance of ceasefires. So to stop the releases, we would have had to declare the ceasefires at an end – when, despite the activities of a few mindless thugs, they were not. The IRA had not gone back to war, nor were they going to. But if we turned round and said the ceasefires were over, prisoners had to be kept in and Sinn Féin kept out of government, there was every chance that the peace process would be finished and large-scale violence would return and the British government would have broken the terms of the agreement. It was a non-starter. So despite all our revulsion at these attacks, we had to be open and say, 'Yes, it was an imperfect peace, but surely that is better than no peace at all?' (Mowlam 2002, p. 269)

The Decommissioning Deadlock

The impasse over decommissioning continued to dog the progress of the 'peace process', but there were, simultaneously, signs of progress. The outrage following murders and bombings could create the space for the peace process to move forward. The murder of three young Catholic boys helped to defuse the Drumcree standoff in 1998. The Real IRA (aided by the CIRA) carried out the worst single atrocity of the conflict by bombing Omagh in July 1998, killing 29 people and injuring 310.

The UUP leadership attempted on several occasions to circumvent the decommissioning impasse but their room for manoeuvre seemed tight (*Irish Times* editorial, 3 February 1999). So the Irish Taoiseach increased pressure on the IRA to move by insisting that failure to decommission was incompatible with participation in an executive (*Sunday Times*, 24 February 1999). The two governments published the Hillsborough Declaration on 1 April 1999, which was supported by the SDLP and the US president, and placed the spotlight on the IRA's failure to decommission. The Hillsborough Declaration did not produce the desired shift in the republicans' position on decommissioning and so, having 'zigged' to put pressure on republicans, the two governments then 'zagged' to put pressure on the UUP to accept devolution without decommissioning. Trimble was prepared to act but, remarkably, the Irish Taoiseach did not believe the Unionist leader would be able to win his party over to such a deal and was jeopardizing his own position. The British government, meanwhile, thought it was up to Trimble to decide what he could or could not sell – which had been the mistake with Faulkner at Sunningdale (Godson 2004, p. 423). In the European elections that followed, the UUP slumped to their lowest-ever share of the popular vote. In July 1999, the two governments produced *The Way Forward*, which favoured establishing devolution but with IRA decommissioning to follow soon afterwards. The UUP leader offered to 'jump together' with Adams – devolution and decommissioning would happen simultaneously. Trimble rejected the *The Way Forward* proposals unless the Irish government and the SDLP promised to specifically exclude Sinn Féin if the IRA defaulted.

The Patten Report on policing was published on 9 September 1999. The report favoured a transformation of policing, including policing as a partnership for community safety; a decentralization of the force; the creation of a human rights culture; the democratic accountability of the police; transparent and open policing; and the composition of a force that better reflected the communal make up of the population. While there was much of 'substance' in the review that was of benefit to unionists, the symbolism was highly damaging, most particularly the proposal to change the name of the RUC. The name change from the RUC to the Police Service of Northern Ireland (PSNI) was seen by many unionists as a betrayal of a force that had suffered more than 302 of their number being killed, and over 8,500 injured during the conflict, which, because of the skewed recruitment of the police, were mainly Protestants. Nationalists welcomed the report, while unionists attacked it. A poll published in the *Irish News* showed 69% of Catholics in favour of the Patten report, while 65% of Protestants disapproved (*Irish News*, 13 September 1999). Pro-nationalist consociationalists demanded that there should be full implementation of Patten, particularly on the 'crucial issue' of 'symbolic neutrality' in spite of the probably disastrous consequences for the UUP leader (O'Leary 2002, p. 321–3). By contrast, a champion of the Civil Society approach, Robin Wilson, argued that opinion polls indicated that it did not matter to most Catholics that any reference to the name RUC be abolished, and suggested that a compromise on the name change, such as 'The Police Service of Northern Ireland (incorporating the RUC)' – which was eventually accepted – might secure cross-community support (Wilson 2000). By 2001, 59% of Protestants felt that RUC reform had gone too far, while 44% of Catholics thought it had not gone far enough (www.NILT).

On 11 October 1999, Peter Mandelson was appointed Secretary of State for Northern Ireland, replacing Mo Mowlam, who was seen by unionists as being too sympathetic to nationalism and republicanism. Mandelson did resist Blair's attempt to make more concessions to nationalists and republicans 'because it is more than the RUC unionist market will bear; I mean they're swallowing God alone knows what' (*Guardian*, 14 March 2007). After the first period of devolution, from 2 December 1999 to 11 February 2000, Mandelson tried to help the UUP leader win his party's support for devolution by making tactical changes on police reform. Once devolution was restored, the British government retreated from its changes and restored the essence of Patten (MacIntyre 2000, p. 584).

Co-operation of Enemies: Devolution, December 1999 to February 2000

From 6 September until 18 November 1999, George Mitchell conducted a review of the 'peace process' which was successful in achieving a breakthrough on the decommissioning impasse and lead to the first period of devolved, power-sharing government since 1974. Pro-Agreement parties took part in negotiations at Winfield House, the US ambassador's residence, in London's Regents Park between 13 and 20 October. At these talks, Mitchell detected an attempt by the parties to understand each other's point of view, this led not to trust but to 'a sense of realistic understanding that they were in this together'. Republicans began to acknowledge publicly the importance of seeing the conflict from the point of view of their opponents, and the importance of resisting the urge to hype or go for short-term advantage. Pro-Agreement leaders had to help one another; Sinn Féin had to help David Trimble to deliver unionism (Dixon 2009). Trimble also acknowledged the constraints on republican leaders, and appears to have believed that there was a real threat to the lives of Adams and McGuinness as a result of the compromises they were making (Godson 2004, pp. 517–18). The run-up to devolution in December 1999 was a carefully choreographed series of co-ordinated statements and initiatives, during which unionists and republicans exerted restraint in the propaganda war in order to help each other manage their audiences There was no explicit promise or guarantee that the IRA would deliver, but there was an understanding that this was what they were trying to achieve (Dixon 2009; MacIntyre 2000, p. 545). Seamus Mallon, of the SDLP, later accused republicans of 'double-crossing' unionists by failing to deliver on decommissioning (Purdy 2005, p. 78).

David Trimble departed from the choreography in order to win a vital vote in support of devolution at his party's governing Ulster Unionist Council. This improvisation took the form of four post-dated resignation letters, from the four Unionists in the executive, which would be lodged with the party president to be submitted in the event that the IRA failed to decommission and the Secretary of State refused to suspend the institutions. This was probably the only way Trimble could have won the support of his party to enter government. The UUC supported the unionist leader by 58 per cent to 42 per cent, representing a gap of just sixty votes. If the UUC was reasonably representative of unionist opinion then, when this was added to electoral support of anti-GFA unionist parties, a majority of unionists did appear to be opposed to devolution, and perhaps also the GFA itself. An opinion poll taken just before the UUC vote suggested that 94 per cent of Protestants (but also 74 per cent of Catholics) wanted some decommissioning before the formation of an Executive. After his victory, Trimble publicly challenged republicans: 'We've done our bit. Mr Adams, it's over to you. We've jumped, you follow.'

On 29 November, the Executive was formed. The DUP took their ministerial posts but refused to sit in the Executive with Sinn Féin; they would instead be 'ministers in opposition'. The d'Hondt procedure for allocating ministerial posts was triggered, with parties claiming their ministries in order. Most controversially, Sinn Féin claimed the high-profile posts of education and health (which accounted for about half of the block grant from Westminster). The final list of ministers was:

First Minister: David Trimble (UUP)
Deputy First Minister: Seamus Mallon (SDLP)
Agricultural and Rural Development: Brid Rodgers (SDLP)
Culture, Arts and Leisure: Chris McGimpsey (UUP)
Education: Martin McGuinness (SF)
Enterprise, Trade and Investment: Sir Reg Empey (UUP)
Environment: Sam Foster (UUP)
Finance and Personnel: Mark Durkan (SDLP)

Health, Social Services and Public Safety: Bairbre de Brun (SF)
Higher and Further Education, Training and Employment: Sean
  Farren (SDLP)
Regional Development: Peter Robinson (DUP)
Social Development: Nigel Dodds (DUP)

On 2 December 1999, power was devolved to a Northern Ireland government. On the same day, Articles 2 and 3 of the Irish Constitution were amended, ending the Republic's claim to Northern Ireland. The North–South Ministerial Council met in Armagh on 13 December, and the British–Irish Council and Intergovernmental Conference in London four days later. After just ten weeks of devolution, the 'seismic shift' in the republican movement that Blair perceived in the summer of 1999 had not resulted in the surrender of any weapons, and the British government – fearing the demise of Trimble's leadership – honoured its guarantees to the UUP and suspended the Executive and the devolution of power on 11 February 2000. The Northern Ireland Act 2000 was rushed through Parliament to suspend the Assembly and preserve the position of the first minister and deputy first minister, thereby preventing a further election which would be likely to weaken the position of the moderate parties. Nationalist consociationalists opposed the suspension as an illegal act that breached the terms of the GFA. The Irish government argued that the GFA provided only for review and not suspension of devolution (*Irish Times*, 5 February 2000). They opposed suspension in spite of the likelihood that it would precipitate the resignation of the unionist ministers and the collapse of devolution. This would probably have damaged Trimble's position within his own party and therefore severely jeopardize the restoration of devolution.

Guns and Government: May 2000–October 2001

On St Patrick's Day in Washington, David Trimble announced that he would go back into an Executive without IRA decommissioning up front, but that issue would have to be dealt with in due course and he would have to persuade his party. This was no easy task, as Trimble had not performed well against a challenge to his leadership, taking just 57 per cent of the vote, against 43 per cent for Martin Smyth. Further negotiations resulted in the choreography of devolution at midnight on 29 May 2000. The British government undertook to further demilitarize and agreed that the name of the RUC would be included in the 'title deeds' of the new police force. The IRA allowed 'agreed third parties' to inspect and re-inspect a number of their arms dumps to ensure that the weapons had not been used. These measures enabled Trimble to win a vote in the UUC by just 53 per cent to 47 per cent to reinstate the Executive and return devolved powers to Northern Ireland. Trimble's vulnerability was underlined in September 2000, when the DUP won South Antrim in a by-election, previously one of the UUP's safest seats.

After a year of devolution, the IRA had still not decommissioned any weapons. In May 2001, Trimble announced that he would resign as first minister on 1 July unless the IRA began to decommission its weapons. This was probably an attempt by the UUP leader to shore up his hardline flank in the run-up to the June 2001 Westminster General Election. In spite of this, the UUP slumped to its worst-ever result, losing two seats to Sinn Féin and three to the DUP. The DUP outperformed expectations and the SDLP's 'Stalingrad strategy' failed to turn Sinn Féin's advances, so the republicans became the largest nationalist party. Even these poor results disguised the bad performance of the pro-Agreement unionists. A fair percentage of the votes for the UUP were probably from anti-Agreement unionists voting for UUP MPs opposed to the GFA. The replacement of the SDLP by Sinn Féin as the leading party of nationalists in Northern Ireland was more unexpected than the UUP's battering.

The election could represent increased support for the hardline parties because they were less compromising, or else it could be a reward for the moderation of their positions. Sinn Féin had moved increasingly onto the SDLP's ground, by signing up to the Good Friday Agreement, distancing itself from the IRA and allowing the inspection of arms dumps. But the IRA had not decommissioned, and continued to be active. The DUP's strong opposition to the GFA was a smokescreen that concealed any moderation of its position. The party had shifted its position from 'smashing' the Good Friday Agreement to 'renegotiating' it, and had taken up its seats in the Executive, but it was not clear whether this was a tactical ruse to undermine wavering UUP voters or a more long-term strategy that would lead to power-sharing with Sinn Féin in 2007.

Growing unionist discontent with the GFA was apparent in the election results, in opinion polls and also in the feud, in 2000–1, between the pro-Agreement UVF, which had seats in the Assembly, and the anti-Agreement UDA, which did not. The casualties as a result of loyalist paramilitary shootings increased from 33 in 1997/98, peaking in 2001/2 at 124 and dropping back to 70 in 2005/6. Loyalist assaults exceeded those of the republicans in every year after the GFA, peaking at 112 in 1998/9. During September–November 2001, the Holy Cross dispute flared in North Belfast, underlining the deep sectarian tensions that continued to exist alongside the peace process. On 10 July, the UFF/UDA announced it was withdrawing its support for the GFA, and by October 2001 the UDA, UFF and LVF were no longer considered to be on ceasefire. Prisoners associated with these organizations who had been released from jail could have their licenses suspended and be returned to jail if evidence was found that they had engaged in paramilitary activity. There was severe rioting in Belfast in both 2001 and 2002. The alienation of unionists was so apparent that the Secretary of State for Northern Ireland, John Reid (who had replaced Mandelson on 24 January 2001) said in a speech in November 2001 that unionist confidence had declined as that of Catholics had risen, warning that 'Northern Ireland must not become a cold place for Protestants, or we will have failed.'

IRA Decommissioning, 2001

David Trimble resigned as promised on 1 July 2001. The two governments presented *The Way Forward* proposals to the pro-Agreement parties at Weston Park on 1 August 2001, but they were rejected by unionists. Peter Mandelson later argued that Weston Park 'was basically about conceding and capitulating in a whole number of different ways to republican demands . . . the Sinn Féin shopping list. It was a disaster because it was too much for them' (*Guardian*, 14 March 2007). They covered four outstanding issues: policing, normalization of security, the stability of the institutions, and decommissioning.

Republican attitudes towards the peace process were thrown into doubt by the arrest of three suspected IRA men in Colombia, who were charged with training FARC guerrillas in the use of explosives and urban terrorism. The atrocity in the United States on 11 September 2001 (9/11) helped to create the context in which the IRA was finally able to deliver its first act of decommissioning, on 23 October 2001. In terms of republican culture, this was a major step and one that the Sinn Féin/IRA leadership had long denied they would take. Trimble and his senior colleagues were careful not to gloat in response to decommissioning: something publicly acknowledged by Adams (*Irish Times*, 27 October 2001). Devolution was restored, but the problem for pro-Agreement unionists was that while decommissioning had taken place, it was not clear whether this represented a significant proportion of the IRA's arsenal or not: it could have been as little as one bullet, one ounce of Semtex and one gun. According to a poll published in the *Belfast Telegraph* in November 2001, while 51 per cent believed de Chastelain when he said that a significant act of decommissioning had been carried out during the previous week, 52 per cent of *Protestants* did not believe the statement, while just 29 per cent did (Millward Brown Ulster, poll taken 30 October 2001).

The Centre Falls Apart

The IRA had cleared an important, symbolic hurdle by decommissioning some weapons, but other parties complained that having an armed, active, paramilitary force was not compatible with participation in democratic politics. The break-in at the Special Branch office at Castlereagh police station on 17 March 2002 raised further doubts about the democratic intentions of the republican movement, and this was confirmed by other evidence that the IRA were still training, recruiting, targeting and procuring arms. On 8 April 2002, the IRA announced a further act of decommissioning, though what proportion of the IRA's total arsenal this represented was not known. This act of decommissioning may have helped Sinn Féin to make significant gains at the General Election held in the Republic of Ireland on 17 May 2002, winning a total of 5 seats (a rise of 4 seats), and increasing its share of the vote from 2.5 per cent to 6.5 per cent. In September 2002, Trimble announced that he and the UUP ministers would withdraw from the Executive on 18 January if republicans failed to demonstrate that they had left violence behind for good. The 'Stormontgate' scandal broke on 4 October 2002, when the PSNI made high-profile, televised raids on Sinn Féin's offices in Stormont and the homes of Sinn Féin officials. The raids concerned allegations that republicans were spying on the British and Irish governments, and had access to transcripts of conversations between the Secretary of State and the British and Irish prime ministers. A target list of 2,000 people – prison officers, intelligence officers, soldiers, police and loyalists – along with their personal details, were allegedly found during raids. The head of Sinn Féin's Assembly administration,

Denis Donaldson, was arrested and had his home searched but it turned out later that he had been working as an agent for the British. The Chief Constable later apologized for the dramatic way the raid had been conducted. In December 2005, the 'Public Prosecution Service' declared that it was not 'in the public interest' to prosecute three republicans accused of involvement in Stormontgate. Unionists tended to see this as part of a deal to keep Sinn Féin 'on board', whereas for nationalists the initial raid was seen as part of a plan by 'securocrats' to undermine the peace process. The UUP and DUP ministers resigned, and at midnight on 14 October 2002 devolution was suspended.

The British and Irish prime ministers said that people now had to choose between violence or democracy, and called for the IRA to be dismantled. Tony Blair, in his 'Belfast Harbour Speech' on 17 October 2002, called for an end to the ambiguities and incrementalism that had characterized the conduct of the peace process, and instead demanded 'acts of completion' from the IRA. The process was coming to a crunch point because some of the compromises with paramilitarism were not only morally wrong but also ineffective in taking the peace process forward. The 'political skills', or, for some, lies and manipulation, that had been used by pro-Agreement politicians to take the peace process forward had created a 'credibility gap'. The audience no longer knew whether the performance it was seeing was 'real' and truthful, or lies and illusion choreographed behind the scenes. For unionists, the prime example of this was Blair's deception during the Referendum campaign (see Dixon 2002a). The British government now demanded:

(a) the transparent decommissioning of IRA weapons;
(b) a statement from the IRA that it does not intend to return to war and that it envisages disbanding; and
(c) an end to paramilitary activity, including 'punishment' attacks.

The Irish government was reported to have been suggesting fresh Assembly elections from the summer of 2001, and continued to do so after the suspension of devolution in 2002. The British government and moderate parties both objected to this proposal because it was likely to result in victory for their hardline rivals which, they believed, would end any prospect of power-sharing and devolution (*Independent*, 10 October 2002).

Stormontgate appeared to vindicate the DUP's claims that the IRA had not turned their back on violence, and undermined the trust that Trimble had placed in Sinn Féin. There were contradictory signals coming from the DUP, both that the DUP wanted to destroy the GFA and that they would renegotiate the agreement. A BBC poll after suspension underlined the polarization that had taken place towards the GFA since 1998. It suggested that only 32.9% of unionists would vote 'Yes' if the Referendum on the GFA were held today, compared to 82.2% of nationalists. When presented with a range of options, only 22.6% of unionists and 38.5% of nationalists favoured the return of the power-sharing assembly from suspension. The most popular options were direct rule from Westminster by 41.7% (3.8% of nationalists) of unionists, and a united Ireland by 38.3% (0.9% of unionists) of nationalists. The majority of unionists, 58% (37% UUP voters; 79.2% DUP voters), opposed power-sharing with either the SDLP or Sinn Féin, while just 27.8% favoured sharing power with the SDLP (see http://news.bbc.co.uk/1/low/northern_ireland/2335861.stm, 17 October 2002). Ironically, the suspension of devolution led to an improvement in the perception of inter-communal relations.

Paul Murphy took over from John Reid as Secretary of State for Northern Ireland in October 2002, and tried to kick-start devolution in time for Assembly elections scheduled for 1 May 2003. It was probably hoped that the more moderate, pro-Agreement parties would receive an electoral boost in the aftermath of a successful restoration of devolution. After talks in March 2003, the deadline for elections was put back to 29 May. A 'Joint Declaration' was published on 1 May 2003 in which the two governments committed themselves 'to undertaking and securing the acts of completion necessary to bring about a peaceful and normalized society': 'In order to re-establish that trust, it must be clear that the transition from violence to exclusively peaceful and democratic means is being brought to an unambiguous and definitive conclusion' (Joint Declaration, April 2003, paras 6 and 7). The Joint Declaration failed to bring about the desired political momentum towards the restoration of devolution. IRA statements were ambiguous about whether they would disarm in return for the full and irreversible implementation of the Agreement. On 1 May the Labour government again postponed the Assembly elections due on 29 May until the autumn, because holding the elections in May was likely to result in the triumph of Sinn Féin and the DUP. On 21 October 2003, the UUP and Sinn Féin attempted unsuccessfully to choreograph the restoration of devolution. Devolution was to be restored after a deal in which Sinn Féin would get new Assembly elections, while the UUP would see a third act of IRA decommissioning. The choreography broke down because General de Chastelain's statement did not include sufficient detail about the extent of IRA decommissioning for David Trimble to play his part in the choreography. Also, there was no video or photographic evidence of decommissioning, which might have helped Trimble to persuade his sceptical unionist audience that substantial decommissioning had taken place. The Assembly elections on 26 November 2003 confirmed the triumph of the hardline parties. Both the SDLP and UUP hardened their positions during the campaign, in an unsuccessful bid to fight off their rivals. Sinn Féin's vote increased by 5.9 per cent (+6 seats) to 23.5 per cent, while the SDLP languished on 17 per cent (−6 seats). The DUP increased its vote by 7.5 per cent to 25.6 per cent (+10 seats), mopping up a lot of the votes and seats of independent, anti-agreement unionists. The UUP's vote went up 1.4 per cent, to 22.7 per cent, perhaps at the expense of the Alliance Party, but, again, the UUP's vote included a lot of voters who might not have voted for the party but rather for the presence of prominent anti-Agreement candidates within its ranks, such as MPs Jeffrey Donaldson and David Burnside, who topped the polls in their areas. Donaldson and two other UUP MLAs – Arlene Foster and Norah Beare – defected to the DUP in January 2004. This brought the DUP's strength at Stormont to thirty-three MLAs, nine more than the UUP, who then had twenty-four MLAs, and confirmed the DUP as the largest Northern Ireland party at Westminster. The 'centre ground' was further squeezed, the Women's Coalition halved its share of the vote and lost both seats. The PUP also had less than half its previous percentage of the vote and lost one of its two seats. Remarkably, the Alliance Party hung on to its seats but was reduced from 6.5 per cent of the vote to 3.7 per cent (see Table 10.6).

The GFA had been built on the 'moderate' centre but this, and the notion of the 'people's peace process', had been overtaken, the future for power-sharing lay with Sinn Féin and the DUP. The alternative to power-sharing was 'Plan B' – which might be moves either towards joint authority (to put pressure on unionists) or a return to direct rule (to pressurize republicans). The two governments announced that there was no viable alternative political framework other than the fundamentals of the GFA, and whether power-sharing between Sinn Féin and the DUP was compatible with 'the fundamentals' of the Agreement remained to be seen.

Table 10.6   Northern Ireland Assembly elections results, 28 November 2003

	Votes	Percentage of vote	+/−%	Number of seats	Seats gain/loss
DUP	177,470	25.6	+7.5	30	+10
Sinn Féin	162,758	23.5	+5.9	24	+6
UUP	156,931	22.7	+1.4	27	−1
SDLP	117,547	17.0	−5.0%	18	−6
Alliance	25,372	3.7	−2.8%	6	+/−0
PUP	8,032	1.2	−1.4	1	−1
Kieran Deeney (West Tyrone)	6,158	0.9		1	+1
NIWC	5,785	0.8	−0.8		−2
UKUP	4,794	0.7	−3.8	1	−4

Source: www.ark.ac.uk.

The Mother of all Deals: the DUP and Sinn Féin, 2003–7

Prior to 2003 there seemed to be little prospect that the DUP would re-negotiate the GFA and share power with Sinn Féin. But in May 2007, devolution was restored to Northern Ireland, with Ian Paisley as first minister and Martin McGuinness as his deputy. This was a turnaround in Northern Irish politics that was probably as remarkable as the negotiation of the Good Friday Agreement itself. Both politicians had made their reputations as militant hardliners who had opposed power-sharing and the first peace process in 1972–4. They were members of parties that stirred up communal antagonisms by exploiting symbolic issues (such as Orange marches, flying flags) and using the most incendiary language to fight the propaganda war over Northern Ireland. After 1974, both leaders and parties showed little interest in the kind of compromise settlement that Sinn Féin were to embrace in the GFA 1998 and the DUP at St Andrews in 2006.

Ian Paisley had been a hardline, anti-power-sharing unionist since the 1960s, successfully building his career by accusing more moderate, mainstream unionists of 'selling out' the Union. The DUP appeared to be wholeheartedly opposed to the peace process and the GFA. David Trimble was attacked as a liar for the 'creative ambiguities' he had accepted in order to take the peace process forward. By contrast, the DUP saw itself as the party of 'honest Ulstermen' who spoke plain and true. A leading figure in the DUP, Nigel Dodds MP, claimed: 'We are looking at a way forward without constructive ambiguity or fudges which turn a blind eye to gangsterism and terrorism' (*Irish News*, 27 April 2005). But behind this smokescreen of rhetoric there was a more subtle, sophisticated and tactical approach to the peace process. The DUP had, for example, behind their 'smokescreen' of hardline rhetoric been careful to anticipate developments and leave itself 'wriggle room' to take up its seats in the Executive in 1999. Subsequently, they had also left open the possibility of participating in some kind of new agreement with Sinn Féin. The 'creative ambiguity' of the DUP's position made it difficult to know whether their stance was a tactical ploy to win over wavering, more moderate UUP voters and become the largest unionist party, or whether it represented a genuine desire to reach a power-sharing compromise.

Martin McGuinness had been leader of the IRA in Derry and was among the delegation that met Secretary of State William Whitelaw in 1972. It has been alleged that McGuinness was a chief of staff of the IRA and, even during the 1990s and up to 2001, a member of the IRA's army council (Moloney 2002, p. 479; Clarke and Johnston 2001, p. 266). The IRA had fought a violent struggle to prevent power-sharing, and to achieve a united Ireland, republican paramilitaries had killed more than 2,139 people and the IRA, 1,771. The IRA designated as 'legitimate targets' about 40,000 people, including anyone serving in the security forces or who had served in the past, including cleaners, builders and other workers who serviced army bases.

The record of these leaders and parties explains why Sinn Féin is the party most detested by unionists, and the DUP the party most detested by nationalists. According to opinion polls, nationalists favour a coalition between Sinn Féin or the SDLP and the UUP rather than the DUP (www.ark.ac.uk/nilt). Similarly, unionists would rather share power with the SDLP than with Sinn Féin. None the less, following their triumph at the 2003 Assembly elections, these hardline parties began to negotiate through and with the two governments. Sinn Féin insisted that the Good Friday Agreement would not be abandoned, and that the IRA would not disband, while the DUP's position ranged from a refusal to share power with republicans to calls for a new agreement. Like the Good Friday Agreement, there was little evidence available to the public that a compromise deal could be achieved, given the hardline rhetoric and positions of both parties. There were several possible scenarios:

1. The DUP and Sinn Féin could appear to be accommodating as a tactic to win the 'blame game' and advance a more hardline agenda. The DUP might make some moderate noises, but this would be in order to shore up its moderate flank and consolidate its electoral advantage over the UUP. The party might also believe that because Sinn Féin would not be able to meet its demands in negotiations, the republicans would be blamed for collapsing negotiations and destroying the peace process. They called on the two governments to permit a voluntary coalition without Sinn Féin, but the SDLP refused this option. Direct rule would return, which unionists could well prefer to sharing power with republicans. For their part, Sinn Féin might believe that appearing to be moderate and compromising would consolidate their advantage over the SDLP and win it the 'blame game' if the DUP pulled out of negotiations. The two governments had threatened the DUP with 'Plan B', which was thought to be either steps towards joint authority or direct rule with a much 'greener' tinge and the full implementation of all other aspects of the GFA. This tactical moderation could be the means by which the parties backed each other into agreement, and some argue this was what happened in the negotiation of the GFA (Dixon 2002a, pp. 731, 734).
2. The DUP and Sinn Féin leaderships could always have intended there to be accommodation between the two parties, but in the intervening period their hardline positions were more effective for winning electoral advantage over their moderate rivals.
3. It is possible that the DUP and Sinn Féin leaderships may not have always intended an accommodation, but as they went through tactical moderations of their positions they became locked into these and both sides calculated that not to go for power-sharing and IRA disbandment/disarmament would be worse for their party.

A Photograph Away, or Sackcloth and Ashes: December 2004

On 8 December 2004, the two governments presented their proposals for a deal between Sinn Féin and the DUP in Belfast. Tony Blair claimed that the only outstanding issue preventing a deal between the DUP and Sinn Féin was the IRA's refusal to allow greater transparency on decommissioning by permitting it to be photographed. Significantly, both governments supported the demand for photographic evidence of IRA decommissioning in order to win over unionist sceptics who did not trust the way the peace process had been choreographed. Republicans claimed that this was an attempt to humiliate them. Ian Paisley reinforced this perception by saying that the IRA had to wear 'sackcloth and ashes', and that those who had 'sinned in public need to repent in public', an intervention that might have been designed to drive Sinn Féin out of a deal. Contrary to Blair's claim, there were other outstanding issues between the parties. The IRA was being asked to produce an inventory of weapons, describe how weapons would be destroyed, and endorse the police. Sinn Féin/IRA refused to recognize 'the need to uphold and not to endanger anyone's personal rights and safety', which would have prevented the IRA from pursuing criminal activities and 'policing' nationalist areas. Sinn Féin wanted the early release of the IRA members who had murdered the Irish detective, Jerry McCabe, an amnesty for 'on the runs', and reform of the Republic's upper house to allow representatives from the Northern Ireland assembly to become members. An IRA statement maintained that the organization would 'conclude the process to completely and verifiably put all our arms beyond use . . . speedily and, if possible, by the end of December'.

On 20 December 2004, the IRA carried out the UK's biggest bank robbery, stealing £26.5 m from the Northern Bank in Belfast. Both the British and Irish governments held the IRA responsible for the raid, which highlighted, again, the problems of Sinn Féin's participation in government while the IRA continued to carry out violent and criminal acts. At the end of January, members of the IRA carried out the brutal murder of Robert McCartney in Magennis's bar near the Short Strand. The courageous and effective campaigning of the McCartney sisters, including winning a brief audience with the US president, again focused attention on the criminality of the IRA, and drew attention to the other victims of the IRA's 'domestic housekeeping' during the peace process. In March 2005, the IRA offered to shoot the IRA members who murdered McCartney, in an apparent blunder that drew international criticism. Martin McGuinness also blundered by telling the McCartney family to steer clear of party politics. The campaign to bring justice to the murderers of Robert McCartney was important, because the McCartney family are Sinn Féin voters who criticized the IRA's descent from 'freedom fighters' in 1994 to criminal thugs in 2005. Gerry Adams' personal rating in the

Republic slumped, and in the 2005 Westminster General Elections there was a significant but minor effect on the Sinn Féin vote in the local elections. The 'pan-nationalist front' that had brought republicans in from the cold to a peace process had broken up. Nationalists, and the US president, were demanding that republicans decommission their weapons, give up their private armies and accept the rules of the democratic game. The Northern Bank robbery and the McCartney murder played into the hands of those within the republican movement who were arguing that the IRA should 'stand down' rather than become a 'Rafia' besmirching the record of 'heroic struggle'.

In May 2005, the local elections and Westminster General Election confirmed the dominance of Sinn Féin and the DUP within their respective communities. The DUP won 34 per cent of the vote, and four more MPs than in 2001, in the Westminster election, and nearly 30 per cent of the first preference votes in the local elections. These gains partly reflected the support that Jeffrey Donaldson and other defectors from the UUP brought with them to the DUP. David Trimble had lost his seat in the process of leading the UUP to its worst-ever election result. He resigned as party leader and was succeeded by Sir Reg Empey. Ian Paisley said during the campaign that 'There is no place in any democracy for terrorists and no place for IRA/Sinn Féin'. He also wrote, 'Let me make it unequivocally clear that the DUP will never enter government with IRA/Sinn Féin.' The Independent Monitoring Commission found the IRA to be 'a highly active organisation' and to have retained the capacity to resume a campaign of violence if that was its intention (IMC May 2005).

2005 General Election: the IRA Stand Down

The appointment of Peter Hain as Secretary of State for Northern Ireland was probably the most partisan appointment since 1972. Hain had been active in Irish issues since 1972 and a long-standing supporter of British withdrawal from Northern Ireland. On 25 March 1996 the *Independent* alleged that Peter Hain was among five Labour MPs who sent their greetings to Sinn Féin's Ard Fheis just weeks after the IRA had ended its ceasefire by detonating a bomb at Canary Wharf on 9 February 1996, which killed two people (*Independent*, 25 March 1996). Peter Hain may have been appointed by accident, or as part of a side-deal of the peace process, to put pressure on the DUP to cut a deal and in return for the IRA 'standing down'.

Hain played 'hard cop', threatening unionists that if they didn't reach a power-sharing deal with Sinn Féin, then 'Plan B' would see the extension of British–Irish co-operation and even joint authority, which Hain had, as foreign minister, tried to push on Gibraltar (Dixon 2006b).

The pressure on unionists to strike a deal was also increased by threatening the abolition of academic selection for secondary schools, the introduction of water charges, the reform of local government, higher rates, an end to the payment of salaries and allowances to Assembly members; and he also pioneered enhanced gay rights. The British and Irish governments now had leading politicians involved in Northern Ireland, Hain and Michael McDowell, the Irish justice minister, who were not championing but putting pressure on their 'allies' in pan-unionism and pan-nationalism to sign the 'mother of all deals'.

On 28 July 2005, the IRA declared that the 'armed campaign' was over and prepared a 'final' act of decommissioning. This major initiative was taken unilaterally and not in return for concessions from the DUP. The IRA 'has formally ordered an end to the armed campaign . . . All IRA units have been ordered to dump arms. All Volunteers have been instructed to assist the development of purely political and democratic programmes through exclusively peaceful means. Volunteers must not engage in any other activities whatsoever.' The IRA would 'complete the process to verifiably put its arms beyond use in a way which will further enhance public confidence'. Irish unity would be achieved through unarmed means, but 'We reiterate our view that the armed struggle was entirely legitimate.' On 26 September, the Independent International Commission on Decommissioning declared 'that the IRA has met its commitment to put all its arms beyond use'. The IRA had carried out a fourth and 'final' act of decommissioning. There was no photographic proof, but Protestant and Catholic clergymen witnessed that 'the arms of the IRA have been decommissioned'. The DUP raised doubts about the IRA's decommissioning and whether all weapons had been put beyond use; some were rumoured to have been retained for self-protection. Ian Paisley said, 'We have a right to know the truth – the day for deception is over, the day for truth, the whole truth and nothing but the truth has come' (*Irish Independent*, 26 September 2005).

The loyalist paramilitaries showed little sign of decommissioning but were beginning to talk of winding down their organizations. The diminishing threat of violence from loyalist paramilitaries also reduced the DUP's negotiating position. Unionist politicians had traditionally been able to warn the British government of the violent consequences from loyalist paramilitaries of failing to deliver to their community. In May 2007, the UVF claimed to have deactivated all active service units, put their weapons 'beyond reach' and stopped recruitment, training, targeting, training and intelligence gathering. The Northern Ireland Office provided £1.2 million to the UDA to help it transform into a community organization, but at the time of writing, the UFF had not yet decommissioned (Spencer 2008). During the peace process, the Orange Order has undergone a radical transformation, leading opposition to the GFA, having 'grave reservations' about the Sinn Féin–DUP power-sharing deal and reappraising its links with the UUP (*Irish Times*, 13 July 2007; Kaufman 2007).

The St Andrews 'Agreement', 2006

In July 2006, Ian Paisley was adamant that he would not betray unionism and go into government with Sinn Féin, but he did so in less than a year. On 12 July, the DUP leader told a gathering of Orangemen

> No unionist who is a unionist will go into partnership with IRA–Sinn Féin. They are not fit to be in partnership with decent people. They are not fit to be in the government of Northern Ireland. And it will be over our dead bodies that they will ever get there . . . Ulster has surely learned that weak, pushover unionism is a halfway house to republicanism. There is no discharge in this war . . . Compromise, accommodation and the least surrender are the roads to final and irreversible disaster. There can be no compromise. (*Irish Times*, 13 July 2006)

On 13 October 2006, the two governments announced the 'St Andrews Agreement' after talks between the parties in Scotland. The agreement set out the choreography which, following a referendum or an election, would result in the participation of Sinn Féin and the DUP in power-sharing devolution by 26 March 2007. The DUP insisted that Sinn Féin/IRA must end paramilitary and criminal activity, remove terrorist structures, endorse the police, actively support the rule of law and this should be 'tested and proved over a credible period'. IMC reports in October 2006 and March 2007 confirmed that the IRA was winding down its organization, was 'firmly committed to the political path', and that the loyalist paramilitaries appeared to be taking some steps in the same direction. Sinn Féin wanted the full implementation of the GFA, the devolution of security and for the DUP to enter power-sharing.

The location of the talks in St Andrews, Scotland, may have been stage-managed to give it an 'Ulster Scots' flavour and thereby make any deal more acceptable to unionists. The DUP had wanted the abolition and replacement of the GFA, while Sinn Féin and the SDLP insisted that the Agreement be upheld and implemented. The failed 'comprehensive agreement' of December 2004 was also a point of reference for the St Andrews 'deal'. There were a number of aspects to the St Andrews deal:

1. A timetable for the devolution of policing and criminal justice by March 2008 was set.
2. The assembly was no longer required to endorse the new Executive.
3. There was a revised pledge of office which committed ministers to support policing, courts, the rule of law and promote the interests of the whole community.
4. A statutory ministerial code tried to create some sense of collective executive responsibility
5. Extra safeguards were introduced to allow three ministers to require a cross-community vote if there was no consensus in the executive. Important ministerial decisions could be referred to the Executive by thirty MLAs.
6. There were also proposed changes to improve value for money and the efficiency of the executive, including minor institutional alterations.
7. The UK government's power to suspend devolution would be repealed.
8. MLAs would no longer be able to change community designation during the assembly term except in the event that they changed party.
9. The agreement committed, among other things, the UK government to: produce a policy on social inclusion, establish a permanent victims commissioner, establish a forum on a bill of rights, produce a Single Equality Act, introduce an Irish Language Act and support 'Ulster Scots', end 50:50 recruitment to the PSNI when the 30 per cent target for Catholic officers was achieved,

increase the powers of the Human Rights Commission, ensure access for EU nationals to the Civil Service, work on the reintegration of prisoners, and propose a new strategy for handling parades.

The two hardline parties had not negotiated face to face and subsequently did not endorse the agreement. Nevertheless, the governments proceeded with the choreography, and on 24 November Gerry Adams indicated that Martin McGuinness would be their candidate for deputy first minister. The DUP leader, Ian Paisley, did not nominate himself, but the speaker claimed that he *had* and Paisley later clarified his remarks, saying that if Sinn Féin delivered on policing and other outstanding issues then he would accept the nomination as first minister. The speaker's interpretation of Paisley's remarks was probably a 'necessary fiction' (Dixon 2002a, p. 737) to keep the peace process going forward.

While the Sinn Féin and DUP leaderships had not fully endorsed the St Andrews Agreement, their moves towards power-sharing were drawing pressure from hardliners. Gerry Adams was informed by the police of death threats from republican dissidents who attempted to exploit discontent with Sinn Féin's moves on policing. There was significant internal disquiet, leading to several Sinn Féin MLAs either not seeking renomination or being de-selected. Nevertheless, Sinn Féin organized a special Ard Fheis, which overwhelmingly passed a motion endorsing the police and support for the rule of law. Ian Paisley responded to Sinn Féin's motion: 'If you had told me 20 years ago that they [republicans] would be repudiating the very fundamentals of Sinn Féin/IRA, I would have laughed, but that is what they have done' (*Guardian*, 30 January 2007).

In the DUP, Jim Allister MEP, led the opposition to the St Andrews Agreement and power-sharing with Sinn Féin. He criticized the St Andrews Agreement for:

(a) the absence of a mechanism for the sole exclusion of Sinn Féin if it defaulted on its commitments to exclusively peaceful and democratic means;
(b) failing to demand that the IRA's army council be disbanded;
(c) committing to an Irish Language Act;
(d) allowing EU applicants, including those from the Republic of Ireland, to apply for jobs in the Northern Ireland Civil Service; and

(e) the absence of a specified period to test Sinn Féin/IRA's commitment to democratic and peaceful means.

Opinion polls suggested that the peace process was not driven from below, and in the aftermath of the GFA there appeared to be a deterioration in perceptions of community relations. This improved in 2003, after devolution had been suspended in 2002 and the DUP had established itself as the dominant unionist party. The improvement in unionist confidence appeared to be demonstrated in an opinion poll question that asked, 'Do you think Northern Ireland will still be part of the United Kingdom in 2020?' In 1998, 69% of unionists had answered 'Yes'. This dropped to 61% by May 2000, recovered to 66% by October 2002, but shot up to 82% by November 2006. In the wake of the St Andrews Agreement, an opinion poll suggested that, while 47% of DUP supporters favoured the deal, 32% opposed it and 22% said they didn't know. According to the poll, the St Andrews Agreement was supported by 49% of unionists, with 26% against; and 62% of nationalists supported the deal, with 20% against. There were significant numbers of respondents who said they didn't know (BBC NI Hearts and Minds Survey, November 2006). Another poll suggested that 45% of respondents would vote 'Yes' on the St Andrews Agreement, just 8% would vote 'No', but 16% would not vote and 28% didn't know how they would vote on the deal (www.ark.ac.uk/nilt/2006/). The St Andrews Agreement was not subjected to a referendum, probably because the DUP and Sinn Féin were concerned that the deal would not win the same level of support that had been won by the GFA.

In the run-up to the Assembly elections on 7 March 2007, it was not clear whether the DUP believed that Sinn Féin had delivered enough for them to go into a power-sharing Executive. Unionists could therefore vote for the DUP, in the belief that this was a vote *against* power-sharing with Sinn Féin. The issues raised during the campaign reinforced the importance of devolution in order to prevent the continuation of direct rule and the threat of the introduction of water charges, a new rating system, the end of academic selection, and reforms in public administration. The result of the 2007 Assembly election reinforced the dominance of the DUP and Sinn Féin, with both parties winning their highest-ever percentage of the vote. The UUP and SDLP had their worst-ever results, but for moderates the consolation was the surprisingly strong performance of the Alliance Party and the election of an MLA from the Green

Party. Republican dissidents and loyalist opponents of the St Andrews Agreement performed miserably. Republican dissidents stood in several seats, but won a pitiful share of the vote: in West Belfast, for example, the Republican Sinn Féin candidate won just 427 votes, or 1.2 per cent of the vote. The UKUP leader, Robert McCartney, lost his seat in North Down, winning only 5.9 per cent of the first preference votes, down 5.7 per cent on 2003.

The choreography in the St Andrews Agreement identified 26 March 2007 as the date for the restoration of devolution. Critics of the DUP leadership argued that joint government was premature, republicans had not fully delivered (the IRA Army Council was still in existence) and a testing period was needed to see if Sinn Féin was sincere in its commitment to the police and the rule of law. Serious opposition within the party led the DUP leadership to request a delay for devolution until 8 May to test Sinn Féin's commitment to supporting the PSNI and 'to manage their party and ensure the ducks were "in a line" before committing' (*Irish Times*, 31 March 2007). On 26 March, instead of devolution, Ian Paisley and Gerry Adams met for an hour and appeared together in public at Stormont to endorse the deal.

The St Andrews Agreement and devolution were presented, like the Good Friday Agreement, differently to different audiences. The Sinn Féin leadership presented St Andrews as having the potential to deliver full implementation of the Good Friday Agreement and being transitional to Irish unity. Martin McGuinness told an audience of republicans, 'As the process progresses, more people are recognising that we have now entered the end phase of our struggle ... I truly believe that we have begun the countdown to a united Ireland, and we are continuing to get that message out as widely as possible. We are on a countdown to a united Ireland.' Republicans had 'entered the final lap in the journey towards a united Ireland, they must try to understand the anxieties of unionists for whom such change was a terrifying prospect' (*Irish Times*, 9 April 2007). The IRA's Easter message endorsed Sinn Féin's position and claimed that partition could be brought to an end through purely peaceful and democratic means.

Ian Paisley claimed that devolution was a victory for unionism, the Union had been secured and republicanism defeated. The Good Friday Agreement had been renegotiated and delivered fundamental changes to the way in which devolution operates, giving DUP ministers a veto on all major decisions. Republicans had been forced to 'bow the knee' and accept DUP demands, and devolution would mean that republicans would be sitting in a British institution taking an oath to support the police, the rule of law and British justice. The DUP leader promised a government 'not preoccupied with sectarianism or the threat of violence, but with the bread and butter issues that matter to everyone in Northern Ireland' (*Newsletter*, 31 March 2007; *Belfast Telegraph*, 2 April 2007; *Washington Times*, 13 April 2007). Paisley also warned his internal critics that if the DUP did not accept the deal, then the British and Irish governments' 'Plan B' could be much worse for the Union.

Devolution Restored

On 8 May 2007, devolution was restored to Northern Ireland, and Ian Paisley of the Democratic Unionist Party and Martin McGuinness of Sinn Féin were sworn in as first minister and deputy first minister, respectively. Interestingly, the DUP was prepared to enter government with Sinn Féin in the North, but political parties in the Republic of Ireland still refused to accept coalition government with the republicans. Like so much else in this peace process, devolution was carefully choreographed. The key strategists 'through the benefit of bitter experience, nailed down the script in advance. There would be no deviation from each side's carefully rehearsed roles. No surprises. We've had enough surprises' (*Irish Times*, 9 May 2007). The Executive comprised:

Ian Paisley (DUP), First Minister
Martin McGuinness (SF), Deputy First Minister
Peter Robinson (DUP), Department of Finance and Personnel
Nigel Dodds (DUP), Department of Enterprise, Trade and Investment
Arlene Foster (DUP), Department of the Environment
Edwin Poots (DUP), Department of Culture, Arts and Leisure
Conor Murphy (SF), Department of Regional Development
Michelle Gildernew (SF), Department of Agriculture and Rural Development
Caitriona Ruane (SF), Department of Education
Reg Empey (UUP), Department of Employment and Learning
Michael McGimpsey (UUP), Department of Health, Social Service and Public Safety
Margaret Ritchie (SDLP), Department of Social Development

Ian Paisley, Jr (DUP), Junior Minister, Office of the First and Deputy First Minister

Gerry Kelly (SF), Junior Minister, Office of the First and Deputy First Minister

Tony Blair's achievement in Northern Ireland was hailed as his greatest as prime minister, and it came just in time for his departure from office. The British prime minister characterized the Northern Ireland conflict as an 'irrational' one in the 'modern world'. Yet he has also sought to portray it as a model for conflict management everywhere, particularly the Middle East. The Secretary of State for Northern Ireland, Peter Hain, argued that the deal on devolution would be stable: 'I am confident that the agreement in Northern Ireland will stick precisely because it was brokered between the two most polarised positions' (Hain 2007, p. 26).

The start of power-sharing got off to a promising start, and the Paisley–McGuinness leadership was dubbed the 'Chuckle Brothers' by the press. But at the time of writing it has not yet been tested by decisions that will have to be made on academic selection, the devolution of security, the reform of public administration, an Irish Language Act, and the continuing existence of the IRA's Army Council. Republican dissidents continue their 'armed struggle' and loyalist paramilitaries, the UDA and UVF, appear to be winding down their activities but have not yet decommissioned. The DUP has maintained its unity, though dissent continues and Ian Paisley submitted to pressure to stand down as the leader of his own Free Presbyterian Church and, later, of the DUP. Jim Allister MEP set up a new party, 'Traditional Unionist Voice', in December 2007 to oppose the DUP's support for power-sharing (www.jimallister.org). Relations between the moderate SDLP and UUP appear to be warming as the two parties attempt to fight back against their hardline rivals.

Evaluating Perspectives on the Good Friday Agreement

At the start of this chapter, seven perspectives on the Good Friday Agreement were described. Here we revisit those perspectives from the vantage point of devolution in May 2007.

1. *Anti-Agreement republicans*. The Real and Continuity IRA collaborated in the Omagh bombing of 1998 and attempted to sustain an 'armed struggle' throughout this period (Tonge 2004). They carried out bombings in Northern Ireland and London, but did

not succeed in peeling off a sufficiently large group of republican activists from the IRA to destabilize the peace process. On 31 July 2007 the British army was able to end officially 'Operation Banner' – its 38-year campaign in Northern Ireland – because the dissident threat was no longer sufficient to justify the presence of a military force (*Irish Times*, 26 June 2007). These dissidents claimed to speak on behalf of the Irish people, but when they stood for election in March 2007 they won only paltry support.

2. *Sinn Féin/IRA*. By 2007 there did not seem to be much evidence that the GFA had brought a united Ireland any closer. There was no sign of majority consent for Irish unity, and unionists were voting for the hardline DUP. Sinn Féin had become the dominant nationalist party in Northern Ireland and now had four ministerial posts. The party was sharing power with Ian Paisley's DUP – the party perceived by nationalists to have been the most sectarian and uncompromising of the main unionist parties. Sinn Féin's poor showing in the May 2007 elections in the Republic of Ireland dashed its hope of being in government in both the North and South of Ireland. The IRA has probably decommissioned nearly all of its weapons, and ended its armed campaign, but has no feasible strategy to achieve Irish unity. The leadership claim that the GFA is a major improvement on Sunningdale 1973, and continue to predict the unity of Ireland.

3. *SDLP*. The implementation of the GFA and the St Andrews Agreement saw the SDLP achieve its key goals, but at the same time it was overtaken by its republican rival. The party criticized the way the two governments marginalized it during the period after the signing of the GFA and the prominence they gave Sinn Féin in negotiations. The party attempted to stem its decline by taking a more assertive position on Irish unity, but to little effect. Leading members of the party were concerned about the balkanization of Northern Irish society.

4. *Pro-Agreement unionists in the UUP* were critical of the British government's failure to support it after the GFA was signed. The UUP leadership claims it has done the hard work of negotiation and compromise, only for the DUP to have reaped the benefits of its work. The DUP, they argued, had cynically denounced the UUP, defeated it in elections and then embraced the St Andrews Agreement, which was remarkably similar to the GFA, which they had denounced the UUP for supporting. The DUP had achieved this and soundly defeated the UUP at the polls.

5. *Anti-Agreement unionists.* The DUP argued that the UUP had sold out the Union in signing the GFA, and deceiving the unionist people by allowing Sinn Féin into government without decommissioning. The 'plain-speaking' DUP then negotiated the St Andrews Agreement and entered power-sharing with Sinn Féin. The DUP justified this move on the grounds that St Andrews was a significant improvement on the GFA; the DUP had forced the IRA to fully decommission; Sinn Féin had endorsed the police; and the institutions of power-sharing were now properly accountable. Robert McCartney of the UKUP and dissenters within the DUP opposed power-sharing with republicans. After his defeat in the 2007 Assembly Elections, McCartney said: 'I believe that democracy and terrorism can never co-exist in government, but clearly the electorate takes a different view.' None the less, it was not clear how popular Sinn Féin–DUP power-sharing was, and there has been a significant backlash from hardliners.

6. *The Civil Society approach* made the mistaken assumption that public opinion is more moderate than the extreme political elites. It accepted the evidence of opinion polls, which have been notorious for overestimating the moderation of public opinion since the start of the conflict, and were given a rude awakening when support for the hardline parties increased. The advocates of the 'Civil Society' approach also emphasized the polarizing effect of the 'consociational' institutions of the GFA on communal relations. There was, however, plenty of evidence of communal polarization *before* the GFA was signed. It is unlikely that the institutions of the GFA, rather than the 'law and order' issues, were significant factors in further polarizing Northern Ireland. The danger of Civil Society assumptions to the peace process was that they underestimated the problems faced by key political actors, most particularly David Trimble, and so insufficient action was taken to shore up his position. Advocates of the Civil Society approach are concerned that the Good Friday–St Andrews Agreements reinforce communalism, and that Sinn Féin–DUP power-sharing is unstable.

7. *Consociationalists* had been too pessimistic to anticipate the development of a peace process in Northern Ireland, let alone an accommodation such as the Good Friday Agreement. Although the GFA was designed to be ambiguous and presented differently to different audiences, pro-nationalist consociationalists are Constitutional Traditionalists who claimed to have the 'authentic'

interpretation of the GFA and demanded that this was implemented, regardless of the political consequences for Trimble and pro-Agreement unionism. They conceded that Trimble had given more in negotiations and that the UUP leadership was under considerable pressure, yet they simultaneously demanded further concessions (O'Leary 2002, p. 343).

Consociationalism, overly focused on the 'institutional fix', showed little realism in its understanding of what was 'the art of the possible'. Consociationalists continue to redefine consociationalism in order to claim Northern Ireland as a support case for their theory, which they want to export to Iraq and other areas of conflict around the globe.

Conclusion

The British government had attempted 'to identify the positive elements within the opposing communities and to encourage and sustain them'. This meant trying to understand the pressures on them from within their own constituency, and 'Ultimately this meant making judgements about the extent to which those pressures were real or tactical' (Hain 2007, p. 21) The British government's success in supporting the moderates and judging which party had more or less room to manoeuvre is less than clear. The government's defenders might argue, with the benefit of hindsight, that the triumph of extremes was inevitable, and that they were successful in delivering power-sharing by 2007. Moderate critics would argue that the evidence suggests that Blair's deception of unionists during the referendum and the dire state of Trimble's position (which was clearly apparent in opinion polls and elections) should have been met by a greater effort among the other pro-peace process actors, including Sinn Féin, to shore up Trimble's position (Dixon 2004a; Dixon 2009). The SDLP also complained of the failure of the two governments to support the moderate parties. Tony Blair apparently told Mark Durkan that his problem was that, unlike Sinn Féin, his party did not have any guns. There is concern that the DUP and Sinn Féin will accelerate communalism and segregation rather than seeking a 'shared future'. As leader of the SDLP, Mark Durkan, asked, could those who have 'given us the worst of our past' provide 'the best of our future'? (*Irish Times*, 8 May 2007) While there is political agreement between the leadership of Sinn Féin and the DUP, there is not much sign of reconciliation at the popular level. Voting behaviour and opinion polls do not suggest that the people of Northern Ireland have driven the peace process forward. Since the late 1990s there have been repeated eruptions of sectarian tension during the marching season, the 'sieges of Drumcree', the Holy Cross dispute, and rioting in Belfast. The 'Troubles' have seen growing residential segregation and there are now fifty-seven 'peace walls', a number that has increased during the peace process (*Belfast Telegraph*, 26 April 2007).

The peace process has seen impressive transformations in and by Northern Ireland's political parties. Politics has worked in bringing about a shift from violent conflict to unsteady, but much less violent, power-sharing. Sinn Féin/IRA's progress has been steady and gradual over a long period. The GFA was a remarkable achievement in itself, coming without any significant shift by public opinion towards the centre ground. The stunning transformation of the DUP since 2003 from implacable opponent of power-sharing to partnership with Sinn Féin has been breathtaking. Unlike Trimble, Paisley appears to have won over a reasonable majority of unionism to the St Andrews Agreement and power-sharing, though this has yet to be properly tested at the polls. Whether the hardline parties can create a sustainable, devolved government, and what the implications of this are for the people of Northern Ireland, remains to be seen.

11

Conclusion: Democracy, Violence and Politics

Introduction

This conclusion reviews and draws together the themes and arguments of the book to show how the concepts of power, ideology and 'reality' can provide a convincing explanation of the recent conflict, and in particular of the peace process. An attempt is then made to assess the, albeit shifting, interests of the key parties and governments to the conflict, and their power – through both the 'real' and propaganda wars – to realize these interests. Why has the British government been unable to impose a settlement on the conflict? What are the limits to its powers and that of other parties? How might a more democratic peace be constructed in Northern Ireland?

Explaining Northern Ireland: Power, Ideology and 'Reality'

As previously noted, there was a widespread expectation in Britain and Ireland at the time of partition that it would only be a temporary measure, and that inevitably, Ireland would be reunited either within the British Empire/Commonwealth or in an independent united Ireland (see Chapter 3; and Dixon 2001a, ch. 3) by, among other things, the forces of modernization. While modernization theory has become discredited, the widespread acceptance of its assumptions produced, and continue to produce, real effects in the attitudes of both politicians and the public. The British and Irish could justify their non-interventionist approach towards Northern Ireland by trusting in the inevitability of a united Ireland. Unionists increasingly interpreted modernization theory as a threat to their position in the UK, particularly perhaps when this theory continues to have such currency

321

in British governments. The attempts of Northern Ireland's prime minister, Terence O'Neill to weld modernization theory to a more 'moderate', accommodating attitude towards Catholics was backed by the British government, the BBC and the *Belfast Telegraph*, but met fierce resistance from unionists both inside and outside his party. This limited the ability of O'Neill to back up his rhetorical gestures towards Catholics with concrete, material concessions, which alienated unionists without satisfying Catholic demands. It was into this volatile environment that the civil rights campaign marched, sparking off an unanticipated explosion from below of Catholic resentment and frustration at discrimination in the expanding public sector. This agitation for civil rights was mixed with more traditional anti-partitionist sentiment, and republicans played a leading role in the movement's establishment (see Chapter 3). Just as O'Neill experienced considerable difficulties leading unionism, so the leadership of the civil rights movement was pushed more from below than led from the top.

During the period 1968–71, the British government attempted to bring Northern Ireland up to 'British standards' of democracy in the hope that this would result in the resolution of the conflict. The British were ideologically ill-equipped to deal with communal conflict, and quickly became disillusioned and frustrated when it appeared resistant to their reformist efforts to resolve it. The desire of the British to limit their involvement resulted in dependence on the unionist government to balance the reconciliation of nationalists without undermining its political position among unionist 'hardliners'. There had been considerable sympathy in Britain for the demands of the civil rights movement, but when the British army was deployed on the streets of Northern Ireland and came into conflict with both nationalists and unionists, a process of British alienation from the region began.

The limits on Britain's power to police Northern Ireland 'impartially' soon became apparent. Leading soldiers dismissed the illusion of a purely military solution; the army could only 'hold the ring' while the politicians reached agreement and feared a 'nightmare scenario' where it found itself fighting a war on two fronts, against both unionists and nationalists. The RUC were too weak to police Northern Ireland, and until the local security forces could be built up – ideally on a cross-community basis – the British Army would have to remain in its 'policing' role. Certainly, it was in the interests of republicans to draw the British army into conflict, but the army's repressive approach to policing also contributed to its deteriorating relationship with nationalists. The British attempted to extricate themselves from Northern Ireland by involving nationalists in the government of the region and recruiting them to the security forces, thereby legitimizing the state. Alienation from the security policy of the Northern Ireland government resulted in a withdrawal of Catholics from the locally recruited security forces.

Dependent overwhelmingly on Protestants to man the RUC and UDR, the danger was that policing the unionist community 'too stringently' could result in a lack of Protestants willing to join the security forces. It could also provoke the army's 'nightmare scenario' of a war on two fronts. It was this kind of calculation – the 'security dilemma' – that has constrained British security policy in Northern Ireland throughout the recent conflict, resulting in a structural bias against the nationalist community. This helps to explain the British state's reluctance and caution in taking on unionists in 1972–3, 1974, 1986 and 1996. The difficulties of managing British security policy were compounded by the strains 'counter-insurgency strategy' placed on civil–military relations and the problem of exerting close political control over the army. The repressive nature of the security policy, and its anti-nationalist bias, conflicted with the attempts of British politicians to bring nationalists into a power-sharing settlement with unionists.

A bipartisan approach was quickly established by the two major parties to fight the propaganda war and maximize the chances of resolving the conflict (see Chapter 4). British counter-insurgency strategy set great store on the importance of 'political determination' in order to defeat the IRA in the propaganda war. However, by 1971, there were signs that this determination was wavering, and that the politicians' definition of the conflict was shifting away from an internal, domestic British conflict towards an 'international' or even 'colonial' one. There was considerable sympathy among British politicians, particularly but not exclusively in the Labour Party, for Irish unity. The introduction of direct rule, the growing involvement of the Irish government and the opening-up of talks between the British government and opposition and the IRA raised further questions about the determination of British politicians to defeat the 'insurgency'. From the point of view of the military's counter-insurgency strategy, the increasing ambiguity of British politicians over the future of Northern Ireland encouraged IRA violence by raising its hopes of victory. This ambiguity also exacerbated loyalist fears of forcible incorporation into a united Ireland. In 1971–4 a 'Protestant backlash' developed, culminating in the UWC strike, partly in response to what loyalists saw as the successful deployment of violence by republicans that had produced major concessions from the British. Loyalist violence and unionist mobilization against both nationalism and the British state was 'successful' in checking the tendency among the British political elite to see Irish unity as an option that could extricate Britain and leave behind a stable Ireland.

There have been important continuities in British policy throughout the recent conflict, arising from the British government's attempts to build accommodation in the centre-ground of Northern Irish politics. There is a certain consistency to the British government's 'inconsistencies and contradictions', which can be explained by its need to achieve 'balance' between unionists and nationalists while pragmatically keeping the lines of communication open to paramilitaries in the hope of drawing them into the democratic process. In order to achieve some kind of even-handedness between nationalist and unionist interests and claims, British governments reassure nationalists (and even republicans) that they are 'neutral', Irish unity can be achieved by consent, and they will be treated fairly in any peace process. At the same time, the British government must also reassure unionists of their place within the Union by championing their cause and opposing Irish unity without the consent of a majority in Northern Ireland. The 'contradiction' in the British position in declaring its opposition to talking with terrorists and then maintaining a channel of contact since the mid-1970 and periodic talks (1972, 1975, 1981, 1990–3) can be explained most convincingly by reference to the propaganda war between the British government and the IRA for the support of British, Irish and international opinion. The IRA and the British army were not likely to defeat one other solely through military means but rather through a combination of the 'real war' and the propaganda war (Dixon 2001b).

Initially, the IRA's emphasis was on the military struggle. Following the example of 'anti-colonial' liberation movements, the IRA hoped to demoralize British politicians and public opinion by killing sufficient soldiers to precipitate a withdrawal. Public opinion polls and the willingness of the British government to talk gave republicans some reason to believe they were winning. Talking to 'terrorists' allowed the British to investigate the possibility of a negotiated settlement, but ran the risk of lending the IRA legitimacy, a valuable resource in the propaganda war. It also raised fears among unionists that 'perfidious Albion' was about to sell them down the river.

There are considerable parallels between the first and second peace processes. The first peace process was unbalanced in favour of the nationalists, and so the chances of a successful settlement were therefore not maximized. Whether even a 'balanced' settlement would have led to a stable settlement in the polarized political climate of 1973–4 is questionable, particularly with both republican and loyalist paramilitaries attempting to bring down power-sharing. Nevertheless, in spite of considerable support for power-sharing from both inside and outside Northern Ireland, from governments and the media, the 'moderate silent majority' failed to materialize and the failure of prime minister Brian Faulkner again illustrated the problems faced by unionist leaders in bringing their supporters to accommodation. During the second peace process (1994–8) the power-sharing experiment of 1972–4 was a reference point for the parties.

Following the collapse of power-sharing in 1974, the stalemate between the parties and governments over Northern Ireland was more apparent. Various parties and governments had the power to combine and veto the preferred settlement of others, but none could impose its own agenda. The defeat of British policy 1972–4 by unionists was hardly compatible with the strand of republican ideology which suggested that unionists were merely the puppets of British imperialism. Learning from this new awareness of unionist power, the Labour government again considered independence for Northern Ireland as a more effective way of extricating itself from the conflict (this had also been debated in 1969). This option, like withdrawal, was thought likely to result in civil war in Northern Ireland, resulting in the destabilization of the island of Ireland with serious overspill effects for the UK.

The diffusion of power among the different parties to the conflict led to stalemate. The unionists had stood up to the British government and its army, and there was no reason to think that the IRA or the Irish government would be much more successful in imposing its will on unionism in the event of a British withdrawal. There was no guarantee that the IRA would cease its 'armed struggle' in the event of a British withdrawal and be content only with a united Ireland run by the 'Free State' parties. The Irish government took repressive security measures to deal with the IRA's military threat as well as attacking republicans in the propaganda war. The IRA was able to sustain violence over a considerable period of time but were not able to force the British to withdraw from Northern Ireland.

Even if it could have done this, the unionists probably represented an insurmountable obstacle to Irish unity.

The British government and the security forces could contain the IRA, but might defeat it militarily only by using extremely repressive techniques, which would probably have been counter-productive in the long-run. These would have alienated international opinion, destroyed the credibility of moderate nationalists (and with them any hope of an accommodation with unionism) and questioned the legitimacy of the British state. The continuing violence of the paramilitaries made attempts to construct an accommodation between unionists and nationalists more difficult. The unionists could prevent a British withdrawal through the threat and use of violence, but could not gain integration or majority rule. All sides could exert their power to try to shift the political agenda in their direction, but this was to some extent constrained by the power of other actors and the threat of destabilization and all-out civil war.

Under the Labour government 1974–9 there was an apparent drift towards integrationism, as both Labour and Conservatives courted the Ulster Unionists; however, it is doubtful whether this policy was seriously pursued. The pursuit of integration would antagonize international (particularly US) opinion, lose the British the co-operation of the Republic and alienate 'moderate nationalism', perhaps resulting in a drift of nationalists towards republicanism and a consequent increase in violence. The importance of underpinning moderate nationalism and winning security gains contributed to the signing of the Anglo-Irish Agreement (AIA). There were also important intra-party and bipartisan pressures constraining both Labour and Conservatives from pursuing an all-out integrationist policy. British public opinion tended to favour extrication from the conflict altogether, but seems to have been appeased by continuing bipartisanship and the strategy of normalization, which decreased army casualties and attempted to contain the conflict. These constraints resulted in a considerable degree of continuity in British policy between Conservative and Labour governments. The extent of the constraints operating on British government policy towards Northern Ireland are apparent in the shift of Conservative government policy under Margaret Thatcher. In 1979–80 the Conservatives rejected their party's formal commitment to integration, and Thatcher picked up where her Conservative predecessor, Edward Heath, had left off in 1974, by pursuing both power-sharing and, in 1980, an Anglo-Irish process.

By the mid- to-late 1970s, the British government and the IRA were settling down for the 'Long War'. In order to win the propaganda war, the British government shifted its presentational approach to the conflict. The IRA were no longer to be treated as a political organization, but were labelled 'criminals' in an attempt to 'normalize' the conflict and to undermine support for the IRA in the propaganda war. The IRA was also altering its propaganda strategy and attempting to mobilize a political as well as a military movement. This 'mass propaganda' strategy resisted British 'normalization' and resulted in the 1981 Hunger Strike and a propaganda victory for the IRA. Behind the scenes, the British government maintained contacts with the republican movement, undermining its own claim that the IRA were a criminal organization. The successful entry of Sinn Féin into the electoral process during the Hunger Strikes damaged the British claim that the IRA was a criminal organization that succeeded only through intimidation. The threat that Sinn Féin might replace the SDLP as the principal party of the nationalists was a powerful force behind the AIA in 1985.

The AIA was not the rational, Machiavellian master-plan of Margaret Thatcher – who signed principally for security reasons – but rather the product of competing agendas in the Civil Service and the cabinet. They were responding to pressure from the Irish and US governments, but also to the turn of events in Northern Ireland, particularly the rise of Sinn Féin. The British government, in order to retain the hope of an accommodation, had to maintain some conception of 'balance' between unionist and nationalist interests. Push unionism 'too hard', as during the first peace process, and unionist public and party opinion would become too alienated to construct an accommodation. Push nationalism 'too hard' and this was likely to manifest itself in the more nationalist drift of SDLP policy in the late 1970s and the political rise of Sinn Féin.

The distinction between 'constitutional' and 'unconstitutional' politicians becomes blurred, particularly when a particular community feels itself under threat, and constitutional means appear an ineffective way of defending political interests (Dixon 2004a, 2004b). The impact of the AIA was largely unanticipated: it provoked unionist rebellion, which the British government struggled to contain, and the security situation deteriorated. Rather than coercing power-sharing, the AIA appeared to polarize politics as the SDLP engaged with republicans instead of conciliating unionism, and unionism drifted away from devolution and towards integration. Yet one of the consequences of the AIA might have been to pave the way for the peace process and the GFA.

Analysing the Peace Process

The key to understanding the peace process is an appreciation of the difficulties that faced political elites in Britain and Ireland in bringing their parties and public opinion towards an accommodation. There is little evidence that public and party opinion, fed by the propaganda war and the experience of twenty-five years of violence and repression, was converging prior to the 1994 ceasefire. The political elites, assuming they were so inclined, would have to work hard to shift opinion to the point where a deal (such as the Good Friday Agreement) might bridge the gap between the parties. It was difficult to see where an agreement might be reached that was capable of being sold to both unionists and republicans. The Sinn Féin leadership had problems bringing their movement, if perhaps not so much public opinion, with them towards a settlement, and these problems were recognized both by the RUC and the British government. The leadership of the UUP also had considerable difficulty in containing and leading unionist opinion. Prior to the IRA ceasefire in 1993, Northern Ireland faced high levels of violence, and communal tensions remained high during the peace process. These manifested themselves in opinion polls, elections and clashes during the marching season, most notoriously at Drumcree. In this environment, how could the political elites lead their voters and supporters to a compromise settlement?

The polarization of politics in Northern Ireland during the late 1970s and early 1980s was not conducive to the construction of an accommodation between unionism and nationalism. The confrontation and clashes between unionism and the British government over the Anglo-Irish Agreement accelerated the ideological development of republicans by demonstrating, once again, the relative autonomy of unionism from the British state and the willingness of the British to 'face down' unionism. Peter Brooke's public claim that Britain had 'no selfish strategic or economic interest' in Northern Ireland echoed similar British statements from the early 1970s. It reinforced the view that the conflict was essentially an internal one, requiring accommodation between unionists and nationalists rather than one driven by British imperialism. The military struggle with the

British was stalemated, and continuing IRA violence inhibited any further electoral progress. In the Republic there was a movement away from traditional republicanism and towards unilateral moves to amend Articles 2 and 3 of the Irish Constitution. This, along with progress in the Brooke/Mayhew talks, threatened to further marginalize the republican movement. The end of the Cold War, and other 'anti-imperialist' struggles in South Africa and Israel/Palestine, also appeared to be moving towards resolution and were used by the Sinn Féin leadership to justify the unarmed strategy.

The view of leading members of the British government was that a faction of the republican movement probably wanted to bring the conflict to an end and enter the democratic process. However, the problem remained as to how to bring the conflict to an end in a way that would maximize the credibility of the SF leadership, and therefore minimize the prospects of a major split in the IRA while encouraging unionists to participate in negotiations. The British and Irish governments, Sinn Féin and the SDLP attempted to wind down the propaganda war by choreographing the peace process (Dixon 2002a, Dixon 2008). The British had to play a 'dual role' and deal with both republican and unionist audiences. The British government needed to draw republicans into a peace process and reassure them that their interests would be protected. Simultaneously, it had to publicly reassure unionists by championing their concerns and interests while attempting to push them towards accommodation. The Irish government played a comparable role among nationalists and republicans. But the British government had the added difficulty of taking responsibility for most of the decisions that moved the peace process forward, which tended to be seen by unionists as 'concessions to nationalism and republicanism'.

This made the British task of retaining the confidence of unionism all the more difficult. There is strong evidence of choreography in the back-channel contacts, the negotiations of the Downing Street Declaration and on decommissioning. Privately, the British government encouraged Sinn Féin and facilitated its path towards a peace process, acknowledging the constraints on the Sinn Féin leadership, while publicly it would reassure unionism by attacking and condemning the republican movement and displaying determined support for the Union. The Sinn Féin leadership needed to show republican activists and supporters that they could exert more power and influence through the unarmed struggle than they could through the use of arms. The choreography of high-profile 'defeats' for the British government (for example, over Adams' visa to visit the USA in 1995) would reinforce the Sinn Féin leadership's argument for the 'unarmed struggle'. The US president's role in the 'pan-nationalist' performance encouraged republicans into the peace process, but at the expense of alienating unionism (Dixon 2006a, p. 85).

The failure of the IRA to declare its ceasefire permanent emphasized the importance of the decommissioning issue. This issue had been raised before the ceasefire, and the British government may have believed it was relatively unproblematic for the republican movement, which had declared its desire to demilitarize and remove the gun from politics. The Framework Documents seemed to be yet another concession to nationalism, and while they might have helped, in the short term, to entrench the IRA's ceasefire, they did so at the cost of alienating unionism, so that UUP leader James Molyneaux's position was fatally undermined. The 'balance' between unionism and nationalism had been upset. The British government conceded further ground to nationalism on the decommissioning issue with 'Washington 3'. Unionists and their allies in the Conservative Party were digging in and insisted on movement on decommissioning before all-party talks. This reflected the alienation of the wider unionist community from the process.

The impasse over decommissioning was not an artificial barrier erected by the British. For unionists, the British government appeared to be in retreat before 'the pan-nationalist front', precisely the appearance that Adams needed to convince republican hardliners that the peace process was preferable to the armed struggle. Unionism was alarmed and destabilized by the British government's apparent failure to defend the Union, and its assertions of neutrality. Unionism's worst suspicions were aroused by the revelations of secret contacts between Sinn Féin and the British government after these had been denied outright by the British government. The Downing Street Declaration (DSD), the Framework Documents and British retreats on decommissioning were further evidence of the ability of the pan-nationalist front to set the agenda. Molyneaux managed to reassure unionism of his influence with the government and mute its reaction to the DSD, although opinion was already shifting against his stance. The British government attempted to get round the decommissioning issue but was constrained ultimately by the unionists, who could not enter all-party negotiations without decommissioning. Quietly, Sinn Féin leaders acknowledged that the British government was constrained over the decommissioning issue by the need to keep unionists 'on board' in the peace process. The ability of unionist leaders to bring their supporters and voters with them towards the 'centre ground' was severely limited, as most indicators of unionist opinion suggested a hardening in that community's position.

The Irish government privately, and to some extent publicly, appreciated the British government's dilemma over decommissioning. However, the Irish government, like the US government, had publicly to fulfil its role in the 'pan-nationalist front' and take the nationalist part in disputes with the British, thereby demonstrating to republicans the effectiveness of the unarmed struggle. An impasse was reached by the end of 1995, with neither unionist nor republican leaders having room for manoeuvre. The subsequent compromise announced by British prime minister, John Major, following the publication of the Mitchell Report seemed to be able to deliver all-party talks without decommissioning. But the end of the IRA's ceasefire dashed these hopes.

The Good Friday Agreement (GFA) of 1998, with its support for power-sharing with an Irish dimension, echoed the Sunningdale Agreement of 1973. As with the first peace process, the problems for the second peace process arose out of the ability of the political elites to sustain the GFA and deliver their respective constituencies to support the deal. The decommissioning issue had been (perhaps necessarily) fudged by the GFA: unionists felt the spirit of the Agreement involved decommissioning, while republicans claimed the letter of the GFA involved no decommissioning before entering the executive. The pro-GFA parties and governments have attempted to choreograph movement on all sides to create an environment of trust and push the process forward. However, the process has foundered repeatedly on the rock of decommissioning and the limits of choreography and 'spin' to get round the 'reality' of no decommissioning. Sinn Féin's fortunes improved and the party overtook the SDLP to become the largest nationalist party. The UUP leadership's position was vulnerable as soon as David Trimble endorsed the GFA, and the pro-Agreement parties and governments, arguably, did not do enough to help the unionist leader fight off the DUP. The electoral rise of the DUP and Sinn Féin was widely thought to end the prospects of power-sharing and signal the demise of the peace process. Remarkably, the leaderships of both parties were able to deliver their parties to the St Andrews Agreement and the restoration of devolution in May 2007. This completed a remarkable transformation in both hardline parties, which was particularly marked in the case of the DUP because this shift took place over such a short period of time with relatively little preparation of its party and voters. The transformation of the party leaderships has not be matched by transformation among the people of Northern Ireland, and the challenge of reconciliation and integration remains.

During the recent conflict, violence and democratic politics have co-existed uneasily. Both nationalists and unionists have, through politics, mobilization and the use and threat of violence, attempted to shift the political agenda in their own direction. Loyalist and republican paramilitaries have used violence, but nationalist and unionist politicians have also used the threat of violence to influence the political process (Dixon 2004b). The relationship between some unionist parties, in particular Vanguard and the DUP, and the loyalist paramilitaries has often been close. When constitutional politics have failed, some unionist politicians have resorted to the threat of violence to prevent the erosion of the Union. Others have acted in ways that could reasonably be interpreted as encouraging violence. The British and Irish governments have attempted to reach accommodation with the paramilitaries but, in the process, have also risked the delegitimization of democratic politics through this process. The attempt to bring paramilitaries into politics has recognized, and to some extent accommodated, the power of street politics and violence, though it should be remembered that liberal democracies often bow to those with extra-parliamentary (for example, economic) power.

Power and Interests

From the evidence presented in this book, we can attempt to define the (perceived) interests of various key actors and their power to realize those interests. Interests and power can vary over time, perhaps as particular politicians or governments learn or forget the 'realities' and parameters of practical politics. It should be remembered that there are competing views and interests within the British and Irish states, unionism and nationalism.

The British government is the most powerful actor, but it has been unable to impose its will on republicans or loyalists in Northern Ireland after thirty years of violence.

British Interests and Power

There have been widely contrasting interpretations of the British government's interests and goals in Northern Ireland. On the one hand, republicans have emphasized the determination of British imperialism to retain the union with Northern Ireland, while some loyalists have claimed that Britain is in the process of withdrawing. Both tend to conceive of the British state as a very powerful, single, rational actor pursuing clearly determined goals. This conception was not borne out by our analysis of the AIA or the autonomy of the security establishment. The British state has sovereignty over Northern Ireland, an enormous capacity for violence and great resources that can be deployed in both the 'real war' and the propaganda war. However, it has been argued here that the *overriding* interest of the British government is for a stable settlement, and its failure to deliver this indicates the limits of its power.

Since 1969, the British government has had no overriding selfish, strategic, economic or political interests in Northern Ireland, and both of the major British parties have considered Irish unity and independence. British politicians and public opinion have often excluded Northern Ireland from Britain's 'imagined community' (Dixon 2001a, pp. 293–4). Even such apparently keen supporters of the Union as Margaret Thatcher, signatory of the Anglo-Irish Agreement, are better thought of as English nationalists or unionists whose interests and priorities do not necessarily coincide with those of Ulster unionists. On the one hand, the limits of Britain's ability to coerce unionists into a settlement were seen by the failure of power-sharing and the AIA, which underlined unionists' ability to make Northern Ireland ungovernable. But, on the other hand, the British political and military elites largely accepted that the IRA could not in the long run be defeated solely by military methods (Major 1999, p. 492). The limited power of British governments to achieve their interests in Northern Ireland is indicated by their consistent inability to achieve a stable settlement. The constraints operating on British policy shape its parameters which, while permitting short-term movement, have led to relative consistency in policy.

Unionist Interests and Power

Unionist interests lie in the preservation of the Union, but they are divided on the means to achieve this. The lack of *overriding* British strategic, economic or political interests in Northern Ireland, and Britain's attempts to create a 'balanced accommodation', has further fed unionist insecurity about its commitment to the Union. The British government has not been the sponsor of Ulster unionism in the way that the Irish government has supported Irish nationalism (Dixon 1995b). Given the 'unreliable' record of successive British governments on Northern Ireland, it is hardly surprising that unionists are insecure about their constitutional position in the UK, and have regarded both the first and second peace processes with such suspicion. Since British governments have not been a great source of support or comfort for unionists, they have fallen back on their own resources, including the threat and use of violence. It is during periods when unionists, with some reason, have seen their constitutional position come under threat (1966, 1969, 1971–1975/6, 1986, 1991–3, 1996, 1998–2001) that they have mobilized and violence has increased. Constitutional unionist politicians (like many other 'constitutional' politicians) have operated in the grey area between democratic politics and the threat and use of violence. Fearing British manipulation of Northern Ireland out of the Union, unionist politicians have taken to the streets, threatened the use of force and advocated independence as the only way of resisting British power and coercion.

At the same time, there has been considerable antagonism between the loyalist paramilitaries and the leaders of the principal unionist parties (including Ian Paisley), who have condemned loyalist violence. There is a difficulty in assessing whether unionist politicians (as with other politicians), in reflecting the outrage of some of their supporters, are attempting to incite further violence or, by venting frustration and letting off steam, limiting the prospect of that anger turning into violence. Without the physical resistance of unionists and the threat of violence, it seems reasonable to suggest that the British might well have eased Northern Ireland out of the Union. When the power of unionism has been demonstrated, as during the UWC strike in May 1974 and after the AIA, British (and Irish) political calculations have been reassessed. The unionists have had little success in the propaganda war, and their power is limited by the lack of sympathy for them both in Britain and internationally. However, unionism's capacity to mobilize its supporters, the violence of its paramilitaries and unionist domination of the local security forces have given unionists the capacity to set limits on British–Irish initiatives.

Nationalist Interests and Power

Nationalists are united in their aspiration to a united Ireland, but are divided over the means to achieve it. The nationalist SDLP has played a pivotal role throughout 'the Troubles'. As the political representatives of the majority of nationalists until 2001, the British government required SDLP co-operation in any power-sharing settlement, and needed the party to be strong enough to fend off its Sinn Féin rival, unless Sinn Féin replaced the SDLP and the IRA guns were silent. This majority status within the nationalist community gave the SDLP prestige and influence in the Republic, Europe and the USA, which it has exploited to significant advantage. The SDLP is able to draw on the sympathy of public opinion in the Republic of Ireland, and this is something that the Republic's political parties and government can ill afford to ignore. The SDLP has been scrupulous in its condemnation of violence from whatever source it has originated. Nevertheless, many of the founder-members of the SDLP were involved in the civil rights marches, which could be interpreted as being designed to provoke confrontation. The violence and success of the republican movement has often rebounded to the SDLP's advantage. Anxious to stem the rise of republicanism, the British and Irish governments have attempted to shore up the SDLP and undermine republicanism by making concessions. After 1985, the SDLP found itself in a pivotal position where it could either advance the peace process or the 'all-party talks' process.

The Irish government has been in a position to exacerbate or ameliorate the conflict in the North. Articles 2 and 3 of the Irish Constitution 'lay claim to Northern Ireland and have been seen by unionists as legitimizing the IRA's violent campaign. In 1969, republicans were encouraged to fight by their perception that the Irish government would come to their rescue. There have also been allegations of the Republic's lack of resolve to deal effectively with the IRA. The 'Arms Crisis' of 1970 involved allegations of Southern ministers funding and arming the IRA. On the other hand, the IRA was, perhaps increasingly, seen by the Irish political elite as a direct threat to the stability of the Republic, particularly once the extent of unionist resistance to Irish unity became apparent. Containing the IRA and preventing civil war in the North from spreading into the Republic have created a strong incentive in the South for a stable settlement to 'the Troubles', and some have detected the emergence of a partitionist, 26-county nationalism. Since 1972, if not before, the British have seen an important role for the Irish government in promoting peace in the North, first at Sunningdale and later through the British–Irish process initiated in 1980, producing first the AIA and subsequently the GFA. British–Irish co-operation has deflected international criticism from Britain and has been effective in the 'propaganda war' against the IRA, particularly in the USA.

The continuing violence of the IRA's campaign during 'the Troubles' has contributed significantly to the polarization of public opinion, and enormous suffering. But it has also proved to be a powerful tool for drawing the attention of the British government to republican grievances. The mobilization of republicans during the Hunger Strikes and Sinn Féin's successful entry into electoral politics were catalysts to the signing of the Anglo-Irish Agreement. While the IRA has been unable to beat the British militarily, its violence has helped to heighten tension and undermine British constitutional initiatives. Sinn Féin has been able to exert electoral pressure on the SDLP to prevent it entering an accommodation with unionists. The history of the republican movement has been a history of splits, and the leadership is constrained in its ability to move towards accommodation by hardline activists within the IRA and the wider republican movement. None the less, the leadership has been remarkably successful in transforming Sinn Féin /IRA from the pursuit of Irish unity through 'armed struggle' to 'unarmed struggle' (see Moloney 2002).

The US government has an interest in actions that gain it Irish-American support and bolster its international and national reputation, but which do not alienate their loyal British ally. The impact of US pressure is difficult to assess, but it has generally been overestimated. During the recent peace process, its influence has been deliberately overplayed to demonstrate to republicans the influence of 'pan-nationalism' and the advantages of the unarmed struggle. But the US president also has an interest in taking his share of the credit for any settlement (Dixon 2006a).

Power, the Media and the Propaganda War

The British state has considerable resources to make a powerful impact on the propaganda war over Northern Ireland (Miller 1994, p. 274). But again, it is important to draw attention to the limits of this power. While the British press and broadcasting media are not subject to direct government control, the state has used its control of information, censorship and intimidation to influence the presentation of 'the Troubles' by the media (Schlesinger 1978; Schlesinger *et al.* 1983). The sensitivity of the British state to media portrayals of Northern Ireland suggests a sense of vulnerability to its impact on public opinion and its implications for the 'real' and propaganda wars against the IRA. The British government, with some reason, seems to have been more concerned with the impact of the portrayal of republicans on British rather than on Northern Irish opinion (Dixon 2000a).

The British media has been largely sympathetic to the government's policy in Northern Ireland, and has shared the government's attempts to rally and promote moderate opinion. The BBC Northern Ireland (BBC-NI) supported O'Neill during the 1960s and attempted to emphasize the positive in community relations, stress the experiences that united the people, ignore sectarian divisions, marginalize 'extremists' such as Ian Paisley, and manufacture consensus (Butler 1991; Butler 1995, p. 47). The *Belfast Telegraph*, the newspaper with the largest circulation in Northern Ireland, and with a cross-community readership, strongly supported O'Neill's efforts at reform, and subsequent unionist 'moderates'. The *Belfast Telegraph* attempted not only to describe the 'moderates' in Northern Ireland but also to rally support for them and create a 'bandwagon' effect. As with much of the British press, the *Belfast Telegraph* underestimated loyalist discontent. Before October 1968, the local broadcast media 'persisted with a bizarrely optimistic account of O'Neillism's command of a fictive centre ground' (Butler 1995, p. 47). The civil rights movement won the media battle, winning sympathy in the British press and in the BBC-NI (Butler 1991, pp. 109–12; Kirkaldy 1984, pp. 175–6; Parkinson 1998, p. 103).

Violence 'is thought to be an un-British way of solving political problems'; after 1969 the conflict was presented increasingly by broadcasters as one 'between equivalent warring tribes' (Schlesinger 1978, p. 236; Butler 1991, p. 110). The introduction of British troops in 1969 and the death of the first soldier in February 1971 further shifted the broadcasters' portrayal of the conflict. The British media supported the army as 'peacekeepers' between two warring factions, responding to events rather than having an impact on them (Elliott 1976). Terrorism became the cause of the conflict, and the IRA, killers of British soldiers and later bombers of Britain, emerged as the principal enemy (Schlesinger 1978, p. 205; Butler 1991, p. 110). Until the introduction of direct rule in 1972 'there was a structured institutional bias in broadcast journalism in favour of the "reformed" unionist position' (Butler 1991, p. 111).

As the violence escalated further following internment in August 1971, the broadcast media came under further political pressure, which established the parameters of future reporting. Although the conflict with the IRA was not officially recognized as a 'war', to avoid giving legitimacy to the IRA in the propaganda war, the conflict was seen by the British government and the military as a war. Therefore, the reporting of the conflict was 'war reporting' and the media were expected to offer support to the state in the propaganda war against the enemy. A myth had arisen in British military circles that it was the media that had undermined the USA's will to defeat the North Vietnamese (Dixon 2000a). William Whitelaw, the Secretary of State for Northern Ireland, warned the media of the dangers of lowering the morale of the security forces and argued that it was not possible to be neutral in the 'fight for freedom': 'Surely one is either for it or against it.' These sentiments were echoed in the right-wing press (Chibnall 1977, pp. 40–1). The broadcasters dropped their commitment to impartiality and came out in clear opposition to the methods of the 'extremists' (Schlesinger 1978, pp. 211–12; Curtis 1984, p. 10).

The British media's reliance on official sources further reduced its capacity for criticism of the conduct of the government or security forces. An indirect form of censorship was imposed which, while allowing reporting, inhibited any analysis of the underlying causes of the conflict. The source of violence was terrorism, 'the result of inexplicable, asocial forces' (Elliott 1976, pp. 5–3). Such covert censorship was arguably a more effective way of influencing public opinion than overt censorship, which would have discredited the media and thereby limited the effectiveness of the information they carried. Interviews with republican and loyalist paramilitaries were almost totally banned. The broadcasters shared with the press a tendency to produce 'a series of decontextualized reports of violence [that] fails to analyse and re-analyse the historical roots of the Irish conflict', which left the British audience with a view of the Troubles as 'largely incomprehensible and irrational' (Schlesinger 1978, p. 243; see also Elliott 1976; Butler 1995, p. 86). There was also overt censorship in the Republic. This may have contributed to Britain's problems in building domestic public support for sustaining its presence in Northern Ireland.

The effect of censorship was to overestimate the strength of 'moderates'. Butler argues:

> Without a wider frame of reference, the view was compounded that a 'few extremists on either side' were the cause rather than a symptom of deeper division. This encouraged the misapprehension that if the British could negotiate a 'reasonable' settlement between the parties, the good sense of the vast majority would prevail, isolating the tiny minority of malcontents. (Butler 1991, p. 111)

The power-sharing experiment attempted to unite moderates and isolate the extremists. The British government was supported by the broadcast media and the *Belfast Telegraph* in its claim to have found a 'moderate silent majority' in favour of power-sharing. The British security services supported attempts to build moderation in Northern Ireland by undertaking a 'psychological warfare' or 'black propaganda' campaign against both republican *and* loyalist 'extremists', including William Craig and Ian Paisley (Curtis 1984, pp. 236–41; Foot 1989). In addition, the *Irish News* favoured Sunningdale, while the unionist *Newsletter* endorsed power-sharing and focused its criticisms on the Irish dimension of the Sunningdale package. The over-optimistic hopes vested in a 'moderate silent majority' were dealt a knockout blow by the 'realities' of unionist politics and the subsequent defeat of 'moderate unionism' at the ballot box. This may have deepened the disillusion of the British public with any kind of settlement of the conflict and boosted support for the withdrawal option.

By 1975, coverage of Northern Ireland was falling away. The British army's 'black propaganda' campaign was being exposed and losing it credibility as a reliable source of information. The British government moved to wind up its operations, with responsibility for information being passed over to the RUC as the conflict was Ulsterized and the army kept a lower profile (Miller 1994, pp. 78–9, 81). Learning from the failure of the broadcast media to create consent in the 1960s, the BBC proposed a state of 'balanced sectarianism', where the broadcast media would 'function as an honest broker, guaranteeing impartial representation between the various sectarian forces in the local polity' (Butler 1995, p. 73). The electoral success of Sinn Féin in 1981–2 represented a powerful blow to British portrayals of the IRA as criminals who sustained themselves through manipulation and intimidation and without popular support. 'Repeatedly obliged to give way to executive pressure, in 1969, 1971, 1974, 1977–78, 1979 and 1985, broadcast journalism had been reduced by degrees to a state of "culpable silence"'. For Butler, the limits of 'permissible reporting' are related to the shifting priorities of the state during the conflict (Butler 1995, pp. 79, 89).

While the British government has considerable power to set and influence the political and media agenda over Northern Ireland, four significant constraints operate on this:

- First, the support from the media for British policy was insufficient to sustain O'Neill or deliver a 'moderate' settlement in the first peace process. Indeed, public opinion appears to have polarized during 'the Troubles'.

- Second, the British government has also failed to persuade the British public against support for the withdrawal of troops. Although British policy emphasizes consent and, despite little public political support for the withdrawal option, opinion polls have consistently indicated that, since the mid-1970s, a majority of the British public supports withdrawal. Interestingly, there is evidence that, in the short term at any rate, IRA bombings and interviews with republicans have hardened British attitudes and reduced support for withdrawal (Dixon 2000a).

- Third, the republican movement has scored 'propaganda' victories against the British government, most notably during the Hunger Strikes and through its ability to reinforce the perception of the conflict as 'colonial'.

- Fourth, David Miller has drawn attention to the role of British television in bringing about the release of the Birmingham Six and the Guildford Four in the face of obstruction by the state. Nevertheless, he argues that 'The media operate within a set of constraints in which power is clearly skewed towards the state' (Miller 1994, p. 277).

The IRA and the republican movement have been the particular targets of the British (and the Republic's) propaganda war. This is probably because republicans target British soldiers, bomb Britain and are seen as the primary threat to the stability of Northern Ireland. The loyalists are perceived to be reacting to republican violence. From the British state's point of view, since the IRA were the principal enemy, it made sense to blame them for some loyalist killings in order to win the propaganda war. It may also have been felt that drawing attention to loyalist violence could lead to demands to take on the loyalists more forcefully and pull the army into its 'nightmare scenario' of a 'war on two fronts' (Elliott 1976, pp. 5–3). This might also add to the disillusion of the British public with the whole conflict and accelerate demands for withdrawal.

There has been a tendency to assume that, because the British media have focused most of their hostility on the republican movement, unionism has received favourable treatment. Some have argued that the media's obsession with IRA terrorism as the cause of the conflict has led to unionism being 'marginalized, absented and ignored'. It is argued that the underestimation of loyalist violence does not represent a pro-loyalist bias but rather a tendency to ignore unionism and its grievances (Butler 1995, p. 114; Parkinson 1998, p. 164). When unionism is considered it 'tends to be (mis)represented as a monolith' personified by Ian Paisley, who has been subject to media hostility since the 1960s (Butler 1995, p. 114; Parkinson 1998). The 'reasonable' British are contrasted with the 'extremists' from both sides in Northern Ireland: 'The insistence on an extremist symmetry makes the Protestants almost as bad as the republicans. Indeed, from the standard British point of view, it makes sense that Protestants and Catholics are morally equivalent, for a binary system of identification legitimates long-suffering British neutrality' (Butler 1995, p. 115; see also Parkinson 1998, pp. 68–70, 166). Unionism has a poor media image, and has largely failed to engage effectively in the propaganda war (Miller 1994, pp. 157–9; Parkinson 1998). The 'moderate' centre is occupied by the nationalist SDLP, which has considerable media sympathy and is contrasted with republican and unionist extremists (Miller 1994, pp. 156–7; Butler 1995, pp. 115–16; Parkinson 1998, pp. 68, 108).

In those sections of the British press that support unionism this tends to be from an English/British rather than an Ulster unionist perspective, sharing Ulster unionist concerns about security and IRA violence, but tending towards support for British government initiatives (Parkinson 1998, pp. 89, 108, 121, 165). While the British press are more concerned with the deaths of 'their soldiers' than the locally recruited RUC/RIR, unionists may correspondingly exhibit greater concern for the locally-recruited forces (Parkinson 1998, pp. 90, 96). The *Daily Mirror* (and the *New Statesman*) have broken ranks in the past to support British withdrawal, but for English/British nationalist reasons – 'bring our boys home' and let the Irish get on with it – rather than out of any sympathy for republicans. In 1981, the *Sunday Times* came out in favour of withdrawal as a prelude to independence, and in recent years the liberal *Guardian* newspaper has taken a position that has been sympathetic towards nationalists, if not republicans. Even right-wing magazines, such as *The Spectator* and *The Economist*, have expressed sympathy for Irish unity, and the right-wing press periodically despairs of Ulster (Parkinson 1998, pp. 49, 101–2, 103). But for the most part the UK press has taken a political stance broadly supportive of the Union but usually from a distinctively English/British unionist perspective.

How do we explain the failure of the British government to win the propaganda war and dominate the audience's understanding of the conflict in Northern Ireland? Important sections of the people of Northern Ireland, both unionists and nationalists, have resisted British propaganda on the conflict. Even British domestic opinion has not proved to be as malleable as the political and military elites might have hoped (indicated by the extent of support for withdrawal). There has been an overemphasis on the power of the media to shape perceptions, and less attention has been paid to the context in which the audience receives media messages (Miller 1994, p. 260). Philip Schlesinger has drawn attention to the excessive way that research on the media has concentrated on the media itself and the privileged role of the state. He argues that we should not ignore 'the activities of other sources as this unnecessarily deprives us of empirical knowledge of how the battle for access is conducted' (Schlesinger 1990, p. 82). Media research suggests that perceptions are not shaped solely from the 'top down', by the state and the national or local media, but perceptions are also shaped by the audience itself. The public 'are active participants in the construction of meaning . . . both media and audiences are part of wider cultural political contexts that may either facilitate or obstruct the acceptance of certain kinds of representations' (Eldridge 1993, p. 31). It is possible to acknowledge the power of the media while at the same time accepting the importance of the cultural and ideological context for the shaping of perceptions. A media message may only be accepted when it reinforces the prevailing ideology and 'dominant values' of the communal group (Elliott 1976, pp. 1–13). The British government's impact through the media may therefore be related to the socialization and ideological disposition of the audience. It has more success when talking to its 'own people' than to members of other communities, but even here, as British withdrawal support indicates, its impact is still constrained.

Just as the British state experiences difficulty in manipulating British and Irish public opinion, so the nationalist and unionist political elites, as we have seen, encounter difficulty in manipulating opinion within their own communities. While local elites may have the power of the party machine, activists and other sympathisers to promote their interests and their account of 'reality' in the propaganda war, there are alternative sources of information available to activists and voters. Local cultures sustain ideological perspectives which compete with those of the British government as well as those of local elites. Local newspapers tend to reinforce communal ideologies and perspectives, but also from time to time appear to have attempted to lead their readers towards the 'centre ground' (notably the *Newsletter* and *Irish News* during the second peace process).

There are important alternative sources of information apart from these local newspapers which compete for the attention of the people. There are the more obviously communal or party political media, the 'alternative press', and the campaigning of pressure groups, but also folk memory, oral history, word-of-mouth accounts of events, rumour, and marching organizations that can sustain an alternative culture, and different perspectives and interpretations of the conflict. Jarman's work on parading draws attention to the way such practices 'have been shaped by the broader political world, and have been an important element in creating that world' (Jarman 1997, p. 253). People's direct experience of the 'reality' of the conflict is also likely to be a powerful influence on perception. If an individual has been beaten up, or witnessed violence or intimidation, then this could well have an impact on that individual's perception of the conflict. It could be argued that because the population of Northern Ireland are, relatively, so politicized, they are likely to be particularly resistant to media or state manipulation. Loyalist and republican paramilitary organizations have a two-way relationship with the communities from which they spring, and there are limits to the toleration of these communities for paramilitary violence and what are deemed to be 'legitimate targets'.

Politics and the 'Art of the Possible'

The concepts of structure and agency have been used to understand the dynamic nature of the Northern Ireland conflict and the power of the various parties. Rather than accept the 'front stage' appearances of politics, there has been an attempt to investigate some of the 'behind the scenes' manoeuvring to gain a more realistic understanding of how the political process works. This focuses attention on the *politics* of conflict management, and politics as 'the art of the possible'. There are many competing 'ideal' 'solutions' to the conflict, but many of these do not seem to have a 'realistic' chance of success. Yet many realists would not have anticipated either the Good Friday Agreement 1998, and power-sharing between Sinn Féin and the DUP in 2007. These are both remarkable achievements by British and Irish politicians, who are usually much maligned. Sinn Féin/IRA have brought about a radical ideological transformation since the 1980s, from the pursuit of Irish unity by violence to unarmed struggle and power-sharing. The UUP leadership struggled to win over unionism to power-sharing but found themselves marginalized in the process. The DUP's transformation to partnership with Sinn Féin is, perhaps, the most astonishing of all, coming over such a short period of time.

The political skills that have been deployed to 'bridge the gap' between unionists and republicans have been criticized as deception, spin and manipulation by dissident republicans and the DUP (Dixon 2002a, p. 737):

- *Conservative realists* argue that the ends justify the means, public opinion is ignorant and the job of the politicians is to exercise their judgement on the public's behalf. Blair's deception during the Referendum campaign and other deceptions by pro-Agreement politicians were justified to achieve peace.
- *Idealists* claim that it is never right to deceive the public. Democracy is violated by secrecy and deception, politicians cannot be held accountable to the people for the power they wield if the public is not properly informed. Deception is not only wrong, but it is also ineffective. Blair's deception during the referendum became increasingly obvious, and this led to growing alienation among unionists and declining support for the GFA.
- *Democratic realists* argue that during the recent peace process the deployment of political skills has been deceitful and manipulative but, to some extent, this has also been necessary in order to wind down the conflict and secure the landmark Good Friday Agreement, and then power-sharing between Sinn Féin and the DUP. Democratic realists, unlike Conservative Realists, do not celebrate the lies and manipulations of the elites. They are concerned

at the threat that these political skills represent to democracy, and want to hold on to progressive, integrationist ideals. Democratic realists want good, political actors to (reluctantly) do morally disagreeable things where necessary, and this genuine reluctance suggests awareness of the moral cost of such actions. On the other hand, democratic realists criticize the naïvety of idealists who fail to appreciate the real moral dilemmas that confront politicians. There are white lies and black lies. Blair's deception during the Referendum campaign was probably necessary to win a 'Yes' vote and take the peace process forward. Subsequently, however, there should have been some attempt to mitigate the impact of this deception on unionism. The 'success' of Blair's deception in Northern Ireland might have emboldened the prime minister to deceive the British public over Iraq in 2002–3 (Dixon 2002a; and see Dixon 2009 for elaboration of these themes).

Manipulation and deceit eats into the culture of democracy, producing cynicism and resentment. The result of this is that power-sharing between Sinn Féin and the DUP is still 'balanced precariously on still seething reservoirs of hatred between unionists and nationalists' (Dixon 2001a, p. 307). The challenge is how to promote reconciliation now that elite power-sharing has been achieved. While Northern Ireland has experienced rapid economic growth since 1990, there has also been rising inequality within both Catholic and Protestant communities. Those in poverty, often located in the most highly segregated areas, have suffered most during the recent conflict, yet have benefited least from the peace (Horgan 2006).

Further analysis on the politics of Northern Ireland can be found on the author's website: www.nipolitics.com

Bibliography

Adams, G. (1986) *The Politics of Irish Freedom* (Dingle: Brandon).

Anderson, D. (1994) *14 Days in May* (Dublin: Gill & Macmillan).

Anderson, J. (2004) 'Political Demography in Northern Ireland'. Available at: www.qub.ac.uk/c-star/.

Armstrong, Lord R. (1993) 'Ethnicity, the English and Northern Ireland: Comments and Reflections', in D. Keogh and M. Haltzel, *Northern Ireland and the Politics of Reconciliation* (Cambridge: Cambridge University Press).

Arthur, P. (1984) *Government and Politics of Northern Ireland*, 2nd edn (London: Longman).

Aughey, A. (1989) *Under Siege: Ulster Unionism and the Anglo-Irish Agreement* (Belfast: Blackstaff).

Barritt, D. P. and Carter, C. (1962) *The Northern Ireland Problem* (London: Oxford University Press).

Bean, K. (1995) 'The New Departure?', *Irish Studies Review*, no. 10 (Spring).

Benn, T. (1988) *Office Without Power – Diaries 1968–72* (London: Hutchinson).

Benn, T. (1989) *Against the Tide – Diaries 1973–76* (London: Hutchinson).

Bew, P. and Dixon, P. (1995) 'Labour Party Policy and Northern Ireland', in B. Barton and P. Roche (eds), *Northern Ireland: Policies and Perspectives* (Aldershot: Avebury).

Bew, P., Gibbon, P. and Patterson, H. (1979) *The State in Northern Ireland 1921–72* (Manchester: Manchester University Press).

Bew, P., Gibbon, P. and Patterson, H. (1995) *Northern Ireland 1921–94: Political Forces and Social Classes* (London: Serif).

Bew, P. and Gillespie, G. (1993) *Northern Ireland: A Chronology of the Troubles 1968–1993* (London: Gill & Macmillan).

Bew, P. and Gillespie, G. (1996) *The Northern Ireland Peace Process 1993–96: A Chronology* (London: Serif).

Bew, P. and Gillespie, G. (1999) *Northern Ireland: A Chronology of the Troubles 1968–99* (Dublin: Gill & Macmillan).

Bew, P. and Patterson, H. (1985) *The British State and the Ulster Crisis: From Wilson to Thatcher* (London: Verso).

Bew, P. and Patterson, H. (1990) 'Scenarios for Progress in Northern Ireland', in J. McGarry and B. O'Leary (eds), *The Future of Northern Ireland* (Oxford: Clarendon).

Bew, P., Patterson, H. and Teague, P. (1997) *Between Peace and War: The Political Future of Northern Ireland* (London: Lawrence & Wishart).

Billig, M. (1995) *Banal Nationalism* (London: Sage).

Birrell, D. (1972) 'Relative Deprivation as a Factor in Conflict in Northern Ireland', *Sociological Review*, vol. 20, no. 3.

Birrell, D. and Murie, A. (1980) *Policy and Government in Northern Ireland* (Dublin: Gill & Macmillan).

Bishop, P. and Mallie, E. (1987) *The Provisional IRA* (London: Corgi).

Bleakley, D. (1972) *Peace in Ulster* (Oxford: Mowbrays).

Bloomfield, K. (1994) *Stormont in Crisis* (Belfast: Blackstaff).

Blumer, J. G. and Gurevitch, M. (1995) *The Crisis of Political Communication* (London: Routledge).

Bowman, J. (1982) *De Valera and the Ulster Question 1917–73* (Oxford: Clarendon Press).

Boyce, D. G. (1995) *Nationalism in Ireland* (London: Routledge).

Boyce, D. G. and O'Day, A. (1996) *The Making of Modern Irish History: Revisionism and the Revisionist Controversy* (London: Routledge).

Boyle, K. and Hadden, T. (1994) *Northern Ireland: The Choice* (Harmondsworth: Penguin).

Brett, C. E. B. (1970) 'The Lessons of Devolution in Northern Ireland', *Political Quarterly*, vol. 41.

Brett, C. E. B. (1978) *Long Shadows Cast Before* (Edinburgh: John Bartholomew).

Brivati, B. *et al.* (1996) *The Contemporary History Handbook* (Manchester: Manchester University Press).

Bromley, M. (1989) 'War of Words: The *Belfast Telegraph* and Loyalist Populism', in Y. Alexander and A. O'Day (eds), *Ireland's Terrorist Trauma* (London: Wheatsheaf).

Bruce, S. (1989) *God Save Ulster: The Religion and Politics of Paisleyism* (Oxford: Oxford University Press).

Bruce, S. (1992) *The Red Hand: Protestant Paramilitaries in Northern Ireland* (Oxford: Oxford University Press).

Bruce, S. (1994) *The Edge of the Union: The Ulster Loyalist Political Vision* (Oxford: Oxford University Press).

Bruce, S. (1999) 'The State and Pro-State Terrorism in Ireland', in R. English and C. Townshend (eds), *The State* (London: Routledge).

Bulpitt, J. (1983) *Territory and Power in the UK* (Manchester: Manchester University Press).

Burton, F. (1978) *The Politics of Legitimacy: Struggles in a Belfast Community* (London: Routledge & Kegan Paul).

Butler, D. E. (1991) 'Ulster Unionism and British Broadcasting Journalism, 1924–89', in B. Rolston (ed.), *The Media and Northern Ireland* (London: Macmillan).

Butler, D. E. (1995) *Trouble with Reporting Northern Ireland* (Aldershot: Avebury).

Byrne, S. (1995) 'Conflict Regulation or Conflict Resolution: Third-Party Intervention in the Northern Ireland Conflict; Prospects for Peace', *Terrorism and Political Violence*, vol. 7, no. 2 (Summer).

Callaghan, J. (1973) *A House Divided* (London: Collins).

Cameron Report (1969) *Disturbances in Northern Ireland*, Cmd 532 (Belfast: HMSO).

Campbell, J. (1983) *F. E. Smith* (London: Jonathan Cape).

Campbell, J. (2004) *Margaret Thatcher, Vol. Two: The Iron Lady* (London: Pimlico).

Canning, P. (1985) *British Policy towards Ireland 1921–41* (Oxford: Oxford University Press).

Carruthers, S. L. (1995) *Winning Hearts and Minds: British Government, the Media and Colonial Counter-Insurgency 1944–60* (London: Leicester University Press).

Carver, M. (1989) *Out of Step* (London: Hutchinson).

Cash, J. D. (1996) *Identity, Ideology and Conflict: The Structuration of Politics in Northern Ireland* (Cambridge: Cambridge University Press).

Castle, B. (1980) *The Castle Diaries 1974–76* (London: Weidenfeld & Nicolson).

Castle, B. (1984) *The Castle Diaries 1964–70* (London: Weidenfeld & Nicolson).

Chibnall, S. (1977) *Law and Order News* (London: Tavistock).

Clarke, L. (1987) *Broadening the Battlefield* (Dublin: Gill & Macmillan).

Clarke, L. and Johnston, K. (2001) *Martin McGuinness: From Guns to Government* (Edinburgh: Mainstream).

Cochrane, F. (1997) *Unionist Politics and the Politics of Unionism since the Anglo-Irish Agreement* (Cork: Cork University Press).

Connor, W. (1972) 'Nation-building or Nation-destroying', *World Politics*, vol. 24, no. 3 (April).

Conservative Party (1969) *Conservative Party Conference Report* (London: Conservative Central Office).

Coughlan, A. (1986) *Fooled Again? The Anglo-Irish Agreement and After* (Cork: Mercier Press).

Coughlan, A. (1990) *C. Desmond Greaves, 1913–1988: An Obituary Essay* (Dublin: Irish Labour History Society).

Coulter, C. (1999) *Contemporary Northern Irish Society* (London: Pluto).

Cox, M. (1997) 'Bringing in the "International": The IRA Ceasefire and the End of the Cold War', *International Affairs*, vol. 73, no. 4.

Cox, M. (1998) ' "Cinderella at the Ball": Explaining the End of the War in Northern Ireland', *Millennium*, vol. 27, no. 2.

Cox, M. (2006) 'Rethinking the International and Northern Ireland: A Defence' in M. Cox *et al.* (eds), *A Farewell to Arms? From Long War to Long Peace in Northern Ireland*, 2nd edn (Manchester: Manchester University Press).

Crossman, R. (1977) *The Diaries of a Cabinet Minister 1968–70* (London: Hamish Hamilton and Jonathan Cape).

Cunningham, M. (1991) *British Government Policy in Northern Ireland 1969–89, Its Nature and Execution* (Manchester: Manchester University Press).

Curtice, J. and Dowds, L. (1999) 'Has Northern Ireland Really Changed?' Crest Working Paper No. 74, September.

Curtis, L. (1984) *Ireland: The Propaganda War* (London: Pluto).

Darby, J. (1976) *Conflict in Northern Ireland* (Dublin: Gill & Macmillan).

Darby, J. (1994) 'Legitimate Targets: A Control on Violence?', in A. Guelke (ed.), *New Perspectives on the Northern Ireland Conflict* (Aldershot: Avebury).

Darwin, J. (1988) *Britain and Decolonisation – The Retreat from Empire in the Post-war World* (London: Macmillan).

Delaney, E. (2001) *An Accidental Diplomat: My Years in the Irish Foreign Service 1987–1995* (Dublin: New Island).

Devlin, B. (1969) *The Price of My Soul* (London: Collins).

Devlin, P. (1975) *The Fall of the N.I. Executive* (Belfast: published by P. Devlin).

Dillon, M. and Lehane, D. (1973) *Political Murder in Northern Ireland* (Harmondsworth: Penguin).

Dixon, P. (1993) 'The British Labour Party and Northern Ireland 1959–74', Unpublished PhD thesis, University of Bradford.

Dixon, P. (1994a) 'European Integration, Modernisation and Northern Ireland 1961–75', *Etudes Irlandaises*, no. XIX-1.

Dixon, P. (1994b) ' "The Usual English Doubletalk": The British Political Parties and the Ulster Unionists 1974–94', *Irish Political Studies*, 9.

Dixon, P. (1995a) ' "A House Divided Cannot Stand": Britain, Bipartisanship and Northern Ireland', *Contemporary Record*, vol. 9, no. 1.

Dixon, P. (1995b) 'Internationalization and Unionist Isolation: A Response to Feargal Cochrane', *Political Studies*, vol. 43, no. 3.

Dixon, P. (1996a) ' "A Real Stirring in the Nation": The Crisis of the British Army over Northern Ireland', in G. Stanyer (ed.), *Contemporary Political Studies* (the collected papers of the PSA) (London: Longman).

Dixon, P. (1996b) 'Explaining Antagonism: The Politics of McGarry and O'Leary', *Irish Political Studies*, vol. 11.

Dixon, P. (1997a) 'Consociationalism and the Northern Ireland Peace Process: The Glass Half Full or Half Empty?', *Nationalism and Ethnic Politics*, vol. 3, no. 3.

Dixon, P. (1997b) 'Counter-insurgency Strategy and the Crisis of the British State?', in P. Rich and R. Stubbs (eds), *The Counter-Insurgent State* (London: Macmillan).

Dixon, P. (1997c) 'Paths to Peace in Northern Ireland (I): Civil Society and Consociational Approaches', *Democratization*, vol. 4, no. 2.

Dixon, P. (1997d) 'Paths to Peace in Northern Ireland (II): Peace Process 1973–74, 1994–96', *Democratization*, vol. 4, no. 3.

Dixon, P. (1998) 'Comment on *The Conservative Stewardship of Northern Ireland 1979–97; Political Studies*, vol. 46, no. 3.

Dixon, P. (2000) 'Britain's "Vietnam Syndrome"? Public Opinion and Military Intervention from Palestine to Yugoslavia', *Review of International Studies*, vol. 26, no. 1.

Dixon, P. (2001a) *Northern Ireland: The Politics of War and Peace*, 1st edn (Basingstoke: Palgrave).

Dixon, P. (2001b) 'British Policy towards Northern Ireland 1969–2000: Continuity, Tactical Adjustment and Consistent "Inconsistencies"', *British Journal of Politics and International Relations*, vol. 3, no. 3 (Autumn), pp. 340–68.

Dixon, P. (2002a) 'Political Skills or Lying and Manipulation? The Choreography of the Northern Ireland Peace Process', *Political Studies*, vol. 50, no. 3, (Autumn), pp. 725–41.

Dixon, P. (2002b) 'Northern Ireland and the International Dimension: The End of the Cold War, the USA and European Integration', *Irish Studies in International Affairs*, vol. 13 (Autumn), pp. 105–20.

Dixon, P. (2003) 'Victory By Spin? Britain, the US and the Propaganda War over Kosovo', *Civil Wars*, vol. 6, no. 4, pp. 83-106

Dixon, P. (2004a) ' "Peace Within the Realms of the Possible?" David Trimble, Unionist Ideology and Theatrical Politics', *Terrorism and Political Violence*, vol. 16, no. 3, pp. 462–82.

Dixon, P. (2004b) 'Contemporary Unionism and the Tactics of Resistance', in J. Coakley and M. Bric (eds), *From Political Violence to Negotiated Settlement: The Winding Path to Peace in Twentieth Century Ireland* (Dublin, UCD Press).

Dixon, P. (2005) 'Why the Good Friday Agreement in Northern Ireland is not Consociational', *Political Quarterly*, vol. 76, no. 3 (July–September), pp. 357–67.

Dixon, P. (2006a) 'Performing the Northern Ireland Peace Process on the World Stage', *Political Science Quarterly*, vol. 121, no. 1 (Spring).

Dixon, P. (2006b) 'Peter Hain, Secretary of State for Northern Ireland: Valuing the Union?', *Irish Political Studies*, vol. 21, no. 2 (June).

Dixon, P. (2006c) 'Rethinking the International: A Critique', in M. Cox *et al.* (eds), *A Farewell to Arms? From Long War to Long Peace in Northern Ireland*, 2nd edn(Manchester: Manchester University Press).

Dixon, P. (2008) ' "A Tragedy Beyond Words": Interpretations of British Government Policy and the Northern Ireland Peace Process', in Aaron Edwards and Stephen Bloomer (eds), *Transforming the Peace Process in Northern Ireland: From Terrorism to Democratic Politics* (Dublin, Irish Academic Press).

Dixon, P. (2009) *The Northern Ireland Peace Process: Choreography and Theatrical Politics* (London: Routledge).

Donoughue, B. (1987) *Prime Minister – The Conduct of Policy under Harold Wilson and James Callaghan* (London: Jonathan Cape).

Downey, J. (1983) *Britain, Ireland and the Northern Question* (Dublin: Ward River Press).

Duignan, S. (1995) *One Spin on the Merry-Go-Round* (Dublin: Blackwater Press).

Eldridge, J. (1993) 'News, Truth and Power', in Glasgow University Media Group, *Getting the Message: News, Truth and Power* (London: Routledge).

Elliott, P. (1976) *Reporting Northern Ireland: A Study of News in Britain, Ulster and the Irish Republic* (Leicester: Centre for Mass Communication Research).

Evelegh, R. (1978) *Peace Keeping in a Democratic Society: The Lessons of Northern Ireland* (London: Hurst).

Fahey, T. *et al.* (2005) *Conflict and Consensus: A Study of Values and Attitudes in the Republic of Ireland and Northern Ireland* (Leiden: Brill Press).

Farrell, M. (1976) *The Orange State* (London: Pluto Press).

Faulkner, B. (1978) *Brian Faulkner, Memoirs of a Statesman* (London: Weidenfeld & Nicolson).

Fay, M. *et al.* (1999) *Northern Ireland's Troubles: The Human Costs* (London: Pluto).

Feeney, V. E. (1974) 'The Civil Rights Movement in Northern Ireland', *Eire-Ireland*, vol. 9, no. 2.

Feeney, V. E. (1976) 'Westminster and the Early Civil Rights Struggle in Northern Ireland', *Eire-Ireland*, vol. 11, no. 4.

Fisk, R. (1975) *The Point of No Return, The Strike which Broke the British in Ulster* (London: André Deutsch).

Fisk, R. (1983) *In Time of War* (London: Paladin).

Fitzgerald, G. (1991) *All in a Life* (Dublin: Gill & Macmillan).

Flackes, W. D. and Elliott, S. (1999) *Northern Ireland: A Political Directory* (Belfast: Blackstaff).

Foot, P. (1989) *Who Framed Colin Wallace?* (London: Pan).

Furedi, F. (1994) *Colonial Wars and the Politics of Third World Nationalism* (London: I. B. Taurus).

Gailey, A. (1995) *Crying in the Wilderness: Jack Sayers: A Liberal Editor in Ulster 1939–69* (Belfast: Institute of Irish Studies).

Gillespie, G. (1998) 'The Sunningdale Agreement: Lost Opportunity or an Agreement Too Far?', *Irish Political Studies*, vol. 13.

Godson, D. (2004) *Himself Alone: David Trimble and the Ordeal of Unionism* (London: HarperCollins).

Goldsworthy, D. (1971) *Colonial Issues in British Politics 1945–61* (Oxford: Oxford University Press).

Goodall, D. (1993) 'The Irish Question', *Ampleforth Journal*, vol. XCVIII, Part 1 (Spring).

Gordon, D. (1989) *The O'Neill Years, Unionist Politics 1963–69* (Belfast: Athol Books).

Graham, J. A. V. (1982) 'The Consensus-forming Strategy of the NILP', MSc thesis, Queens University Belfast.

Gudgin, G. (1999) 'Discrimination in Housing and Employment under the Stormont Administration', in P. J. Roche and B. Barton (eds), *The Northern Ireland Question: Nationalism, Unionism and Partition* (Aldershot: Ashgate).

Guelke, A. (1988) *Northern Ireland: The International Perspective* (Dublin: Gill & Macmillan).

Hadden, T. and Boyle, K. (1989) *The Anglo-Irish Agreement, Commentary, Text and Official Review* (London: Sweet & Maxwell).

Hadfield, B. (2001) 'Seeing it through? The multifaceted Implementation of the Belfast Agreement' in R. Wilford, *Aspects of the Agreement* (Oxford: Oxford University Press).

Hain, P. (2007) 'Peacemaking in Northern Ireland: A model for conflict resolution?' (London: Northern Ireland Office).

Haines, J. (1977) *The Politics of Power* (London: Jonathan Cape).

Hamill, D. (1986) *Pig in the Middle, The Army in Northern Ireland 1969–85* (London: Methuen).

Harkness, D. (1977) 'The Differences of Devolution: The Post-War Debate at Stormont', *The Irish Jurist*, vol. xii.

Harkness, D. (1993) 'Never the Twain: Belfast–Dublin Relations since 1920', *L'Irlande Politique et Sociale*, vol. 1, no. 3.

Harkness, D. (1996) *Ireland in the Twentieth Century: Divided Island* (London: Macmillan).

Hart, V. (2001) 'Constitution-making and the Transformation of Conflict', *Peace and Change*, vol. 26, pp. 153–76.

Hay, C. (1995) 'Structure and Agency', in D. Marsh and G. Stoker (eds), *Theory and Methods in Political Science* (London: Macmillan).

Hay, C. (2002) *Political Analysis* (Basingstoke: Palgrave).

Hayes, B. C. and McAllister, I. (2001) 'Sowing Dragon's Teeth: Public Support for Political Violence and Paramilitarism in Northern Ireland', *Political Studies*, vol. 49.

Hazelkorn, E. and Patterson, H. (1994) 'The New Politics of the Irish Republic', *New Left Review*, vol. 207.

Heath, E. (1998) *The Course of My Life: My Autobiography* (London: Hodder & Stoughton).

Hewitt, J. (1991) 'The Roots of Violence: Catholic Grievances and Irish Nationalism during the Civil Rights Period', in P. J. Roche and B. Barton (eds), *The Northern Ireland Question: Myth and Reality* (Aldershot: Avebury).

Hillyard, P. (1988) 'Political and Social Dimensions of Emergency Law in Northern Ireland', in A. Jennings (ed.), *Justice under Fire* (London: Pluto).

Hogg, Q. (1975) *The Door Wherein I Went* (London: Collins).

Holland, J. and Phoenix, S. (1997) *Policing the Shadows* (London: Coronet Books).

Horgan, G. (2006) 'Devolution, Direct Rule and Neo-Liberal Reconstruction in Northern Ireland', *Critical Social Policy*, vol. 26, no. 3.

Howe, G. (1994) *Conflict of Loyalty* (London: Pan).

Hunt Report (1969) *Report of the Advisory Committee on Police in Northern Ireland and Belfast* (London: HMSO).

Hurd, D. (1979) *An End to Promises* (London: Collins).

Hurd, D. (2003) *Memoirs* (London: Little, Brown).

ICBH (Institute for Contemporary British History) (1997) Anglo-Irish Agreement Witness Seminar, 11 June.

Ignatieff, M. (1996) 'Articles of Faith', *Index on Censorship*, no. 5.

Irish Political Studies (1986–2000) Yearbook of the Political Studies Association of Ireland (Limerick: PSAI Press).

Irwin, C. (2002) *The People's Peace Process in Northern Ireland* (Basingstoke: Palgrave).

Jarman, N. (1997) *Material Conflicts: Parades and Visual Displays in Northern Ireland* (Oxford: Berg).

Jenkins, R. (1991) *Life at the Centre* (London: Macmillan).

Kaufmann, Eric (2007) *The Orange Order: A Contemporary Northern Irish History* (Oxford: Oxford University Press).

Kelley, K. J. (1988) *The Longest War: Northern Ireland and the IRA* (London: Zed).

Kelly, H. (1972) *How Stormont Fell* (Dublin: Gill & Macmillan).

Kennedy, D. (1988) *The Widening Gulf* (Belfast: Blackstaff).

Kenny, A. (1986) *The Road to Hillsborough* (Oxford: Pergamon).

King, C. (1975) *The Cecil King Diary 1970–74* (London: Jonathan Cape).

Kirkaldy, J. (1984) 'Northern Ireland and Fleet Street: Misreporting a Continuing Tragedy', in Y. Alexander and A. O'Day (eds), *Terrorism in Ireland* (London: Croom Helm).

Kirkaldy, J. (1986) 'English Cartoonists: Ulster Realities', in A. O'Day (ed.), *Ireland's Terrorist Dilemma* (Lancaster: Martinus Nijhoff).

Kremer, J. and Schermbrucker, I. (2006) 'Difference and the Psychology of Conflict', *The Psychologist*, vol. 19, no. 3.

Kyle, K. (1975) 'Sunningdale and After: Britain, Ireland and Ulster', *The World Today*, November.

Labour Party, (1969) *Labour Party Annual Conference Report* (London: Labour Party).

Lawrence, R., Elliott, S. and Laver, M. (1975) *The Northern Ireland General Elections of 1973* (London: HMSO).

Lawson, N. (1992) *The View from Number Eleven* (London: Bantam).

Lichbach, M. and Zuckerman, A. (1997) *Comparative Politics* (Cambridge: Cambridge University Press).

Little, A. (2004) *Democracy and Northern Ireland: Beyond the Liberal Paradigm?* (Palgrave: Basingstoke).

Loughlin, J. (1995) *Ulster Unionism and British National Identity since 1885* (London: Pinter).

Lustick, I. (1997) 'The Oslo Peace Process as an Obstacle to Peace', *Journal of Palestine Studies*, vol. 27, no. 1.

Lynn, B. (1997) *Holding the Ground: The Nationalist Party in Northern Ireland, 1945–72* (Aldershot: Avebury).

MacIntyre, D. (2000) *Mandelson: And the Making of New Labour* (London: HarperCollins).

Mair, P. (1987a) 'Breaking the Nationalist Mould: The Irish Republic and the Anglo-Irish Agreement', in P. Teague (ed.), *Beyond the Rhetoric: Politics, the Economy and Social Policy in Northern Ireland* (London: Lawrence & Wishart).

Mair, P. (1987b) *The Changing Irish Party System* (London: Pinter).

Major, J. (1999) *John Major:The Autobiography* (London: HarperCollins).

Mallie, E. and McKittrick, D. (1997) *The Fight for Peace: The Secret Story of the Irish Peace Process,* revd edn (London: Mandarin).

Mallie, E. and McKittrick, D. (2001) *Endgame in Ireland* (Hodder & Stoughton: London).

Marsh, D. *et al.* (1999) *Postwar British Politics in Perspective* (Oxford: Polity).

Marsh, D. and Stoker, G. (2002) *Theory and Methods in Political Science* (Basingstoke: Macmillan).

Mason, R. (1999) *Paying the Price* (London: Robert Hale).

McAllister, I. (1977a) 'The Legitimacy of Opposition: The Collapse of the Northern Ireland Executive', in *Eire-Ireland*, vol. 12, part 6.

McAllister, I. (1977b) *The Northern Ireland Social Democratic and Labour Party: Political Opposition in a Divided Society* (London: Macmillan).

McCann, E. (1969) 'Interview with Peoples' Democracy', *New Left Review*, no. 55, May–June.

McCann, E. (1974) *War and an Irish Town* (Harmondsworth: Penguin).

McCullagh, M. (1983) 'The Political and Sectarian Significance of Changes in the Occupational Structure in Northern Ireland', *Social Science Teacher*, vol. 12, no. 2.

McDonald, H. (2000) *Trimble* (London: Bloomsbury).

McGarry, J. and O'Leary, B. (1995) *Explaining Northern Ireland* (Oxford: Basil Blackwell).

McKeown, M. (1997) 'The Impact of the 1947 Education Act upon Roman Catholic Access to Academic Secondary Education in Northern Ireland', *Irish Education Studies*, vol. 16 (Spring).

McKittrick, D. *et al.* (2004) *Lost Lives: The Stories of the Men, Women and Children who Died as a Result of the Northern Ireland Troubles*, 2nd revd edn (Edinburgh: Mainstream).

McNair, B. (1995) *An Introduction to Political Communication* (London: Routledge).

Millar, F. (2004) *David Trimble: The Price of Peace* (Dublin: The Liffey Press).

Miller, D. (1993) 'Official Sources and "primary definition": the case of Northern Ireland', *Media, Culture and Society*, vol. 15, no. 3.

Miller, D. (1994) *Don't Mention the War: Northern Ireland, Propaganda and the Media* (London: Pluto).

Miller, D. and McLaughlin, G. (1996) 'The Media Politics of the Peace in Ireland' *Harvard International Journal of Press/Politics*, vol. 1, no. 4 (Fall).

Mitchell, G. (1999) *Making Peace* (Heinemann: London).

Moloney, E. (1980) *The IRA, Magill magazine.*

Moloney, E. (2002) *A Secret History of the IRA* (Penguin: London).

Moloney, E. and Pollak, A. (1986) *Paisley* (Swords: Poolbeg).

Morgan, M. (1987) 'The Catholic Middle Class in Northern Ireland: Myth or Reality?', *Ireland: Politics and Society*, vol. 1, no. 3.

Morgan, M. and Taylor, R. (1988) 'Forget the Myths: Here's the Real Story', *Fortnight*, October.

Mowlam, M. (2002) *Momentum: The Struggle for Peace, Politics and the People* (London: Hodder & Stoughton).

Murray, G. (1998) *John Hume and the SDLP* (Dublin: Irish Academic Press).

Nagel, J. and Olzak, S. (1982) 'Ethnic Mobilisation in New and Old States: An Extension Of the Competition Model', *Social Problems*, vol. 30, no. 2.

Needham, R. (1998) *Battling for Peace* (Belfast: Blackstaff).

Nelson, S. (1984) *Ulster's Uncertain Defenders: Protestant Political, Paramilitary and Community Groups and the Northern Ireland Conflict* (Belfast: Appletree).

Niens, U. *et al.* (2003) 'Contact and Conflict in Northern Ireland', in Owen Hargie and David Dickson (eds), *Researching the Troubles* (Edinburgh: Mainstream).

Northern Ireland Office (1972) *The Future of Northern Ireland: A Paper for Discussion* (Belfast: HMSO).

Norton-Taylor, R. (2005) *Bloody Sunday: Scenes from the Saville Inquiry* (London: Oberon Books).

O'Brien, B. (1993) *The Long War: The IRA and Sinn Féin 1985 to Today* (Dublin: The O'Brien Press).

O'Brien, C. C. (1972) *States of Ireland* (London: Hutchinson).

O'Brien, J. (2005) *Killing Finucane: Murder in Defence of the Realm* (Dublin: Gill & Macmillan).

O'Clery, C. (1986) *Phrases Make History Here* (Dublin: O'Brien Press).

O'Clery, C. (1996) *The Greening of the White House* (Dublin: Gill & Macmillan).

O Connor, F. (1993) *In Search of a State: Catholics in Northern Ireland* (Belfast: Blackstaff).

Ó Dochartaigh, N. (1997) *From Civil Rights to Armalites: Derry and the Birth of the Irish Troubles* (Cork: Cork University Press).

O'Doherty, M. (1998) *The Trouble with Guns: Republican Strategy and the Provisional IRA* (Belfast: Blackstaff).

O'Doherty, M. (2007) *The Telling Year: Belfast 1972* (Dublin: Gill & Macmillan).

O'Farrell, J. (1998) 'Divided People, Divided Press – Interpreting the Poisonous Silences in a Fractured Society', *Media Studies Journal*, vol. 12, no. 2.

O'Halloran, C. (1987) *Partition and the Limits of Irish Nationalism* (Dublin: Gill & Macmillan).

O'Kane, E. (2007) *Britain, Ireland and Northern Ireland since 1980: The Totality of Relationships* (Basingstoke: Palgrave).

O'Leary, B. (1997) 'The Conservative Stewardship of Northern Ireland, 1979–97: Sound-bottomed Contradictions or Slow Learning', *Political Studies*, vol. XLV.

O'Leary, B. (2002) 'The Belfast Agreement and the British–Irish Agreement: Consociation, Confederal Institutions, a Federacy, and a Peace Process', in A. Reynolds (ed.), *The Architecture of Democracy* (Oxford: Oxford University Press).

O'Leary, B. and McGarry, J. (1996) *The Politics of Antagonism*, 2nd edn (London: Athlone).

O'Malley, P. (1983) *The Uncivil Wars: Ireland Today* (Belfast: Blackstaff).

O'Malley, P. (1990) *Biting at the Grave: The Irish Hunger Strikes and the Politics of Despair* (Belfast: Blackstaff).

O'Malley, P. (1994) 'Northern Ireland – A Manageable Conflict?', *The Irish Review*, no. 15 (Spring).

O'Neill, T. (1969) *Ulster at the Crossroads* (London: Faber & Faber).

O'Neill, T. (1972) *The Autobiography of Terence O'Neill, Prime Minister of Northern Ireland 1963–69* (London: Rupert Hart-Davis).

O'Rawe, R. (2005) *Blanketmen: An Untold Story of the H-Block Hunger Strike* (Dublin: New Island).

Owen, E. A. (1994) *The Anglo-Irish Agreement: The First Three Years* (Cardiff: University of Wales Press).

Ozkirimli, O. (2005) *Contemporary Debates on Nationalism* (Basingstoke: Palgrave).

Parkinson, A. (1998) *Ulster Loyalism and the British Media* (Dublin: Four Courts Press).

Patterson, H. (1986) 'British Governments and the Protestant Backlash 1969–74', in A. O'Day (ed.), *Ireland's Terrorist Dilemma* (Lancaster: Martinus Nijhoff).

Patterson, H. (1997) *The Politics of Illusion: A Political History of the IRA* (London: Serif).

Porter, N. (1996) *Rethinking Unionism* (Belfast: Blackstaff).

Portland Trust (2007) *Economics in Peacemaking: Lessons From Northern Ireland*, (Portland Trust: London).

Power, P. F. (1977) 'The Sunningdale Strategy and the Northern Majority Consent Doctrine in Anglo-Irish Relations', *Eire-Ireland*, vol. 12, no. 1.

Pringle, D and Jacobson, P (2002) *Those Are Real Bullets: Bloody Sunday, Derry, 1972* (Grove: London).

Prior, J. (1986) *A Balance of Power* (London: Hamish Hamilton).

Purdie, B. (1983) 'The Friends of Ireland: British Labour and Irish Nationalism 1945–49', in T. Gallagher and J. O'Connell (eds), *Contemporary Irish Studies* (Manchester: Manchester University Press).

Purdie, B. (1986) 'The Irish Anti-Partition League, South Armagh and the Abstentionist Tactic 1945–48', *Irish Political Studies*, vol. 1.

Purdie, B. (1988) 'Was the Civil Rights Movement a Republican/Communist Conspiracy?', *Irish Political Studies*, vol. 3.

Purdie, B. (1990) *Politics in the Streets* (Belfast: Blackstaff).

Purdy, M. (2005) *Room 21: Stormont Behind Closed Doors* (Belfast: The Brehon Press).

Rawnsley, A. (2000) *Servants of the People: The Inside Story of New Labour* (London: Hamish Hamilton).

Rees, M. (1973) 'The Future of Northern Ireland', *Contemporary Review*, vol. 223, part 1290.

Rees, M. (1974) 'Northern Ireland', *Contemporary Review*, vol. 224, no. 1297.

Rees, M. (1985) *Northern Ireland: A Personal Perspective* (London: Methuen).

Rose, Paul (1981) *Backbencher's Dilemma* (London: Muller).

Rose, Peter (1999) *How the Troubles Came to Northern Ireland* (London: Macmillan).

Rose, R. (1971) *Governing Without Consensus: An Irish Perspective* (London: Faber & Faber).

Rose, R. (1976) *Northern Ireland: A Time of Choice* (London: Macmillan).

Rose, R. *et al.* (1978) *Is There a Concurring Majority about Northern Ireland?*, Studies in Public Policy No. 22 (Glasgow: University of Strathclyde, Centre for the Study of Public Policy).

Rowan, B. (1995) *Behind the Lines: The Story of the IRA and Loyalist Ceasefires* (Belfast: Blackstaff).

Ruane, J. and Todd, J. (1996) *The Dynamics of Conflict in Northern Ireland* (Cambridge: Cambridge University Press).

Ruane, J. and Todd, J. (1999) 'The Belfast Agreement: Conflict, Context, Consequences', in J. Ruane and J. Todd (eds), *After the Good Friday Agreement* (Dublin: University College Dublin Press).

Ryder, C. (1992) *The Ulster Defence Regiment: An Instrument of Peace?* (London: Mandarin).

Ryder, C. (1997) *The RUC: A Force Under Fire* (London: Mandarin).

Scarman Report (1972) *Violence and Disturbances in Northern Ireland in 1969*, Cmd 566 (Belfast: HMSO).

Schlesinger, P. (1978) *Putting 'Reality' Together* (London: Methuen).

Schlesinger, P. *et al.* (1983) *Televising Terrorism: Political Violence in Popular Culture* (London: Comedia).

Schlesinger, P. (1990) 'Rethinking the Sociology of Journalism: Source Strategies and the Limits of Media Centrism', in M. Ferguson, *Public Communication: The New Imperatives* (London: Sage).

Seldon, A. (1997) *John Major* (London: Weidenfeld & Nicolson).

Sharrock, D. and Devenport, M. (1997) *Man of War, Man of Peace? The Unauthorised Biography of Gerry Adams* (London: Macmillan).

Sinn Féin (1993) *Setting the Record Straight* (Sinn Féin: Belfast).

Sluka, J. A. (1989) *Hearts and Minds, Water and Fish: Support for the IRA and INLA in a Northern Ireland Ghetto* (London: JAI Press).

Smith, D. and Chambers, G. (1991) *Inequality in Northern Ireland* (Oxford: Oxford University Press).

Smith, M. L. R. (1995) *Fighting for Ireland? The Military Strategy of the Irish Republican Movement* (London: Routledge).

Smyth, C. (1987) *Ian Paisley: Voice of Protestant Ulster* (Edinburgh: Scottish Academic Press).

Spencer, G. (2008) *The State of Loyalism in Northern Ireland* (Basingstoke: Palgrave).

Stuart, M. (1998) *Douglas Hurd: The Public Servant, An Authorised Biography* (London: Mainstream Publishing).

Sunday Times Insight Team (1972) *Ulster* (Harmondsworth: Penguin).

Sutton, M. (1994) *An Index of Deaths from the Conflict in Ireland 1969–93* (Belfast: Beyond the Pale).

Sutton, M. (1999) *An Index of Deaths from the Conflict in Ireland.* Available at: www.cain.ulst.ac.uk/sutton/index.html.

Taylor, P. (1997) *The Provos: The IRA and Sinn Féin* (London: Bloomsbury).

Taylor, R. (1988) 'Social Scientific Research on the "Troubles" in Northern Ireland: The Problem of Objectivity', *The Economic and Social Review*, vol. 19, no. 2 (January).

Teague, P. (1993) 'Discrimination and Fair Employment in Northern Ireland', in P. Teague (ed.), *The Economy of Northern Ireland* (London: Lawrence & Wishart).

Thatcher, M. (1993) *Downing Street Years* (London: HarperCollins).

Tonge, J. (2004) ' "They haven't gone away, you know". Irish Republican "Dissidents" and "Armed Struggle" ', *Terrorism and Political Violence*, vol. 16, no. 3 (Autumn).

Tonge, J. (2006) *Northern Ireland* (Cambridge: Polity Press).

Urban, M. (1992) *Big Boys' Rules* (London: Faber & Faber).

Utley, T. E. (1975) *Lessons of Ulster* (London: Dent).

Wallace, M. (1982) *British Government in Northern Ireland* (Newton Abbot: David & Charles).

Walsh, P. (1989) *From Civil Rights to National War, Catholic Politics 1964–74* (Belfast: Athol Books).

Welch, D. (1999) 'Powers of Persuasion', *History Today*, August.

White, B. (1984) *John Hume: Statesman of the Troubles* (Belfast: Blackstaff).

Whitelaw, W. (1989) *The Whitelaw Memoirs* (London: Aurum Press).

Whyte, J. (1983) 'How Much Discrimination Was There under the Unionist Regime, 1921–68?', in T. Gallagher and J. O'Connell (eds), *Contemporary Irish Studies* (Manchester: Manchester University Press).

Whyte, J. (1990) *Interpreting Northern Ireland* (Oxford: Clarendon Press).

Wilson, A. J. (1995) *Irish America and the Ulster Conflict 1968–1995* (Belfast: Blackstaff).

Wilson, H. (1966) *Purpose in Power* (London: Weidenfeld & Nicolson).

Wilson, H. (1974) *The Labour Government 1964–70: A Personal Record* (London: Weidenfeld & Nicolson).

Wilson, H. (1977) *The Governance of Britain* (London: Sphere).

Wilson, H. (1979) *The Final Term: The Labour Government 1974–76* (London: Weidenfeld & Nicolson).

Wilson, R. (2000) 'Order on Policing: Resolving the Impasse over the Patten Report', *Democratic Dialogue*, October.

Wilson, R. (2003) *What's Going Wrong?* (QUB, Institute for Governance). Available at: http://www.qub.ac.uk/schools/SchoolofLaw/Research/InstituteofGovernance/Publications/briefingpapers/Filetoupload,47659, en.pdf.

Winchester, S. (1974) *In Holy Terror: Reporting the Ulster Troubles* (London: Faber & Faber).

Windlesham, D. (1975) *Politics in Practice* (London: Jonathan Cape).

Wright, F. (1973) 'Protestant Ideology and Politics in Ulster', *European Journal of Sociology*, vol. 14.

Wright, J. (1991) *Terrorist Propaganda: The Red Army Faction and the Provisional IRA 1968–86* (London: Macmillian).

Young, H. (1989) *One of Us?* (London: Macmillan).

A guide to further reading, articles and sources on Northern Ireland are available at www.nipolitics.com.

Index

BC	12/08